NI DE AQUI, NI DE ALLA

"Not from here, Not from there"
A Memoir by Yesenia Garcia
YESENIA GARCIA
PUBLISHING 2025
THIS IS MY TRUTH!

For permission requests, please contact:

Yeseniagarcia.store

ISBN (Paperback): 979-8-9937338-0-7

DEDICATION

For Julian and Issac.

My reason, my rhythm, my redemption.

You've seen every chapter of me, even the ones I barely survived.

Because of you, I've never given up.

I pray you grow into strong, tender-hearted men

who protect, provide, feel deeply, and lead with grace.

May you always know when to be soft, and when to stand firm.

I truly feel like one of God's favorites.

He knew exactly what He was doing when He made me your mom.

You are my greatest gift, my favorite title,

and the truest love story I've ever written.

And last but not least

God, thank You for protecting me.

Thank You for loving me.

Thank You for creating me exactly as I am.

DEDICACIÓN

Para Julian e Issac

Mi razón, mi ritmo, mi redención.

Ustedes han sido testigos de cada capítulo de mi vida, incluso los que apenas sobreviví.

Gracias a ustedes, nunca me rendí.

Ruego que crezcan siendo hombres fuertes y de gran corazón que

protejan, provean, sientan profundamente, y lideren con gracia.

Que siempre sepan cuándo ser suaves… y cuándo mantenerse firmes.

De verdad me siento como una de las favoritas de Dios.

Él sabía exactamente lo que hacía al hacerme su mamá.

Ustedes son mi regalo más grande, mi título más valioso,

y la historia de amor más real que he escrito.

Y por último, pero no menos importante

Dios, gracias por protegerme.

Gracias por amarme.

Gracias por crearme exactamente como soy.

INTRODUCTION & AUTHOR'S NOTE

"The Blood Remembers"

Growing up in a Single Wide in Oregon and living with family in Texas full of chaos wasn't just my reality it was my normal.

We were the kind of family that ate 12 grapes at midnight on New Year's Eve, one for each wish we hoped would come true. We threw lentils over our heads and ran around the house with suitcases to bring in travel luck. Wild, I know but in our world, that was just tradition.

At home, I spoke Spanish with my parents. The second I stepped outside, it was English with the rest of the world. I was constantly bouncing between cultures, schools, cities, and friend groups never really knowing what settled felt like.

I watched my parents hustle their way through jobs that demanded everything and gave so little in return. From farm fields to warehouses to whatever paid that week I saw it all. I heard it all. We moved, we migrated, we adapted.

That ever-changing rhythm shaped me. It taught me how to read a room, how to code-switch before I even knew there was a term for it, and how to survive chaos by learning to dance in it.

Before I was born, the story already had a pulse.

Before I took my first breath, my people had already learned to survive droughts, losses, and long seasons of silence.

I didn't come from peace I came from grit.

From fields and freight trucks. From gamblers and chiefs.

From mothers who cried quietly and fathers who couldn't follow because they were born to lead.

This is not a fairytale.

This is the map of my lineage.

The memories we don't speak of but carry in our posture.

The trauma we inherit and the healing we choose.

Back then, I didn't realize how much I was carrying. I just thought, "This is what life is."

But now, looking back, I see the beauty, the struggle, the trauma, and the resilience and it all needs to be told.

I'm not writing this for pity or praise I'm writing because truth deserves a voice.

Because silence never saved me.

Because my past doesn't define me but it damn sure built me.

So here it is. The real, unfiltered, bilingual, back-and-forth, heart-heavy, laugh-out-loud, messy, magical journey that made me, me.

If you see yourself anywhere in these pages I hope you feel less alone.

And if you don't I hope you listen anyway.

This is my story.

My survival.

My becoming.

I'm the daughter of grit, gamble, and grace.

And this time, I'm holding the pen.

Welcome to my crazy-ass life.

This is my truth.

I'm so glad you're here.

— Yesenia

TRIGGER NOTE

A gentle message before we begin…

Before you step into this story, I want to take a moment not just as the author, but as a woman who lived every word on these pages.

This book holds pieces of me that once felt too heavy to name. It includes memories of trauma, loss, heartbreak, and survival. Some chapters are soft and tender. Others might feel like open wounds.

If any of it ever feels like too much I hope you give yourself permission to pause, breathe, or come back later. You do not owe your healing to any timeline, and you do not owe your discomfort to anyone not even this book.

I didn't write this to shock you.

I wrote it to free myself.

And maybe, just maybe free something in you too.

So take your time.

Hold what you need.

Leave what you don't.

You are not alone.

You never were.

— With love,

Yesenia ♡

Tómate tu tiempo. Estoy compartiendo esto con el corazón en la mano.

Contents

"The Last Valentine I Didn't Say I Love You & The Grown-Up Good-bye"

The Woman San Antonio Softened

Chapter 1

Middle of Chaos, Mexican parents, granddaughter of Cassiques

Just to give you a little backstory.

Before I ever took my first breath, my story had already begun.

Before there was me, there was hustle. There was grit. There were two people building something from nothing together.

I come from a lineage of people who survived by instinct and endured by force. People who lived off the land who knew the rhythm of planting and the ache of harvesting. Who understood that survival wasn't just physical, it was spiritual. It lived in your hands, in your spine, in the way you showed up for your family tired, sweating, and unbreakable.

My grandfather on my father's side was what they called a Cassique — a chief, a leader within his indigenous community. A man whose title meant more than authority; it carried weight. Culture. Responsibility. Protection. Power.

If you look up the word "Cassique" today, you might find a simple definition but to us, it meant so much more. It meant: He walked ahead so others could follow.

And even though I never met him, I carry his name in my blood like a quiet anthem. A pulse. A drumbeat I didn't ask for but one I now understand.

He wasn't just a father to my dad.

He was the father the one that shaped everything after him.

He was tough. Unforgiving. A force to be reckoned with.

"Or so I've heard".

Not an easy man to be around or deal with.

"Again, so I've heard".

I never got the chance to feel his presence for myself. But I've felt the

aftermath.

He owned land in General Bravo, Nuevo León, a tiny rural town near the Texas border. Population? Maybe 5,500 people. Maybe less.

It sits just about 1 hour and 20 minutes from the McAllen-Hidalgo

International Bridge and 1 hour and 50 minutes from the Pharr–Reynosa bridge. It's the kind of town where everybody knows your business, where stories carry weight even after the people are gone.

That's where my father was born. Where our roots are buried. Where my grandfather grew corn and grain until eventually, like many others in search of something more, he brought his wife and children to the U.S. for farm work.

They weren't chasing the American Dream they were chasing survival. A paycheck. A future. And that's where everything shifted. The land changed. The language changed. The rules changed. But the grind? That stayed the same.

Tragically, my grandfather died young struck and killed by an 18-wheeler while driving a company truck. It was sudden.
Brutal.
Instant. They say he didn't suffer. I hope that's true.
They transported his body back across the border and laid him to rest in his hometown right back in General Bravo, the very soil he once worked.

His death left behind a widow my paternal grandmother and a family who never really spoke of it without a hint of pain in their voice.

But if there's one thing I'll say about that woman?

She is a STALLION.

A powerhouse in the quietest form. Nearly 90 years old now, and to this day she has never remarried.

Loyal. Unshaken. Elegant. She chose solitude over compromise.

We'll talk about her more in a later chapter.

(Maybe. I haven't decided yet.)

As for my dad he never finished high school.

They said he couldn't follow instructions. Couldn't sit still.

But personally? I don't think he was built to follow.

He was born to lead.

I can't even blame the man I'm so much like him.

I relate to him fully… and not at all, all at once.

He was expelled from middle school.

Not for skipping class or getting caught cheating.

Nope, my dad got expelled for fighting a teacher.

First, he got paddled. Then suspended. Then warned.

And when he came back? He fought the teacher anyway.

My grandmother God bless that woman probably aged five years that week.

She'd already been through enough by then.

Now she had a wild, fearless teenage son out here throwing hands with educators.

I used to laugh when my mom told me that story. Still do.

But now that I'm a parent, I don't just laugh I feel it.

It wasn't just funny.

It was wild. Bold. Uncontainable.

The kind of kid you don't raise you brace for.

Maybe that's why I feel like I carry him in my blood like both a warning and a torch.

The strength, the chaos, the charm, the rebellion.

He walked away from classrooms and straight into the fields.

He became a farmer before he was even a man.

And in those same fields somewhere between the sweat, the soil, and the seasons he met my mother.

Actually… if I'm remembering correctly, they technically met at school first. Just a glance. A moment.

My dad had already been expelled, but one day, while picking up his

brothers, for a funeral, one of his other brothers had just passed,

"my mom saw him".

A small seed was planted.

The kind of spark that simmers in silence and then blooms when the timing is right.

(We'll get to the meat and potatoes of their love story soon. LOL.)

Now my maternal grandfather my mom's dad

He came from major wealth.

I was told his family once owned nearly all of Reynosa, Tamaulipas,

Mexico a city that today has a population of about 750,000. Back then? Probably closer to half a million. Still, much bigger than my father's tiny town of 5,000.

The story goes like this:

They didn't just own land. They owned Reynosa.

Over 400,000 hectares — nearly 1 million acres.

Let me put it this way:

Jerry Jones may own a stadium, but my great-grandfather?

He owned a city.

Land. Schools. Pharmacies. Beauty salons. Businesses. Studios.

A legacy of wealth and power that ran through everything.

Until it didn't.

He fell into obsessive gambling.

Little by little, he lost everything, land, property, opportunity.

Anything he could put on the table for one more shot.

And just like that, poof the empire slipped through his fingers. But pride? He never lost that.

Even in his later years, he stood tall with quiet dignity.

Not long ago, already well into his late eighties, he earned his dual citizenship a powerful, full-circle moment for a man who had once owned so much and sacrificed even more to start again in a new country.

His mother my great-grandmother was from Spain.

An elegant woman. Refined, light-skinned, with soft features and a poised presence.

It makes sense to me now the blue eyes, the fair tones, the gentle softness that shows up randomly in our gene pool.

People often say, "You don't look Mexican," and I just smile.

My maternal grandmother, on the other hand, was from Jalisco, Guadalajara rooted in Native Indigenous ancestry.

Her beauty is quiet. Earthy. Strong. Timeless.

What a mix, huh?

Spain and Jalisco.

Privilege and perseverance.

Legacy and loss.

And then… there was my mother.

Let us not forget Mom.

She was born in Reynosa, the same border town mentioned earlier

A city bustling with traffic, vendors, families, and frontera culture.

The streets were loud, the air thick, and life moved fast.

Even back then, Reynosa was busy. Big. Much bigger than where my dad was from.

But my mother?

She never got lost in the noise.

She was the backbone of the family in all the ways that go unnoticed.

While my father was already riding four-wheelers through the fields like a boss, managing crews, getting expelled (lol), and doing donuts down the street to loud música norteña…

My mom was in the trenches.

Hands in the dirt.

Sweat on her collarbone.

Balancing school and farm work.

Handling responsibilities with no applause. No credit. No drama.

She was sharp. Strategic.

A quiet powerhouse.

That's the thing about women like her

You don't always see their strength right away.

But it's there.

Silent.

Unshakable.

Sacred.

Turns out, I didn't just inherit her height and tenacity or my father's loud laugh, natural dominance, and relentless hustle.

I carry both lineages and everything in between.

I inherited the Cassique's boldness.

The gambler's edge but with a little more control. (LOL, kind of.)

Anyone who knows me knows I love a good Vegas getaway.

I inherited my paternal grandmother's loyalty, elegance, and stillness.

My maternal grandmother's grace, humility, and quiet fire.

I am the sum of many contradictions

Rich blood and rough beginnings.

Patriarchs and paddlings.

Indigenous royalty and dusty trailer parks.

My bloodline has always been a paradox:

Powerful. Unpredictable. Unstoppable.

From Dirt Roads to Donuts in the Street

My mom didn't have a choice either but for different reasons.

She wasn't rebellious like my dad.

She didn't walk away from school.

She was pulled out.

She did what she was told.

Worked the fields. Went to school. Balanced both until her family needed more hands than homework.

She completed elementary school in Mexico, then moved to Texas with her parents and siblings.

There, she attended sixth, seventh, and eighth grade all while working in the fields after school.

Eventually, her parents withdrew her from school entirely.

She was needed full-time now.

Her dreams could wait.

We'll get to the heart of that later, but for now...

During those early years, both of my parents worked for farms like "Helly Farms" and "Griffin & Brand" familiar names for anyone who's picked in the Rio Grande Valley.

They harvested whatever the season called for — melons, onions, green bell peppers, and eventually, as they became more skilled, even cauliflower, which took more care and speed.

Once my mom was pulled out of school, the grind became her full reality.

No more bell schedules. Just crop cycles.

And oddly enough, she said that meant she got to see more of Dad.

Apparently, my dad was always a wild one.

He was fearless when it came to machinery.

Tractors, trucks, trailers he didn't care if he'd never driven it before.

He'd hop in, figure it out, and by the end of the day, he was shifting gears like he'd been doing it for years.

Classic Dad.

Big engine energy. No formal training. Just vibes.

They started dating while working in Texas.

And trust me, this is where the story gets hilarious.

My dad had this beat-up old car — covered in Road Runner stickers like a Looney Tunes NASCAR tribute.

He was obsessed with the Road Runner.

Speed, noise, chaos sounds about right.

He'd drive by my mom's house, windows down, music blasting.

The soundtrack? Los Barón de Apodaca — specifically "Y Por Esa Calle Vive" on repeat.

If you don't know the song, look it up, heartbreak, drama, intensity… the perfect anthem for a young man in love and out of control.

He'd burn tires, do donuts in the street, pass by her house three, four, five times.

A one-man parade with cheap speakers and big feelings.

One time, he even spun out and drove straight into a neighbor's fresh concrete foundation. Yup. Destroyed it.

Then drove off, terrified but obviously got in trouble later. Who did this man think he was?!

I shouldn't laugh, but I can't help it.

It's so him. So over-the-top. So dramatic. So bold.

The stories make him feel close again.

They dated for three years on and off. Even long distance.

Since this was the pre-cell phone era, they stayed in touch by writing love letters.

Every year, my mom's family migrated to Washington State to chase higher wages working seasonal crops.

While she was gone, they wrote.

Letters full of longing and teenage promises.

Both in Texas and Washington, some farms offered shelter.

Not glamorous by any means just migrant camps built for temporary laborers.

There were usually multiple camps per farm, with about ten families per camp.

Each family was given a single small cabin two beds max, regardless of how many kids or adults were in the family

Everyone shared communal bathrooms one for men, one for women located in the center of the camps.

Wild, right?

Humbling.

Raw.

Real.

My dad hated her leaving every year.

He'd get jealous, they'd argue, they'd break up and always end up back together.

But one year, when she returned from the Washington fields, everything changed.

He told her he wanted to marry her.

She told her parents.

They prepped the house for a celebration.

Family members were invited aunts, uncles, cousins, neighbors. It

was going to be a real engagement moment.

You know, Mexican style loud, festive, full of food, and everyone in your business.

But he didn't show.

Not on time, anyway.

He showed up late that night.

My grandfather?

He was furious.

He pulled out a machete, chased him off the property, and told him in no uncertain terms that marriage wasn't a game.

(Side note: If you've never seen a machete
"Imagine a sword made for work, not war. Long. Heavy. Thick. And sharp enough to make anyone

rethink their life choices".)

But guess what?

Three months later, my mom left with him anyway.

They snuck off without telling anyone.

My dad was so paranoid her family would come after them, he even

removed the Road Runner stickers from his car to avoid being recognized.

They hid in a field nearby, just long enough to let the tension cool off.

Eventually, they made it to his mother's house.

But even she wasn't happy about it.

She slapped him across the face and separated them for the night.

My mom slept with the girls.

My dad with the boys.

The next morning, my mom's parents came looking.

Words were exchanged.

And two weeks later, the families arranged the wedding.

Once they were married, they joined Mom's family on the road migrating to Washington to continue working contracts together.

Farming didn't stop just because they were married.

If anything, it intensified.

Not long after, Mom got pregnant with my older brother.

And still they hustled.

They worked asparagus fields in the heat.

Then later, in Yakima, Washington, they picked strawberries and blueberries for extra money.

The work was hard.

The days were long.

The pay? Never enough.

Mom would carry my brother in her arms as she worked.

If he got too heavy, she'd sit him in the dirt beside her while she filled buckets.

Other families did the same.

Babies crawling in the shade of a bucket.

Toddlers sleeping between rows of crops.

It was normal.

Unspoken.

Passed down.

That life those fields became home.

Not by choice, but by necessity.

They didn't have the money to return to Texas.

So they stayed.

Worked.

Saved.

Planted roots.

Oregon Was Everything

Three years later…

I came into the picture.

Born in a small town called Hermiston, Oregon, my arrival marked the

beginning of a whole new chapter for our family not just as parents of two kids, but as entrepreneurs in the making.

Around the time I was born, my parents made two major moves:

They bought their first home a modest single-wide trailer and my dad purchased his first two semi-trucks.

While they were still working the fields during the day, they had those trucks running routes and contracts.

My mom handled payroll, paperwork, and as much of the business side as she could… until I showed up.

Now, there were two of us:

My older brother their firstborn.

And me their December baby with a loud laugh and a wobbly little walk.

From the very beginning, I was different.

Mom swears I came out independent the only one of her four kids who refused to breastfeed.

She said I always seemed to have my own mind, even as a newborn.

Everyone in Hermiston adored me.

Neighbors and family friends would bring over tiny dresses, shoes, and headbands.

Mom says people couldn't help but want to hold me dress me up spoil me just a little.

I walked early.

I had a weird little sense of humor.

I'd waddle around making ridiculous faces and noises, going absolutely feral in the jumper or swing.

If I was in the walker?

Good luck catching me.

But once I learned to walk for real, it was game over.

I started climbing up onto chairs, unlocking the front door, and sneaking out.

I gave my poor mom so many heart attacks she should've gotten hazard pay.

Sound familiar?

Like father, like daughter giving the women in our lives gray hairs before their time.

The family always said I wasn't a "girly-girl."

I didn't care for Barbies or pink frilly stuff.

I wanted Hot Wheels, and I'd steal my brother's toy cars every chance I got.

But I did have a thing for dresses and shoes.

Even if they weren't pink, I wore little heels and dresses everywhere.

Mom said my little belly always puffed the dresses out in the front, making everyone laugh.

And I loved it, loved the attention.

I loved the camera, too.

If someone was filming or snapping photos?

There I was front and center with the cheesiest smile.

Always ready.

Always extra.

I was a happy baby.

When I started school, I became the class translator.

I was fluent in Spanish and English something that would follow me for the rest of my life.

At home, Spanish was the first language.

None of my grandparents spoke English.

But at school, everything was in English.

So I became the bridge.

The go-between.

The bilingual baby translating conversations between teachers and

classmates, parents and principals.

Even before I knew the word bi-cultural, I was living it.

And let me tell you

Living in Oregon felt like magic.

I was a winter baby, born in December and to this day, winter is still my favorite season.

The snow, the scarves, the puffy jackets, the stillness in the air.

The way the cold stings your cheeks but makes the world feel fresh.

I remember how the fields looked after a frost.

How the house felt warm when you came inside.

It was beautiful.

Safe.

Peaceful.

Oregon was joy.

Oregon was stability.

Oregon was home.

While our little family settled into what felt like a "normal" life, the business was growing too.

The year after I was born, my dad bought three more trucks bringing his total to five.

That was a huge deal.

He now had a small fleet, and since his trucks were under contract with the farms, he was allowed to park them right on farm property during the off-season.

No warehouse. No commercial lot.

Just open land and big dreams.

That setup worked.

It kept things flowing.

We didn't have to move back to Texas.

Didn't have to chase work in the same way.

And as the seasons passed, so did the miles and memories.

We ended up living in Oregon for nearly seven years straight without ever returning to Texas.

For a while…

Oregon was everything.

Chapter 2

The Oregon Years

During those seven years we lived in Oregon, we did a whole lot of living. Our days were simple but full the kind of full that sticks with you when you're older and looking back. My dad, along with a few of our family members who were also living nearby at the time, made it a point to gather on weekends. Cookouts, soccer games, random get-togethers at the park it was always something. We'd pack into the car and head to Marina Park, our go-to spot for family outings. That little park held more memories than most places ever could.

Dad loved playing soccer. Nothing serious just pick-up games with his friends, mostly other men who had grown up with the same grit and rhythm of fieldwork and long days. Soccer was their release, their joy. I don't know if they ever kept score or if it even mattered. The game was just part of the weekend, like sunshine or laughter.

We'd also visit the Portland Zoo, and one of my favorite parts was the long train ride that circled the entire place. I still remember the anticipation of hearing the train whistle, watching it curve through pine trees and little hills. There was an eagle show too a full performance where they'd release this massive eagle, and you'd watch it soar through the Oregon skies, above the hills, gliding between pine-covered ridges before returning home to the zoo. It was magic. Real magic. And I remember feeling so small, but also so amazed like anything was possible.

Looking back, we lived what I like to call a pretty normal, humble life. And I mean that in the best way possible. It wasn't flashy, but it was full of heart. It was a life that made room for joy, even when money was tight or stress was high.

Somehow and I don't even remember how it started. I got into dancing while we were in Oregon. I used to perform for Florcorico during Cinco de Mayo celebrations. Every year, the town hosted a festival at Marina Park. There were vendors, live music, food, and cultural performances. I was one of the girls who danced in full traditional Mexican attire big, colorful dresses, hair braided to the side, faces painted with full glam (well, as glam as a little girl could get). Red lipstick. Rosy cheeks. Thick eyeliner. It was the only time I got to wear makeup, and I felt like a star.

We wore those hard-bottomed shoes that made loud clacking sounds against the concrete. I can still hear the echo. Click, clack, click — like music all on its own. Every girl had her own braid style, but we all shared that same electric energy, that pride of being on stage, dancing to rhythms rooted in generations of culture.

My mom still has pictures of me from those days and I love looking back at them. Little me, trying to dance seriously but cheesing hard the whole time. I remember catching glimpses of my dad's face in the crowd while I danced. His eyes would light up, and he'd nod along with the beat, pride all over his face. It made me feel seen. Like I mattered. Like I was part of something bigger than just my small body and loud shoes.

I even learned how to dance the lambada, though I was a stiff little thing. They'd always tease me about my hips, trying to get them to move the right way. But I eventually got it. Dad would blast cumbias in the living room or corridos, depending on the mood and dance with my mom like they were teenagers again. And when the music changed, it was our turn. My brother and I would twirl around the living room, dizzy and giggling.

Music did something to our house. It brought it to life. There's something about music and Latinos it stirs up joy like a pot of caldo on the stove. It doesn't matter how the day's gone or what worries are on your chest. When the music hits, it shifts the whole atmosphere. Suddenly the stress melts away, and for a few minutes, it feels like everything is okay. Everything is beautiful.

The marina really was the heart of the town. It was where everyone went to breathe. They had picnic tables, space to walk dogs, and even a full

RV campground paved and ready for families to pull in and settle for the weekend. If you've ever seen Free Willy, the scene where the whale jumps over the rocks that's exactly what the marina looked like. No exaggeration. Oregon sunsets reflected over the water like gold spilled across glass. The kind of view that doesn't need a filter or a caption and when it was warm enough, we swam. Not pools. Not splash pads. Real water. The river was cold, and it would shock your bones at first, but after a while, it felt perfect. The kind of cold that reminded you you were alive. We'd run in squealing, splash around, and dare each other to swim further or dunk under longer.

To me, Oregon always felt cold year-round, if I'm being honest. The mornings were crisp, almost icy. By midday, the sun warmed things up just enough to take off a jacket. But by 6 PM, the chill returned like clockwork. I got used to it. I became an Oregon girl, through and through. Puffy jackets, cozy socks, cold breath in the air that was my backdrop.

Those years were soft in the way that only childhood can be. Oregon was more than a place. It was a feeling. A safe one. A grounded one. A chapter of life where everything felt possible and nothing felt too heavy. I didn't know it back then, but I was gathering joy real, lasting joy to carry with me into the harder chapters ahead.

Mom and Dad still had their regular arguments, like every other couple. I was too young to understand what all the tension was about, but even then, I knew something wasn't right. I've pieced things together over the years, but I believe there was a point when my dad got in trouble with the law and was taken to the county jail. I'm not sure if it was just for a couple of months or closer to a full year everything from that time is a bit of a blur. I don't remember visiting him. I don't remember seeing him in an orange jumpsuit or behind any glass. But I do remember the silence. I remember catching my mom crying by herself in their bedroom more than once quietly, with the door cracked, sitting on the edge of the bed, as if she was trying to hold herself together and come undone all at once. I don't think she ever realized I saw her. I never told her. But those images stayed with me her small frame, her silent sobs, her trying to be both mother and father while keeping the house from falling apart.

The details were never fully explained to me, but from what I've heard in bits and pieces, it might've had something to do with drinking and driving maybe reckless driving. That wouldn't surprise me. My dad was a fast driver. Everything about him was fast the way he talked, the way he handled business, the way he moved through life. He lived like he had something to prove. Like he was in control of the world and wanted to keep it that way. He liked things done his way all the time. That part of him never really changed.

Despite everything, he still made space for us to feel special in our little town. There was a small hotel nearby that had a restaurant attached to it, and on occasion, he would take us there. Looking back, it was just a modest diner inside a basic roadside hotel. But to us kids who lived a humble life it felt like luxury. The booths were shiny, the menu had more than just tacos or hamburgers, and the drinks came with little lemon wedges. It was nothing extravagant, but it felt like everything. That's the thing about growing up with less the little things hit different. They sparkle. They stick.

Most of the people we knew our school friends, our parents' coworkers, our relatives lived in simple trailers, small mobile homes, or even campers. Everyone was trying to make it. No one was rich. A dinner out like that wasn't common. It wasn't something we could do every weekend. So when we did go, we dressed a little nicer, sat up straighter, and soaked it all in like we were at a five-star restaurant. Dad never really told us no, but we also didn't ask for much. Not because we were selfless kids, but because we didn't know what else was out there. What we had was enough. Or at least, it felt like it at the time.

One of my favorite childhood memories is tied to a gift from my grandma P my mom's mom. One visit, she gave me a little cassette radio shaped like a duck. Yes, a literal duck. It was bright and goofy, small enough to carry around, and the sound wasn't anything special no bass, no fancy speakers but to me, it was magic. A duck radio that played music? That was it. That was peak happiness.

I remember popping in my favorite cassette: Los Tigres del Norte or Los Tiguerillos something upbeat and rooted in Mexican rhythm. I'd play that cassette over and over, flipping it when it ended, turning it back around, and pressing play again like it was the soundtrack of my entire childhood. I didn't need anything else. That duck radio became my whole world.

My parents always said I was an early bird even when school started at six or seven in the morning, I'd be up by five. This wasn't a one-time thing; this was every day. Through elementary, middle school didn't matter. I'd wake up early, turn on my little duck radio, and start my day with music while the rest of the house tried to sleep. My mom used to say, "You have no business being up that early!" but I never stopped.

Sometimes I'd even leave the cassette playing through the night, and when it stopped, I'd wake up, flip it, and start it again. That cassette deck worked overtime. Now that I'm a mom myself, I laugh when my boys do the exact same thing. Playing the same songs or videos on repeat, waking me up before the sun is even out. It's full circle now. Like mother, like sons, I guess.

Dad worked hard like really hard. I didn't understand the weight he carried until I got older, but now I see it. He was trying to juggle everything. Long hours, odd jobs, risky moves all of it with the goal of getting my mom out of the working fields. To him, the ultimate luxury as a man was to be able to take care of your woman in a way that she didn't have to clock in and out for anyone else. He didn't want her laboring in the sun or working for some company that didn't value her. He used to say it clearly and proudly: "Why would I let my wife work for another man's business when she could help build mine?"

He didn't just want to provide. He wanted to create something that belonged to us. A business. A legacy. Something that would outlive the back pain and the stress and the struggle. He was intense, but he was smart. I'll give him that.

My mom might've been a little slow to catch on at first at least that's how she tells it but she learned fast. She studied him. She listened. He mentored her in his own way. It wasn't always pretty or patient, but it worked. She started helping him in small ways, learning the ropes, and doing her part to support the dream. They were building something together, whether they realized it or not.

And that was the beginning of a new kind of partnership between them one rooted in survival, ambition, and the kind of teamwork that can only come from knowing what it means to have nothing... and still try anyway.

I know I've mentioned this before, but my dad practiced control. And when I say that, I mean control over everything. Over decisions. Over routines. Over the mood in the room. Even in his most humble beginnings, he moved like a man who needed to be in charge. He didn't just want control he believed it was his duty to lead, protect, provide, guide, and yes, control. To him, that was part of being a man.

He used to say, "Leadership and control cost money." That was one of his mottos. If you wanted to be the man of the house, you had to fund the house. Provide for it. Earn your seat at the head of the table. It wasn't just about masculinity it was about responsibility. That was his whole mindset.

But let's not paint him as just some strict, traditional, hard-nosed Mexican dad. That man knew chivalry. As short-tempered and hot-blooded as he could be, he was also incredibly thoughtful and romantic in his own way. He had charm. He had rhythm. And let me tell you that man could move. He didn't just dance; he commanded a dance floor. He had that natural sway, that confidence, that smoothness that made people watch.

Underneath the fire and grit, he was caring, funny, and full of life. He had that irresistible combination ambition and humor, street smarts and softness. Who doesn't love a man with drive? He was goal-oriented, competitive, and calculating but at the same time, he was a family man to his core.

He would do thoughtful little things for my mom from time to time. And one thing about this man? He paid attention to details. He knew how to give a good gift like, really good. Even when we didn't have much, he somehow found a way to make her feel special.

Looking back now as an adult, I'd say one of his strongest love languages was gift giving. Not the flashy, overpriced kind, but the "I saw this and thought of you" kind. The kind that made you feel known.

Another one of his love languages was definitely music and dance. I've said this before and I'll say it again music lit up his soul. There were so many nights I'd catch him slow dancing with my mom in the kitchen of our little single-wide trailer, or grabbing her by surprise while she was cooking, smacking her on the butt and making her jump. She'd yell and then burst into laughter. I remember thinking it was kind of cute, even if I pretended to roll my eyes. It was like watching two people still choosing each other, even in the chaos.

Some of my favorite memories of him are tied to my younger brothers being born. I remember both times when my mom went into labor the energy was always high, and the house felt different. The first thing my dad would do was try to make breakfast for me and my older brother... and fail miserably. The man could not cook to save his life. One time, he tried to make toast and somehow still managed to burn it. The entire house smelled like charred bread and disappointment. I can still picture his face frustrated, standing in the kitchen with the spatula in his hand, smoke in the air, and that short-tempered energy building up. He tossed everything in the trash, threw his hands in the air, muttered under his breath, and marched off to get us ready instead. "Screw this," basically. Next thing you know, we were dressed and in the car, headed to a little restaurant called Granny's.

As soon as we stepped into that place, he was back in his element. Calm. Collected. Regal. Like he was walking into his own throne room. He always ordered the same thing, no matter where we went: sunny-side-up eggs, crispy bacon, hash browns, and toast. Always in that exact combination. And he never just ordered one drink he had a system. Coffee, orange juice, and a glass of water. Three drinks. Always. If we were home, my mom knew that when she served him, she had to prepare the drinks the same way. It was just how he functioned. That's how particular he was even when he was just a broke farmer trying to feed his family, or later when he became a landlord running multiple properties. Whether he had $20 in his pocket or $20,000 in his bank account, he wanted three things on his plate. A complete, proper meal: protein, carbs, and veggies all separate, all portioned right. No exceptions.

Now that I'm older, I laugh because I kind of inherited that mindset. I'm definitely more relaxed the millennial mom version but deep down, I get it. Presentation matters. Routine matters. Order matters. Some things just stick with you when you grow up watching them day in and day out.

That was my dad. Complex, funny, infuriating, warm, structured, full of rules and somehow, full of love.

One thing about my dad he did not believe in leftovers. There was no way on earth we were going to box up unfinished food at a restaurant and take it home. And don't even think about reheating something from the night before. If it wasn't fresh, he didn't want it. My mom, on the other hand, didn't mind. She'd wrap things up and save it for herself, knowing full well that he wouldn't touch it. For him, it had to be a hot, freshly made meal every single time. He believed in quality, even in the smallest details.

Now circling back to those sweet mornings when my mom went into labor after we finished our breakfast at Granny's, my dad didn't just drive us straight to the hospital. No, he made it a whole experience. He took my brother and me to the store to pick out gifts for Mom roses, bouquets, chocolates, cards, all the little things. He made sure each of us had something to carry so that when we walked into the hospital room, we'd surprise her together.

I'll never forget the look on her face when we arrived. It was like her entire soul lit up. The exhaustion, the pain, the hospital smell it all faded for a second. She smiled so big, tears in her eyes, and I remember thinking this is what love looks like. The moment felt perfect. I would do anything to relive it again. It's one of those core memories that stays tucked in your chest, always warm when you go back to it.

At the time, my parents were still hustling hard. To help manage

Everything, they leaned on the kindness of the community. There was a small local daycare that sometimes watched us, and neighbors or family friends would step in when needed. The town was tight-knit. Everybody knew everybody, and my mom's friends were always generous with their time and love. We weren't rich in money, but we were rich in community.

It was around this season of life that we began spending part of the year in Texas. We'd go back for a couple months at a time, but Oregon still felt like home it was our full-time place. Most holidays were spent in Oregon, and let me tell you Halloween was the best of them all.

I don't know if it was the small-town feel, the cold weather, or just the magic of childhood, but Halloween in Oregon hit different. The sky would turn a deep gray, the air crisp and cool, and the leaves would crunch under our feet as we walked house to house, trick-or-treating through the neighborhood. It felt like something out of a movie. Everyone handed out good candy none of that off-brand nonsense. Whole chocolate bars, fun-size Snickers, Reese's, Twix, the works. We had the best time.

Mom would layer us in warm clothes under our costumes, zipping up our jackets tight while trying not to ruin the "look." She took us door to door, smiling and chatting with neighbors, while Dad stayed home and passed out candy. But my favorite part? We would knock on our own door and Dad would open it like we were just any other neighborhood kids. "¡Trick or treat!" we'd yell. And without breaking character, he'd reach into the candy bowl and drop two big handfuls into each of our bags, like he had no idea who we were. We'd run off laughing, high on sugar and pretending we tricked him every time.

It was wholesome. It was simple. It was safe.

You couldn't really do that in Texas. The neighborhoods were different, more spread out, and there was always a little bit of tension in the air. In that small Oregon town, we could walk anywhere — to the corner store, to school events, to a friend's house. If my mom needed milk or tortillas or something last-minute, we'd throw on a hoodie and walk to the store to grab it. It was no big deal. Just part of daily life.

That kind of simplicity sticks with you. It carves a space in your heart. Oregon wasn't just the place where we lived it was the place where everything felt safe. Where things were normal. Where life had rhythm, community, and breath. We didn't know how good we had it… not yet.

But we'd come to learn.

Chapter 3
A Single-Wide Simplicity

Life in Oregon was probably the most peaceful time for us as a family. You'll understand why that matters so much later but for now, just know that it was the closest we ever came to feeling something like "normal." Maybe it was the trailer a narrow little single-wide that forced us into closeness, whether we liked it or not. You couldn't go anywhere in that home without hearing someone laugh, cry, cook, or cuss. Privacy didn't exist, but somehow that created a kind of intimacy. We were in each other's lives, fully and completely, every single day.

Like I mentioned before my dad used to play soccer at the local park on weekends, showing off like he was trying out for a team. He had a way of making even a pickup game feel like a championship match. Afterward, he'd take us out to eat, and we'd all pile into some humble family-owned restaurant where the food tasted like love and the waitresses already knew our names. My parents had good, salt-of-the-earth friends they hung out with and so did my brother and I. We'd go to school carnivals, church events, holiday parades, and community gatherings where the whole town showed up. People waved. People remembered you. We were part of something, even if it was small.

And maybe that's what made it feel so safe. So free. Anytime I was in Oregon, I didn't feel judged, not for how I looked, not for what I wore, not for the single-wide we called home or the beat-up truck we drove. Nobody cared. Or if they did, they kept it to themselves. Life felt... simple. Peaceful. Uncomplicated.

Until it wasn't.

We came from a town so tiny that if you burped, sneezed, or farted at the corner store, five people down the street would know it was you. And as annoying as that sounds, I still crave that kind of knowing

That kind of safety. That feeling of being seen, not as a spectacle, but as someone who belongs. I think I've spent most of my adult life trying to recreate that trying to find it again in bigger cities, in new circles, in my work, in my relationships. Maybe I've got a small-town heart with big-city ambition. Maybe I'm both.

Our life followed a seasonal rhythm, like clockwork. Every year, we'd live in Oregon for the fall months September, October, and November just long enough to feel settled. And then we'd pack everything up and head back to Texas for the rest of the year. It was a cycle. Oregon. Texas. Texas. Oregon. One life traded for another like a set of clothes we kept changing out of. I got used to it. But that doesn't mean it didn't cost me. Every move meant leaving something behind. We'd leave behind friends, teachers, routines. Every time we got to Oregon, I felt like I was playing catch-up in school. The curriculum never matched. The way they taught math or reading or science it was always just different enough to make me feel lost. The kids already had their inside jokes and classroom cliques. I'd walk in with a new backpack and the same old nerves, hoping someone remembered me. Hoping someone would say hi.

Most of the teachers in Oregon didn't speak Spanish, and I don't think a single one of them ever pronounced my name correctly. It seems small, but when you're a kid trying to belong, every syllable matters. Being called the wrong name in front of a whole class feels like being erased in real time. Like whatever identity you brought with you from Texas just got snatched out of your hands. I started shrinking into myself. Started dreading roll call. Started wishing my name was something anything easier.

Real talk? Oregon made me hate my own name. I hated the way it sounded in their mouths. I hated the long pauses and confused stares before they even tried. I hated that my name always came with a question mark. Yuh-sin-ee-uh? Yess-uh-nigh-uh? It was like watching people try to solve a riddle with their eyebrows. And every time they stumbled, I felt myself disappear a little more. I swore I was going to change it the moment I turned eighteen. I was already practicing fake names in my head, dreaming of something short and sweet, something nobody could butcher. In Texas, there were always a few other Yesenia's. I blended in, even if just a little. But in Oregon? I was the only one. The only one. Which meant I stuck out and not in the cute, special way. In the awkward, always explaining yourself kind of way.

And don't even get me started on the nickname Yesi.

My grandma said it with love. My mom's side of the family yelled it like it was part of their daily routine. My brothers would scream it from across the house like it was my legal name:

"¡YESI!"

"Hey, Yesi, come here!"

"YESI, VEN PA'CA."

Every time I heard it, I rolled my eyes so hard I could practically see my childhood trauma. I hated how exposed it made me feel. It sounded like a cartoon character. Like Jessie from Toy Story too peppy, too country, too… not me. I didn't want to be called anything that made me feel more out of place than I already did.

But now? Now I am Yesi.

Now I wear my name like armor soft but unbreakable. I have a necklace that spells it out in delicate gold and a matching ring that wraps it around my finger like a secret only I fully understand. I even have it in silver for the days when I want to switch up the vibe. People compliment it all the time they say it sounds beautiful, elegant, rare. Powerful.

And it is.

Because I am.

No lie every time I sign my name, whether it's on a check, a contract, or a Starbucks cup, I feel it. That little girl who wanted to change her name is still inside me, but now she's protected. Now she's celebrated. Funny how you grow into the very thing you once tried to run from.

And don't even get me started with the closet. LOL. Just thinking about the way I dressed in Oregon vs. Texas cracks me up now. It was like I lived two completely different lives one laid back, the other buttoned-up. My outfits had personality shifts depending on the zip code.

Oregon? Oregon was chill to the core. Laid-back vibes everywhere. You could step out of the house in leggings, a hoodie, and some beat-up sneakers, and nobody would care. I mean nobody. You could roll into Walmart in pajamas, and there was a good chance half your school was there doing the same thing. That was the weekend move grocery store strolls, random aisle hangouts, seeing who else had the same idea. A dress with sneakers? Cool. Baggy jeans and a tee? Even cooler. No judgment, no performance. Just comfort and vibes.

Texas? Oh, honey. Texas was a whole different production.

Even a quick trip to the gas station felt like a mini fashion show. And not the fun kind, the pressure kind. Like: do your hair, fix your lashes, pick the right outfit, walk with purpose. I swear, the way people turned heads at H-E-B (which, by the way, is our Texas version of heaven in grocery store form) you'd think it was a runway.

Everything in Texas felt a little extra. Like, pop-your-collar, full-face-of-makeup, matching set to take the trash out kind of energy. It wasn't just about being presentable it was about showing up polished, loud, and noticeable. The best nails. The name-brand bag. The fresh blowout. The full aesthetic. There was always this unspoken contest of who could do the most while pretending it was casual.

And honestly? That energy used to stress me out. Because some-times, even when I didn't mean to, I'd carry little pieces of Oregon with me in how I dressed, how I moved, how I spoke. I'd slip up and say something with a soft "up north" twang, and my Texas friends would be quick to clown me:

"Why are you talking like that?"

Cue the pit in my stomach.

It was such a subtle thing, but it cut deep. It made me feel like I didn't fully belong anywhere. Like I was always too much of something and not enough of something else. I can't remember a single time my Oregon friends made me feel that way. In Oregon, I was "the Texas friend." In Texas, I was "the Oregon girl." Always in between.

We traveled a lot, too even beyond the Oregon-Texas back-and-forth. As I got older, my dad started taking us to Mexico. He'd say it was for family. For culture. For fun. And as a kid, I believed him. I soaked up every beach town and quiet pueblo like it was vacation. I played with my cousins, ate fresh fruit off roadside stands, marveled at the colors, the smells, the music, the dirt roads that kicked up behind our truck like powder. I didn't know there was more to it. I didn't understand the layers of business, family ties, or unspoken logistics behind those trips.

Back then, it just felt like an adventure. A beautiful blur of new places and old traditions.

But if I'm being real, I was terrible on road trips. I wasn't trying to be dramatic I just never learned how to pop a squat. No joke. It became a whole thing. I'd hold it for hours, sometimes even a full day, just to avoid having to pee in a porta potty or behind a bush. I refused to go unless I had access to a proper toilet.

In Mexico, that was tricky.

My dad's mom, my abuelita had a real bathroom in her house, so I always said yes to those visits. But my other grandma, the one who lived more humbly in a ranch-style home, didn't have plumbing like that for the longest time. I'd skip the trip altogether if I knew we weren't going to have a toilet. It sounds so silly now, but it was a real issue back then. I'd help wash dishes outside, sleep on the floor, pluck fruit, feed the chickens no problem. But pee in a bucket or squat in a field? Absolutely not.

Eventually, she got a toilet installed, and when she called to let us know, she said, "Now you have no excuse." And she was right. From that day on, I went. I showed up.

Despite all the places we traveled, all the life I got to experience at such a young age, I still lived under a rock in a lot of ways. My dad was strict. He ran our house like it was boot camp. I wasn't allowed to know too much. I wasn't allowed to do too much. I didn't have a phone. No social media. No TV in my room. Not even a stereo or CD player. It wasn't about money. We could afford it I just wasn't allowed.

I didn't get to live out the kind of childhood most of my classmates did. I didn't have posters on my wall or favorite radio stations. Most of the world outside of our family bubble felt far away. I lived in my own little world strict, sheltered, quiet.

But Oregon?

Oregon was my breath. My pause. My in-between.

It was where life slowed down just enough for me to notice the way the leaves changed in the fall. Where I could walk to school without worrying about what I looked like. Where dinner meant conversation, not chaos. Where I could just be for a moment before the next storm of change.

It was never perfect.

But it was peaceful.

And sometimes… that was more than enough.

Now, with everything I've shared so far, you'd probably think I had this perfect, tight-knit relationship with my parents especially my dad. But nope. You'd be wrong.

I remember being five or six maybe seven standing in our tiny trailer doorway like a pint-sized soap opera star, telling anyone who would listen, "My dad doesn't love me." Dramatic. Full telenovela mode. I'd say it to family members, friends, random visitors. Like a little Latina with a flair for theatrics and a lot of feelings.

But deep down, I knew it wasn't true. I knew both my parents loved me I could feel it in the things they did, even if they didn't say it. They just had this old-school, emotionally unavailable, Mexican parent way of showing love. No hugs for no reason. No "I'm proud of you" unless you hit a major milestone. No deep talks. Just tough love, sacrifice, and the occasional plate of food handed to you without a word. If you know, you know.

As I got a little older and as a little bit more money started rolling in I discovered the one thing I hated the most: sharing. Not my toys, not my snacks... but my parents. We were Catholic, and because of that, my parents were constantly getting asked to be god-parents. And not just once or twice I'm talking often. Usually to baby girls. And I hated it.

It felt like there was always another madrina moment waiting around the corner. Every birthday, every holiday, every Christmas, they'd buy me and their goddaughters the exact same gift. Like, down to the same doll or outfit or little accessory set. And I couldn't wrap my little brain around it. Why? I was their daughter. Not just another godchild. Not someone else's kid. I wanted to feel special and instead, I felt replaceable.

We'd walk into a party and their goddaughters would come running up, arms wide, screaming "¡Madrina!" and "¡Padrino!" while throwing themselves into my parents' arms like it was a reunion scene. And there I was standing off to the side, watching. Trying not to look like it bothered me. But it did.

Little Yesenia definitely held a grudge. Quiet, invisible, bubbling up inside kind of grudge.

Things shifted with time and you'll see how in the chapters ahead but during these early years, I felt like I was constantly fighting for a spotlight that should've been mine without question. Like I had to earn a kind of love and attention that should've already been mine by default.

Still, even through the jealousy and confusion, there were sweet memories too. Moments that belonged only to me. My dad and I connected through music and dancing. Our little trailer didn't have much space, but somehow we always found room to dance. He taught me how to dance cumbias and the lambada right there in the living room. My mom would step in to help too correcting my footwork or clapping along with a smile. We'd slide the coffee table out of the way and turn up the music like we were at a party. It was loud. Joyful. A little chaotic. But it was ours.

Later, I danced folklórico in school and performed for Cinco de Mayo and yes, I'll tell you about that later but those early dance sessions with my parents were special. They planted something in me. A love for rhythm. A pride in my culture. A way to move my body that made me feel seen.

One of my favorite memories the one that always plays in my mind like a movie was riding shotgun next to my dad on one of our road trips between Oregon and Texas. I was always the best co-pilot because I refused to fall asleep. I'd keep him company, DJ the ride, and point out things along the way. He'd blast Cher's "Do You Believe in Life After Love?" while we rolled through Vegas at night city lights blinking, windows down, wind blowing through the car. Just vibes. Pure freedom.

I can still picture the pine trees lining the roads as we got closer to Oregon. That moment when the air shifted cooler, cleaner and I could feel that we were almost home. Oregon home. Even my parents seemed to breathe easier the moment we crossed into that state. Like some invisible weight came off their shoulders. They laughed more. Smiled more. We played more music. Stopped for snacks. Sang louder. They were more alive there.

Eventually, they started baptizing not just family members' kids, but friends' kids too. It added another layer to my jealousy but by then, I'd grown up just enough to shrug it off. Sort of. Okay, maybe not completely.

But Oregon softened us. The music, the dancing, the weekend community events they brought us closer in ways that Texas didn't. There was less pressure. More presence. And I'll never forget the Portland Zoo. That place blew my little mind. Hands down, one of my favorite family weekends of all time. Even now, as a mom, I want to take my own kids there so they can feel that same magic I did.

Back to my parents, though. Like I mentioned before, we were raised Catholic. Heavy on tradition. They enrolled me in Catholic school so I could make my First Communion and Confirmation. We had weekly Bible classes during the week and Sunday church services. Very small-town, very structured. Ask me if I actually learned anything from those classes though? Sadly… I didn't.

I knew the basic prayers. I could do the whole Catholic stand up, sit down, kneel, repeat routine like clockwork. But emotionally? Spiritually? I wasn't really connecting with it. It felt more like going through the motions than anything deeply meaningful.

Still, I'll never forget my Communion day.

That might've been the first time my dad showed love in a way that I actually felt it. Not because it was loud or dramatic but because it was just for me. After church, still dressed in my white communion gown with the updo, the sparkly crown, my tiny white Bible clutched in my hands he let me ride in the front seat.

That simple act? It meant the world.

He could've said no. He usually would have. But that day, he didn't. He let me ride shotgun all dolled up like a little bride and in that moment, I felt seen. The image is blurry now, but the feeling stuck. I held onto it like a keepsake.

We didn't do stuff like that in Texas. Honestly, we didn't even go to church every Sunday over there. It was harder to keep up with tradition in Texas. Everything was inconsistent. Rushed. Chaotic. Oregon was slower, softer and for that reason, more memorable.

If I'm not mistaken, around this time my parents were still working the fields or farm warehouses. I can't remember exactly the time-line's fuzzy but the big money hadn't rolled in yet. We were still in that single-wide trailer, living at that dusty little trailer park where kids ran barefoot, rode bikes until the sun went down, and collected scrapes and bruises like trophies.

Well… they rode bikes.

I didn't know how until later.

I remember my dad trying to teach me one afternoon. He held onto the seat, told me to trust him, and gave me a push. I pedaled for maybe three seconds before slamming straight into the back of a parked pickup truck. I can still feel the sting both on my knees and my pride.

I was always a bit of a girly-girl when it came to outdoor stuff. Even in our most humble beginnings, I leaned more towards sparkles than scrapes. But I tried. I really did.

And sometimes, those little efforts were the biggest acts of love we had.

School was walking distance from our trailer close enough that even when it snowed, we'd still bundle up and walk. I remember thinking it was magical at the time. The white snow covering everything like powdered sugar, the cold biting our cheeks, our little boots crunching against the frozen ground. It felt like we were in one of those Christmas movies. Meanwhile, my dad would step outside like it was no big deal barefoot in shorts, completely unbothered. My mom would just shake her head and laugh, calling him crazy, while I stood at the door like, Isn't he freezing?!

This was still elementary school age we were tiny. Innocent. Still playing with toys and believing in Santa.

The owner of the trailer park was this grumpy but kind of sweet older woman who had a love/hate relationship with all the kids. She thought we were wild which, to be fair, we probably were. She'd always hand out those strawberry Twizzlers like they were gold, and none of us wanted them. We thought they were so lame back then. We'd be like, "Ugh, why not Hot Cheetos?" Now? I can't lie Twizzlers are one of my favorite snacks. It's funny how taste changes with time, and so do your memories.

That trailer park had a name too or at least a nickname. Everyone called it "Tijuanitas" or something like that. To this day, I still don't know why. I never even asked. That's just what it was. I didn't question it. It was our world.

We lived in that single-wide for years. By then, my medium brother had just been born, making us a family of five my older brother, me, the baby, and eventually, my youngest brother who came two years later. I was the only girl in a sea of boys. That was my identity big sister, little girl holding it down while Mom and Dad worked the fields.

My parents were still deep in the farm and warehouse grind at that time. Early mornings, long days, aching backs, dirty boots. So I stepped up. I helped cook. I swept. I held the baby when he cried. I played with him when my mom needed a minute. I changed diapers. That's just what it was. No complaints, no awards. Just life.

Weekends? All my parents wanted to do was sleep. I hated that back then. I didn't get it. I thought they didn't want to spend time with us. But now? Now I understand completely. That kind of labor takes everything out of you. Physically. Mentally. Emotionally. They weren't avoiding us. They were surviving.

But right around that time… things started to get messy.

There was one day I'll never forget it, the school was doing those random lice checks. The nurse combed through my thick, long Mexican hair and paused. Just like that, I was sent home with instructions to be fully treated before I could return. I was mortified. Embarrassed. And confused. That had never happened to me in Texas.

While I was out of school, I stayed home and helped my mom around the trailer. On one of those mornings, she packed a warm lunch for my dad to take to work. It was something she did often. And before leaving, she looked at me and asked, "Mija, you okay staying home for a bit?"

I said yes I wanted to help. I was proud she trusted me.

But then, there was a knock at the door.

Cops.

Someone had called them. Said a child was left home alone.

My heart dropped.

I remember feeling frozen as they asked me questions one after another, like I was on trial. I tried so hard not to say the wrong thing. I told them the truth: that my mom had just stepped out to deliver lunch, that she'd be right back. I wasn't scared of being alone. I was scared of what would happen to her.

The whole thing lasted maybe fifteen minutes, but it felt like forever. When my mom got back, she stayed calm. She explained everything. The officers eventually left. We never found out who made the call a neighbor, maybe. Honestly, I don't even care anymore.

What stuck with me was what my mom said after. She looked at me and said, "I'm proud of you." And that was everything.

But still… after that, they cut my hair. Took my long locks and chopped them to my shoulders probably to make it easier to manage, to avoid another scare like that.

I cried...Hard.

I didn't feel like me without my long hair. It felt like a piece of my identity had been taken away like the world was punishing me for something I didn't even do wrong.

Eventually, it was time to head back to Texas. Again.

We always knew we were close when we saw the tall water tower and the rows of palm trees swaying in the warm breeze. That was our signal: home. Texas home.

We'd stay at my grandma's house my dad's mom and without fail, she'd greet us with fresh gorditas de azúcar. Always warm, always wrapped in foil, always made with love. She made them when we arrived. She packed extras when we left. I can still smell the sugar and feel the softness of the dough breaking in my hands. That kind of love stays with you.

It was the same routine every year from the time I was in daycare through elementary school. At first, it felt sweet. Cozy. Familiar. But over time, it started to feel heavy. Tiring. Repetitive.

I loved it — until I didn't.

And that haircut? It looked cute for a day, maybe two. Then I just felt... like a boy. I didn't like what I saw in the mirror. No one in Oregon cared, but I did. I missed my hair. I missed feeling pretty. I missed feeling like me.

We withdrew from school again. Said goodbye to friends again. And hit the road, again.

But this time, the excitement started to flip.

Because every year, those long drives came with problems. We'd hit hard snowstorms heading north, and my parents would have to pull over to put chains on the tires. Our cars weren't new. They weren't reliable. Something always came up the engine would overheat, the brakes would squeak, or a tire would go flat. Every trip came with a story.

My parents would take turns driving. Just one vehicle. One car stuffed with kids, bags, snacks, and exhaustion. When they couldn't push through anymore, we'd pull into a truck stop. They'd close their eyes for a few hours in the front seats, just enough to keep going. No fancy hotel stops. No real rest. Just grit.

It was exciting, sure. But it was also exhausting.

And somewhere in the middle of all that back-and-forth Texas to Oregon, Oregon to Texas I started to feel split in two. Like I was never fully from anywhere. Like I belonged to both places, but also... neither. I'd feel at home in Oregon, but crave the culture and rhythm of Texas. Then I'd settle into Texas, only to miss the peace and freedom of Oregon.

It's confusing.

I know. It's confusing in my head too.

But that was life.

From here and there. From neither and both.

Just me caught between palm trees and pine trees. Sugar gorditas and strawberry Twizzlers. Soccer fields and snow boots. Texas roots and Oregon dreams.

Somewhere in between, I was growing up.

Chapter 4

Back to Grandma's / The Slight Transition

TRIGGER WARNING:

This chapter contains memories of emotional tension, childhood neglect, and shifting family dynamics. While it does not contain graphic descriptions, the emotional tone may be heavy for some readers. Please take care as you read.

When we got back into the Texas routine, things weren't anywhere near as good. We didn't see my dad as often and when we did, it didn't feel like him. His presence was different. His fuse was shorter. His voice carried this edge, this weight. He didn't laugh the way he used to. His eyes looked tired like he was in the room, but not really in it. And some days? He just... disappeared. No explanation. No goodbye. He'd be gone for hours, sometimes even overnight, and we were left guessing when or if he'd come home.

But what did increase during that time were our trips to Mexico.

My dad was still deeply connected to his roots in Bravo, Nuevo León. That part of him never changed. My grandparents owned a home and property there, and we visited often sometimes for holidays, sometimes just for the weekend, and always for big family events like weddings, baptisms, or quinceañeras. It wasn't a long drive either the Mexican border was only about thirty minutes from our place in Texas. A short stretch of highway, a quick border crossing, and boom new language, new money, new air.

That kind of proximity shaped so much of my childhood. We could be in another country before we even finished a bag of chips.

Around that same time, my parents were also house hunting for the very first time.

I was still a kid, so the details were blurry, but I felt the tension. I think things were starting to get a little sticky at my grandma's house my dad's mom where we were all still living. And honestly? I don't blame her. We were a full-blown family of six by then: my older brother, me, my younger brother, and now the baby. Four kids. Two tired parents. All under one roof. That's a lot of bodies in a small space. A lot of footsteps. A lot of voices. A lot of stress.

There's an old saying: "Even a dead body starts to stink after three days."

Same goes for extended stays with family. It's cute in the beginning shared meals, late-night talks, the comfort of home cooked food and familiar faces. But after a while? You start bumping into each other in the hallway one too many times. Fridge doors get slammed. Boundaries blur. Tension builds. Eventually, someone's gotta pack a bag and bounce. LOL.

I say that with love, but also with honesty.

To be fair, I think my dad had a deep emotional attachment to his mother. It wasn't a secret. He adored her. Respected her. Protected her. And I truly believe he wanted to make sure she was always okay especially since she had been widowed young and never remarried. In his eyes, it was his duty to stay close and take care of her. And I respect that.

But at the same time… my mom was done.

She wanted her own space. Her own kitchen. Her own rules. Her own bathroom where no one left the toilet seat up or barged in while she was washing her face. She had raised kids, worked in the fields, and been a respectful daughter-in-law but now? She needed a home she could breathe in.

It was time.

We'll come back to that later.

Remember how I said we didn't see my dad much anymore? And that when we did, he was sharper, more on edge?

Well… it got worse.

My parents started fighting. Not just snappy arguments or passive aggressive digs. I'm talking full-blown, door-slamming, yelling from the lungs fights. And sometimes though I wish I could say otherwise it got physical. Nothing too graphic, but enough to shake the walls. Enough to make me scared.

It was the first time I became aware of the darkness in our home. A shadow I hadn't noticed before. Or maybe it was always there and I had just grown old enough to see it.

Let's not forget: my dad's father my grandfather was called a Cassique. A chief. A man of power, presence, and control. I never met him, but the stories I've heard? They paint a clear picture. He was respected. Feared. And maybe even a little dangerous. And somehow… that legacy lived in my father too.

The loudness. The pride. The intensity. The rage.

It wasn't just aimed at my mom. It touched all of us me and my brothers included. He could be rude. Dismissive. Cold. Sometimes even cruel. There was a heaviness in him stress, ego, trauma, pain… maybe all of it combined. And while I couldn't name it back then, I felt it. I knew something was off. The man who used to teach me to dance, sing along to Cher on road trips, and laugh with his whole chest… he was disappearing.

And someone else was showing up in his place.

Sometimes, when my mom knew my dad was about to come home, she'd go into this quiet kind of panic mode. It wasn't screaming or crying it was a sudden urgency in her movements. She'd lower her voice and tell us:

"Go to your room."

"Don't talk to him."

"Don't bother him."

"Don't even eat at the same table."

She didn't say it with fear in her voice not exactly but with that kind of sharp, clipped tone that lets you know this isn't up for debate. Like she knew one wrong move could tip the whole house over. Like she was trying to keep a bomb from going off.

I'm a mother now. And looking back, I know exactly what she was doing. She wasn't trying to scare us or make us small. She was trying to protect us. Trying to keep the peace. Trying to keep us safe even if it meant teaching us how to shrink. Even if it meant making the kids quiet so the house wouldn't explode.

At the time, I didn't understand any of it. I was too young. Too busy being a kid to see the bigger picture.

I must've been around eight or nine years old still an elementary school kid. So let's do the math: my older brother would've been about 12. That would put me at 9. My middle brother was five years younger than me, so he would've been 4. And the youngest? Just 2 years old at this point. Four kids. Two parents. One roof. One ticking tension.

To cope, my mom started taking us to her mother's house my other grandma just to unwind. Sometimes she'd just make coffee, cook a small meal, and sit quietly while the TV murmured in the background. My grandmother loved her animals dogs, cats, birds and her yard was full of life. She was always outside pulling weeds, watering plants, or feeding some stray creature. She tended to her plants like they were her children. Her hands were always in soil, always growing something. She and my grandfather had a little farm and land in Mexico too just like my dad's parents only in a different town. My mom was born in Reynosa, Tamaulipas like I mentioned before.

We didn't spend a lot of time with my mom's side of the family. My dad never really allowed it. I still don't know why. It just wasn't something we did. So maybe that's why I clung so tightly to my other grandma my dad's mom. She was the one I saw the most.

The one I could sneak off to be near.

I remember sneaking out of bed more than once, tiptoeing across cold tile floors, careful not to wake my siblings, and slipping into her room just to curl up next to her. The smell of her lotion. The softness of her nightgown. The sound of her quiet breathing. Those moments felt like safety. The next morning, my parents would be panicked, searching the house for me. And there I'd be curled up next to my grandma like nothing was wrong. I didn't understand the stress I was causing. I just wanted to feel safe.

Everything during this time felt fragile. Like our whole life was being held together by a few frayed threads. They still hadn't found a house of their own. We were still at my dad's mom's place a family of six trying to keep the peace under one roof. Everyone was walking on eggshells. Everyone was trying to keep things calm.

But calm never lasted long.

There's one night I'll never forget.

I can't remember the exact time. I don't remember why it started. I don't even remember what words were said. The details are a blur. But the feeling? The feeling is burned into me.

I was in the house when I heard them my parents yelling in the garage. It was different this time. Not the usual tension. Something in the tone made my heart race. I don't know what triggered the fight, but it was bad. I could tell from the crash of objects, the low rumble of voices turning sharp, the energy in the air.

We all rushed to the garage. I remember seeing my grandmother standing between them, her arms out, trying to shield my mom like a human barrier. She was small, but her presence was huge in that moment a wall between chaos and my mother.

I didn't know why my mom needed defending. I just knew that she did.

And then I saw it.

My dad slapped my mom across the face.

It was fast a flash of movement, a sound that cracked the air. Her lip bled. And I froze.

Time slowed down. My ears rang. My stomach knotted. My heart felt like it left my body.

That moment was the first time I understood, really understood that the tension in our house wasn't just words. It could spill over. It could leave marks.

And as much as I wanted to move, to say something, to run... I couldn't. I just stood there, a nine-year-old girl, holding my breath in a garage full of grown-up pain.

I don't know if it was truly the first time, but it was the first time I saw it with my own eyes. And that was enough. That one image burned into my memory like a scar you don't notice at first but can always trace with your fingers later.

My grandmother tried to calm him down, to get him off my mom. I think there were other people in the garage too relatives, neighbors maybe but it's all a spinning, aching blur. Shouting. Movement. Heat. I just remember crying. Crying so hard I couldn't breathe. My tiny chest heaving. My heart pounding out of my body. Thinking, My dad's acting like a monster.

And my mom... she barely said a word. She just stood there, bleeding. Silent.

She never fought back. Not then. Not with him. She stayed quiet, shoulders rounded, like she was trying to make herself small enough to disappear. She was so submissive to my father in those moments, and I hated it. But she always tried to shield us during the arguments and the fights. She'd tuck us into bed like it was armor, whispering instructions:

Stay quiet. Don't come out. Don't jump on him. Don't talk to him. Don't eat at the same table.

She wasn't being cold. She was trying to keep us safe. She knew what could set him off. She knew which triggers could flip the switch.

Now that I'm a mother, I understand that kind of fear. That kind of survival. She wasn't weak. She was protecting. She was doing the only thing she knew how: keeping us alive in a house that sometimes didn't feel like one.

At this point, I know anyone reading this might be thinking, Well, why didn't she just leave?

But let's not jump to conclusions.

My dad wasn't always a monster not completely. There was a lot going on behind the scenes that even now, as an adult, I'm still piecing together. That doesn't excuse anything. Let me be clear: nothing justifies the way he treated her. No one deserves to be spoken to like that. No one deserves to feel afraid in their own home.

Still, as a little girl, I didn't have that nuance. I just knew what I saw. And I started to hold it against my mom. I couldn't understand why she wouldn't stand up for herself. Why she let it happen. Why she stayed.

But I was just a kid. My world was small. My perspective even smaller. I promise we'll get deeper into all of that later in the book. For now, this was our life. This was what was happening behind closed doors while we were still living at Grandma's house.

And then, something shifted.

My mom found a house she loved.

I don't even think it was for sale at first. But my dad made it happen anyway. From what I remember, there was still a family living there. He offered them cash on the spot. She wanted it. He got it.

The house wasn't far just a few miles from both of my grandmothers' homes. (Yes, both of them. Each had their own house in Texas, plus land and homes in Mexico. I know it sounds confusing, but that was our world, two cultures, two countries, always over-lapping.) But this house? This was different. This was ours. A real brick home.

It reminded me of our Oregon trailer, but in Texas only now in brick and tile instead of wood and aluminum. And let me be clear: our trailer in Oregon was ours too. It might not have had fancy floors or high ceilings, but it had peace. That home held some of our happiest memories. It was the place where Mom and Dad laughed more, where we danced in the living room, where the air felt lighter and love felt easier.

It was where I learned how to ride a bike (even if I crashed into a truck), where the snow piled high and Dad still walked barefoot like a fool, where scraped knees and frozen noses didn't matter because life felt... safe. Simple.

That home wasn't just a building. It was a pause in the chaos. Stability, even if it looked humble on the outside.

So yeah, this new brick home in Texas was bigger and shinier but it wasn't our first taste of having something to call our own. Oregon was ours too, in a softer, quieter, more meaningful way.

In our Texas home, though, everyone finally had their own room with private doors and space to breathe. The floors were a glossy honey-colored tile or maybe marble, I'm not even sure but they were shiny, almost like glass. I remember sliding across them in socks, laughing like we were in a movie. The walls were smooth ivory, and the kitchen cabinets were a warm honey-brown wood. The whole house just glowed.

It finally felt like we had something of our own. A real home. A fresh start.

I remember moving into the house and not having a single piece of furniture yet. Just mattresses on the floor. But we couldn't wait. We were too eager. As long as there was power and a place to sleep, we were moving in and we did.

I was so excited. Some of my cousins on my dad's side were excited too. They even asked if they could spend the night. When my parents said yes, I was over the moon. Finally, I had family over at our new house. In my beautiful room.

My room had such a girly touch that it felt like it had been designed just for me. The window wasn't a regular square window either. It was big, facing the front of the house with a rounded arch at the top, like something you'd see in a castle. My very own princess window.

There were two long closets side by side each with two wooden bi-fold sliding doors, totaling four. And above them? Five little show lights, each with its own switch. You could dim them or angle them to light up different parts of the room. I remember thinking that was the coolest thing ever. It made the room feel magical, like I was finally living in a storybook instead of a crowded trailer.

I had just started sixth grade. Middle school. Everything about life felt like it was shifting, like I was standing on a bridge between childhood and teenagehood. For the first time ever, I could ride the bus straight from my own driveway. That alone felt like a huge deal. No corner stops. No waiting at a random sign. The bus pulled right up to our gate on the main road. Everyone on that bus saw where I lived.

And suddenly, I was "that girl."

The one with the big house.

The one with the gate.

I never felt like I was better than anyone else, but it didn't matter people assumed I did. I didn't have friends over. I wasn't allowed to go to anyone else's house. And if I'm being honest, sixth grade ended up being one of the hardest years of my life.

I remember everyone had those trendy Mudd jeans the ones with the little hand logo on the back pocket. Everyone and their mama had a pair. But me? I wasn't allowed. Not because we couldn't afford them but because my dad didn't allow me to wear what was "in." He was extremely overprotective.

No makeup.

No plucking my eyebrows.

No straightening my hair.

I didn't even own a real hair tool at the time. It wasn't about money.

It was about rules. Control.

I used to sit in class and watch the other girls show up with their glossed lips, cute bracelets, stylish jeans, and light makeup. Their hair straight and shiny. Their sneakers perfectly clean. And I hated that I couldn't do the same. In our Mexican culture at least in my family a girl didn't get to "dress up" or express herself until after her quinceañera. I hadn't had mine yet.

So I was stuck somewhere between a little girl and a young woman wanting so badly to be seen, to express myself, to belong.

It was a lot.

To be seen as someone who "had it all" because of my house, while secretly being bullied for how I dressed.

To live in a beautiful home, but not feel beautiful in my own skin.

To feel like I was finally settling into something… only to be told it was time to go again every year.

This particular year, we took a trip to Mexico. My dad is from Nuevo León, but this time we were heading to Monterrey City. He said he was going to take us to Plaza Sésamo basically Sesame Street Park. It was like our own Mexican version of Universal Studios or Six Flags. We didn't get to do things like that often, so we were head-over-heels excited for the trip.

I can still remember the anticipation. Packing my bag. Imagining the rides. Thinking about how it would feel to walk into a real theme park with my whole family. That kind of excitement was rare.

But behind the scenes? My parents were still arguing. Still battling each other in ways I couldn't understand. Why? I didn't know. I just knew the tension followed us everywhere. Even in the new house. Even on the way to "fun" things.

Because no matter how shiny the tile floors were or how magical my princess window felt, there was still something broken between them that a new house couldn't fix.

My dad had recently lost a younger brother. He had passed away suddenly, and with his passing came a wave of family chaos details I still don't fully know even now.

Here's a little very brief insight on that: my uncle (my dad's brother) was married to my mother's sister. Together they had four kids of their own, who were like brothers and sisters to us because we were related on both sides mom and dad. They were also my Godparents. They baptized me as a baby. Remember, I grew up Catholic. (I hope all this is making sense!)

With that being said, my dad felt responsible for helping and being there for my aunt and her children after his brother's passing. And I understand that now. I have my own nieces and nephews, and there isn't anything I wouldn't do for them. I love them like my own. I get it.

Anyway, back to the Plaza Sésamo trip. My dad had mentioned this trip to my aunt, and somehow it turned into an agreement that my cousins would come with us to Mexico too. We were leaving early the next morning.

When morning came, as we were getting ready and loading the car, my parents were at it again. Arguing over heaven knows what. I honestly don't even know. It was just another fight in a long string of fights.

We drove to the border to cross into Mexico, and I remember my older brother and I looking at each other, whispering, "Aren't we going to pick them up?" We wouldn't dare say it out loud. Dad would lose it, and it wouldn't be pretty. So we stayed quiet. Not a word was said.

When we finally arrived in Monterrey, it was... fine. A good time, but not the kind of trip you brag about at school. Nothing crazy fun. My dad was always so uptight on trips, and it rubbed off on my mom. She was slowly becoming a bit bitter too, tired, maybe even resentful.

Either way, we made the best of it. We tagged along. It's not like we had an option. lol

My dad met up with some friends while we wandered with my mom.

After that, he took us to the beach. We ate outdoors right by the water with some of his friends, the smell of salt and grilled food mixing in the air. One of the wives was pregnant, and I remember taking a slow walk with her along the sand. We didn't stay long, but we did get to enjoy a little bit of it a brief pause in the chaos.

When we arrived back in Texas, my dad and my aunt my mom's sister ended up in an argument over what had happened with my cousins. I have no clue how it ended. It was just another grown up problem I wasn't allowed to understand.

Eventually, life went back to our normal routines. The school year faded. The months passed. And then the packing began.

Leaving for Oregon always came with a different kind of chaos. My parents ran around the house cleaning every inch, unplugging the toaster, the waffle maker, the TV anything that could be turned off while we were gone. The fridge had to be emptied. Beds stripped. Curtains drawn. It was like putting the house to sleep before disappearing for months.

At the same time, my dad had hired workers to build a luxury brick fence around the entire property. It was tall and elegant, with a large gate that opened with a remote or a pin code. There was even a keypad built right into the brick wall at the driveway. When I got dropped off after school, I'd walk up to the gate and punch in the code, and just like that, the gate would glide open for me.

It made me feel… important. Like I was walking into a little kingdom.

Even if inside that gate, I still felt lost sometimes. And just like that while the cement was still drying on the new fence and the last suitcase was zipped shut it was time to go. Not long after we had moved in, it was already time to migrate to Oregon again.
This time, though, it felt different. We weren't just leaving a place behind we were leaving our home. A real home. Our gorgeous brick house with the glowing tile floors and my princess window. It felt heavier this time. We packed up, loaded every car we had Mom in hers, Dad in

his pickup. Some of my cousins followed too, carpooling with their families for a shot at the same work waiting up north. Before hitting the road, we stopped by Grandma's, hugged her goodbye, and picked up a warm dozen of gorditas de azúcar to go the kind that melt in your mouth and make everything feel okay for a minute.

I remember staring out the window as we drove off, sugar on my fingers, dust in the air, and a lump in my throat I couldn't name yet. We had just started building a life… and now we were leaving it behind. Again.

Three long days on the road ahead of us.

Chapter 5

The Double-Wide and the Dream

This trip to Oregon was a little different. And by different, I mean… my parents had a little more money this time. Not a lot, but definitely more than we'd ever had before. Enough to notice. Enough to make the road trip feel less like survival and more like a real journey.

For once, we didn't have to sleep in the car. We actually got to stay in a hotel with beds, a bathroom, a real door to lock behind us. I remember the feeling of checking in, laying on clean sheets, and thinking Wow… this is what rest feels like. Normally, when we traveled in one car, Mom and Dad would take turns driving, which made the trip shorter, but more exhausting. If we needed to stop, we'd pull into a truck stop, park in some quiet corner, and try to catch a few hours of uncomfortable sleep before hitting the road again.

But this time? It was different. There were more cars. More people involved. The vehicles were bigger, newer, nicer. No overheating. No breakdowns. No packing duct tape in case something rattled loose. We had a little more breathing room literally and financially and that alone made the trip feel special.

When we arrived in Oregon, I remember the way word traveled fast. The town was so small that everybody knew when "the Texas family" was back. And since we had Texas plates, it didn't take long for people to figure out it was us. It was low-key kind of exciting pulling up and knowing we were already being talked about. And honestly? Dad's rules loosened up a little too. He was still strict, but nowhere near as intense as he was back in Texas. I could actually run next door to the neighbor's house to see my friends without getting yelled at. I could step outside without it turning into a lecture. It was a breath of freedom even if it was small.

But here's the thing: this time when we got back to Oregon, we didn't return to our usual hometown. And we didn't go back to the trailer we had grown up in.

I'm not gonna lie I was confused. And because of my dad's temper, neither my brother nor I had the guts to ask any questions. We didn't dare ask where we were, where we were going, what happened to the old place, or why anything had changed. We had been raised to keep quiet.

Since we were little, we were taught that when adults were talking, we needed to be in a different room or at the very least, silent. But let's be real... I was a nosy little kid. If my grandma was in the kitchen, I was right there, watching her every move what spices she used, how she stirred the beans, when she flipped the tortillas. And when all the aunts were gossiping in the living room, I'd play with something close by and keep my ears open. I didn't always understand what they were saying, but I'd catch on quickly. So when we got to Oregon and ended up somewhere unfamiliar, I knew something had changed. But I also knew better than to ask. And just like Mom always told us, we kept quiet.

Turns out, my parents had upgraded without telling us.

They sold the old trailer we grew up in the one that held so many of our earliest memories. To who? How? When? No clue. They must've done it during one of those solo trips they always took. What happened to our stuff? Our furniture? Our clothes? I honestly don't know. And now that I'm writing this... I'm wondering about it for the first time. I might have to call my mom after I finish this sentence because now I'm really curious. LOL.

Anyway the new place was in another small town called Irrigon, Oregon. Just a few miles before our hometown of Boardman. Still quiet. Still rural. Still familiar... but different. The new house was a cute little double-wide. Still a trailer home, but much nicer, bigger, and more updated. It felt like a real step up newer, cleaner, roomier. What's even crazier? The double-wide was right across the street from my new middle school. I could literally walk to school. The football field and running track were directly in front of our door.

It felt surreal.

So we settled into the new home, got enrolled in school again, and started to build a new routine.

But this time… it hit different.

Even though it was the same people I had grown up with the same town energy, the same familiar faces everything felt new. A different town. A different store. A different house. And now, a whole new school.

I had graduated elementary and was now officially a middle schooler. That shift alone was major. The school was way bigger than our little elementary building. And the transition from having one classroom and one teacher to suddenly managing seven different classes and a rotating schedule? It was overwhelming. I had a binder for every subject. I had to learn how to use a locker. I had to memorize classroom numbers and learn how to walk quickly without getting lost in the hallways.

It was a lot to take in.

And just like everything else in my life back then it was sink or swim. No one sat me down to prepare me. No one explained how to transition into this next version of myself. It was just: here's your new school, here's your new life. Figure it out.

Middle school.

I think this is when I first started to feel a shift both in who I was and who I was becoming.

My friend group started to change. I didn't live in the same small, humble trailer park I had grown up in anymore, and as silly as it sounds, even my outfits made a difference. The styles between Texas and Oregon were totally different, and trying to keep up felt impossible.

When I dressed up for school in Oregon, I just wanted to blend in to not feel like the new girl from out of town. Everything there was more laid-back, more relaxed, but somehow that made it even harder for me. The pressure to be effortlessly cool, to wear the right shoes, the right hoodie it weighed on me.

And school itself? Felt ten times harder.

We had lockers now. Schedules. Seven different classes a day. Memorizing locker combinations, trying not to be late, figuring out where each classroom was it was a lot of change in a short amount of time. I felt like I was always rushing to catch up, always trying to make sense of everything new around me.

Around this time, my parents' business was also growing. What started as just a couple of trucks turned into something much bigger. They started hiring more drivers, more help, and suddenly my brother and I had responsibilities too.

We'd help with paperwork, or tag along to the yard on weekends when the trucks were parked and there wasn't any farm work to do. My dad would use that time to work on the trucks changing parts, welding, fixing whatever needed to be fixed. He was an incredible welder and mechanic. Even if he didn't say much, you could tell how proud he was of what he had built.

By then, my older brother was already in high school and fully helping out. He was even driving the work truck and hauling equipment. My mom handled the errands she'd run to Napa Auto Parts where my dad had a business account, pick up what he needed, then rush back to the yard.

Sometimes, she'd send us to go grab food for everyone. Then we'd all eat outside in the open air, tacos, burgers, pizza, whatever was quick and hot. I remember my dad always kept a bottle of this weird orange liquid it was like an industrial-strength hand cleaner. He'd pass it around so everyone could scrub the grease off their hands before eating, then we'd all sit on the back of a truck bed to eat together like it was a picnic and even though I wasn't allowed to be around the heavy equipment or a lot of the workers my dad was very over protective, especially if there were a lot of men around I still felt part of it in my own way. Sometimes he'd leave me in the truck with the windows cracked or let me stand outside for just a few minutes. Other times, he'd drop me off with my grandma, my mom's mom, and I'd play with my cousins from her side of the family.

But one time? He let me help.

I don't remember what exactly I was doing probably something simple and safe but I remember the feeling. I had asked him if I could help, expecting him to brush me off. But instead, he handed me a grease gun and showed me how to slide under the truck and lube up the joints underneath.

What it was called? I had no idea.

What I was doing? Still don't really know.

But in that moment, I didn't care.

I felt so proud.

I felt like I was part of something. Like I wasn't just the little sister who tagged along I was helping. I was learning. I was included. It might sound small or silly to someone else, but to me? It meant everything. That moment still makes me emotional. It was one of the few times I felt like my dad saw me not just as his daughter, but as someone capable. Someone he trusted.

Another thing I remember clear as day: every time we returned to Oregon from Texas, the trucks would still be sitting at the yard completely covered in tape, plastic, and cardboard to protect them from the winter. Dad had figured out ways to shield the mufflers and vents from the snow and ice.

The moment we got there, my dad and brother would get to work peeling all the tape and coverings off. But here's the thing sometimes bees had made little nests inside the truck frames or under the hoods.

So every now and then, as soon as that cardboard came off, bees would come swarming out and suddenly you'd see all of us running around the property like maniacs, screaming and swatting the air, trying not to get stung. It was chaos.

And it happened almost every year. No matter how prepared we thought we were the bees always got us. Looking back now, it was hilarious. At the time, not so much. But still... one of those family memories you never forget.

Another thing I started to notice in middle school: we stopped going to church like we used to.

We used to go every week, sometimes more. It was a big part of our lives especially when we were younger. But after moving back and forth so much, and with the business growing, and with all of us being so busy, it just kind of... faded. I don't know if anyone else noticed, but I did.

Texas had changed us.

It changed our routines. It changed our rhythm.

My mom wasn't working in the fields anymore. She was now fully invested in helping my dad with the business. They were still hustling maybe harder than ever but now it was their hustle. It belonged to them.

I'd run errands with my mom go with her to deposit checks, pick up invoices, cash out payments so the employees could get paid every Friday. On payday, the workers would come straight to the house, and my parents would have their checks ready, lined up and counted out.

I got to witness all of it. I got to be part of it even at such a young age.

Especially because their English wasn't perfect. They could speak it, they could write it, but there were always small gaps and my brother and I became the bridges. We translated. We called. We figured things out.

My older brother handled more of the physical labor with Dad welding, tools, equipment. I stayed back with Mom doing the office work, answering calls, helping her organize files or send faxes.

And honestly? I'm glad.

Because I heard my dad could be really rough on my brother when they were out in the yard.

It was that old-school, macho, man-to-man dynamic. And with my dad? If you didn't hold the flashlight just right you were getting yelled at. If you couldn't find the wrench fast enough? You were getting chewed out.

With Dad, you always got chewed out. It was part of the job.

And trust me, he didn't care if you were his kid or not.

Still… there was teamwork.

There was hustle.

There was us.

And that mattered more than anything.

On weekends, when there wasn't too much maintenance left to do at the truck yard or when all the trucks were finally clean and parked Dad would take us to Washington for a day of shopping. Since we lived so close to the state line, it became one of our regular things.

Costco was a favorite. Dad loved that store.

That was his playground the one place where, without fail, he'd buy things we absolutely didn't need. I'm just going to say it exactly how I remember it: the man bought so much random shit.

One year, he bought a chimney.

I'm serious. A whole-ass chimney. Well… technically it was a pellet stove, but as a kid I called it a chimney and that name stuck with me.

It was one of those bulky, heavy-duty heaters that needed special wood pellets to run. This thing had a marble top, I mean real marble and weighed a ton. It was gorgeous, expensive, and completely unnecessary. He also bought the pellets in bulk like mountains of them as if we were about to live through a snowstorm in the middle of Texas.

And the funniest part? To this day, I don't think that stove ever got installed. Not once.

Where was he planning to put it?

What did he even buy it for?

Still don't know.

Even now, as a grown adult writing this, I'm cracking up because I know for a fact that expensive ass pellet stove easily over $3,000 just sat there, collecting dust.

This was peak Dad behavior. He'd load up on all kinds of things "for the house" or "for Texas," and I never really questioned it at the time. I just tagged along. I didn't need to understand it. But now, as I'm writing and reflecting, more and more of these memories are coming back and it's a lot to process.

My dad carried an entire world of unspoken meaning in his hands.

By the end of the season in Oregon, once all the work was wrapped up, we'd be buzzing with excitement. We were headed back to our beautiful Texas home.

That year had been a good season. Not perfect, but peaceful.

Settled.

Hopeful.

But as soon as we returned to Texas, the pattern started again.

Dad would disappear for long periods days, sometimes over a week and then reappear as if nothing happened. He'd go back to being strict. Real strict. I wasn't allowed to do much at all.

I had one best friend who lived right behind our house. We had been close for a long time. The town was small, so even if you lived a few blocks away, you almost always ended up in the same school.

But since I wasn't allowed to have friends over, and I wasn't allowed to go over to her house either, we made do with what we had.

We'd climb up and sit on the brick fence that wrapped around our property just to talk, joke, and catch up. We'd sit there for hours, laughing about school, gossiping about boys, talking about teachers and family and everything in between.

But even for that, I had to ask permission.

One time, I forgot to ask and Dad lost it.

When I say he went ballistic I mean full-on yelling, slamming things, pacing, the whole thing. Over sitting on a fence. But that was the control. That was the weight we always felt around him.

And yet, that same man the one who scared me for sitting on a wall could throw some of the biggest parties in the entire town.

Everyone knew that Mr. García could throw a legendary event.

We're talking mariachis, live bands, music blasting till 3, 4, even 6 a.m. sometimes. His parties weren't just gatherings they were productions. Loud, wild, unforgettable.

That December, my mom let me have my very own birthday party. Girls only, no outside friends, just family. But I didn't care. I was so excited. I picked out the cutest birthday dress, and Mom made sure we had everything: hot dogs, burgers, chips, sodas a whole feast for the cousins. The moms hung out inside while all of us kids played out on the back porch.

We had a little speaker and played every hip hop song we could think of. We laughed so hard that night our stomachs hurt. We were crying from how much we were laughing.

I even had a disposable camera that year to take pictures and you better believe I filled it with memories. That party is still one of my favorite birthdays ever. All my cousins from my dad's side were there, and for once, everything felt light. My parents even started going out more dressing up for dinners, stepping out to the clubs.

They were enjoying themselves again.

It made it really hard to leave for Oregon again.

On some weekends, Dad would take us across the border to Reynosa, Tamaulipas, Mexico. We'd park and walk into downtown the plaza was always full of life, packed with stores selling everything from candy and snacks to CDs, clothes, and souvenirs.

There were barbers and beauty salons everywhere. Mom and I would stop to get our hair trimmed and treated, while Dad shopped. And when I say shopped, I mean shopped.

Music was everything to him so he'd stock up on piles of CDs. Entire stacks. Anything he could get his hands on.

Sometimes our cousins came with us, and the whole day felt like an adventure. Crossing back into the U.S., my parents had a nice Yukon with a custom stereo system. And let me tell you the music was loud. Always.

We'd be blasting:

"We Like to Party" – Vengaboys

"Boom, Boom, Boom, Boom"

"Up and Down"

"Barbie Girl" – Aqua

"Blue" – Eiffel 65

Oh my god — the jams were elite.

I didn't even know half the lyrics, but I sang with confidence. For years, I thought the song said "We're going to eat pizza" instead of "We're going to Ibiza" and honestly, my version was better.

We'd all be packed in the Yukon, windows rolled down as we crossed the bridge near the checkpoint. And just for fun, we'd rock the truck side to side all of us until it looked like the Yukon itself was dancing to the music.

Street vendors would rush over, selling Mexican candy, fresh fruit, churros, light-up toys, and little gadgets. Dad would always buy us a few things.

Even the men who cleaned your windshield for a peso would come by, giving the glass a quick swipe with their rags.

It was chaotic, colorful, loud, and full of joy.

Good old times.

Memories I'll never forget.

Moments that didn't always make sense back then, but now, now they feel like pieces of a puzzle that built the girl I was becoming.

There was this one restaurant we used to visit often in Reynosa a place that, to this day, lives in my memory like a scene out of a movie. It was called La Fogata, and it felt fancy fancy. Like, boujee. Cloth napkins, low dimmed lighting, chandeliers dripping from the ceiling, thick table linens, and everything I mean everything served on real glassware and sparkling wine glasses.

From the moment we walked in, it felt like we were someone important. The waiters would gently pull out the chairs for the women and place the folded napkins on our laps like we were royalty. And then, they'd bring over this steaming little bowl with slices of lemon floating in it.

Now… me being me I thought it was lemon juice to drink. I remember looking at it thinking, "Hmm, kind of smells like tea…"

Spoiler alert: It was not tea.

It was actually a hand-washing bowl meant to cleanse your hands before the meal. And right after that, they'd hand us warm towels to dry off with.

The whole experience felt luxurious, especially for a kid who wasn't used to that kind of dining.

But let's talk about the salads. Oh my God, their salads were next level. Everything was homemade even the dressing. They would toss and plate it right at your table. The way they presented it made you feel like you were at some high-end show.

Off to the side, there was a visible cooking room with a fire pit where dozens of cabritos young goats were hung up, roasting. You could actually choose which part you wanted, and they'd weigh and plate it to your liking. It felt primal and elegant all at once.

The bar? Stunning. Top-shelf everything:

Blue Label. Clase Azul. Don Julio Reposado. Buchanan's Scotch. The best of the best.

One of those visits, I even got to take half a shot. Just a little sip but I was over the moon. It was Mexico, so age didn't matter much, and my dad gave me the okay. I felt grown. And I loved that moment.

Back in Texas or "The Valley," as we'd call it, my mom started to enjoy life a little more too. She wasn't just working hard; she was finding little ways to express herself and connect with other women.

She started selling Jafra and Avon for fun and I thought it was the coolest thing ever. She'd host what she called "home material parties," where ladies would show off expensive home décor: fancy china, decorative frames, glass vases, and wall art with thick golden trim. It was the era of Tupperware parties too. My mom would make those tiny triangle sandwiches chicken salad, tuna, ham and serve them with chips and soda while all the moms sat in the kitchen and living room, laughing and gossiping.

She'd light up during those moments. I could see it.

During that same season, my baby brother was attending Head Start, and I believe my mom volunteered there. She was so involved and so present. It was one of the few seasons I can remember her having a little bit of her own life outside of just being a mom and wife.

As for me? I was killing it in school.

I had just started a keyboarding class you know, where they teach you how to type properly. I don't even know if those classes still exist, but I loved it. I was the fastest one in the class, I'd finish my assignments long before anyone else. My teacher would look at me, amazed, while the rest of the class was still pecking away at the keys.

To this day, I can still hear that sound the click-clack of keys being tapped in rhythm almost like music. It was so soothing to me.

Even my grandma used to say I had "perfect fingers for the piano." She wasn't wrong, long, skinny fingers that danced effortlessly over the keyboard. I was a natural.

That same year, I got into my first fight ever.

Technically, it was on the bus not in the school but they still made us go back to the building afterward. They wouldn't let us off at our stop, and instead called our parents.

And yes… the fight was about a boy. Of course it was.

Even worse it was with a friend.

Let me paint the scene: I dragged that poor girl by her hair from the very back of the bus all the way to the front. It was wild. Dramatic. Loud.

When the school called my mom, we both agreed not to mention why we had fought. She didn't know it was over a boy and we were going to keep it that way.

For punishment, the school made us wipe down every cafeteria table after each lunch shift. Everyday. For weeks.

At first, we w ere bitter. S ilent. P issed off. But eventually, we'd glance at each other across the table and just… crack up. We got over it. That's how it is with kids. You fight. You clean. You laugh. You move on.

Meanwhile, my dad was traveling a lot again. When he was gone, I got more freedom at school more space to join clubs and do extracurricular stuff without having to ask permission.

One day, I needed money for a school activity, and my cousin ended up being the one to drop it off. When she saw me, I had a little makeup on. I thought I looked cute blending in with the other girls, finally.

She quickly handed me her spare shirt and told me to wipe it off.

"Your mom's right behind me," she whispered.

I rushed to the hallway and took it all off before my mom saw.

Because as much as I wanted to fit in, I wasn't allowed to wear trendy clothes or makeup. All the other girls were flashy hair done, cute purses, lip gloss popping. I was always behind in that sense.

And I got bullied for it.

But I still tried. I wanted to feel like I belonged.

That summer, Dad took us on a few trips to Mexico and one of those trips was to Playa del Carmen. To this day, that's still one of my most cherished memories.

Even though he was strict didn't let us swim much or run off unsupervised just being there was enough for me. We took boat rides and even visited this hidden little market spot tucked away under trees. It was dimly lit, but filled with restaurants, street vendors, and people literally sitting in the water while ordering drinks at the bar.

The mariscos the seafood was my favorite part. Anyone who knows me knows seafood has always been my weakness. Give me a tostada de ceviche and I'm good for hours.

Those Mexico trips became more frequent.

At first, I struggled I didn't like using public restrooms unless they were super clean (I mentioned this earlier in the book it was a thing for me). I also noticed the way we spoke Spanish was a little different from the locals. We didn't always blend in.

And truthfully, Dad's temper had started to get worse. He was more impatient, more reactive, and the tension lingered heavier. Not every trip felt peaceful.

Coming back home always felt like relief.

Like taking a vacation from the vacation.

There was nothing like crashing in your own bed. Familiar walls, your own pillow, your own rhythm.

But time flew by like it always did.

Birthdays came and went. Cookouts, school events, weekends with family all a blur of laughter, food, and life. And just like that… it was time to head back to Oregon.

This time, we had stayed long enough to finish the full school year in Texas, and we were actually going to start the next one in Oregon on time.

No mid-semester transfers.

No weird gaps.

Maybe just maybe this time we'd get to pick some classes we actually liked.

Chapter 6

"El Sol de la Calle"/ "The Ranch Built Me Too"

The trip back to Oregon this time felt lighter in every way. For once, the drive wasn't so exhausting that we had to eat in the car or skip meals altogether. We actually stopped for breakfast at a small roadside café. It wasn't anything fancy a little diner with a few worn booths, the smell of coffee thick in the air, and the sizzle of bacon on the grill. But attached to it was something I'd never seen before: a tiny casino tucked inside, filled with oldschool slot machines and bright neon lights.

I was obviously underage, but curiosity got the best of me. While my parents were ordering food, I wandered over and, without thinking much of it, slipped a single quarter into one of the machines. I pulled the lever and suddenly the lights started flashing, bells ringing, and coins pouring out. The machine went crazy.

I panicked.

I called for my parents in a full-on freak-out. They came rushing over, eyes wide and immediately dragged me out. But not before realizing I had actually hit the jackpot. The look on my dad's face was a mix of disbelief, pride, and panic. Because if the staff had found out a minor was the one who hit it, not only could we have gotten in serious trouble, but they wouldn't have been able to cash out the winnings at all.

My dad never forgot that moment. From that day forward, he started calling me his lucky charm and he meant it. I'll get more into that later, but that memory stuck. It became one of those family stories that got retold again and again, each time with a little more dramatic flair.

This trip to Oregon felt more like a vacation than a stressful migration. My parents' vehicles kept upgrading each season shinier, newer, bigger. Our convoy was growing, and so was our sense of pride.

Getting out of Texas always took forever it felt like a whole journey in itself but once we passed into New Mexico, things shifted. The views became more scenic, and we actually made time to stop and enjoy places we used to only zoom past.

One of my favorite stops was in Phoenix, Arizona, at a spot called Hole-in-the-Rock. It was this natural geological formation that looked like something out of a movie. We climbed, explored, and took tons of pictures. I still remember how the red rocks glowed under the sun and how small we felt standing inside them. We even grabbed some souvenirs from the gift shop little trinkets and magnets we'd later stick on the fridge back in Texas.

After Arizona, we made another stop the Hoover Dam, just outside Boulder City, Nevada, straddling the border between Arizona and Nevada. It was massive, majestic, and felt like something you only see in textbooks. We walked along the edge, stretched our legs, grabbed some snacks, and breathed in that dry desert air.

My dad was obsessed with capturing every moment. He had one of those big, bulky cameras with the zoom lens that you could twist back and forth. He'd film everything from tractors to traffic to us just sitting in the backseat. Anything he could point the lens at, he would. He even had those little mini-tapes to record it all. Sometimes he'd narrate the videos himself, saying where we were or what we were doing. It felt like we were starring in our own family road trip documentary.

Even though we passed through these areas every year, we had never really seen them. Usually, we drove straight through exhausted, in the middle of the night, just trying to get there. But this year, everything was different. For once, we were awake, we were present, and we were seeing it all during daylight. It felt like life had slowed down just enough to enjoy it.

Then came Las Vegas.We didn't stop, but we passed right through the strip, and I remember pressing my face to the window, mesmerized by the glowing lights. Everything sparkled. Even the sky seemed brighter. I told myself, "One day, when I'm grown, I'll come back and see what all of that is really about." I wanted so badly to explore it. But I also remember another year we passed through Vegas during the day, and it felt... different. The glamor disappeared in the sunlight. All the magic I saw at night seemed to vanish with it. It reminded me of what my dad used to say: "Las Vegas is the city that doesn't sleep." And it truly looked like it came alive only when the sun went down.

As we crossed into Idaho, I remember the first time I looked out the window and actually noticed how beautiful it was. Rolling hills, open skies, and green that stretched for miles. It was peaceful like the land itself was telling us we were getting closer to home. The rest of the drive felt quick after that. Compared to Texas, every other state felt like a blink.

But Oregon that was always the real homecoming.

I'll never forget how our ears would pop driving up and down the steep mountain roads leading into the state. You could feel the elevation. And unlike flat Texas, Oregon had terrain that made you pay attention. It was wild and hilly, but so damn beautiful.

Because my dad hauled so much work trucks full of compressors, equipment, and heavy-duty tools he had installed trailer brake systems in our pickups. These weren't just regular brakes. They were powerful systems built specifically to help slow down and control a heavy load on steep hills. That's how intense the Oregon terrain was.

You couldn't drive through it with basic setups. You had to prepare. And my dad, being the meticulous man he was, never cut corners when it came to safety or machinery.

Sometimes I miss that sound the hiss of the air brakes, the weight of the trailer shifting behind us, the rhythmic click of the blinker as we climbed uphill. There was something comforting about it. Something that made me feel like we were really going somewhere like we were part of something bigger than just another drive.

Looking back now, I realize this trip was more than just miles on the road.

It was the moment I started to feel the shift in our life from chaos to stability. From surviving to thriving. From rushing to arriving. And in the middle of it all, I was just a kid, riding in the backseat, quietly collecting the memories that would one day become the foundation of everything I'm writing now.

Once we got back home Oregon home it was like pressing play on a routine we knew by heart. School started back up. Mom and Dad went back to work. I went back to helping with payroll and doing whatever was needed for the family business. Same double-wide, same little town, same everyday grind just with a few new upgrades.

That year, Dad decided to get a little fancy. He gave out gas cards to everyone on the crew. It was his way of showing appreciation and also keeping things running efficiently. He made sure Mom's truck, his work equipment truck, the service pickup, and all the bulk-bed trucks used for potato season were fueled up and ready to go. I remember how official it felt like our family business was leveling up, and I got to witness it from the inside out.

He also started putting more effort into carving out time for us, especially on Sundays. He'd take us to this cozy little local café in town. The kind of place that knew your name and your order by heart. The smell of pancakes and bacon would hit the second we walked in. Everyone would smile when we came in like we were regulars at a diner in a movie. Those mornings felt like peace. For a couple of hours, life felt balanced. Not perfect. But definitely lighter.

Dad still had a temper that short fuse never really went away but it wasn't as explosive. Not yet. It was manageable. He was still strict, still sharp-tongued when pushed, but there was more softness in between the edges. I was old enough to notice the difference. Mom had a little more breathing room too. She'd hang out with her sisters-in-law, cook together, gossip, laugh. By this point, most of her family had officially settled in Oregon, even though they still migrated to and from Texas depending on the season. It was more stable now. Oregon was becoming their permanent home too. Most of Dad's family, though, had stayed back in Texas. A few of them had migrated with us in the early years, when I was just a baby, but eventually they stopped making the trip. I didn't mention much about that in the earlier chapters, but I always noticed it. The shifting dynamics. The missing faces. The way the old stories faded when the people weren't around anymore.

And as for me? I was definitely getting spoiled. I still had to follow a thousand rules. Still wasn't allowed to wear makeup or dress how I wanted. But Dad was starting to give me a little more freedom when it came to everything else. I had my ways of getting what I wanted. I knew how to pout, throw on the sad eyes, and work my magic. Plus, I was the only girl in the house three brothers and me. That alone gave me a certain kind of leverage. Being the baby girl had its perks. When school started again, I went back to that same middle school across the street from our double-wide. I had walked those hallways before, seen those faces before but something about this year felt harder. Different. I was spending more time in Texas now, and the shift was starting to affect my friendships. It used to be that we lived in Oregon almost the entire year, especially during my toddler and early childhood years. Oregon was home base, and Texas was seasonal.

But now it had flipped.

We were only in Oregon for potato season maybe two or three months, max and the rest of the time was spent back in Texas. Because of that, I started to feel disconnected from everyone. My old friends still lived in the nearby trailer park where I'd grown up, but I wasn't around enough to hang out anymore. Even though it wasn't far, I didn't go and I definitely wasn't old enough to drive myself over. That distance, even if it was just a few miles, started to feel like a whole different world.

That was also the year I got assigned to an athletics class. Out of nowhere boom, they put me in track. And honestly? I didn't mind it. I had never really done outdoor sports before. Back in Texas, I had tried dance and cheer, but always behind Dad's back. I wasn't allowed to participate in anything he considered too girly or distracting. But track? That was neutral. Harmless. Something he wouldn't complain about.

I'll never forget the day Mom brought home my new P.E. clothes. She went shopping and came back with a bright green top and matching green shorts. I was mortified. It was the most embarrassing outfit I had ever worn in my life. I looked like a damn turtle running around the football field. Not even exaggerating I still remember hearing some kid call me "The Green Turtle," and it stuck. To this day, I laugh at the image of me jogging that mile like a neon lizard.

But you know what?

I got second place in that mile run. Second place! I don't care if I looked like a turtle doing it I was fast. And it felt good to be recognized for something physical, something I didn't even know I was capable of. For a brief moment, I wasn't the girl with the rules, or the outsider bouncing between states. I was just someone doing something well. That stuck with me.

My friend group had started shifting too. Faces changed. Some kids moved away, others grew apart. But it was still a small town, and small towns never really let you become invisible. Everyone knew everyone. People remembered where you lived, who your parents were, what car your dad drove. Even if I felt like my life was constantly split between two states, everyone else still saw me as the same girl from that double-wide across the school. And even though things were changing slowly, surely a part of me started to change with them. I was becoming someone in-between worlds, learning how to float through both without ever fully belonging to either. That feeling would never quite go away.

But for now, I was just a green turtle with second-place bragging rights and a heart full of stories that hadn't even happened yet. My parents' company kept growing, and so did the fleet. Dad had invested in even more trucks that year big, loud, powerful ones and when it was time to get them prepped for the season, he did it with intention. He didn't just maintain them he honored them. He greased every part himself, handled all the maintenance, made sure each truck was running like new. Then, he had them lined up, one by one, like a showcase. They were washed, waxed, buffed, spotless from top to bottom. You'd think they were headed to a car show, not a worksite.

When the drivers showed up to take the trucks to the yard, it was late I remember it being pitch black outside, except for the long stretch of glowing headlights cutting through the night. We were on the highway, all the trucks driving in a perfectly straight line, and I could just see my dad's eyes in the mirror glassy, proud, locked onto the scene like it was a dream he had waited years to witness.

I'll never forget his face in that moment.

It was joy. Not the loud kind. The kind that lives in the chest, swells quietly, and says, "I made it." He didn't say it out loud. He didn't have to. I felt it. I saw it.

He pulled out his camera, recording the entire line of trucks driving behind us like a caravan. The trucks weren't just driving they were glowing. Dad had installed special lights on all the live bottoms and bulk beds, so when they drove together at night, it looked like a moving light show. A convoy of giants lit up like a parade like something out of a movie.

Honestly, it looked like a carnival of trucks rolling toward the yard. I've never seen anything like it since. There's no perfect way to describe it. It was magic, mechanical magic, and my dad had built it with his own two hands. And quietly, even though I didn't say it out loud, I was so proud of him.

My older brother was still driving the white dually service truck. I'm pretty sure my mom had the white Tahoe at this point, although my memory's a little fuzzy there. And Dad? He had his big white dually, too another beast in the lineup.

Now that I'm grown and I look back on it all, I can say with full confidence that my dad had OCD and was a perfectionist in the best, most intense way. Every truck had to match. Every color had to be exact. The way he lined them up at the yard, parked perfectly side by side, evenly spaced... it does something to my brain even now. Like when something fits just right or clicks into place it was satisfying, almost therapeutic to watch. That man had vision. Precision. Pride.

And that year, he started a new tradition company dinners at the end of every season. He'd host them at the local Mexican restaurant, renting out the party room or a big section just for his employees. The truck drivers would show up in their best sometimes with their wives, sometimes solo and we'd all be there. My mom, my brothers, and me. It felt like family. Like a celebration. Dad would pass out seasonal bonuses at those dinners. That was his way of showing love through generosity. He had also started getting company shirts, caps, and hoodies made with the business logo and name stitched across the front. He'd hand them out at the dinners like trophies.

And for me? I got my own custom gear. My name on it. Personalized pieces a zip-up sweater, a hoodie, and even a black Letterman-style jacket with leather sleeves. I still have it. That jacket made me feel important. Like I belonged to something bigger. Like I wasn't just the daughter of the boss I was part of the story.

People started calling me "Patroncita." Little Miss Boss. Dad was El Patrón, The Boss. Mom was La Patrona. My brothers and I? We were Patroncitos the little bosses. It started as a joke, something people would say at the yard or at family dinners, but it stuck. And deep down, I think I carried that name with quiet pride. I laughed when they said it, but it meant something.

Because people really respected my dad. He did right by everyone his family, his friends, his employees, his nieces and nephews. He showed up. He helped people. He gave people opportunities. And even though I was still too young to understand all the ways he carried everyone, I could feel it in the way people talked about him. The way they smiled at him. The way they showed up when he called. That same year, when it was time to head back to Texas, Dad bought the jankiest looking truck I'd ever seen. I'm not even kidding it looked like Tow Mater from the Cars movie. Rusty, loud, beat-up, crooked smile and all. He loaded it onto a flat trailer and hauled it behind one of the pickups all the way back to Texas like it was a prized possession.

And in his eyes? It was.

Dad had an obsession with vehicles cars, trucks, tractors, anything with an engine. But especially oldies. The kind most people would toss or scrap, he saw potential in. He loved them for their character. Their stories. Their power. It was like a language only he spoke one I grew up understanding just by being near him.

I guess a lot of men are like that their hearts beat in pistons and tailpipes. But with my dad, it was more than that. Machines were a reflection of who he was: built to endure, made to move, full of noise and purpose and a little rough around the edges.

And in that season, everything was moving forward.

The trucks. The business. Our lives.

And even though I didn't have the words for it back then, I knew something was shifting. We were building something that felt permanent. Rooted. Loud. Unapologetic.

And I was growing up right in the middle of it all.

When we got back to Texas, it was like flipping a switch. Back to our regular schedule. Back to what had become our "normal." School enrollment started all over again for me, for my brothers, for everyone. And just like that, I was back in middle school, walking through the same doors, but somehow feeling like a slightly different version of myself. The kind that had seen more. Grown more. Changed just enough to notice.

On the first day, I picked up my schedule and immediately noticed something was off. Somehow, I hadn't been enrolled in P.E. like usual I had been placed in "Athletics." And if you've ever been a non-sporty girl in a Texas middle school, you know exactly how terrifying that is. I remember staring at the word on my schedule like it had betrayed me. ATHLETICS? Me? No way.

Still, I walked into the gym building, hoping maybe I had misunderstood. But the second I stepped inside, I could feel it I didn't belong there. The whole vibe was different. Everyone already had their groups, their confidence, their rhythm. It smelled like sweat and competition. Girls were already warming up, stretching, tossing volleyballs, sprinting laps like it was the Olympics and then I saw her, my best friend at the time, the one who lived right behind my house. The same friend who used to sit with me on top of the brick fence while we gossiped and planned our futures like two little daydreamers. But here? She was in her element. Her legs were thick and strong, like they were made to run and jump and leap. She looked like a natural-born athlete. And me? I was this tiny, skinny little thing all dance class and sparkly notebooks. I felt so out of place it almost made me want to disappear.

I walked up to the coach, trying to find the courage to ask for a schedule change. "Hi… is there any way I could transfer out? I think there's been a mistake."

She didn't even blink. She pointed to the door and barked, "IF YOU DON'T WANT TO BE HERE, GET OUT."

Loud. Sharp. Echoing through the gym.

I didn't flinch. I didn't cry. I didn't feel embarrassed. I felt relieved.

Her yelling didn't scare me. What scared me was having to pretend to be someone I wasn't. So I turned around, walked straight out the doors, and headed to the office to fix my schedule. And guess what? They placed me right back in dance class exactly where I wanted to be. What nobody at school knew and what I had to hide constantly was that I wasn't even allowed to be in dance class. My dad was 100% against it. I wasn't allowed to join cheerleading, be part of the drill team, go to school dances, or even attend football games. None of it. To him, all of that was inappropriate. So every time I stepped into that dance room, it was like stepping into a secret identity one where I could express myself, even if it meant breaking the rules.

And little did my dad know, I was actually good. So good, in fact, that I was placed in the front row of every routine. Dead center. The spotlight. I danced at pep rallies, school festivals, class performances anywhere they needed energy and movement, I was there. Smiling, dancing, leading. And none of it was allowed.

I was also let's just say quietly rebellious that year.

There was a little boy I talked to often. Behind my dad's back, of course. Just a crush, nothing serious. But for someone like me, living under constant rules and restrictions, it felt dangerous and thrilling all at once. Maybe I'll talk more about that later… maybe.

This year in Texas was different. Harder. Heavier. I started to feel the weight of not belonging. The teasing turned cruel. The laughter didn't feel playful anymore it felt pointed. The way I talked, walked, dressed, looked everything about me became a reason for other girls to make fun of me. And for the first time, I experienced what it felt like to be truly bullied.

I got jumped that year more than once. Some girls just didn't like me and didn't need a real reason why. Maybe it was because I was quiet. Or maybe it was because of who liked me. Or maybe it was just because I was different a little girl from Oregon trying to figure out how to fit in with a Texas-sized attitude.

The school itself was huge, built to keep up with the town's rapid growth. Each grade had its own building and hallway sixth, seventh, eighth separated but connected through shared spaces: the cafeteria, gym, main office, nurse, and outdoor courtyard where everyone gathered in between classes. That courtyard became a battlefield some days if not physically, then emotionally. It was my first year at this particular school. The previous year, I had been at a different campus, but with so many new families moving in, the district started building more schools. I was transferred here, dropped into a world that felt unfamiliar and not very welcoming.

There was this one eighth-grade boy who had a crush on me. I wasn't supposed to be talking to boys at all let alone older ones but we'd pass notes and smile at each other in between classes. Apparently, he had just broken up with another eighth-grade girl before he started talking to me. And she wasn't having it.

One day, she stormed into the seventh-grade hallway which was totally against the rules and brought a group of girls with her, all ready to jump me. I was just walking to class when it happened. My math teacher, Mrs. Flores one of the kindest and most protective women I've ever met was standing at her door, watching everything unfold.

I don't know how she saw it coming, but she moved fast. She reached out, grabbed me by my hoodie, and yanked me into the classroom before the girls could touch me. Then she slammed the door shut. I still remember the sound. It was the sound of being rescued.

The principal and office staff got involved after that. I didn't have to deal with the girl again, at least not physically. But every time I walked through the courtyard or waited for my ride after school, the whispers and laughter continued. They laughed at me for anything my clothes, my voice, my walk. And I couldn't shake the feeling that I didn't belong.

In my heart, I was still an Oregon girl. That part of me never faded. Oregon felt like fresh air and freedom. Texas started to feel like pressure rules, judgment, and noise. I began to carry a quiet resentment toward my life in Texas. I felt torn between two homes, but only one of them felt like me.

I couldn't explain all of it then. But I felt it deep in my chest.

The ache of not being understood.

The heaviness of pretending.

The loneliness of growing up in between two worlds.

And I was only in sixth grade.

That year, Mom and Dad started traveling a little more for work.

Nothing extravagant just short flights back and forth from Texas to Oregon, or road trips if my dad needed to handle errands or check in on equipment. Sometimes he'd ask my mom to tag along and keep him company. Whenever that happened, my grandma P., my mom's mother, would come and stay with us.

Now, let me just say this... that was not exactly the best experience.

My parents always made sure we were as comfortable as possible. They'd let Grandma stay at our house so we didn't have to adjust our routines or sleep somewhere unfamiliar. They even left money behind so we could order food or step out if we needed something. It was supposed to be easy, familiar, and smooth.

But Grandma P. was strict. And I mean strict strict.

We'd ask her to buy us a burger or something simple from town, and she'd immediately say, "I don't have money," even though we knew full well there was money in the house. So we just stopped asking. When she cooked, she made small portions enough for one plate per person and nothing more. If we didn't sit down at the exact time she called us to eat, we missed our chance. And I'm not exaggerating if you didn't eat when she said it was time to eat, you didn't eat again the rest of the day.

And even when we did sit down in time, seconds were not an option. One plate. No more. That was the rule. We were kids, growing, hungry, but there was no room for extra. And honestly, I don't even think we told our parents the full story. It just felt annoying. Even now as an adult, I think back and it still makes me shake my head.

The only slightly redeeming thing about Grandma watching us? She let us sleep in a little later than Mom and Dad ever would. When Dad was home, there was no such thing as sleeping in. Not even on the weekends. He'd walk down the hallway, knocking on every door before the sun came up, yelling:

"GET UP! TIME TO GET UP!"

Didn't matter if it was Saturday. Didn't matter if we had nowhere to be. According to him, there was always something that needed doing something to fix, something to clean, something to handle.

That year, Dad bought a speed boat.

It was one of those with a built-in cooler and a stereo system that thumped with bass. The paint job was metallic blue with glittery sparkle, the kind that shimmered in the sunlight. It looked like something straight out of a catalog. And of course, he bought a bunch of safety jackets for everyone no one was getting on without one.

He would take us to this local lake called Anzalduas Park. He'd pull up to the boat ramp, back the trailer in, and unload the boat with the same level of pride he had for his trucks. We'd sit on the old wooden bleachers by the water, watching speed boats and jet skis fly past, their engines roaring and spraying water into the air. People were always smiling, blasting music, flipping into the lake. The energy was wild loud, colorful, chaotic. A lot of my cousins and uncles would come too, so it felt like a family event. It was kind of like the days we'd go to Marina Park in Oregon, but with a completely different energy. Oregon was chill, earthy, and calm. Texas was loud, fast, and always a little extra.

And like I've said before and I'll probably say again my parents' personalities would completely shift depending on what state we were in. Their moods, their pace, their interactions it was like two versions of the same people.

Now… here's a confession: I didn't know how to swim. I was terrified of the water.

So that safety jacket? I clung to it. I wasn't trying to play brave I was a proud little chicken, and I'll admit that.

But my dad, in true dad fashion, wanted me to get over my fear. So he'd grab me, count to three, and throw me off the boat. Not in a mean way more like, "You'll get used to it." And eventually, I did. After being tossed in a few times, the panic wore off. I started floating without freaking out. But did I ever really learn how to swim? Nope. To this day, I'm probably the only one in my entire family who still doesn't know how. Outside sports were just never my thing, and honestly? I've made peace with that.

Still, those lake days were good while they lasted. Those were the few moments where everything felt lighthearted when family surrounded us, and music played, and for a while, no one was yelling.

But then… there was always the return home.

My mom used to say something about my dad that stuck with me "El sol de la calle, la obscuridad de la casa."

The sun in the streets, the darkness at home.

It sounds prettier in Spanish. But the meaning? It hit hard.

It meant that Dad was charming, magnetic, full of life and laughter around others especially in public. But at home? He could be cold. Heavy. Dark. The version of him we got was different. It made those fun trips feel almost fake. Like something you couldn't fully enjoy because you knew what waited on the other side of the door.

Let me explain.

One year, during a migration trip up north, we were all packed into the truck my dad driving, me and my brother in the backseat. The stereo was playing some hip-hop or rap CD, and we were vibing, just riding. Ironically, this was music we knew he listened to when no one was around, but we were never allowed to play ourselves. Something must've set him off that day, because mid-drive, he suddenly reached over, ejected the CD, cursed under his breath, and whipped it into the backseat. The CD flew through the air and hit my brother in the forehead.

Just like that. No warning.

My dad had a temper. A real one. I don't think many people outside our home saw that version of him. But we did. And often. My mom per usual stayed quiet. She had grown more vocal over the years, more willing to call him out and hold him accountable. But honestly? Dad didn't care. Not enough to change.

What made it even more confusing was watching him be so laid-back around friends. That same music? He'd nod his head to it, joke, play it loud without a problem. But at home, it somehow became disrespectful. Offensive. A reason to lash out.

It didn't make sense then. And truthfully, it still doesn't.

But it's one of the many ways we learned to live in two realities the one the world saw, and the one we lived in when the doors were closed.

Around this time, my dad bought a ranch. Not just any piece of land a real ranch, with gates, barns, animals, and acres of open land surrounded by mesquite trees and dusty Texas roads. He named it Rancho Las Águilas, which means "Eagles Ranch" in English.

It was located just outside of the city, tucked into the rural outskirts where life moved slower, the skies were wider, and the work never stopped. It was beautiful like something you'd see in a Mexican novela. And my dad? He poured his everything into it time, money, and sweat. The ranch quickly became his sanctuary, his obsession, his second home. Actually, scratch that it was probably his real home. That's where he spent most of his time.

The Farm Operation

Dad decided to start growing sorghum or as we call it in Spanish, "sorgo." It's a grain crop that looks like tall grassy stalks with red-dish seed heads. It's used for livestock feed, biofuel, and sometimes even food. He bought all the John Deere equipment to get things rolling those giant, signature green machines with yellow trim that took over the fields like dinosaurs. One of the main machines he used was a green header combine, a massive piece of equipment that cuts down the stalks and feeds them into its belly. Inside, the machine separates the grain from the leaves and stalks through a process called threshing, it's this fast, mechanical dance that's loud, gritty, and powerful.

Once everything was harvested, my dad, my brothers, and our cousins would spend entire days out there, stacking sorghum bales in the sun, sweat soaking through their shirts. The ranch had a huge warehouse Dad had built from scratch, and that's where they'd store the bales to dry and prep them before taking them to the local farm auction to sell. It was a full-blown operation, and for Dad, it was just another piece of his growing empire.

The Animals & Ranch Hands

The ranch was always busy. It felt like something was happening all the time. My dad had employees and ranch hands managing everything the hay, the goats, the cows, the equipment, the horses, the land. There were people mowing the grass, feeding animals, driving machinery, repairing fences, and doing nonstop labor.

And while we kids tried to help when we could, my dad didn't really let me do much. He believed certain things were "a man's job," and since I was a girl, I was expected to stay inside with the air conditioning away from the sun, the sweat, and especially the men. He'd say, "You don't need to be around a bunch of guys. That's not your place."

I hated that.

Still, I got to sneak in a few experiences, moments I treasure even now.

The Horses

One of the coolest things was the horse walker he bought. It was this circular, mechanical contraption used to exercise the horses in a slow, controlled rotation. He had a ranch manager who would bring out the horses, tie them up, and let them take turns walking in circles to stretch and strengthen their muscles.

But these weren't just regular horses, no. My dad bought high-end, luxury horses some for show, some for racing. Full-blooded, sleek, strong. He even had a professional jockey who raced them on weekends. We'd sometimes go to the races to watch. It was hot and dusty, but exciting. The kind of event where you could feel the tension in the air as the horses lined up at the gate and people screamed with excitement when the bell rang. I loved those days. We didn't get many calm family outings, but when we did they were fire.

The Goat Business

My mom helped run the goat side of the business, especially during birthing season. Goats were a huge deal in our community in Mexican culture, "cabrito" (baby goat meat) is a delicacy, especially around the holidays. My dad sold well-fed, healthy goats at a premium price because people trusted the quality. He made sure they were raised with high-end feed, and because of that, they were in high demand.

I even got to help my mom deliver a few baby goats during one particularly cold winter. It was messy and beautiful and weirdly cool watching life happen right in front of me. I felt like a real ranch girl in that moment.

But… I never touched cabrito again after a certain day.

We had this huge family party at the ranch, and I happened to see someone kill one of the goats. I wasn't supposed to be near that part of the ranch, but I wandered off and saw everything. My grandpa on my mom's side was amazing at cooking and also skilled at hunting, cleaning, and prepping animals for meals. But seeing it with my own eyes? That was it. I was done. I couldn't eat cabrito again if you paid me. The image never left me.

My Favorite Ranch Memory

There was one rare moment where my dad actually let me help and it's something I'll never forget.

We were tagging cows for auction. They had built a tight alley of fencing that funneled the cows in single-file. My job? To climb up and straddle the fence like I was about to mount the cow (which I wasn't, lol), and use a big air-powered tagging gun to pierce each cow's ear. Each tag had a number on it that's how they were tracked and identified at the auctions.

At first, I was nervous. The cows were huge and fidgety, and I didn't want to hurt them. But once I got the hang of it, I actually loved it. There was something empowering about being trusted with real work even if it was messy and a little scary. It made me feel capable.

Included. Like I belonged.

I can still remember the sound of the tag clicking into place, the dust in the air, the way the cows mooed and shuffled forward. I'll never forget it. That day meant a lot to me.

The ranch was life year-round, every day, all day. It was work. It was pride. It was chaos and joy and tradition all rolled into one. Even if I didn't always have a place in the center of it, I still carry the memories like they were stitched into my childhood. Because they were.

As the ranch became the heart of our lives, even the way we celebrated changed. The parties were no longer held at our city house they had officially migrated to Rancho Las Águilas.

My dad went all in.

He had a massive palapa built right behind the ranch house a traditional thatched-roof hut made from dried palm leaves, which in Spanish culture is used as a shaded structure for gatherings, shade, music, food, and life. In English, they're called "palm huts" or "pavilions," but palapa just hits different.

It was beautiful. Handcrafted. Big enough to hold tons of people. Right in front of the horse corrals. You'd be sitting under the palapa, sipping on a soda or plate of food, and you'd hear the horses neighing or walking around behind you. The sounds of laughter and music blended with the hooves in the background. It was pure magic. The placement couldn't have been better.

At night, my dad would light the whole place up. He had strings of lights, loud music, and plenty of chairs and tables set up under the palapa. The cousins would run wild, and the adults would dance, laugh, and eat into the late hours. Sometimes, he'd even bring the horses or four-wheelers out during the party and let us ride around for a little while. It was chaos in the best way.

One of my favorite memories was seeing him convince Grandma Z his own mom to get on a horse and there she was, up on this tall animal, holding on for dear life while everyone cheered and clapped.

He was wild like that. Bold. Full of energy. Always wanting to impress people, make a moment out of everything.

Behind the Scenes: The Work Never Stopped

What most people didn't see behind the fun was just how demanding the schedule was, especially for my dad, my brother, and his loyal team of workers. And to be fair he had a solid team. A crew of hardworking men who believed in what he was building. They didn't clock out at 5 PM. This was sunup to sundown and then some.

At this point, my dad had leased even more land to expand the grain and sorghum operations. The fields had to be watered constantly, and because he was using a method called furrow irrigation, it was a delicate science. The fields were carefully leveled with a slight slope, and water had to run through these narrow furrows or rows. If anything wasn't timed correctly, the crop could be ruined it was that serious.

There were no automatic timers or high-tech sensors. This was manual labor at its most demanding.

They had to be out there at 1 AM, 2 AM, even 3 AM, driving four-wheelers through muddy paths, checking that the irrigation furrows weren't overflowing or drying up. If an alarm went off or something broke, they'd all spring into action no matter the hour. I remember one night I begged to go. Just once.

Eventually, he gave in and let me tag along. Just that one time.

It was dark, damp, and honestly kind of magical. The headlights from the four-wheelers cut through the mist, the air was thick with humidity, and the mud was everywhere. Wheels got stuck. We got dirty. But I felt like I was part of something bigger even if my dad insisted I stay out of the way. "Too messy," he'd say. "This ain't for girls." But I loved being included, even if it was just to observe.

The Day Everything Changed at John Deere

Whenever my dad needed new equipment or repairs, we'd all pile into the truck and head to the John Deere dealership. We were always told: look, but don't touch. And we listened for the most part.

One trip changed everything.

We were all at the yard, walking around the giant tractors and machines, when my youngest brother who must've been around two or three years old at the time wandered off. He was so little, curious, always trying to explore. I don't know exactly how it happened, but he must've gotten too close to one of the pieces of equipment.

Suddenly, we noticed he was hiding his hand behind his back. Pale. Quiet. Not saying a word.

And that silence? It wasn't normal. That was fear.

We all froze. My mom and dad rushed over. He still wouldn't say anything. And honestly, we knew why, Dad's temper. He could explode at the smallest thing, and we were all raised to stay quiet to avoid making things worse.

But my mom didn't hesitate. She grabbed his arm gently and turned his hand over. That's when we saw it.

His little finger was sliced almost completely off, barely hanging by a thread.

Chaos erupted. They rushed him to the emergency room, trying to keep calm, trying to keep him from passing out. It was terrifying. The entire drive was a blur, and I remember thinking: this is it. Everything is about to change.

Thankfully, the doctors were able to save his finger. A miracle, honestly.

But let me tell you that was the last trip we ever took to John Deere with Dad. Officially retired from "family errands." Lol"

That entire chapter of life the ranch, the long days and late nights, the harvests and horse rides, the chaotic parties and irrigation alarms it was a world of its own.

Texas wasn't just where we lived it was a lifestyle. Fast, loud, gritty, beautiful, exhausting. And in the middle of it all was my father, orchestrating every piece like a conductor running an unpredictable symphony. There was always something to build. Something to grow. Something to fix.

And even though I was often kept on the sidelines because I was a girl, I was watching everything. Every detail. Every contradiction. Every triumph. Every scar.

And I never forgot.

Chapter 7

We Had Everything but Peace

TRIGGER WARNING:

This chapter contains memories of emotional tension, childhood neglect, and shifting family dynamics. While it does not contain graphic descriptions, the emotional tone may be heavy for some readers. Please take care as you read.

Just because we didn't get to go back to John Deere didn't mean Dad stopped bringing us along for other hings. He absolutely did. Dad had an enormous fleet of farm equipment lined up like showpieces always washed, always clean, and always ready to be fired up. Everything from tractors to trailers to plows gleamed like trophies under the Texas sun. He even had a massive gas tank installed on the ranch just to refill the machinery onsite. No gas station stops. No need to haul anything into town. He ran the operation like a full scale business sleek, convenient, efficient. Maybe all farmers did it that way, or maybe that was just him. I couldn't tell you if it was the norm, but in my eyes, it felt next-level. Boujee, even. He had invested so much during that season of our lives. The hustle was real. The ranch looked like something out of a western movie rugged but intentional. Driving to the property was an experience in itself. It was all dirt roads, miles of fields, citrus groves, and quiet ranch homes scattered in between. Some of the gates had their family last names proudly displayed in elegant letters. Others had water fountains in their front yards large, decorative ones that sparkled in the heat. Everything about it felt like its own little hidden world. Once you passed the gates to "Rancho Las Aguilas" The Eagles Ranch the energy shifted. To the left, you'd see a wide open stretch of grass and a poured concrete slab where cars could park.

But the detail that stood out most was this beautiful vintage wagon Dad had placed near the entrance. It had these massive wooden wheels and a full-on old-school ranch aesthetic. It wasn't just decor it set the tone. It made you feel like you were arriving somewhere special.

Then came the house. The ranch house itself was long and stretched out, facing directly toward the entrance like it was watching every visitor pull up. It had at least ten tall windows across the front maybe more and two wide, wooden double doors that opened from the center. Those doors were so big and heavy, but they made moving furniture easy. You didn't have to twist and struggle things through narrow entryways. You just opened both doors, and boom the house let you in.

To the right of the house, there was a huge warehouse my dad had built from the ground up. That's where all the John Deere equipment sat in a perfect row like military tanks. Beyond the warehouse was the horse walker and the bathing station where the ranch hands would hose down the horses after training or long days in the sun. You could hear the sounds of water splashing, the snorts of the horses, and the rhythm of boots moving across gravel and mud. It was alive with work. Tucked away past all that was my dad's office his headquarters, his hideaway, his man cave. That little building had its own vibe. It was fully decked out in a masculine, ranch-style version of Scarface energy leather furniture, shelves filled with cigars, and racks of expensive liquor he rarely drank. My dad wasn't a big smoker or drinker at all, but he collected like he lived: all in. And during special occasions, he'd light a cigar or pour a drink with his friends while they sat around gambling or talking business.

I wasn't allowed in there often, but the few times I was, I felt like I had walked into a secret world. A world where adult men laughed loudly, counted money, and passed around dice cups like it was ritual. And in those rare moments, he'd invite me into the fold in his own way. He'd hand me the cup before rolling the dice and say, "Blow on it, Lucky Charm." And I would. Every single time. And somehow, every single time, he'd win. The room would cheer, or money would slide his way, and he'd flash me that proud smirk.

The ranch house was a mix of deep brown and reddish brick, warm and textured, nestled against the backdrop of endless Texas sky. It wrapped around with a porch that curved like a soft hug complete with western-style wooden benches and rocking chairs that creaked with the wind. My dad made sure everything fit the vibe. Inside, the house was furnished entirely in Western ranch style. Every room carried a heavy sense of intention wood, leather, and rustic charm.

Even the smell of the house felt like it belonged in a storybook. It reminded me of the scent you get when you walk into Boot Barn rich leather, aged wood, a bit of dust, and something warm and earthy that you can't quite name but never forget. It smelled like the kind of life my dad had always dreamed of building.

The kitchen had this big round glass table, and what held it up was so unique three hand-carved horse heads made of polished wood, facing outward like guardians of the space. The matching wooden chairs completed the set, and everything looked custom made, even if it came with the house. The kitchen itself was surprisingly spacious with more storage than I'd ever seen before. The cabinets were this deep jade green color a bold, unusual shade I'd never seen in another house. Paired with the cracked tile counter tops that had an uneven, imperfect charm, the whole kitchen felt like something out of an old countryside magazine. I don't think my parents would've chosen those design elements on their own, but they added character like the house already had a soul when we moved in. Just off the kitchen was the formal dining room, where a massive wooden table sat surrounded by what had to be twelve chairs all the same heavy, western-style build. It mirrored the setup we had in our city house. We weren't a fancy family, but we were structured.

At mealtimes, everyone had an assigned seat no exceptions.

My dad always sat at the head of the table in a larger, throne-like chair.

My mom was on his right, my older brother to his left, and I sat next to him, followed by my younger siblings. It was one of those unspoken traditions that just became law. You didn't sit anywhere else. Everyone knew their spot.

The living room was just as styled a massive western sectional stretched across one side of the room, soft but structured, always smelling like leather and saddle oil. A large cowhide rug covered the floor, and in the center was a chunky wooden table that looked like it had been carved straight out of a tree trunk. Against the wall stood this towering entertainment center almost touching the ceiling housing the TV, cowboy memorabilia, and framed photos. Behind the couch, there was a built-in wooden bar with hanging racks for wine glasses, shelves for whiskey or tequila, and a full bartending setup. The back of the bar had a stool for the "bartender," and the front had space for people to sit and sip. Everything and I mean everything in that house was solid, heavy, and hard to move. It wasn't just furniture. It was presence.

Each bedroom kept the theme too big wooden bed frames with headboards and footboards, matching dressers, rustic lamps, and cozy chairs for sitting or throwing your clothes on after a long day. There was something about that house that made you feel like you were stepping into another world, one where the air itself had texture warm, masculine, earthy. The kind of place you remembered with all your senses.

Outside, behind the house and past all the farm equipment, stood the long line of horse corrals. Each pen was carefully sectioned, and nearby was the feed room a small barn-like structure packed with hay, grains, and supplies. Some areas were shaded and covered to protect the animals from the harsh Texas sun. The rest of the land was divided by fencing a patchwork of sections that served different purposes. Some fields were for grazing cows, others were used for growing sorghum and rotating crops. Every inch of land had a purpose, and my dad made sure it was used well. During the weekdays, we lived in the city house. That was our base. But come the weekend, it was ranch time. Sometimes, depending on the season or school schedule, we'd stay at the ranch during the week too. It wasn't too far from town, so getting to school wasn't a big issue especially if we left early enough. I always looked forward to those weeks. Ranch mornings felt different.

That's when I started riding horses with my dad. He had bought me my very own horse a beautiful white one named Palomo because white was (and still is) my favorite color. I'll never forget him. His coat was so bright it almost shimmered in the sun, and he had the gentlest eyes. Dad would ride in front, holding onto the rope, while I rode behind him on Palomo. He never let me stray far. Those rides usually happened early in the morning, right as the sky started turning from dark blue to soft gold before the Texas heat set in. He taught me how to take care of my horse how to bathe him correctly, how to brush and comb his mane, and even how to braid it "just for looks." He showed me how to approach the other horses too how to place my hand over their nose in a calm, firm way so they'd get familiar with me. It was his little trick, something he'd picked up over the years. It worked. The horses always remembered me.

I got to feed them, watch them get new shoes when the farrier came, and even sit nearby during their checkups. I loved everything about it the smells, the sounds, the rhythm of the ranch. It probably sounds weird, but I even liked the smell of the stables. Hay, sweat, earth, leather… it was strangely comforting.

Those were the moments when I felt most free, most alive. And even if Dad didn't say much, being next to him during those rides or feeding sessions felt like something sacred like a soft language only we understood.

Dad taught all of us how to ride four-wheelers even my younger brothers. We were just kids, but he didn't believe in limiting us when it came to learning how to move with power. He was wild like that. He had no fear, and he made sure we didn't either. I still remember him showing off, riding the four-wheeler on just two wheels, leaning into the curves like he was born to do it. He wasn't just that way with the ATVs, even at the lake or the beach, he'd pull off the same wild stunts with jet skis. He'd dip the entire jet ski under the water, disappearing for a second, and then come shooting back up like some kind of water cowboy. It was wild, and it made everyone stare. But to us that was just Dad. Eventually, he got dirt bikes for my brothers. I never got to ride those, but I didn't mind. I had my own four-wheeler, and that alone made me feel like I could go anywhere. We'd spend hours riding around the open fields filled with citrus trees, weaving in and out of rows of oranges, or racing down the dusty dirt roads that stretched beyond the ranch. We even had the freedom to ride all the way to the corner store and back. No one stopped us. That's just the kind of place it was open, wild, and ours.

But as much freedom as we had out there, things inside started to shift especially after we settled more permanently in Texas. By this time, we had a bigger house, we were no longer bouncing between places, and from the outside looking in, it probably looked like we were thriving. And we were, in some ways. But in others? Things got complicated. You have to understand I had grown up in a completely different environment. Oregon felt like a whole different universe. The way people talked, the way they dressed, the pace, the air everything was different. I was different. And when we moved back to Texas, that difference followed me everywhere. It clung to me like an accent I couldn't shake.

Every time we got together with extended family, I could feel the stares. The side-eyes. The tension in the room. I'd barely walk in before one of my cousins would mumble, "Ahí viene la prima presumida." In English, that means, "Here comes the conceited cousin," or "Here comes the show-off." And let me be clear I had never bragged about anything. I wasn't flashy. I wasn't loud. I wasn't trying to outshine anyone. But to them, my difference was threatening. Maybe it was the way I spoke, or how I carried myself. Maybe it was my clothes. I don't know. But I felt it, and it cut deep.

I didn't feel like I had more than anyone else. I wasn't raised that way. Sure, my parents had nice things. Sure, we were going to fancier places, eating better food, maybe wearing more polished clothes. But I was still in a strict household. I wasn't allowed to do half the things they were allowed to do and that was the part they never saw. They only saw the outside.

And it wasn't just my cousins. Even my own tias my mom's sisters would throw shade. One of them once said my facial features were too sharp, and that I had a cara de caballo a "horse face." And even though I laughed it off in the moment, that comment stayed with me. For years. Into adulthood. Sometimes even now, I'll look in the mirror and hear that voice. It took time and a lot of growing to let that go.

And as much as it hurts to say, it wasn't just my mom's side of the family. Some of the cousins from my dad's side weren't much better. Not all of them but enough to feel it. Enough to know that competition and comparison were alive and well behind the smiles and hugs. I think a lot of that tension came from the parents the way families would subtly compare who had more, who was doing better, who got further. I didn't care about any of that. I just wanted to feel like I belonged. But often, I didn't.

What they didn't know what they never asked about was how much I had already seen. I knew exactly what it was like to live in a cramped trailer. I knew what it was like to share a room, to hear my parents fighting through thin walls, to hope the lights stayed on. And I also knew what it felt like to have abundance a big house, my own things, new boots, Sunday dinners with a seat at the table. I lived both realities. I had known what it was to have, and I had known what it was to go without. That's not something you forget. It's not something you throw in anyone's face. If anything, it teaches you humility and hunger.

It was both a blessing and a curse. A gift and a scar.

Back in Texas, my dad still had his shopping addiction. Every time we were in town with a little downtime, he'd take us to Boot Jack, Boot Barn, or Cavender's and go wild. He had this thing for boots but more specifically, for shoes. I guess that's where I get it from, because let's be real… I love shoes.

To me, shoes are magic. You can wear the same exact outfit and just change the shoes, and boom whole new vibe. Whole new character. It's like an outfit rewrite. And I've always believed:

"Give me the right pair of shoes, and I can conquer the world... fashionably." It was one of those things Dad and I quietly bonded over the flair, the attitude, the unspoken language of showing up sharp. Even when everything else was shifting, even when family tension ran high, we still had those moments. The rides. The shopping trips. The styling. The freedom. It didn't fix everything. But it helped.

When I told you I wasn't allowed to wear what was trending I meant it. That wasn't just me being dramatic. Even at this point in my life, my dad still controlled what I wore. He would buy me piles of expensive Western wear head-to-toe Wrangler, button down shirts, pearl snaps, thick denim jeans but it was never what I wanted. It was only what he chose. What they approved. I could go to school wearing a full Wrangler outfit while everyone else was in flared jeans, cropped hoodies, or sneakers they saved up for. I stood out but not in the way I wanted. My dad? He wore boots every single day. Seven days a week, 365 days a year. That man's feet were never in sneakers like, ever. The only exceptions I can even recall were rare: maybe when he played soccer with his friends, once or twice at the Portland Zoo when we still lived in Oregon, and in prison. But... we're not there yet. Let's not skip chapters.

That year, my parents were still traveling a lot doing business, making moves, chasing bigger dreams. We got to tag along a few times, and it felt like a treat. They'd take us on trips to Dallas or Irving, Texas, and while my dad disappeared into business meetings, we'd spend time with my mom at the malls. Sometimes, we were allowed to pick something out and when Dad was with us, it was almost always a guarantee he'd say yes. Mom? Not so much. She was stricter with money and way more practical. But Dad had that "just throw it in the cart" energy. That carefree spending energy.

I'll never forget one specific trip to Irving. It got chilly one evening, and we didn't have enough warm clothes packed. My dad walked me into the store and without a second thought, bought me one of the nicest jackets I've ever owned. It was a denim western-style jacket, trimmed with long brown fringe down the arms and across the back. Thick, heavy, and stylish a real statement piece. I think it was over $200, and he bought it like it was nothing. Just saw it, liked it, handed it over. That was him. And even though it wasn't necessarily "my style," I treasured it. Because it made me feel chosen. Seen. Spoiled, even and not in a bad way.

And remember how in earlier chapters I said I wasn't great at using porta-potties or popping a squat outdoors while we traveled? That hadn't changed either. On that same trip, I had a little accident nothing major, but enough that we had to stop for new clothes. My mom bought me a few extra things at the mall, and I remember feeling embarrassed but also cared for. It was a strange in-between feeling. Looking back, I used to think those were family vacation trips... but now I know they were really business trips. What kind of business? We'll leave it at that for now. That same trip, my dad surprised us by taking us to Medieval Times. I had never experienced anything like it. The giant arena, the horses galloping under strobe lights, the knights with their swords clashing mid-air it was magical. And the food? Incredible. We were right up front, too. Amazing seats. It was like stepping into a movie, and I remember being completely hypnotized by it. I haven't been back since, even now as an adult, but that night stuck with me. It was one of those core memories you carry for life.

Around that time, my parents started making more time for themselves too. They began attending Mexican concerts live bands, loud music, a full cultural experience. Dancing was a big deal, and my mom would dress to impress. Always. She was a natural beauty with stunning tight curls and a sharp sense of fashion. She loved high-end clothes from Dillard's, always wore the nicest sets, and had her face permanently done her eyebrows were microbladed to perfection before most people even knew what that was. She had class, style, and presence. But still my dad controlled everything. If her outfit didn't match his standards, he'd send her back to change. No discussion. He'd say, "Do you know whose wife you are?" as if her clothing choices were a direct reflection of his reputation. It was aggressive. Overbearing. It wasn't just control it was image management. And it wasn't just with her. He had the same expectations for all of us, even as kids. Everything had to be pressed, polished, and perfect. If even one shoe had a scuff, he'd make you change. But Mom bore the brunt of it. Always.

Sometimes, we'd tag along to those events. My brothers and I would be seated at their table, dressed up, hair combed, shoes spotless only to fall asleep in the chairs by midnight while they danced into the early morning hours. That was the rhythm of Latino events. Loud. Long. And full of life.

Dad's closet looked like it belonged to a country music mogul. Dozens of crisp white long-sleeve button-ups. Every pair of boots you could imagine ostrich, python, traditional leather, in every shade of brown and black. Western pants, pleated and pressed so sharply they could cut glass. If they had a double line on the front a pressing mistake he'd toss them out without hesitation. No mercy. He was that particular. He knew what he liked. And he had it his way, every single time.

My parents' bedroom smelled like power and elegance. His signature Carolina Herrera cologne lingered in the air, while my mom's Oscar de la Renta perfume was always layered softly behind it. The mix of both was intoxicating. Masculine, feminine, bold, refined just like them. Just like us.

On the days we stayed at the city house, especially when my dad had the yard guys working fixing up fences, planting fresh palm trees, or doing maintenance it felt like an unspoken invitation for family to gather. Dad would call over some of our cousins, even a few uncles and aunts, and without fail, he'd create a whole vibe in the front yard. He had bought this beautiful cement-style table with matching benches from Mexico. It looked like something carved out of stone heavy, detailed, and made to last. We'd all pile around it under the Texas sun, and he'd come back from Jack in the Box with paper bags full of dollar tacos, fries, curly fries, cheeseburgers, and whatever else he could carry. And always, always giant slices of watermelon, chilled and juicy, cut right on the spot. Eating watermelon outside like that was probably one of my favorite things ever. Sticky fingers, juice dripping down our chins, but nobody cared we were outside, and we were kids.

My parents had even built an outdoor bathroom specifically for these gatherings. It matched the house perfectly same brown brick, same roof tiles, same sturdy structure. They built it so guests wouldn't have to go inside during parties. That way the house stayed clean, and everything guests needed was just a few steps away. Next to it was a custom garage not just a place to park the cars, but a whole setup. The garage also matched the house with the same brick and roofing, and it had a smaller, attached storage room for tools and house supplies.

But to my dad, that garage was his kingdom. His toy box. He kept his prized cars there the real treasures. You remember how I told you he had a thing for cars? That obsession never left him. In addition to the old, beat-up truck he brought with him from Oregon (which had its own story), he owned two beautifully preserved vintage trucks. One was a baby sky blue that looked like it belonged in a 1950s postcard, and the other was a green-blue hybrid, almost like a turquoise sea foam, with a wood-toned wagon trim that made it look like it drove straight out of a time capsule. Every time you honked the horn on that wagon, it would let out a wild, ridiculous sound something like "baaaa-ZOOO-gaaa!" that had all of us cracking up every single time. Those trucks weren't just for driving they were show cars. He'd take them to exhibitions and truck meets where people would take pictures, vote, compete, win money or trophies. He didn't just keep them clean; he customized them. One of the trucks had a full surround sound system installed in the truck bed massive blue leather-covered speakers that matched the exact color of the truck itself. When the music blasted, you could feel the bass vibrating through your chest before you even stepped outside. It was the loudest, coolest thing ever. I remember one trip we made as a family to South Padre Island for a big truck show at the convention center. The plan was to enter all the trucks into the competition. I don't fully remember if we had to leave early due to bad weather, but what I do remember is how exciting it was to ride in a convoy of custom cars like we were royalty on wheels.

So much happened that year. It felt like it lasted longer than twelve months. It was one of those years that stretches and bends in your memory so full, so layered, it practically becomes a whole era.

At one point, my mom had to leave on her own for a trip something she never did. One of my aunts was seriously ill and needed her help, so she left us behind with Dad for the first time. And let me tell you... we had a blast. We got to see a side of my dad we rarely saw. He was goofy, loud, silly. He let loose. He let us be kids. We ate out every day. We went to arcades. He took us to Peter Piper Pizza a place kind of like Chuck E. Cheese, with greasy pizza, sticky game tokens, and flashing lights. And to make it even better, he invited the whole extended family. Our cousins came, our uncles came. The men sat around pitchers of beer while the kids got wristbands and token buckets and ran wild. That night turned into a monthly ritual. Peter Piper Pizza became our spot. Everyone was close during that time the kind of closeness that feels like a warm blanket around your whole family.

Around that same time, my parents were also planning my older brother's 18th birthday party. For us, that was a huge deal almost like a quinceañera. In our culture, girls usually get a big celebration at 15, and sometimes again at 16 or 18. But for boys? An 18th birthday is the moment to step into adulthood with pride and my parents weren't going to miss the chance to throw something big. The party was set to be at the ranch. They installed giant white party tarps to cover the dance floor and seating area in case the weather turned ugly. It was Western-themed, of course but still had plenty of modern touches. There was a bounce house for the younger kids, a full spread of food and drinks, and space for dancing under the stars. My mom planned almost all of it from decorations to desserts while my dad oversaw the big-ticket items like the band, the DJ, and any logistics involving sound systems or security. They kind of whipped the party together last minute, considering most quinceañera-style parties take years to plan. But because they didn't have to rent a ballroom or fancy venue the ranch was the venue it took some pressure off. Still, it was no small feat.

That whole year was fast, loud, extravagant, and emotional a constant mix of fun and tension, memories and moments that would stick with me for life.

When the big event finally arrived, my brother stood tall in his crisp jeans, sharp boots, and a clean button-up fully dressed in western gear like my dad. It was a proud moment, and he looked like a man stepping into adulthood. All of us girls my cousins and I matched in black pants and red western shirts. We looked like a little performance group, perfectly coordinated around him. The party was a huge success, and the photos came out beautifully. They had mariachis playing live, loud enough to shake the walls of the house and hearts of the guests. Every corner of the ranch was filled with music, laughter, and the clinking of drinks.

The bar was fully stocked. There were giant coolers full of beer, wine, and my personal favorite perros salados. If you've never had one, it's basically a spicy, tangy, salt-rimmed tequila drink with lime and grapefuit juice. Of course, I wasn't supposed to drink but I did anyway, just a little bit. It was one of those "I'm grown" moments I snuck in without anyone noticing. Or maybe they did, and just let it slide.

Catering had always been a thing at our family events. Long before it became a trend, my parents were hiring taqueros, chefs, servers making sure everyone was fed and full without having to lift a finger. So when I started attending birthday parties or school events where we had to get up and serve ourselves hot dogs, or prep our own burgers, it felt... odd. Not in a judgmental way, just in a cultural shock kind of way. I wasn't used to that. Even in earlier days, before my parents could afford catering, the women would serve the food. Always. First the men, then the kids. That's just how it was a deep-rooted, unspoken rule of tradition.

Back to the party, we got to take pictures around the haystacks and all the Western-themed décor: wagon wheels, saddles, burlap banners, and mini boots on the tables. It looked like something out of a country music video. My mom seemed so proud of how everything turned out, but you could tell she was just as relieved when it was over. She always exhaled the loudest after the last guest left. And honestly, the tension that built up before any party or trip was no joke. My parents would argue every single time they had something big to plan whether it was a party, a trip to Oregon, or even crossing into Mexico. The stress always made them snap at each other. I used to joke in my head that they were "chewing each other's necks" because that's what it felt like watching them go back and forth in frustration. That's part of the reason my parents started planning my quinceañera nearly five years in advance hoping that the early planning would reduce the stress and the blowups. (Spoiler alert: it didn't. But they tried.)

Around this time, my dad gifted my older brother a full professional DJ setup. It was huge. We're talking lights, speakers, turntables the works. It was his way of pushing him toward starting a business of his own, something lighter than the hard labor he grew up doing. Dad and my brother both loved music. They thrived in social environments, loved entertaining, and this setup was perfect for that. Before long, my brother was booking weekend gigs after school, loading up the ranch trailer with all the equipment, and setting up for weddings, quinceañeras, and other events. He took it seriously. It wasn't just a hobby, it was hustle.

Sometimes I got to tag along not for long, and not to do much but just to watch. It made me feel included, even if I wasn't quite allowed in the spotlight yet.

But something inside me was changing.

I was growing tired of being labeled "the rich girl who lived in the White House." Not because I was rich, but because people assumed I was. I hated it. I hated the way people whispered about me, the way they stared, the way they twisted everything I did into something it wasn't. The truth is, I didn't feel rich. I didn't feel special. I felt restricted, watched, judged, and muted. I couldn't straighten my hair. I couldn't pluck my eyebrows. I couldn't wear makeup or trendy clothes like the other girls. I was tired of wearing handpicked outfits from western stores when I just wanted to look like me.

Even though Texas schools had uniform policies, kids still found ways to make their outfits pop. Polo shirts had just the right cut, jeans had high-end stitching or trendy fits and I couldn't even get close. My mom was too strict about everything, and my dad only bought what he thought was appropriate. If it didn't match his standards, it was a no. But one day, I realized something.

I had asked my dad for a lot of things before… and he had rarely said no. I think my mom trained us so well to stay quiet that we never dared to ask. We assumed everything would be denied or punished. But when I started asking properly respectfully, but with confidence I noticed something shift. If I played my cards right, I usually got what I wanted. That small realization changed everything for me.

Still, Mom was becoming more bitter, more short-tempered. I didn't know if it was stress, resentment, or something deeper behind closed doors with Dad. Maybe all of it. She always seemed like she was carrying something heavy that she couldn't talk about. Something was shifting in her too.

We also weren't allowed to have any pets. Not even goldfish. But I really, really wanted a hamster.

Eventually, I started losing the fear.

There's a saying: You don't get what you don't ask for. So I started asking. Little by little, I spoke up. I started testing the waters first with money, then with clothes, and finally with things I had longed for as a kid but never dared to ask for. And surprisingly… my dad never said no. Not once.

Every time I asked for money to go shopping or get something for school, he'd do the same funny gesture. He'd lift his hand, pinching his thumb and forefinger together, and say:

"¿Así o más?"

"Like this just a little? Or should I fill the gap?"

Then he'd stretch his fingers apart and laugh.

I'd always respond, "Fill the gap!" and he would. He thought it was hilarious. And that moment that small, lighthearted gesture marked the beginning of me finally stepping out of the shell I had been raised in. I started shedding the fears I'd been groomed to carry. Slowly, I started claiming a voice.

I even got brave enough to ask for a hamster.

That was probably the worst mistake of my childhood because they stink. I swear, I will never in my life own a hamster again. But back then, I was so proud. My parents bought me a full enclosure, and my mom even got me one of those clear plastic balls so it could roll around the house. I don't remember exactly what happened to it that whole chapter is kind of blurry now but I know I had it for a while. The only thing that's still clear in my memory is how awful my room started to smell. Like, bad.

Shortly after that, my mom got her own puppy.

At first, it was a flat-out no. My dad hated dogs, and pets were forbidden especially inside the house. But somehow, my mom pulled it off. She brought home a tiny puppy, and just like that, my dad fell in love with it too. It didn't take long.

That little dog was loyal to my mom. So much so that one morning, when my dad walked into the kitchen and playfully smacked my mom on the butt while she was cooking breakfast, the puppy went wild barking, growling, ready to attack. It was the funniest thing ever. Even my dad couldn't stop laughing.

Around that time, my dad was more relaxed at home than usual. On weekends or after school, we'd sit around the living room eating pancakes and waffles, bacon and eggs his favorite. SpongeBob would be playing on the giant surround-sound TV. Music and sound systems were always a big deal in our house, even outside in the yard. Every space had a stereo. He'd walk out of the bedroom in his pajamas, shake his head at the TV, and say in Spanish:

"¿Otra vez ese pinche queso?"

"Not that damn cheese again."

We'd die laughing.

We'd yell back: "He's not cheese! He's a sponge!"

But he knew. I think he said it just to hear us laugh. He had his moments like that silly, playful, warm. And we held onto them like sunlight during storm season.

But don't get me wrong his temper never disappeared. The fights didn't stop.

He was still 100% strict. When he walked through the front door after work, the house had to look like a showroom. Everything polished. No dishes in the sink. No shoes in the entryway. No socks on the floor. He had eyes like a hawk and a trigger temper. If he spotted anything out of place, someone was getting smacked.

There were days when my mom and I would spend hours on our knees polishing the bases of furniture with wood oil the kitchen table, all the lower cabinets, the legs of every chair. We had this special liquid cleaner just for wood. And he expected every surface to squeak under the rag. That's how clean it had to be.

He'd do closet inspections too. If one drawer was out of place, if one shoe was crooked, it was game over.

And if you dared to roll your eyes, purse your lips, or even breathe too loudly in response to something he said, you'd get slapped immediately. You didn't need to talk back with words your face was enough. Talking back, even silently, was punishable.

This is also when his relationship with my older brother hit a breaking point.

They started fighting like two grown men. Fist to fist. Yelling, pushing, cursing. I always tried to defend my brother. I couldn't help it. I'd throw myself in between them, even if it meant I'd get shoved or slapped too. I'd scream at my dad, "Mess with someone your own size!" and I meant it. I didn't hold back.

I must've been 13, maybe 14 full of rage, full of bravery, full of something. I would shout right back at him, refuse to back down. I'd get punished every time but I didn't care. I refused to cry. That was the one thing he couldn't take from me.

There was a time I remember it vividly when my mom and dad said they were actually terrified of me. Not because I was violent or wild, but because I would stare them straight in the face, stone cold, without a tear. That silence... that rebellion... that was my power. That was the start of the hate that began to grow in my chest. I couldn't stand watching him hit my brothers, or me, over something stupid. I couldn't take it anymore.

One morning, I was standing at the sink, washing dishes for my mom. I wasn't even thinking I was just scared, trying to avoid being yelled at. Suddenly, my dad dragged my brother into the kitchen, mid-argument, and barked at him:

"Look at your sister she's being productive! Why can't you be more like her?"

As if I wanted to be there.

Let's be honest I wasn't doing dishes out of love. I was terrified. I did it because if I didn't, I'd get punished. I wanted to scream at him, "This isn't praise. This is survival."

My blood boiled. I wanted to kick him. Punch him. Something. But I didn't.

And I think... that's when I first realized the cracks in our home weren't just in the walls. They were inside us.

As my dad became more successful, he also became more distant. The more money he made, the more businesses he launched, the more land and trucks and properties he acquired the less he was at home. And when he was home, it felt like walking on eggshells. One good day didn't make up for the six that were hell.

The house got bigger. The bank account got bigger. But so did the tension.

The pressure.

The arguments.

The silence.

And that changed the way I see everything.

To this day, I don't associate success with peace. I associate it with pressure, absence, and pain. And that's something I still have to unlearn.

I just feel like the more money started rolling in, the messier everything became. The cracks that had always been there silent, tucked beneath duty and tradition suddenly got louder. Sharper. My mom, who had always kept her head down and tried to keep the peace, began to shift. I think this was the season where she started to find her voice.

There was one fight I'll never forget.

My dad had recently bought her a little brown Jeep a boxy, rugged one that she loved. That car was her freedom. That day, we were supposed to be headed to a party. Me and my brother were both part of the celebration. I don't remember if we were in the program or just specially invited, but we had a role. I had my outfit ready, and I was told to wear a bit of makeup not too much, just a little.

But that was enough to set my dad off.

He lost it. Said if I didn't wipe the makeup off, he would scrape it off my face himself. Said he didn't care if it hurt. Said no daughter of his was going to show up looking like that.

I froze. But my mom didn't.

She snapped.

I still remember her standing in the driveway, hands shaking, yelling at him to back off. When he didn't, she revved the engine of that little brown Jeep and nearly ran him over. No one got hurt but the message was loud and clear.

"ENOUGH."

That was the moment she stopped letting him control every part of her. That was the beginning of her pushing back. She had taken years of his temper, his commands, his fists, his silence and now she'd had it. That fight cracked the foundation, and not long after, they split up.

Dad moved to the ranch.

We stayed in the city house.

During the months they were separated, life felt lighter. My mom let me go to my best friend's house more often. I didn't have to sneak around or ask for permission in a whisper. I could just go. And her home… it felt like a different universe.

Her family was so warm, so welcoming. I called her parents Mom and Dad, too. They treated me like I was theirs. Her dad would come home with fast food the kind that comes in a greasy brown paper bag and he'd hand it to me like it was a five-star meal. He'd always say, "I know you're probably not used to eating this kind of stuff," or he'd hand me a glass of tap water and say, "I hope that's okay."

Little did they know…

I grew up drinking out of a hose. I was raised on survival meals and trailer park hustle. I wasn't some spoiled rich kid just because we had money now or lived in the white brick house. I didn't care about bottled water or fancy food. I cared about feeling safe. And in that house with my best friend and her family I did.

It felt like a glimpse of normal.

Just a regular family.

In a wooden house.

With laughter in the air.

Me and my best friend were inseparable. Her parents became like second parents to me. Her mom once told me how much she loved when my dad threw parties that they were legendary. The kind that lasted until 3, 4, sometimes even 6 a.m. The music would be loud, the energy buzzing, and everyone had a good time.

But little did anyone know…

Behind closed doors, it wasn't always a celebration.

Behind the music, sometimes there was shouting.

Behind the lights, sometimes there were bruises.

No one knew the weight we carried once the guests left and the last song stopped playing.

And when it came time to go back to Oregon like we did every year it got harder and harder to leave.

Every time we packed up, it wasn't just clothes and luggage. It was memories. It was friends. It was a sense of normal that we were saying goodbye to again. Oregon was familiar, yes. But it wasn't always home.

It never got easier.

Even though we knew it was just for a few months…

Even though we'd always come back…

It still hurt.

It was the ache of living between two lives the loud one, the lavish one, the chaotic one and the quiet, peaceful one we got to taste only in borrowed moments.

And every year, I felt that ache a little deeper.

Chapter 8

"Rebeldia (Rebellion):

Life Under Surveillance in a Gilded Cage

TRIGGER WARNING:

This chapter contains memories of emotional tension, childhood neglect, and shifting family dynamics. While it does not contain graphic descriptions, the emotional tone may be heavy for some readers. Please take care as you read.

The last few years that we took the trip to Oregon were a complete nightmare. There was no way any of us were going to make it through without being yelled at, spanked, smacked, or slapped something always happened. Dad's attitude was at its worst, and my mom was more stressed than ever.

Even though our house was being left behind in good hands with the workers, Dad had the whole place locked down like a fortress. Surveillance cameras were posted everywhere around the garage, on the gates, along the fence line. Every single door and window had alarms. In their bedroom, Mom and Dad had a screen where they could see live footage from all the cameras at once. Nothing happened without them knowing. Not even a leaf moved without being recorded.

Eventually, Mom and Dad made up sort of. When it came time to pack up for Oregon, they were speaking again, but the tension between them was thick and heavy. I think they had even taken a trip to Mexico on their own to handle some business while we stayed behind. During that time, my older brother and I got to do our own thing a little more freely. He had a truck, so we'd go shopping and hang out, and it honestly felt like a little breath of fresh air. But once they got back, that awkward tension returned like it never left.

Then came the usual yearly routine. We unplugged everything in the house, waffle makers, toasters, stereos, everything, like we did every summer. Then it was back on the road, three long days headed to Oregon again.

This time, the road trip felt different. The energy was off. We still made our usual stops, but no one was joking around or enjoying it. It felt like business. Even when we pulled into our Oregon home, it didn't feel like home anymore. Our hometown didn't feel like ours. The connection to our childhood friends had faded, and the older we got, the more distant and awkward it all felt. I still tried to make the best of it tried making new friends but there were more rules now. More control.

By then, I wasn't even allowed to talk to boys. Male friends were completely off-limits. My dad didn't believe in friendships between girls and boys. It was strictly forbidden. If I was ever caught even speaking to a guy, it was guaranteed I was getting spanked didn't matter that I was a teenager. The rules never changed.

I could have anything I wanted from my dad anything as long as it wasn't a boy. When people say I might have "daddy issues," I don't think that's accurate. If anything, it's like a reverse daddy issue. I always got what I wanted... except freedom. Boys? Nonnegotiable. Period.

He used to tell me, straight-faced, that I wasn't allowed to move out, date, or even think about marriage until after I was twenty-five. He started saying that when I was little, and it never changed. I used to think he was joking... but he wasn't.

That year, I didn't get to see much of the ranch work going on. I was getting older, and that meant more restrictions. My dad wouldn't let me be outside around the men, even if it was just to water plants or watch the yard get mowed. I wasn't even allowed near the workers. The only time I got to leave the house was to run errands with my mom. Around that time, she had a white Avalanche truck that my dad had bought her, and we'd cruise around together in that.

One evening, we were heading home and had our blinker on to turn left into our neighborhood when a car came speeding from behind and slammed into us. It was a full-on accident cops were involved. When we called Dad, he rushed to us without hesitation. I had never seen him look so panicked. He was frantic checking on us, making sure we were okay, and once we were cleared to go, he brought us straight home. That was one of the few times I felt like he let his guard down out of pure worry.

To be honest with you, that entire year is a blur. It was strictly business, strictly school. No fun. Nothing exciting. Just tension. Dad was on edge 24/7, and Mom wasn't far behind. Clutch issues kept coming up with the trucks. Maintenance problems were nonstop for my dad, my brother, and their crew. I remember seeing Dad take a call about a breakdown, and this man always in his crisp white button-down and starched jeans would immediately slip into his work coveralls and boots he kept in the back of his truck. He'd drive straight to the problem, fix it himself, then clean his hands with that strong-smelling orange cleaner and keep pushing through the day like nothing happened.

The hustle never stopped. I respected that about him, even when I hated how angry he always seemed. It's that love-hate thing, you know?

I ended up arguing with my dad during that Oregon stay again. As I've mentioned before, I had a short fuse with him. I was over it. Over being yelled at. Over watching everyone get chewed out daily. I wasn't scared of him, not like the rest. I didn't flinch when his voice raised. I was the one who'd push back.

One day, I walked home from school, and one of the girls I knew offered me a cigarette. I had never smoked before, but I said yes. Curiosity, rebellion maybe both. The moment I walked through the door, my dad caught the smell on me. He didn't ask questions. Just whacked me, instantly. He told me if I liked cigarettes so much, I could go ahead and smoke an entire pack back to back, and then we'd see if I'd ever want another.

Honestly? It worked. I didn't pick up another cigarette for years after that. At the time, it pissed me off... but now I kinda laugh. Fair enough, I guess.

On our way back to Texas, we had never been so relieved. Don't get me wrong we still loved Oregon, and I held onto those memories of our old life there. But deep down, I had started falling in love with our new home. Not because everything was perfect it wasn't. I didn't like the weather, or the kids at school, or the way I never quite fit in. I didn't feel like I blended with anyone in Texas. But Oregon didn't feel like home anymore either. The friends, the schools, the business drama it had all changed.

I felt stuck in-between.

Ni de aquí, ni de allá.

Not from here, nor there.

Every time we returned to Texas and I started school again, it felt like I had to brace myself for the bullying. And it was never for anything serious it was always the little things. The way I walked, the way I talked, how I looked.

I had this habit of leaning forward slightly when I walked, and I did this little hop with each step. The girls would laugh behind me and mock the way I moved, pointing and whispering just loud enough. It made me want to disappear.

The boys weren't much better. Every time I walked by in the hallways or cafeteria, I'd hear them shout out, "Limones!"

It was their way of mocking my chest, small and undeveloped at the time. "Limones" meant "limes," referring to my flat chest. I laughed along with them sometimes just to survive it, but it stung bad. I didn't choose my body. God made me that way. But I was too young and too unsure of myself to know how to defend myself.

The girls would also make comments about my hair. It was never styled or done like theirs. Not to shame my mom, but she never really taught me how to be a "girl." I didn't own a single hair tool, no blow dryer, no round brush, no curling iron, not even a straightener. I didn't know how to detangle my hair properly, let alone style it. No shaving, no waxing, no makeup. Nothing.

I was just out here... raw.

Middle school was already tough, but growing up with strict Mexican parents and being a migrant kid made it feel ten times harder.

Still, once we were back in Texas, things fell back into their usual rhythm. If there was one thing Dad knew how to do, it was go all out for Christmas. He didn't play. Lights covered every inch of the house the bricked fence, the garage, the gates, even the tiny building outside we used as a bathroom. He had a decorator's eye, for real. If it involved spending or hustling to make something happen, he was all in. I can definitely see where I get that side of me from now.

That year, I started working on my self-image quietly, in my own way. Sounds wild, but I actually begged my older brother to help me straighten my hair with a clothing iron.

Yup. A real iron.

I had looked it up online: how to straighten your hair without a flat iron. The instructions were insane like laying your hair flat on the ironing board and carefully pressing it down with a towel between your hair and the hot iron. It was risky, but I was desperate. I offered to clean my brother's room or help with his homework if he just helped me out. We figured it out together somehow and my hair was pin-straight by the end of it. I don't recommend it. Seriously. But I was just a little girl trying to feel pretty, even if it meant getting creative. And hey it worked.

My mom loved Las Posadas, and she didn't miss a single night.

Posadas run from December 16th to the 24th. The word "posada" means "the inn". In Spanish symbolizing the biblical story of Mary and Joseph searching for shelter. Each night represents a month of Mary's pregnancy, and the celebrations are filled with music, candles, food, and carols.

That meant tamales, pozole, buñuelos, atole, ponche, and café de olla, rich and sweet and warming your hands and heart at the same time. Whether we were hosting a Posada or preparing for Nochebuena (Christmas Eve), the whole week was full of preparation and joy. My mom thrived in that season.

And despite all the chaos, despite how rocky things could be the holidays were when my family felt whole. We'd have our big extended family events, but we also carved out our own private Christmas day with just us. Those were the best. Pajamas all day. Cookies baking in the oven. Gifts stacked under the tree. Dad became a big kid during the holidays grinning like crazy, shaking wrapped boxes, starting snowball fights with wrapping paper. And Mom? She was in her element. Full kitchen mode. Loud music, big pots simmering, flour everywhere, and love in every dish. Those are the memories I still hold onto the tightest. Oh gosh... I'll never forget this Christmas. It stuck with me for years and honestly, it still used to upset me until not that long ago.

My parents had gone out to do their usual Christmas shopping, and I got to tag along with my mom for some of it. She asked me for ideas on what to get my older brother. I remember being so excited to help. I told her we should look at laptops he'd been wanting one forever. He was older, always working or driving, and it made sense.

And me? I had one small dream that year: I wanted my very own radio something like a karaoke machine or stereo, anything that would let me blast my music and sing my heart out. I didn't need anything fancy. Just a way to feel like I had a space of my own, where I could listen to whatever I wanted and escape into the sound. Mom and I took a trip to Best Buy. I was so excited to even be there. I helped her pick out the laptop bundle since she wasn't really into tech or electronics and I felt proud of myself for guiding her through it all. We found something nice, and I just knew my brother was going to love it. I kept it a total secret. Didn't say a word. I wanted it to be a true surprise.

While we were there, Mom let me explore the aisle with all the karaoke machines and stereos. I remember staring at them like they were magic imagining which one I'd get, dreaming of opening it on Christmas morning. Just me and my music. That's all I wanted. But when Christmas came... I was crushed. We all gathered around to open gift & I watched my brother unwrap his laptop just like I predicted, he was ecstatic. So grateful. He deserved it.

Then it was my turn.

And what I opened was an ab machine.

An ab machine.

Even now, writing this, I know it sounds ungrateful. I feel the guilt creep up in my chest. But I was only 14. A kid. A sensitive kid who wanted music, not crunches. I remember holding back tears while everyone kept unwrapping gifts and smiling. I knew my parents loved me. And I did love fitness, to be fair I always have. But that moment left a mark on me.

It wasn't about not liking the gift. It was the disconnect feeling like no one had really heard me or seen me. I think that's what hurt the most. That feeling haunted me even into adulthood. We're past it now. But still... it's one of those memories that lingers quietly.

During the holiday season before, on, or after Christmas my parents would often arrange a big Tamalada with all the family. It was a whole event. Even the men got their hands dirty that year! We took tons of pictures cousins, aunts, uncles, everyone lined up, working together in the kitchen like a well-oiled machine.

Mom would set up long tables with everyone having their own little tamale station, spreading, filling, and folding like it was second nature. It was loud and beautiful.

And if you've never experienced a Tamalada, let me paint the picture for you.

It's more than just making food. It's a vibe. A real, emotional, cultural experience.

The room fills with the sound of stories being told, loud laughter, generations of memories spilling across the table. You hear the scraping of spoons in metal bowls, the soft soaking rustle of corn husks, and the background hum of festive Latin music. The whole house smells like masa, chiles, simmering spices, and warmth.

Everyone has a role: the masa mixers, the spreaders, the fillers, the wrappers. It's like an assembly line of love and legacy. Elders teach the younger kids the same techniques they were taught growing up. Secrets get passed down between the folds of every tamal.

It's not just about what we're making it's about who we are. The Tamalada is how we keep our roots alive. How we pass on recipes, stories, and cultural pride. It's connection. Tradition. Healing. It's history wrapped in corn husk.

And for us, it was always a party.

Music blasted. Party tarps were thrown up in the yard. Folding tables everywhere. The drinks were flowing Perros Salados, margaritas, beer, whiskey for the grown-ups. Capri Suns for the kids. Laughter in every corner. Tamales in the kitchen. Fireworks on the street.

With Christmas, my birthday, and New Year's all back to back... it was like a week of nonstop celebration. Straight-up party mode. No sleep. Just vibes.

New Year's Eve in our household was more than just fireworks and champagne it was a full-on spiritual and cultural reset. Every woman in the house including me, my mom, aunts, cousins would wash and prepare green grapes. Technically, they could be red too, but green grapes were our go-to. They represented good luck and money, and we didn't play when it came to starting the year off right.

Each person would receive 12 grapes, either served in a cup or skewered onto little wooden sticks. And as soon as the clock struck midnight not a second before or after we'd eat each grape, one by one, making a silent wish for every month of the year. Twelve months, twelve grapes, twelve wishes. No wish was too big or too small. You could pray for love, engagement, marriage, healing, success, peace, babies, or even travel. The universe was listening, and we were ready.

And speaking of travel you better believe we had suitcases ready too. Another fun, slightly chaotic tradition was running around the house with your luggage to bring in travel energy for the new year. The faster you ran, the further you'd go! And for those hoping for abundance and luck? Lentils. Tossed over your head, sprinkled in your wallet, or scattered near the door it was all part of the magic.

It's a Hispanic thing. If you know, you know.

We didn't need Pinterest to feel festive we had tradition in our blood.

And just when you thought the celebrations were winding down, January 6th came around, and it was time for La Rosca de Reyes The King's Bread. It's a soft, ring-shaped sweet bread, beautifully decorated with candied fruit to represent the jeweled crowns of the Three Wise Men. Hidden inside the bread was a tiny Baby Jesus figurine, and whoever found it in their slice? They were responsible for hosting the next tamalada on Día de la Candelaria, February 2nd. Sometimes, two or three people found a baby, and they'd co-host the next family get-together with food, drinks, and more tamales.

La Rosca was always paired with a warm mug of Abuelita hot chocolate or thick atole, sipped slowly while everyone laughed, teased the "winners," and made future plans. It was always such a warm and communal feeling like we were closing the holiday season with one last exhale of joy.

But once the parties ended, real life picked back up quickly.

That year, there was a lot going on. My parents had decided to renew their vows and plan a real wedding ceremony, since they had never actually had one they'd only eloped when they were younger. At the same time, my quinceañera planning was already in full swing. Add in my older brother's high school graduation, and there was barely any breathing room. We started going to tour ballrooms big, beautiful venues where the event could be held and I quickly realized this wasn't going to be a small party. My parents had already drafted the guest list and we were looking at over 1,000 guests. That made finding the right venue hard since most local ballrooms had a capacity of 500–800 people max. It took some serious digging to find one that could fit all the friends, family, and connections they wanted to invite.

My quince colors were classic soft light pink, just how I

envisioned. Even the dress. My dad was extremely picky when it came to this process, and I get it now the quinceañera isn't just about the daughter. In many ways, it's also a rite of passage for the parents, a symbolic moment where they present their daughter to the world as a young woman. In Mexican culture, tradition says that if a girl has a quinceañera, she must be pure as in, she must not have been with a man yet or the celebration would be frowned upon. So yeah… dating or even talking to boys was strictly forbidden in our household. My dad enforced that rule like a bodyguard.

But back to the dress…

My quince dress was being custom made by a local designer who was originally from Monterrey, Mexico. She was the real deal gifted, detailed, and deeply passionate about her craft. My mom and I worked together to design the entire thing from scratch. It was going to be iconic.

The dress was convertible with multiple pieces that gave me three full looks in one. A structured corset mini dress for dancing, a huge, poofy ballgown skirt with a dramatic long train for the reception, and a detachable long-sleeve topper for the church service. Think luxury meets tradition. Layers of high-end chiffon, soft pink hues, Swarovski crystals embroidered into every seam. Double crinoline layers underneath for that perfectly exaggerated shape. It was a dream. A whole fantasy.

And my mom's wedding dress? Whew. Showstopper.

She was also getting two looks made one for the vow ceremony and another for the reception. Both dresses were stunning, dripping in crystals and made with the same care as mine. We'd go to the seamstress's home weekly to check on the progress, try on what was completed, and give feedback. The process was long but magical. I kept telling my parents I didn't want just any quince. I wanted something traditional but also uniquely mine and they really made that happen.

That spring, we took a family trip to Tepic, Nayarit, Mexico during Easter break. It was unforgettable.

We stayed with close friends of my dad's who had a beautiful home tucked into the hillside. But before we arrived, we made a stop along the way in a busy street market the kind that reminds you of a Mexican version of Las Vegas, minus the neon lights and slot machines. Picture rows of tents and open booths on both sides of the street, with vendors selling everything from handmade clothes to clay pots, yard decorations, food, and candies. You could cross back and forth between streets freely no traffic lights, no rules. Jay-walking didn't even exist here.

When we finally arrived in Tepic, it was like walking into a postcard. We ate street tacos, rode around the plaza, and soaked up the local beauty. If I ever had to pick a place to live in Mexico, Nayarit would definitely be in my top five. It was lush, lively, and full of soul.

The house we stayed in was built on a steep mountain, and since it rained often that week, water would rush down like a mini waterfall through the streets. Our parents were extra cautious, reminding us not to go near the edge of the sidewalk or patio. But the kids oh, the kids we made the best of it. We folded paper boats and set them loose in the water, racing them down the sloped streets with the other neighborhood kids.

It was such a simple thing. But to this day, that memory feels like pure joy no stress, no pressure. Just the sound of rain, paper boats, and a bunch of happy kids playing together in the mountains of Mexico.

After a few days in Tepic, my dad surprised us with a drive out to a small, hidden village nearby called Jesús María del Nayar, Nayarit a place you definitely couldn't find on a tourist map. There was no airport, no major bus stop. If you wanted to get there, it had to be by car or in a local van with other travelers. The roads were all dirt, winding through steep mountain terrain/rugged, uneven, and at times, genuinely terrifying. One wrong turn, and you could tumble off the edge.

This little mountain town had a population of under 1,700 people, and by some stroke of fate, we happened to visit during Semana Santa their Holy Week celebration. What we didn't realize until we arrived was that Semana Santa in Jesús María wasn't like anything we had ever seen. It was called the Semana Santa Cora, named after the Cora Indigenous people who lived there. The entire town transformed into a sacred spiritual space, a deep ancestral tradition handed down through generations a living ritual inside the heart of the sierra.

On our way up the mountain, we were stopped at what looked like checkpoints. There were men stationed along the dirt road, and we were told we couldn't pass unless we either paid a fee or purchased a symbolic item usually something resembling a coyote tail or part. Once we had it, we'd hang it from the rear view mirror as a pass that allowed us to continue without interruption.

At each checkpoint, we were greeted by men in elaborate costumes masks that resembled demons, long wigs, detailed face paint, and layered outfits. They were the Cora performers, enacting a symbolic dance between good and evil. At the time, none of us knew what was going on. My dad was confused, and so were we. But after doing some research years later, I realized we had witnessed something sacred a cultural reenactment of spiritual resistance and devotion that had survived centuries.

When we finally reached our host's home, it was tucked deep into the mountains no power, no electronics, and definitely no cell signal. People used "el río" the river to bathe, clean clothes, wash dishes, everything. It was raw. Stripped down to the basics. But honestly? It was beautiful.

Experiencing life without electricity made me grateful for everything we had back home. The quiet, the simplicity, the way people adapted it all stayed with me.

During one of the spiritual performances, the local men asked that all women stay inside, away from the ceremony. From a distance, we could hear the drums, guitars, chanting, and flutes, and we watched as they selected local women to cook and wash their clothes for the week. It was part of the ritual symbolic servitude during Semana Santa, and by the end of the week, everyone returned to normal life.

It was wild, surreal, and honestly, a little unsettling. But it was also deeply fascinating. The artistry of the face paint, the handmade instruments, the fabric of the masks it all looked like it came from skilled artisans. Everything had meaning, from the rhythm of the drums to the symbols on the flags. This wasn't a performance. This was ancestral memory in motion.

After the ceremonies ended, the kids we were staying with took us to the river. Locals carried huge blue jugs of water over their shoulders to use for bathing, cleaning, cooking anything they needed. And the water? Crystal clear. We splashed around, played games, and soaked in the simplicity of life there. It was humbling and unforgettable. One of those experiences you don't really understand until years later.

We didn't stay too long in Jesús María, but before heading back to Tepic, we stopped at a local house that doubled as a restaurant. No electricity. No menu. Just a wooden table, a tiny fire pit, and a woman with magic in her hands. She made us fresh tortillas and a breakfast I can still taste to this day. I've never had anything like it again not even close. It was simple, homemade, and hands-down one of the best meals of my life.

The night we got back to Tepic, the neighborhood threw a small gathering on the patio. The men pulled out their instruments guitars, harps, bongos, trumpets, and accordions and formed what we call a "Fara Fara" band. Think of it as a rural-style mariachi, less formal but just as soulful. You hear that style often in Texas too especially at parties or family barbecues.

People danced under the stars. The vibe was alive. But the dancing style in Tepic was different more rhythmic, more grounded. They called it "Wicholo style", and it was specific to that region. My older brother and I danced together, and to this day, we still call it "Tepic style" when we break into those same moves. It's our little inside joke a memory tucked between two siblings that no one else fully understands. Well... now you do.

Later that week, my dad took us even deeper into the mountains the kind of road that makes your stomach drop. One mistake, and you're gone. The cliffs were steep, unguarded, and dangerous. I gripped the seat the entire time.

But the destination? Unbelievable.

My dad had purchased land and a gold mine. A real, functioning mine where gold was extracted straight from the earth. We got the full tour heavy machinery like John Deere-style equipment, loud and powerful. Dad pulled out a wooden tool called a Colombian Assay Spoon a horn-like instrument used to test gold samples.

He showed us how to "Colar el Oro", which means to filter or sift through the gold. He said the real gold rises to the top, while fake or impure pieces get lost in the mud. I didn't realize it then, but that stuck with me.

Of course, I was the curious one, asking questions every few seconds. I asked what happened after you found the gold what next? And my dad said he had a contract with a jewelry store to sell the refined gold to be turned into necklaces, bracelets, earrings. Real, pure, expensive stuff. To me, in that moment, my dad wasn't just a businessman he was a magician. Holding dust and turning it into treasure. He carried a whole world of unspoken meaning in his hands.

After the trip, we returned home and jumped right back into routine.

Vacations are great, but sometimes, you need a vacation from the vacation and for me, that meant coming home.

Mom would drop me off at school again. I still woke up at 5 AM to get ready, always the early bird. The bus came around 6:30, and I'd wait near the gated fence, surrounded by cameras my dad had installed all around the property for safety.

But one morning… something terrifying happened.

A man tried to lure me to his side of the gate.

I didn't move but he kept trying. Calling me over.

My parents saw the footage in real time and rushed outside immediately.

Thankfully, the gate kept me safe. But after that day, I was never left alone again. Our live-in maid made sure to wait with me every morning until I got on the bus. She'd prep breakfast, make the beds, and keep watch over me like a second mother.

My dad was always protective over me and my mom. He used to say, "Women are the most treasurable accessory a man can have. It's my job to protect mine."

It sounds beautiful, right?

But let's be real he had a short fuse.

I used to tell him that all the time.

He'd laugh and say, "It's just tough love, mija."

Tough love.

Still trying to decide how much was love… and how much was just control.

And remember how I mentioned my parents were finally planning their real wedding?

Yeah… crunch time had officially arrived.

The house was filled with stress, timelines, appointments, dress fittings. Mom was also going through some health issues, and although we didn't know exactly what was wrong, she hadn't been feeling well. It got worse over time. Eventually, she went to the doctor and learned she would need surgery.

She chose to delay it not wanting to interrupt the Oregon trip, my quince prep, or the wedding ceremony.

That was Mom. Always putting everything and everyone ahead of herself.

Even when her body was begging her to slow down, she kept going.

That year marked something big for me.

For the first time ever, I was trying out for the official Drill Team at my school.

I'd always been active cheer, dance team, and even choreographing routines for fun but I had to do it all behind my dad's back. Cheerleading especially was off-limits in his eyes. He didn't like the idea of male teammates lifting girls during stunts, and it made him uncomfortable in a way that felt... possessive. So I always had to play it safe and stay quiet about what I loved.

But the Drill Team felt different. More structured, more uniformed, less "exposed." I thought maybe this time, he'd actually approve. It felt like the kind of organized activity he might respect.

Weeks before tryouts, I remember telling my mom how badly I wanted it how hard I'd been pushing myself in dance class, staying after to practice the routines and fine-tune every step. I was laser-focused. There was even a solo performance component, and I'd been working on mine for days in secret, hoping it would be enough to set me apart.

When tryout day finally came, it was chaos.

There were so many girls competing for a spot that we ran late way late. By the time it ended, most of the girls had someone waiting to take them home. I didn't.

I stood outside with my bag, watching the cars roll away one by one until I was the last one standing.

With no other option, I had to ride the school bus home something I already knew was going to be a problem. My dad had a strict rule: I was not to ride the bus. He didn't like the mix of kids on there, didn't trust who might sit next to me, didn't think it was safe. But I didn't have a choice that night.

I got home around 9 PM, exhausted but proud of myself.

I had done it. I'd faced my fear. I'd tried out. I'd stepped out of the box I had been trapped in for so long.

But the second I stepped into the house, everything exploded.

My dad was furious.

Not just annoyed, livid.

He demanded to know where I'd been, accusing me of sneaking off with boys, of lying to his face, of being "disrespectful." I begged him to check the security cameras. The footage would show the school bus dropping me off. But he refused to look. He didn't want facts he wanted control.

His anger wasn't just loud it was violent.

He lashed out at both me and my mom, shouting so loudly it echoed through the house. And despite me standing there in my tryout clothes, still carrying the pride of what I'd just done, he refused to listen. In his mind, I wasn't a dedicated student chasing her dream. I was a reckless teenage girl defying his authority.

When I tried to explain myself, to share the good news that I had made the team, that I was finally part of something competitive and real he cut me off. He wouldn't hear it.

He spanked me not gently, not like a parent disciplining a child. It was rage-fueled, and I was fourteen.

I stood there, humiliated.

Burning with anger.

But I didn't cry.

Not because it didn't hurt.

But because I was done letting him break me.

I had worked so hard for this.

I had earned it.

And I was proud something he couldn't take away.

All I ever wanted was the freedom to exist, to express myself, to be a part of something bigger than the four walls of our house. But my reality? I wasn't even allowed to wear cute bracelets, wax my eyebrows, wear lip gloss, or buy trendy clothes like the other girls. I couldn't participate in school dances. I couldn't even ride in someone else's car.

From the outside, people thought I had it all.

The big house. The security gates. The fancy clothes bought for family parties. The good grades. The family name.

But the truth?

I had no freedom.

No voice.

No space to be myself.

And that night, something shifted inside me.

I was furious, numb, and completely done with trying to play the obedient, soft-spoken daughter who didn't ruffle feathers.

That night… I hit my rebellious era. I didn't know it at the time, but that moment was the spark. The first fire. The slow unraveling of a rope I had clung to my entire childhood. Because when a girl isn't allowed to breathe, She learns to roar.

And I was just getting started.

Chapter 9

"Two Homes, One Secret Life"

Finally, the days were getting closer to my mom and dad's wedding, and I was still very much not on my dad's good side to say the least. He wasn't on mine either. We were both incredibly alike: guarded, headstrong, and proud. Now that I'm older, I look back and laugh a little. I'm superstitious, love astrology, and totally blame our tension on him being a Sagittarius (a fire sign) and me being a Capricorn (an earth sign). SEND HELP. Two prideful, successful fighters—butting heads with the same intensity we carried into everything we did.

One afternoon, my dad was out working on one of the properties he had leased to grow sorghum. He was on his John Deere tractor, doing what he did best. I was the only one home at the ranch house. My mom was out running errands, and my older brother was working one of the other farms for my dad.

Suddenly, the house phone started ringing.

I was outside by the horse corrals when I heard it. My dad had these huge farm speakers wired outside, so when the landline rang, the sound echoed through the whole property. I ran back inside to answer. It was him.

We weren't exactly on speaking terms at the time, but he didn't seem to care. He asked if someone could come pick him up from the other farm. I told him no one was home it was just me. Without hesitation, he told me to grab the keys to the pickup and come get him.

He didn't ask. It was an order.

I was terrified. I had never driven a vehicle before not even on a dirt road. It wasn't far, just a few acres down, but it still felt huge to me. I wasn't going to be driving on a highway or anything, but it was still a big deal. I hesitated, but he wasn't having it. He was yelling through the phone, his voice booming and intense, saying I needed to listen and get there fast. No excuses.

So I did.

With my heart racing, I grabbed the keys, got behind the wheel, and drove out to pick him up. My hands were sweating. My stomach was in knots. I was panicking the whole way there, but I made it safely. He climbed into the truck, and without missing a beat, drove us back home.

Then, out of nowhere, he told me he was proud of me.

Just like that, the ice between us cracked.

It was one of those moments I'll never forget. My dad was absolutely terrifying when he was mad, but somehow, that small moment of pride from him meant everything to me. It didn't fix everything but it was a start. A shift.

Meanwhile, my mom was under serious stress. The woman who was custom-making all of our dresses had started falling behind, and the wedding date was creeping up fast. On top of that, she was also supposed to be working on my quinceañera dress. Nothing was going as planned.

Mom already had her wedding gown (like I mentioned earlier), but she was also having a separate after-party dress made. I had my own party dress being made for the wedding day too, in addition to my quince dress. That was four dresses four major outfits all in the hands of this one lady. And this wasn't a last-minute situation either. Everything had been planned with plenty of time.

To make matters even more overwhelming, both of my parents were finishing their religious classes at church so they could be married in a Catholic ceremony. As I mentioned before, we were Catholic, and that meant additional requirements and responsibilities leading up to the big day. Everything felt like a race against time.

Then, with only a few weeks left until the wedding celebration…

The unthinkable happened.

Something we'd only ever seen in movies or heard whispered about in distant headlines became our horrifying reality:

My dad got kidnapped.

It started off like any normal day. He was out at the farm, working just like always. He was at one of the far ends of our property, riding the John Deere tractor, when suddenly everything changed.

His workers came rushing back to the ranch house in a panic. They told my mother that he had been taken.

At first, they thought it was some sick prank. Maybe some of his friends were trying to be funny, pulling something wild just before the wedding. But hours passed, and we heard nothing. No calls. No signs. No dad.

Mom knew immediately something wasn't right.

I didn't know all the details at the time I was too young, and the adults kept everything quiet. Mom did her best to protect us and shield us from what was happening, but we could still feel the fear in the air.

While my dad was missing, we weren't allowed to go anywhere. The house felt like a fortress. We were so scared that we'd literally crawl on the floor just in case someone tried to look through the windows. We didn't even walk upright across the rooms.

I believe the police were contacted, and a report may have been filed initially, but then everything got hushed. I later found out my mom told the cops it was a prank likely to avoid drawing more attention and to keep my dad safe. Whatever was going on behind closed doors, we had no idea. All we knew was that every hour he was gone felt like forever.

That moment changed everything.

After that, things shifted. Drastically. We stopped riding the bus to school. We weren't allowed to participate in extra-curriculars. We didn't hang out with friends like we used to. Everything suddenly felt dangerous. Fragile. No one said it out loud, but it was like the rules of our world had changed overnight.

Eventually after what felt like a lifetime we got my dad back.

I don't know what kind of exchange had to happen, but years later, I found out he had been left completely naked, blindfolded, and dropped off behind a store for pickup. At the time, though, we weren't told anything. The adults kept everything from us. When he came home, I remember noticing the bruise on his face. It was right in the middle of his eyebrows, between his eyes and across the bridge of his nose. Later I'd learn that it happened when they pushed him off the tractor and struck him with a gun. Just like that.

And the craziest part? The wedding was now just a day away.

As if that wasn't enough, the dress situation exploded too. The seamstress never finished any of our dresses. My mom's wedding gown and after-party dress were incomplete. My quinceañera dress hadn't even been touched. And the woman kept giving my mom the runaround, dodging calls, making excuses. She had already been paid over $2,000 for my quince dress alone yet there was nothing to show for it.

Everything felt like it was falling apart at once.

Fast forward to the day of the event. My dad had to have makeup applied to cover the bruising on his face, and my mom was still dealing with the chaos of the dresses. I had nothing to wear because my dress wasn't finished either. In a scramble, I ended up "closet shopping" in my mom's room and found a nice dress to wear. Crisis averted.

We all got our hair and makeup done, trying to hold it together, but everything felt like it was held by a single thread. When it came time to leave for the church, my mom didn't even have a ride. Everything was still all over the place. The dressmaker, who had caused so much stress, ended up doing last-minute touch-ups on my mom's gown and personally drove her to the ceremony where everyone was already waiting.

And somehow despite everything once the ceremony started, things began to smooth out. Pictures were taken, the church was full of family and friends, and the wedding turned out beautiful.

Afterward, we headed to the party at the ranch. My mom had hired people to decorate and arrange everything inside the big warehouse. The round tables were dressed with crisp linen cloths. Their wedding cake towered in layers, wide and tall like something out of a magazine. A custom-designed backdrop stood ready for photos, and live music filled the air.

You could still feel the pressure and tension humming under the surface, but everyone kept their composure cool, calm, collected. The surveillance was ten times heavier than usual. My dad had extra people protecting the area, eyes on every entrance. His driver stayed glued to him, step for step. Even so, the party went well.

Mom finally got her after-party dress finished just in time, and she looked stunning. Later that night, I noticed both my mom and dad relaxing a little, finally breathing, watching everything flow the way they had hoped. The dancing, the catering, the music perfect.

Life didn't go back to normal after that, but my parents tried. My dad kept working the ranch, and my mom handled her responsibilities the best she could. I threw myself into drill team, focusing on dancing and school. I even made it to the competition in South Padre Island at the convention center. Honestly, I didn't think I'd be able to go. One of my teachers stepped in and paid for my share and my team shirt so I wouldn't miss out.

I tried to stay as busy as possible extra classes, practices, anything to avoid the heaviness at home. My grades stayed strong, which meant I was never pulled from dance or banned from school performances and pep rallies.

I don't remember every detail of that year maybe because I've spent so long trying to forget it but the memories that do come back are heavy.

I remember a fight. Not how it started, not even the girl's name just the way it felt. A group of girls trailing behind me, whispering and calling me names. Then, someone grabbing my hair from behind outside the cafeteria.

It was the first time I stood up for myself.

I had to. If my dad found out I'd been in a fight and hadn't defended myself, I would've been punished at home too. He always told us we needed to stand up for ourselves, to be courageous, or we'd "get dealt with" at home. Tough love, huh?

No one stepped in to stop the fight not a teacher, not a security guard. A circle of classmates formed, almost like they were watching a show. I've always been soft when it comes to fights or arguments. It doesn't matter if it's a stranger on the street or a scene in a movie my first instinct is to tear up. I think it's because so many arguments and so much tension happened at home.

I remember stumbling into the bathroom alone afterward, trembling, pulling clumps of my own hair from my hands like proof it had all been real. That day stayed with me even when the rest of the year blurred.

Later that year, we had a school dance my brother DJ'd it. (You might remember me saying in a previous chapter that my dad had bought him a full DJ system. Our school actually hired him for events.) That night, the same girl who had fought me came up to me and spoke. We pretty much squashed whatever had happened between us, even if the other girls didn't. I let it go. After that year, I never saw her again. Another memory: calling my mom from the school phone over and over, begging her to bring me clean clothes because I had stained through mine. My body was changing faster than I could keep up. My cycle felt like a war every month. The cramps were so bad I'd cry, but I still had to go to school.

That year wasn't just middle school. It was the beginning of becoming a woman before I even understood what that meant. My mom didn't allow tampons in our house, so I had to wear pads thick, bulky pads that felt like a diaper at school. I wasn't really taught anything about my body, my cycle, or how to care for myself. I learned bits and pieces from other girls in the hallway, during whispered conversations in the bathroom. Some classmates told me their parents had taken them to the doctor to get on birth control pills to help regulate their cramps and cycles.

Mine would go on for over a week, heavy and painful. They'd tell me, "You should ask your parents to do that for you." But it never happened. My parents were too old-school. It simply wasn't an option.

Oh, but some of the best moments during that school year came from dancing tucked somewhere in the middle of all the pain, the awkwardness, and the chaos. When I danced, even if just for a few minutes, I could escape. School performances gave me something to look forward to, a reason to hold my head up even when everything else felt too heavy.

I don't remember every classroom or teacher's name, but I do remember the stage lights, the echo of the gymnasium, and the rhythm in my body the one thing I still had control over. One of my favorite performances that year was a routine choreographed by our dance teacher using music from the 1960s. We danced to Rock Around the Clock by Bill Haley & His Comets, and it was so full of energy and joy it felt like stepping into another era.

I had a super tall and strong dance partner who made every stunt feel effortless. When it came time for the lifts and spins, I felt like a feather floating through the air. I remember hearing gasps and cheers from the crowd people were genuinely shocked at how high I flew and how fun the performance was to watch. We all wore matching uniforms and shoes; the look was so cute and coordinated, it felt like we were in a real dance troupe. That performance is one I wish had been recorded one I could replay for the rest of my life.

During class, we'd sometimes get free time, and that's when the real fun happened. We'd connect someone's phone or an old CD player and play cumbias or música norteña, turning the dance room into a makeshift Mexican club. We'd pair up and practice the spins and partner steps like we were dancing at a quince or a wedding reception. It was silly and pure and exactly what I needed back then a little slice of joy I could hold onto.

The rest of the year… it's foggy. Maybe that's okay.

Maybe some years aren't meant to be remembered in perfect order, but in fragments the kind that still echo in your spirit even if the timeline doesn't quite line up.

This was definitely the year when my rebellion began to take root. It wasn't loud at first. It started with small things straightening my hair, sneaking on a little makeup, talking back when I would've stayed quiet before. But soon it grew louder. My dad wouldn't let me go to the movies with friends or out to eat with anyone. Dating was completely off the table. He wouldn't even let me dress up for school.

So, I found my ways.

I started borrowing shirts from friends and changing once I got to school. I'd leave the house late at night after everyone had fallen asleep, sneaking out just to feel free for a little bit. My parents had alarms and surveillance cameras installed all over the house, but somehow, I always managed to get around them quiet, quick, careful.

We lived just 15 to 20 minutes from the border to Mexico, and back then it wasn't nearly as dangerous as it is now. Crossing over and coming back was easy, especially for teens who knew how to blend in. I even went to a few clubs across the border. It made me feel grown and independent, even if deep down I was still just a kid trying to find her place. One night, my parents were out of town, and my grandma was staying with us, like she often did when they traveled. I thought I could sneak out like usual but I was wrong. She caught on. The windows and doors were locked when I tried to come back. We were stuck outside, forced to knock and ring the doorbell until she opened it.

And just like that she told them everything.

When my parents got home, we had a serious talk. My older brother and I both got in trouble, but I took the brunt of it. I wasn't allowed to go out, couldn't drink, couldn't do anything. I had zero privileges. But something shifted after that.

At least for a moment, my dad softened just slightly.

He started giving me a little bit of spending money. A tiny bit more freedom. Nothing major, but enough to feel like a crack in the wall I'd been living behind. It didn't last long.

I started noticing a pattern: the more money my dad made, the more successful he became, the less present he was at home. It was like the bigger the house, the emptier it felt. The more the bank account grew, the heavier the atmosphere got.

And with that growth came stress. Bigger responsibilities. Bigger tempers. Bigger arguments.

That year changed how I saw everything. I began to realize that having more didn't always mean feeling safer. That a bigger house didn't automatically mean peace. I felt isolated and deprived surrounded by everything, but emotionally starving.

My dad's moods became unpredictable. One second he was laughing, the next he was furious. It was like walking on glass never knowing which version of him would show up.

It was the year I started growing up, whether I wanted to or not.

Speaking of rebellion, you remember how I mentioned we lived in the city house during the week and stayed at the ranch on the weekends? Well... that never really stopped. The routine continued for years, even as everything else around us changed.

Whenever I was at the ranch, I'd ride around on the fourwheeler by myself wind in my face, music in my ears feeling like I had my own little slice of freedom. That's when I started meeting new friends in the area. Quietly. Without telling my dad. I also met a really sweet boy who I'd talk to often. Nothing wild just conversations, laughs, teenage moments. But of course, once my dad found out, that was over. I wasn't allowed to be friends with him anymore. Still, I kept making new friends, especially after we moved into the bigger house. A few of the girls I got close to would come over to the ranch with their own four-wheelers. We'd ride, race, play music, and snack on chips and candy under the Texas sun like we had no worries in the world. They all lived nearby and came from families like mine parents who had roots in the same parts of Mexico. We spoke Spanish the same way, listened to the same songs, and grew up on the same food. There was comfort in that. Belonging. A kind of unspoken understanding.

And in the middle of all this quietly woven into my coming-of-age was a boy I've only barely mentioned before. If you remember, I told you I had a little crush back in sixth grade. Well… that didn't just go away. We stayed in each other's lives, even after we got sent to separate schools. He stayed at the one where we'd met, and I got transferred to a different campus closer to our new house.

We didn't tell anyone, but he'd still come by to see me. We kept in touch in our own secret little ways. He played sports, and I danced, so our paths crossed during events. And when I'd migrate to Oregon, he'd be heading off to California with his parents.

We didn't have cell phones back then not the way kids do now. My parents, my brother, and even some of my cousins all had phones or beepers. But I wasn't allowed to have either. So he'd call me on our house phone from California. These were long-distance calls back then, and they charged extra. We were just kids, but we tried to be smart about it. He'd call me super late at night, when rates were cheaper. And because of the time zone difference, he'd either wake up extra early or stay up late just to catch me. My mom, surprisingly, helped me sneak a few of those calls. She'd answer first and then rush to hand me the phone before my dad could hear it ringing.

We were never official in the way other people were. We never even went on a real date or hung out outside of school or games. But there was something sweet and adrenaline-filled about it. The secrecy. The timing. The constant worry of having to hang up quickly before the bill got too high or before my dad caught on. That little thrill made everything feel more intense. That was the rebellion in us, talking louder than logic. And even though it was innocent, it felt real at the time.

When the school year ended, everything in me dreaded going back to Oregon. I wasn't ready. I was going to miss my Texas friends, my routines, my drill team, the rhythms I had finally gotten used to.

By then, I had officially entered my freshman year of high school. Our school had created a separate campus just for ninth grade, which meant 10th, 11th, and 12th graders were in their own building. Still, we all shared the same sports fields, the arts pavilion, the drama department, and the dance hall, so it felt like a tease of high school life, not quite all the way in.

But the changes just kept coming. And the older I got, the harder it became to process them. Everything felt like it hit deeper, moved faster, demanded more of me. It was harder to blend in, to adjust, to keep up.

Once again, I felt like I was floating somewhere in between never fully belonging to one place or the other.

Ni de aquí, ni de allá.

A phrase I'd come to understand more deeply with each passing year.

Chapter 10

"The Last Valentine I Didn't Say I Love You & The Grown-Up Goodbye"

TRIGGER WARNING:

Before You read this - A Note from Me to You.

I want to take a second before you step into this chapter not just as the author, but as a woman who's lived it. This part of my story is one of the heaviest I've ever carried. And before you carry it with me, I want you to know this:

I care deeply about your nervous system. I care about your healing. I care about the younger version of you who maybe went through something similar. And I care about the version of you reading this now the one who picked up this book looking for truth, connection, or maybe even just a sense of being understood.

This chapter includes physical abuse, emotional trauma, medical recovery, and police involvement. There are hard moments here ones I've never spoken out loud until now.

If you need to pause, skip, or come back later, please do. You do not owe anyone your discomfort.

I didn't write this to shock you I wrote it to set something free. In me… and maybe in you too.

You are not alone. You never were.
— With love,
Yesenia
Tómate tu tiempo, estoy compartiendo esto con el corazón en la mano.

What we didn't realize at the time was that this would be our last trip together to Oregon. We packed up, just like we always did, loading the car with bags, snacks, and that quiet tension that always came with long drives. It felt like a routine by then, but looking back, it was the end of an era.

This year was different for another reason too my brother was a senior. For the first time, I'd get to share the same school with him in Oregon, even if only for a short while. We'd ride together in his car most mornings, music playing low, windows cracked, just the two of us. It made me feel grown, like I was stepping into his world a little.

Sometimes my dad would need him for work and my brother would leave early, which meant I'd have to ride the bus like everyone else. But most days, I didn't. Most days, I had that small luxury of not waiting at the bus stop in the cold.

I wasn't ever able to get deeply involved in sports or extracurriculars in Oregon because we were never there long enough just a few months at a time. But this year felt like maybe, just maybe, I'd get to attend a dance or something normal for once.

I could almost see it me in a dress, laughing with friends under the dim gymnasium lights.

By then, a lot of my mom's family was working with my dad. Some of my uncles were driving for him, others had their own trucks, but they were all tied to the same industry. That meant we saw family more often, not just at holidays. Our lives overlapped with work and bloodlines.

And just like in Texas, I started making friends in Oregon too. I began to step out more. Dad was pulling heavy hours with the trucking business, and when he was buried in work, the pressure around me loosened just a little. I went to a few soccer games from school, some pep rallies, even hung out on the sidelines where everyone else stood laughing and gossiping. For a brief moment, I felt like a normal teenager.

At this point, I was talking to a guy from school too. It was innocent, just like most things at that age, but of course, my dad didn't know.

Then everything blew up.

I had a huge fallout with my dad during this season. One evening after school, the boy I was talking to came by to see me. It felt harmless. But then my dad's truck pulled up while he was still there. Everything inside me froze.

The next moments are a blur. I think my dad may have even chased after the boy family members were at the house, and chaos was erupting everywhere. Even my grandma P., my mom's mom, was there that day.

As soon as I stepped back inside the house, my dad lost it. His rage snapped like a whip.

He came at me fast, yelling, his face twisted with anger, and then the yelling turned into hitting. I ran to my room, slammed the door, and slid down to the floor, pressing my back against it, bracing my feet to keep it shut. My heart was pounding so loud I could hear it in my ears.

But he was stronger.

He forced the door open, yanked me out, and I fell hard to the floor. He was over me in seconds. Slaps. Punches. Kicks. My mom and my grandmother's voices broke through the chaos pleading, crying, desperate.

"Stop! You're going to kill her!"

"You're a monster!"

Their words cracked through the air like glass shattering, but they couldn't stop him. I curled up, arms over my head, trying to cover my face from the swings.

Then, for the first time, my mom stood up to him.

She grabbed a "palote" the same wooden rolling pin she used to roll out flour tortillas and swung it at my dad. The sound of it cutting through the air was something I'll never forget. She planted herself between us, swinging, shouting, crying.

My dad had always been abusive when he was angry or when things didn't go his way. He was unstoppable, untouchable. No one could get in his way, not even us. But this time was different.

There were other people there. Uncles. Cousins. Grandma. Witnesses.

And for the first time, my mom's fear cracked open into something else. Into action. Into resistance.

That moment was a turning point, even if I didn't fully understand it then.

The rest of that night was a blur. Everything felt muffled, like sound underwater. After that I've always had a sensitive nose probably from all the spankings growing up so whenever I got hit in the face, I bled easily. That night was no different. My nose bled, my skin burned, and I had marks everywhere.

I can still hear my dad's voice echoing in my head from that night. He yelled that he disowned me, that he never wanted to speak to me again. He said my quinceañera was permanently canceled, no discussion. Gone. Just like that.

When it came time to go back to school, I almost couldn't do it. My body hurt. My spirit hurt even more. I was afraid people would see the bruises on my arms, my back, my face afraid they'd ask questions I couldn't answer. That morning, I picked out jeans and a long-sleeve shirt to cover the marks. Getting dressed felt like a punishment in itself. Every move hurt. My arms, my back, my ribs they were bruised and swollen. But somehow, I pulled it together.

When I got to school, it felt like everyone already knew something.

Word must have spread about my dad catching the boy at our house, because the way people looked at me changed. Whispers. Side-eyes. The boy I'd been talking to wouldn't even look at me anymore. He completely ignored me. I couldn't even blame him. My dad was terrifying powerful, unpredictable. There were no limits to what he might do.

Things didn't get better after that.

Shortly after, the boy I had been talking to got into some kind of trouble himself, someone keyed his car. Somehow, I got blamed for it. The school office called me in, and my parents were notified. I wanted to scream. If only people knew what had just happened to me, they'd know there was no way I'd risk doing something like that, knowing what would come next. Wearing clothes hurt. Taking showers hurt. My hair hurt. My head and neck throbbed. The marks on my back were so deep that drying off with a towel would make me cry all over again. And yet, here I was, being accused of something I didn't do.

I begged my parents to believe me. My mom said she did, but my dad wouldn't even look at me, wouldn't speak to me. He was stone. And still, they had to go to court. My parents ended up paying for damages for something I had no part in. The rest of my time in Oregon that year was a nightmare. People looked at me with disgust, assuming I had done it. School became a place of silent shame.

And then, like a storm finding its peak, my dad got arrested.

I don't know the exact reason behind it. By that point, he was reckless. We were all scared of him. I can't remember the charges, but I know he didn't serve hard time. He was bailed out. The season ended, and soon it was time to pack up and go back to Texas. On the drive home, my dad refused to speak to me. He and I didn't share a single word. Instead, I rode in the truck with my mom. She wasn't doing well by then. Remember how I mentioned she was going to need surgery? By that time, she had gotten worse.

Her pain was unbearable. She was bleeding heavily and struggling with severe uterine issues. On that long drive home, she had to make multiple stops to change her clothes. She barely made it. Watching her like that broke me in a way I can't explain. It was a tough, silent, painful ride just me and my mom, trying to hold ourselves together as everything around us fell apart.

When we finally made it home, the silence between my dad and me was solid as a wall. We didn't speak for about three months November, December, January. It was so bad that if he was at the dining table, I'd stay in my room. If I was at the dining table, he'd stay in his room. If we crossed paths in the hallway, he'd look right, and I'd look left. It sounds childish now, but it was our reality. Pride met pride. Silence met silence.

When we got back to Texas, my mom was immediately checked by doctors to figure out what was going on. They confirmed she would need surgery. They told her she was going to need a full hysterectomy or her uterus removed. Conceiving more children had never been part of their plan at that point, but hearing it out loud still felt final. This was the only solution to stop her pain, and she accepted it. It was the end of a season in more ways than one. To make things worse, my mom eventually had a falling out with my dad too. Around that time, one of her sisters one of my aunts was staying at our house. I believe she was going through a divorce or separation, but I never knew the full details. What I do know is that my dad had a wandering eye, and my mom caught him.

My dad would take advantage of the fact that my mom wasn't feeling well and spent most of her time in the bedroom recovering. He used that space to do whatever he wanted. The maid handled everything else in the house, chores, cooking, cleaning, laundry, ironing, meals every single detail. My mom, even while sick, would still oversee what needed to be done because my dad was very particular about things. Even the smallest details mattered to him, like the way the clothes were ironed. We weren't allowed to use paper plates or cups in our home everything had to be glass or ceramic, even back in our trailer-home days. Dad would never in his life eat off a paper plate, and by extension, neither would we. Our maid took note of all these rules, from the ironing lines on his shirts to the exact way the kitchen was kept. She was super sweet to us one of the few who actually stayed. We'd gone through several maids before her, and none had lasted, but this one felt different. We all liked her.

Somehow, my mom and dad worked things out after the "wandering eye" incident. I never knew what actually happened or what was said. I just saw my mom handle it with such quiet strength. She carried herself with so much grace, and I will always look up to how she handled that situation, even though I knew she must have been hurting inside.

Shortly after that, winter settled in. The rainy days were almost constant. My dad had always loved the rain. He'd open all the blinds and even the back porch door just to hear the thunder and watch the sheets of water pour down. Rain and snow had been his favorites his whole life. Even now, I can see him standing there, listening, calm for a moment.

But that winter felt heavier than most.

The holidays passed. My birthday passed. My quinceañera never happened.

The lady making my custom dress never gave it to us. I didn't get a single fitting or a single photo of it. She kept lying to my mom, saying it was absolutely gorgeous, that she had entered it into a competition in Monterrey, Mexico, and that it would be back within a few days. But it never came. We never saw the dress, and we never got our money back. The dresses and our hopes were gone.

On Christmas and New Year's Eve, we still gathered with family. I could hear people talking and laughing about my upcoming quince, not realizing it had been canceled. Nobody knew what had happened in Oregon except for the ones who were there. I didn't say a word about it, not one. Not a single detail about that night ever left my mouth.

I remember sitting there, listening to people giggling and joking with my dad about me "growing up" and how he'd better be ready for me to start dating. He'd laugh and joke back, saying I wasn't allowed to date or get married until after 25, that I didn't need to settle because he wouldn't allow it. He'd even say things like, "If he ain't good to my daughter, we'll bury him face down we've got plenty of land and John Deer's on standby."

I'd roll my eyes when I heard conversations like that. Part of me wanted to shout, "Aren't you supposed to set the example?" But I stayed quiet. He also liked to go on about how I had a career ahead of me. "I'm going to send you to law school," he'd say. "You're going to be a lawyer." For the longest time, I thought I didn't want that. But as I got older, I started realizing how much I loved winning debates, loved arguing my point, loved anything to do with politics and law. A part of me really did think I might become a lawyer one day.

Then, somewhere around that time, I got really sick. After winter break, I caught a nasty flu that knocked me out. I had a high fever, shivers, and couldn't go to school.

I remember one day, I was laying on the couch in the living room, shivering under a thin blanket, and my dad walked by. He stopped when he saw me like that. Without saying much, he brought me a heavier blanket and laid it over me.

It was the first time my dad and I had any kind of contact or communication since our fight in Oregon. Even writing about it now, I feel a knot in my throat. He was the one who broke the ice, but I was still so angry, so wounded. When he asked if I was okay, I answered coldly, "I'm fine."

Then my mom came in and checked my fever. She didn't hesitate she went straight to the doctor to get me medicine. I've always hated injections I still do but that year, she gave me no option. "It will work faster than pills," she said. She was right. I got better quickly.

That small moment my dad placing the blanket on me wasn't forgiveness. It wasn't even healing. But it was the first tiny crack in the wall between us.

My mom had finally scheduled her surgery. Knowing she'd need downtime to recover, she made sure everything in the house was organized before hand lists, instructions, routines so things could run smoothly while she was gone.

My dad had been traveling on and off during that time. Sometimes he'd be gone for a few days, sometimes a couple of weeks. He was in and out, as usual.

Mom's surgery went well. She had to stay in the hospital for a few days, so we stayed home with the maid and my dad. The house was quiet while she was gone. Everyone knew what needed to be done, and we mostly kept to ourselves especially staying out of my dad's way.

During that week, the boy I mentioned in earlier chapters the one from sixth grade who used to migrate to California was still around. Still trying to talk to me. By this point, he was already driving. He'd sneak in a call here and there, and even though I'd heard plenty of rumors about him flirting with girls between classes, I still entertained the idea of talking to him again.

He was handsome. Popular. And now he had a nice truck, too. He came from a good family, and whenever he went to Mexico with them, he somehow managed to find a way to call me from there, too. I don't even know how he did it. But he always made the effort.

After I got back from Oregon, things between us got a little more serious. I even told my mom about him. No one else knew. One day, he drove by my house and asked if he could stop by. I begged him not to.

My dad and I still weren't talking, and I could not risk another beating. No one knew how bad things had really gotten. I was doing everything I could to keep the peace. But he insisted said he just wanted to see me for five minutes outside. I told him it was a bad idea. Our house was covered in surveillance cameras. My dad had workers all around and a personal driver who practically lived on standby. But after some back and forth, we came up with a plan.

He'd park at the very end of our long brick fence, where the camera wouldn't catch him. I'd walk over, say a quick hello, and head straight back in. No trace. Just a moment. He agreed.

I had the biggest crush on him since sixth grade. Seeing him again, older now, with that same soft smile it brought the butterflies rushing back. He pulled up with his windows down, blasting music by: "Duelo" through the speakers. He always was a little bit of a romantic.

But just as quickly as that moment came, it passed. As I was walking back toward the house, slipping past the gate, one of my uncles, my mom's brother spotted me. He happened to be working for my dad at the time.

He saw me and instantly started shouting, "Wait until your dad gets home, you little brat!"

My heart sank.

This uncle was usually respectful. He knew me. He had known that boy for years, too. Nothing inappropriate had ever happened between us. He had never even tried to kiss me. He kept his hands to himself. But none of that mattered now. My uncle was going to tell my dad.

And I knew what that meant.

If my dad had nearly killed me in Oregon, this time with no one home to stop it not even my mom there to step in... I didn't know what he'd be capable of. My mind spiraled. I knew I had to act fast.

Not long after, my dad pulled into the driveway. I ran outside, heart pounding, and grabbed his arm. "I need to talk to you," I said. I don't even know how I got the words out. I was shaking. I knew I had to beat my uncle to it or things would get so much worse.

I'll never forget that moment. I pulled my dad by the arm into my room, my princess room with all the white furniture and he leaned against the dresser while I stood in front of him, fidgeting with my hands, too scared to look him in the eye.

I wanted to cry. My voice cracked when I finally said,

"I don't know how to say this... but I don't want you to hit me."

He looked at me quietly, then interrupted in a surprisingly soft tone:

"You have a boyfriend?"

Like he already knew.

I was stunned.

I nodded slowly and told him yes. I promised him I hadn't done anything wrong. That I liked him, and that was it.

He just looked at me and said, "Okay."

Nothing more.

I know he had once told me he disowned me. That he hated me. That he never wanted to speak to me again. But he was still my dad. And deep down, I knew what I needed to do.

The next day, we were scheduled to pick up my mom from the hospital. My dad asked me if I wanted to come with him. He didn't say much, but the fact that he asked at all felt like a small olive branch. I agreed quietly.

The weather that day was terrible. It was storming hard, and my mom was scheduled to be discharged in the evening. On the way, my dad pulled into a small Mexican restaurant so we could eat. It was just the two of us.

Even now, writing this, it's hard not to get emotional. It was the first time he and I had sat across from each other like that with no yelling, no silence, no interruption. Just us.

While we were sitting there, the restaurant lost power because of the storm. But they had a backup generator and were still able to cook.

I ordered a Mexican plate and started making tacos from it. He watched me for a while, then said,

"Well, if you didn't want a plate, why didn't you just order tacos?"

Then added, "Do you want me to get you some so you don't have to do all that work?"

I looked up and quietly replied,

"I like making my own. Thank you."

It wasn't much. We didn't say a lot. But we both sat there, eating in silence, listening to the rain hitting the window beside our booth. And somehow, that silence said more than any words could.

When mom finally came home, the house stayed calm for a while. My dad was still traveling for work, in and out. But the energy was quieter.

And this time, when that boy wanted to come by... he could.

I told my mom I had spoken to dad about the boyfriend situation, and he had given permission. Slowly, carefully, life began to shift.

February 14

Valentine's Day.

I didn't know it then, but it would be the last day I'd ever see my dad.

He hadn't been home much before this. Work, traveling, always in and out. But that day, he came home with a kind of grandeur that only he had. He walked through the door with a huge bouquet of roses for my mom and an oversized stuffed animal for her, classic, bold, showy. And then he handed me a smaller bouquet of roses and a smaller stuffed animal, my own miniature version of hers.

But that wasn't all.

He laid out jewelry for us to choose from gold bracelets, gold necklaces, gold earrings, anything we wanted. He had access to luxuries like this through his gold mine and jeweler contracts, so to him it was nothing. But to me, it felt surreal. I remember my mom being hesitant, almost embarrassed to take any of it. She didn't reach for the jewelry. But my dad insisted, putting some on her and then some on me too. That was it. No big speech. No big moment. Just gifts, gestures, and silence.

My mom still wasn't moving much after her surgery. She spent most of her time in sleeping gowns, loose and soft against her healing body. You could tell the surgery had been painful, but she was glad it was finally over.

Later that day, I was getting dressed for my own Valentine's dinner. My boyfriend had surprised me with a beautiful red dress, kneelength and a delicate hair pin inside a white box for me to wear he added a note saying: "wear this tonight". It felt like a tiny piece of normalcy.

As I stood there in my room, pinning my hair, my dad passed by. He stopped, looked at me, and told me I looked beautiful. Said he couldn't believe how grown up I was already. His voice was soft, almost wistful.

It felt strange. Off. But also sweet.

I smiled, said "thank you," and went about my day. But deep down, I felt something. I didn't know what it was, but it was heavy. Rare as it sounds, I think he felt it too.

I wanted so badly to let down my guard in that moment to just hug him, tell him I loved him, show him that despite everything he was still my dad. But I couldn't. I was too hurt, too guarded, too mistrusting. All I could manage was distance. Short answers. Cold conversations. If I didn't need to speak to him, even better.

I didn't know it was goodbye.

February 15

I got picked up early from school that day. The person who came to get me said quietly, "Listen, something happened earlier. Just stay calm. Your mom will talk to you when you get home." My heart sped up. I had absolutely no idea what was going on. Not a single thought crossed my mind about what it could be.

When we got home, the truth unraveled.

Our home had been raided. My dad had been arrested.

My mom told me what happened. Dad had been in the shower, and she was in the kitchen with the maid checking on dinner when police surrounded the entire property.

They had also been to the ranch. People had tried to warn my dad, but he missed the calls because of the shower.

Mom said the cops wanted to knock down walls to search for whatever they were looking for. One officer told them not to, he said it wasn't necessary. "You can tell this is a family home," he said.

But not all of them were gentle.

My mom said one officer was aggressive with her, asking why she was holding her stomach while she walked.

They wanted to search her too. She told them she had just had surgery days before. They didn't care.

Then they went into the master bedroom, cuffed my dad, and arrested him.

That was it.

The image of roses and stuffed animals and gold, followed so quickly by handcuffs and police boots on our floors, never left me. Valentine's Day turned into something else entirely, an ending I didn't know was coming, a moment frozen in my memory.

Chapter 11

We Were All Falling Apart — And I Missed Him and Hated Him Too

TRIGGER WARNING:

Before you turn this page, I just want to say this next chapter is hard.

It holds pain I've carried for a long time. Pain I tried to forget. Pain I wrote through with trembling hands and a guarded heart.

It includes sensitive experiences: physical abuse, emotional trauma, neglect, and a moment of deep violation I've never shared publicly before. If you've ever been through anything like this or are currently healing from something heavy please read gently, slowly, or not at all if that's what you need.

You matter more than the page.

Con todo mi corazón, te cuido a ti también.

I don't remember a whole lot after my dad was taken to jail.

He and I still weren't on speaking terms, and that silence between us just lingered, heavy and unresolved.

Mom wasn't doing well. Her recovery from surgery was slow and painful, and there was so much happening with my dad's case. This wasn't one of those quick DWI situations or something that would be handled with a fine and a weekend in county. This time felt serious. Way different. Everything around us was heavier, quieter, and far more complicated than I could make sense of.

For a while, I carried the guilt. I blamed myself for what was happening. I thought my dad was in jail because of what happened back in Oregon the situation that had shaken our family in private ways no one ever really talked about out loud.

I was still just a teenager. I didn't understand the legal system. I didn't even understand our own family system most days. But when you're that young and you're used to feeling responsible for things you can't control, you start connecting dots that don't even belong on the same page.

Looking back now, I know how naïve I must've seemed.

But at the time, it wasn't naïve it was survival. If you had grown up in the kind of home I did, with the culture, the rules, the silence, the traditions, and the unspoken expectations, you'd understand why I didn't know more. You'd understand why everything felt so far from my control.

I didn't know anything about hair. I didn't know how to do my makeup. I didn't know how to dress in the "cute outfits" like the other girls. I didn't even understand what was going on with my own body. No one had prepared me for any of it.

I didn't have a cell phone.

I didn't have a computer.

I didn't even have a radio in my room.

I wasn't allowed to shave.

Wasn't allowed to wax.

Wasn't allowed to go to sleepovers or have friends over casually.

Wasn't allowed to go to other people's homes.

Wasn't allowed to just "hang out" the way other kids did.

I grew up sheltered, and not the kind of sheltered people romanticize I mean isolated, policed, kept small.

So when I say I had no clue what the word "conspiracy" even meant, I mean that literally.

When someone said something about drug charges or conspiracy or trafficking I was stunned. Completely thrown. I didn't even know what a drug deal really was. My dad had always been so strict about what we watched, what we listened to, what we had access to. Our cable was monitored. The internet was barely allowed. Even movies were filtered. Our home was controlled to the max.

There was a lot of activity around the house during those days. People were constantly coming in and out, uncles, aunts, cousins talking in hushed voices with my mom behind closed doors. I never really got to hear what they were saying, and truthfully... I didn't care at the time. That probably sounds cold, but it's the truth.

I genuinely thought this was going to be like all the other times a quick in-and-out. Dad would handle it. He always did. I knew he was a powerful man. Whatever this was, he'd fix it. He always fixed everything. So I didn't ask questions. I didn't want details. I just went numb and kept moving.

Things shifted quickly. So quickly it felt like the ground under me disappeared overnight. Everything changed and I don't just mean emotionally. Tangible things started disappearing too. The lifestyle, the movement, the presence of money and ease. It all started slipping away.

And yet, in a strange way, I started finding little pockets of freedom.

Since I no longer had to wear a uniform to school, I finally got to go shopping. I bought a few outfits nothing wild. I started dressing up a little more, adding some style and confidence to how I walked through the halls. Fridays at school were like unofficial dress-up days, guys wore western gear or preppy outfits, and the girls wore heels, cute jeans, nice tops. For the first time, I got to join in. I fixed my hair, wore a fitted pair of jeans, and looked in the mirror feeling...different.

I was still in shock over everything happening at home, but outwardly, I was evolving.

I grew closer to my friends the ones who had always come out to the ranch to ride four-wheelers or go horseback riding. We started going out on the weekends. I know it sounds a little wild now, especially considering how young we were, but things weren't as strict back then.

We could get into clubs, cross the border into Mexico, and somehow thanks to the people we knew we always made it in. We met DJs, bouncers, club owners, bartenders. Everyone seemed to know someone. And just like that, I slipped into this double life.

That boy I mentioned before, the one from California? His family owned a sports bar, and that became our hangout. We weren't partying hard or doing anything reckless by today's standards we were just trying to feel grown. Trying to taste independence. Trying to have fun and feel beautiful and free.

And I was definitely breaking every rule I had grown up with.

The girls and I even started our own little car club complete with nicknames on the windows and matching stickers. It was goofy and fun and rebellious and exactly what high school was supposed to feel like.

It was a weird time.

Everything felt like it was falling apart, and yet… in the middle of the unraveling, I was finding pieces of myself I didn't even know I was allowed to have.

After Dad got taken in, Mom started making big changes fast.

Even though she wasn't fully healed from her surgery, she got rid of the house help. She started cutting back anywhere she could and I mean everywhere. I don't know the full breakdown of how the finances were managed, but I know people were let go. Vehicles and equipment started disappearing almost immediately. I remember watching things leave our driveway that had once been staples of our life trailers, trucks, machines. Things I'd seen my dad use every day. Gone.

She said she needed extra cash for the lawyers. I think there were three of them working on my dad's case, but don't quote me on that. I just remember overhearing it in bits and pieces low conversations behind doors, phone calls she tried to take quietly in the kitchen. From what I gathered, his case was serious. Heavy. Not something that would get swept under the rug. Everyone seemed to know it, even if no one said it directly.

Mom had a lot on her plate. She was trying to heal, trying to be a mom, trying to manage court dates and lawyers, and still get my little brothers to elementary school on time. On top of that, my older brother had just gotten into a new relationship and was talking about moving out or having his girlfriend move in. Everything was changing around me, fast. Life wasn't waiting for anyone to catch up. I think my mom tried really hard to keep things feeling normal, or at least familiar. She'd still go back and forth between the ranch house and the city house, just like we used to do with my dad. But it was obvious that things weren't the same. Not even close. Dad used to run everything the businesses, the bills, the employees, the maintenance, the land. Every detail ran through him. Without him, it was like the whole machine started falling apart. And Mom was left trying to hold the pieces together with her bare hands. She started leaning on me a lot more to help with my younger brothers and even though I was still just a teenager myself, I didn't push back. At least not at first.

Week by week, more things disappeared. More equipment got sold. I even remember my brother's truck being sold off, something I never thought would happen. Mom told us she needed to sell what she could to keep paying the attorneys. I didn't understand what that meant at the time. I wish I'd been older, more aware, more grounded I wish I could've offered real help. But the truth is, I was deep in my rebellious phase, and even deeper in my own confusion. I was too young to fully grasp how serious everything was.

Mom even held yard sales to sell furniture, home goods, and whatever else could bring in cash. She didn't say much about it she just did what needed to be done. I remember overhearing one of Dad's calls where he told her she had enough property and things to sell that she'd be fine, that she could pay what mattered and still live comfortably. But what did that even mean? He didn't know how long he was going to be gone. And it's not like life pauses just because one parent disappears.

He would call all the time constantly checking in from wherever he was being held, trying to control everything from a jail phone. He'd ask about the farm, the lawyers, the finances. I'd overhear some of those conversations, and let me tell you they weren't loving calls. There was no softness in his voice. He would yell at my mom, threaten her, curse at her. Even when we were around. He didn't seem to care. I remember hearing his voice rise, the anger building so quickly that sometimes the calls got cut off completely. I always wondered if the prison staff was listening if they were monitoring the calls and ending them when they got too aggressive.

The house phone would ring all day with collect calls. My mom always accepted them. Every single one. I think at one point the bill was close to $1,000 a month just from those calls and nearly all they did was argue.

If I'm being completely honest... none of it mattered to me at the time.

Let's not forget my dad and I weren't in a good place before all of this happened.

Just because he'd given me jewelry for Valentine's Day or shared a meal with me didn't erase the damage from before. It didn't fix the hurt. It didn't undo the control or the fear I had learned to live under.

So while all of this was falling apart, I felt something I didn't expect: freedom.

I finally got to do what I wanted without having to hide.

I didn't feel afraid every second.

I didn't feel watched.

And truthfully, I didn't miss the material things.

I was never old enough to truly own anything in that world anyway.

I didn't have designer bags or name-brand wardrobes. That was more my mom's reality. My dad made sure she always looked sharp that was part of his image. She had to look the part, even if it came at a cost.

But me? I was just the girl on the sidelines, starting to feel what it was like to breathe on her own for the first time.

A few months later, my girlfriends and I did something I had never done before we skipped school.

It was completely out of character for me. I had always been terrified of getting in trouble, but that day, something in me was just down for it. I was curious. Nervous. Excited. We planned it out carefully like we were in some kind of movie, we'd get picked up right from the campus, go to the mall, shop for a while, and then get dropped back off just in time to make it look like we'd never left.

At first, everything went smoothly. We were laughing, feeling rebellious, feeling like we were part of a world I had only seen from the sidelines. By this time, I'd gotten my first cell phone my mom had given it to me because she wanted to stay in constant contact with me and my brothers. It wasn't some luxury accessory. It was a leash. A way for her to know where I was at all times. That same phone rang while we were out.

It was my older brother. He sounded tense. He told me Mom was looking for me she had sent him to my campus to pay for one of my drill team events. Do you remember back in 6th grade when something similar happened? This was like déjà vu all over again. He told me the school had said I wasn't in class and he was trying to warn me.

Panic set in immediately. We rushed back toward the school, thinking we'd slip back in unnoticed. But before we could even make it onto campus, we got caught. A security guard spotted us, and instead of quietly escorting us in, they called for backup. We ended up being driven back to school in police cars.

The humiliation was unreal.

As we stepped out of the cop car, dozens of students were pressed up against the windows, watching us like it was a scene out of a TV show. I felt my face burn with embarrassment, my heart hammering as we were escorted straight to the principal's office.

Later that evening, when I got home, the rebellion ended with another kind of punishment. My mom lost it. She spanked me and slapped me across the face a few times. I remember my head turning sharply with one of her slaps, and then almost in slow motion seeing blood splatter across my ivory colored furniture. My sensitive nose, the one that had bled through so many spankings as a kid, didn't spare me that day either.

I was grounded for skipping school.

And something shifted inside me.

I started resenting my mom for laying a hand on me. It wasn't just the slap it was everything it represented. The exhaustion, the double standards, the silence about everything we were going through, the expectation that I'd always be the one to help with my brothers, to cook, to clean, to be second mom while she came and went.

I don't want to sugarcoat it. I was fed up.

I was angry. I was tired.

I'd go to school all day, come home, and do chores, babysit, manage my brothers. It felt like my life wasn't mine. Like I was living inside a role that had been assigned to me before I even got to grow into who I was supposed to be. And the resentment just grew.

It was during these moments that I started telling myself: When and if I have kids of my own, I'm going to do it differently. But I'll be honest, I never wanted kids. I said this over and over again.

As a little girl, I used to joke that I'd grow up to be "the rich hot aunt" who traveled and had nice things. It was my way of saying I wouldn't be trapped. That I'd have freedom. That I'd have a life that was actually mine. And yet here I was, at 15 or 16, already feeling trapped by responsibilities I never signed up for.

I don't blame everything on my parents but at the same time, I do.

I held a quiet grudge against my mom for not showing me the things I thought moms were supposed to show their daughters. How to do my hair. How to shop for myself. How to be a girl in a world that expected so much from women. Those moments never happened, not even now as an adult.

Around this time, Mom started meeting people and having conversations about my dad's case. She would vent to them about what was going on, trying to find solutions. Most of it is a blur now, and maybe that's my mind protecting me. But there is one moment I'll never forget.

A man told my mother that he could get my dad released from prison for good with one condition.

Even writing that now, my chest tightens.

It breaks my heart to think about how young I was when I heard it, and how much older I feel now putting it into words. But I promised myself and you that this book would be raw and real. So here it is.

This man offered to "free" my dad for me, in exchange.

Even writing that now makes my stomach turn.

I'm not going to go into the details of what he asked for, but yes... it happened. And yes, I was terrified. But at that time in my life, I didn't know how to show fear. I had learned to swallow it, bury it, pretend it wasn't there. I never shed a tear. Ever.

He was either drunk or high, I'll never know. I was far too young to even understand what I was looking at. All I know is that he got up from his office chair, stumbled, and urinated all over himself. And me. He was incoherent, falling over, unable to form words.

It's a memory I've tried to block out. I don't remember every detail of that night, and honestly, I'm grateful I don't.

I just remember the moment I grabbed a phone trembling but trying not to look scared and made a call for someone to pick me up. I remember getting home safe. That's it. The rest is a blur, like static.

But what I do know is that something in me changed that night.

Something froze.

I went ice cold inside.

I stopped caring. About Mom. About Dad. About the whole extended family drama.

The only people I still felt fiercely protective over were my brothers. It was like I grew a hard shell overnight. I became a little girl with a grown woman's fire and attitude. Nobody was going to make me feel small again.

After that, my communication with my mom almost disappeared. I withdrew completely. Things between us only got worse from there.

Toward the end of the school year, my brother's graduation day arrived. The tension and drama in the house were still sky-high, but he still got to celebrate. He deserved that. Mom put together a party at the ranch with a DJ, snacks, chips, and finger foods for him to offer his friends and guests. She made sure there was something for him, even if everything around us felt broken.

That summer, things took another strange turn.

Mom started bringing us into the lawyers' office. They wanted to question the kids. They also wanted us to write letters about Dad. Letters saying what a good father he was, how much we missed him, how much we needed him at home. The lawyers said the judge needed to see that he had a family that cared.

I remember sitting there thinking, How is this even fair?

We were just kids.

We didn't even understand what was happening, but we were being pulled into this legal hurricane like little pawns on a board we didn't choose to play on.

Dad's court dates kept getting pushed back sometimes at the last minute, even on the same day. This dragged on and on, like a nightmare you can't wake up from. I hated to admit it, but the situation in Oregon, when Dad had been arrested months earlier, was also part of the case against him. It wasn't just an isolated event. Everything was connected.

The lawyers started showing us things videos, pictures, evidence. I didn't even understand what I was looking at. It was like watching a movie in another language with no subtitles. All I could do was sit there, stunned, confused, trying to piece together something that didn't make sense.

And then I heard the words.

The only words that stuck.

"Your dad is facing life in prison."

Life.

Forever.

I remember sitting there numb, like the air had been sucked out of the room. Not understanding a single legal term, but understanding that one word: "Life."

Was I never going to get my dad back?

What had he done that was so big, so serious, that it could take him away forever?

I knew my dad wasn't perfect. I knew he could be cruel. But I still couldn't see him as the man they were describing.

Even with all this chaos, we still ended up going back to Oregon for my parents' trucking company. Mom wanted to keep the business alive, to manage the trucks for the season as if Dad were still there. My older brother knew the ropes, so he gave her a hand, pushing through the work and trying to keep everything afloat while paying off debts.

Meanwhile, we were just waiting.

Waiting to see what would happen to Dad.

Waiting to see if life as we knew it would disappear for good.

This experience was shocking, unbelievable. I felt how hardened I was becoming, even to protect myself. The situation was really surreal.

At some point, Dad told Mom to have my older brother help her out more or to just sell the company altogether. He said the work was too heavy, too overwhelming for her to carry on her own. He instructed her to manage everything wisely and to prioritize paying off the smaller things first like her car so that she wouldn't lose what really mattered. Even behind bars, Dad was still trying to control the narrative, still giving orders from the other side of a phone line.

But I think Mom and my older brother had a falling out. I don't know what was said between them, but the business went down almost immediately after. It collapsed like a house of cards fast, and without much warning.

I was only 15 years old. I didn't know how to run a business. I didn't even understand what the hell was going on half the time. I was just a teenage girl filled with anger and adrenaline, doing whatever I wanted. I was wild. I was careless. I felt free and in all the wrong ways. I was driving without a license, sneaking out, going out constantly, and avoiding home as much as I could.

That same year, I finally got to go to the school dance. Dad wasn't around to say no, so things shifted quickly. Mom had rented a small place, and we were temporarily living in a camper to save money while she tried to keep the trucking company going. It was cramped, messy, and uncomfortable. But at least I wasn't stuck at least I had a little breathing room, even if the whole world felt unstable.

I didn't ask Mom to drive me to school in the mornings anymore. I preferred catching a ride with friends. That became my tiny pocket of peace one of the only parts of my day where I got to feel like a normal kid. The friend who drove us had this long yellow car that we all jokingly named "the banana boat." It was this beat-up, oversized car that looked like an actual banana, and it barely fit all of us. We'd pile in, sit squished in the backseat, and laugh our way through the ride to school. When we hit speed bumps, the whole car would bounce like a trampoline, and we'd be screaming and laughing so loud, you'd think we were on a carnival ride.

It was all good until one morning, the sun was so bright, our friend couldn't see, and he accidentally clipped a side mirror on something. After that, he stopped driving us. I think his parents might've found out and shut it down. Honestly, I couldn't blame them.

By the time we went back to Oregon, I had stopped talking to "the California boyfriend." That's what I'll call him here going forward "the one from Texas and California". He and I broke up not long after everything went down with my dad. I actually found out later that Dad had approved of me dating him all along, because he knew the family and had some connection to them. It's wild how he never said anything when he was around but after the fact, I learned he was okay with it.

Anyway, since that chapter was closed, I started talking to someone else. One of my parents' drivers. He was Mexican tall, built, attractive, and hands down one of the hardest working guys on the team. He worked harder than all the other drivers combined. I knew it for a fact because I helped write out the checks on payday. His check was always the biggest.

I admired his work ethic. That stood out to me more than anything. He also had a wild, hilarious sense of humor. We never dated officially, never went out, nothing serious like that. It was just casual talking, and I'd see him on payday or whenever I was helping out. It was harmless or at least I thought it was.

But somehow, even this turned into drama. Apparently, he had recently broken up with someone I went to school with, and that caused tension for me on campus. I tried to stay out of it and avoided the drama as best I could, but I swear... every time I dipped my toe into dating, something messy would follow.

And when my dad found out I was talking to an employee? Oh, he lost it.

He told my mom I had hit rock bottom all because I was talking to a driver. I was shocked. I told her, "Do y'all not remember being employees at one point too?" Like, come on now. What if this guy works his way up, builds something great for himself? I saw his drive, his ambition. That's what I liked. I wasn't going to entertain anyone lazy or with no future. I had standards. I just didn't have the same standards they did. If only my parents knew, Fast forward, he really did become someone bigger. He owns his own company now. He tries to stay in contact with me till this day.

Anyway:

I was young. I wasn't getting married. I wasn't having kids. I had dreams, big ones and I didn't need anyone trying to micromanage my every move just because I was dating. They were old school. In their minds, if you dated, it better be for marriage. But I didn't see life that way. I didn't even picture myself getting married or having kids at all back then. I had too many other things I wanted to do. But in their eyes, dating a driver was unacceptable. Unforgivable. Something they needed to "put a stop to." To me? It was just another example of how no one really saw me not for who I was, what I valued, or the kind of life I wanted to live.

I had a very popular, successful, and powerful father, and I was constantly reminded that I needed to hold a good reputation and image because of that. But I didn't care. Not really. I was too young to be making my own decisions, and in the end, everything came down to whatever my parents said was best or right or acceptable. I didn't have a say. I just followed what was expected of me. One of the sons from another major trucking company in Oregon started messaging me around this time. I talked to him for a little while. His family was extremely well known probably one of the biggest names in the industry out there. I'll admit, I liked him. And for once, he wasn't an employee so I figured maybe this would be easier. But there was one problem: he was the son of one of my dad's "frenemies." A direct business competitor. My family would've hated the idea of me being involved with him even casually.

One time, he invited me out. He was older than me, so he had a few drinks. I obviously wasn't old enough to drink, so I just sat there and talked with him. We had a long conversation about life, family, the trucking business, and everything that was falling apart in my world. I told him things had been hard lately. That I missed my dad, even after everything. That despite the chaos, I still loved him and couldn't wrap my head around him being gone like this.

And then he said something that changed everything. He looked at me, smirked a little, and said: "What did you think? That everything you all had was legal? All the trucks, the land, the money? Come on. You know better than that."

My entire body froze.

I was instantly disgusted. Who the hell did he think he was to talk about my family like that? I was a kid when all this happened. I had no clue what my father was doing or not doing. I thought our lives were built off hard work. I thought the vacations were earned. I thought the long nights of Dad being gone meant he was working overtime. I never imagined otherwise.

I was so offended that I never spoke to him again. He tried to reach out for years actually but I shut it down every time. The way he looked at me when he said those words… like he pitied me. Like I was naive. And sure, I was but he had no right to throw it in my face.

Eventually, we left Oregon and went back to Texas. The business was in shambles by then. Mom had done what she could, but she and my brother kept bumping heads, and honestly, I had no idea what was even going on anymore. That wasn't my story to tell. I didn't have the full picture. I was too busy being a rebellious teenager who felt like she had just escaped from a woman's-only prison. Around that time, my older brother officially moved his girlfriend in with us. Things were changing so fast while Dad was away, and we still didn't know what the outcome of his trial would be. But he was furious we knew that much.

He was getting updates somehow, and it drove him crazy knowing things were falling apart without him. His daughter was going out and dating. Mom was selling off everything and going out too. My older brother was in a full relationship. My younger brothers were being left alone more often, and even the youngest one was starting to act out and he was still in elementary school.

It was a wreck. We were unraveling.

When we got home to Texas, the court proceedings and lawyer appointments picked right back up. Dad hadn't been transferred yet he was still sitting in some grimy, raunchy county jail, waiting. He wouldn't be moved until he was sentenced, or at least close to it.

I remember one day I went to the lawyer's office with my mom. He pulled out some footage and asked us to watch. Mom leaned over to me quietly and said, "Don't say a word." So I stayed silent.

I saw my dad in some of the clips. It was him. Clear as day.

And some of the places even looked familiar…

We'll get into that later.

By then, this had already been dragging on for so long. My mom was still trying to fight. Still trying to hold things together. Still paying lawyer after lawyer. She had started selling off even more equipment from the business. She put the ranch up for sale. Sold the animals. She started having weekend yard sales to get rid of everything we owned from the house, the garage, and anything that could help ease the financial weight.

I don't remember any of it. I don't even think I was there. I must've been at school or off with friends. I said it before, and I'll say it again I didn't care about the material stuff. I truly didn't. But something else had changed:

Mom wasn't Mom anymore. She had shifted into a completely different person. She was fighting depression, crying constantly, and picking up habits that were never hers before going out, escaping, anything to feel something else. Anything to cope.

And even though I had tried to harden myself, I'll admit it now I was starting to miss my dad.

He wasn't always bad. He wasn't always the problem.

He was my father.

That bond we had since I was a little girl was still there, buried under the anger and hurt.

We had always been close, even when we fought hard.

He taught me how to dance to every kind of music cumbias, the lambada, you name it.

We'd dance at parties, at home during dinner on regular weekdays, and especially on my birthdays and holidays.

I was ten years old dancing with my dad, smiling, spinning, feeling like I could fly.

My footwork came naturally.

I could learn choreography just by watching.

It's something I've always had in me.

So yeah…

I missed him.

I missed him showing up.

I missed him leading.

I missed him providing and protecting, even if I challenged that control every step of the way .

And if I'm being honest, I missed feeling like we were still a family.

Chapter 12

"From Prada to Prison"

GENTLE TRIGGER WARNING:

This chapter includes sensitive topics such as incarceration, emotional trauma, and prison violence. If any part of this feels too heavy, it's okay to pause or come back to it later. I'm walking with you through this you're not alone. <3

Mom finally took us to go see Dad.

He must've been in that county jail for at least two years by then. That meant he'd missed the shift in me from a 14-year-old girl who was still soft, still awkward, still clumsy in her own skin, to a 15, 16-year-old young woman. That kind of transition might not sound like much on paper, but when you're living it... it's everything. The curve of my body, the drop in my voice, the way I started carrying myself it was noticeable. I wasn't a little girl anymore. And I knew he would see it the second I walked in.

I remember walking in feeling completely numb. Like I was floating, disconnected, like my body had entered the room before my spirit could catch up. I felt nothing, and somehow, I felt everything all at once.

I had light makeup on just a flavored, chocolate-brown Lip Smackers gloss that made me feel grown, even if it was just for the day. I wore a long brown cardigan with jeans. Covered. Clean. Discreet. That morning, I made sure not to wear anything too loud or noticeable. I still technically wasn't allowed to wear makeup, but I had started sneaking it on anyway. That soft, quiet rebellion most teenage girls go through. Something about it gave me a little power.

The place itself stank. The kind of smell that clings to the inside of your nose and sits there for hours. A thick mix of sweat, bleach, and something else I couldn't name but one whiff and your stomach turned. I hated that smell. Still do. And I hated even more that we couldn't touch him. A sheet of foggy plastic and tight wire fencing separated us. It made everything feel colder. Inhuman.

The people around us were different. I'm not saying that in a judgmental way I promise I'm not but it was noticeable. Some of the visitors were loud, dressed wild, moving with no grace. And even though we'd lived in trailer parks before, this was a different kind of poor. This was generational, systemic, survival-mode poor. You could see it in their faces. A lot of the women looked exhausted. Some angry. Some just... empty. A few clung to their children like they were life rafts, while others just let them scream unattended. You could feel the tension echo off the cinder block walls crying babies, crying wives, bitter girlfriends, women who looked like they were holding in ten years' worth of pain. I stood still. Frozen in line. My hands folded tightly in front of me like I was in church. I always greeted the guards with a soft "hello," using my best manners. I knew better than to give them a reason to make things harder. Head down. Eyes open. Always watching.

Every visit, I was just... observing. Absorbing. Soaking in everything like a sponge, even though I didn't know what I was supposed to be learning. I didn't even know who I was anymore. Had I ever really known? And did any of it even matter?

That first visit was hard.

Dad and I hadn't spoken in months. We weren't on good terms because of a fight we'd had before he got locked up. So I wasn't exactly walking in there with open arms. I was only there because Mom made us go and because the lawyer said it would "look good" if the family showed up. That was it. Another performance. Another day of doing what I was told. I stood behind my mom as we walked into the visitation room. And out of nowhere, Dad broke the silence.

"You're wearing makeup?"

I can't lie I felt proud. I tilted my chin up a little and answered, "Yes," without blinking. I knew he couldn't do anything about it from where he was. And I took that moment. I wasn't trying to be disrespectful or bratty, but part of me was still holding anger. Anger at how he treated Mom over the phone. Anger at the things he said about me. The yelling. The threats. The control. I hadn't let it go.

I was young, upset, and smack in the middle of my rebellious teenage years. I was only there because Mom took us, and I wanted him to know that.

After a few seconds, he softened. He looked at me, almost like he didn't recognize me at first. And then he said quietly, "You're growing up." Followed by, "You look beautiful."

And just like that, it cracked me. It hurt like hell.

You remember how I told you I never cried when I got spanked? Even then, sitting across from my dad behind prison glass, hearing those words I still didn't let a single tear fall. I wanted to. God, I wanted to. But I refused to let anyone see that weakness in me. I had to be strong for myself, but especially for my mom. So I smiled. I nodded. I joked. I laughed. I played the role of a daughter who was holding it all together, like nothing was wrong.

But inside? It felt like something was dying.

There was this deep, aching, physical pain in my chest and stomach, like my body was rejecting the moment entirely. I remember walking into the house afterward and heading straight to the bathroom. I turned on the sink faucet just to drown out the sound and I threw up everything I'd eaten that day.

I didn't want my mom to hear me. I didn't want her to ask what was wrong. I didn't want to talk about it.

That first visitation broke something open in me. I had never seen my father so low. Never.

He looked like a shell of himself. Depressed but still angry. Wounded but still full of pride.

The worst part? People inside the prison were talking about him, mocking him. Word had gotten around that he cried every single day. My dad. The man who never cried. The man who walked like an eagle and acted like one too proud, unshakable, free. He had always done whatever he wanted, whenever he wanted. And now he was locked in a cage. Four walls. No freedom. No power. No control. I can't even begin to imagine the psychological trauma of a shift that drastic. One day you're running the world, the next you're reduced to a number on someone's list. One day, you're feared and respected. The next, you're just another man in a beige uniform who doesn't get to choose when to eat or when to speak. You never get to go home again. You never get to feel like yourself again.

And even though the visits were supposed to keep us close, sometimes they only showed how far apart we really were. Dad would still go off on Mom right in front of us. He'd tell her she wasn't doing enough, that she wasn't fighting hard enough to get him out. The pressure was constant, relentless. Around that time, we finally got news of his sentence. From facing life, it was now reduced to thirty-six years in federal prison. Thirty-six. It felt like some kind of miracle and a death sentence at the same time. He was finally being charged officially: drug lord, conspiracy, and a stack of other charges on top of that. But my dad refused to settle. He told my mom to keep appealing, to keep pushing. He didn't care how risky it was. Even though the lawyers warned that appealing again could backfire that he could end up with life again if it didn't go well he still wanted to take the chance. That was just the kind of man he was. He didn't believe in surrender. He didn't know how to lose. And he sure as hell didn't know how to live in a world where he wasn't in control.

Visitation continued on the weekends, but sometimes there were prison fights or emergencies and visitation would be canceled. It was an hour-long drive, so if that happened, we had no way of knowing until we showed up. We didn't have an option but to go and hope visitation was allowed. After that first visit, Mom made it a routine for all of us to go every weekend. We were there either Saturday or Sunday. As long as there was visitation, we were there.

The guards and security people already knew us by name. Dad would tell us that every time we left, they would compliment him and say what a beautiful family he had and how well-spoken and well-behaved we were. For him, those words must have been small bursts of pride in a place where dignity gets stripped from you piece by piece.

But my dad looked really down during that time. The place was ugly inside and out, and the uniforms were exactly what they look like in the conspiracy movies. He had to wear these ugly sandals to each visit. He'd be cuffed until he came to the designated visiting area. Sometimes they cuffed him so tight you could see the red marks on his wrists. It broke something inside me to see him like that reduced, restrained, his hands bound where I used to hold them.

As time went on, we all just did what we could at home and school. During my days off, I would step out and go dancing or play pool with my friends anything to escape the heaviness that hung over our lives. The same boy from 6th grade the "California boyfriend" happened to swing by again. He'd been out and about before stopping by my house, but this time he rammed into the front metal gate and busted the front of his truck. Nothing happened to the gate; it was heavy and solid. My mom saw the truck smoking through the camera and ran to my room to tell me he was outside shouting my name and refusing to leave. I had stopped answering his calls and ignored him completely when I'd run into him, so I guess he thought this was the only way I'd talk to him.

I stepped outside and told him to behave if he wanted me to open the gate, and so he did. He asked for ten minutes of my time, which I gave him. We ended up talking again, but it was an on-and-off thing the whole time. My mom called his parents, and they apologized and came to get him and the truck. His mom would let me come over sometimes, she'd even take us to school, and he was able to come visit me from time to time too.

I had started hanging out with friends who didn't have the best intentions, backgrounds, or influence. I was even going to Mexico with my friends, since most of them and their parents had houses there too. Remember the border was only about fifteen minutes away. It was an easy cross-over. I would do anything with anyone in order to be away from home, to avoid dealing with anyone there, or to avoid being left behind to watch my brothers. I met a whole lot of people during this time even grown men at cookouts or get togethers who knew who my dad was. I heard stories, rumors, and so much gossip about him. I just took it all in quietly. I planned to someday have a conversation with my dad about all of this. I would mentally note these things, storing them like evidence. I've always been into journaling, so writing helped me cope with everything that was happening.

These people would hand me a drink, a cigarette, a smoke, anything. You name it, they had it. As I said before, not the best influence, but I stayed. Because at that point, staying in those spaces felt easier than staying home.

Later that year, I picked up a side job. It wasn't glamorous, but it gave me cash in hand and, more importantly, freedom. I already knew a lot about trucks from growing up in my dad's world, so a company hired me to help them book loads for their trucks and drivers. At sixteen, that felt like a big deal. I'd leave home without saying a word, slipping out quietly. One day I even asked my boss if he had a car I could borrow. He raised an eyebrow and asked me why, and I told him I had a very important visit to make.

He said he wanted to see me drive first before making a decision. So I did slid behind the wheel, hands at ten and two, showing him I knew what I was doing. After that, he tossed me the keys to a Harley Truck. It was beautiful sleek, powerful, and way out of my league. I felt like I was holding a piece of gold. I took such good care of it, every mile, every turn, knowing it wasn't mine. I felt privileged that he even trusted me.

That day, I drove an hour away and got my own state ID. And then, for the first time in my life, I went to go see my dad completely on my own. No one knows about this to this day. I walked in, spoke to him, and stayed as long as I could. Dad had no idea I was coming, but the prison was small word spread fast. By the time I arrived, the guards had already told him I was there, even describing the truck I had driven in. Once we sat down, anything he asked, I answered. I told him about the job, the truck, and how things were at home. I told him I felt lost. I told him I needed guidance. I made sure to let him know I was still upset with him over how he handled the fight in Oregon, but that I needed us both to just talk. At first he gave me attitude, but when he saw I didn't budge, he cooled down. Dad already knew who I was working for and asked me to thank my boss for helping me. Turns out my boss had known exactly whose daughter I was all along. Like I've said before, Dad was a very important, very known man.

As time went by, I kept escaping and going to see my dad without saying anything to anyone. At least twice a month, I'd make that drive. It became my secret routine just me and the road, trying to hold my life together in silence. Then one day they moved him further away and I couldn't travel like that anymore.

First it was Carnes City. He was still staring down a sentence of thirty six years, and as I've mentioned before, Dad was not taking "no" for an answer. He insisted on appealing, pushing Mom to keep going. Then he got moved to Houston, Texas. We never went to see him there. He asked my mom not to take us because the facility was ugly and dangerous. He said he would let us know when the time was right. His final small facility ended up being Raymondville, Texas. There was a lot of moving around during those last couple of months as the court process came to an end.

That year, we went back to Oregon during the potato season again. Mom was hoping she'd get new contracts for the trucks, but this time she was denied by a lot of companies. It was a real struggle. School was just school nothing special. I'd always end up talking to some guy or another, but as I've said before, I wanted nothing serious. How could you when you traveled as much as I did anyway? That was my mindset.

I did get to hang out with the friends from the previous year. By then, some of us were already driving even without licenses. We'd leave for Washington, go out to the teen nightclubs, or just cruise around, windows down, music up. I even went to my first live concert. It should have felt exciting and new, but even my fun carried a shadow. I picked up unhealthy habits. Drinks. Late nights. Bad company. All of it was because I wanted to be as far away from home as I could. I was still holding on to grudges, still upset at how everything was unraveling.

That season flew by. It felt like we arrived and left in a blink. And deep down, I think I knew it would be my last official trip to Oregon with my mom.

When we returned to Texas, my dad's court case was finally coming to an end. I have no idea what happened on the actual day of his sentencing because I don't think we were told or taken. I just don't remember attending a court hearing at all.

During that time, Dad had been transferred to a few different facilities before being sent to the one he'd stay in for the long term. And while all this was happening, he ordered my mom to start lining up all the work trucks for sale. He told her the business didn't stand a chance without him. That selling the business and selling the ranch was the only way to survive. By then, Dad had officially been sentenced for twelve years.

Everything about that moment felt final.

This was when I found out my parents had gotten a loan over our house. Remember how Dad bought the house cash? Well, later he went to the bank with Mom and asked for a small loan. It might have been around $50,000 or so. Nothing major, at least in my opinion, for the house we had. The payment might have been only $500-$600 a month. Dad told Mom that if she followed his instructions to sell what needed to be sold and use that money to pay off the house she would be set. Even with all the rest, she would still have money left for day-to-day things. At least, that's what he said.

If there was one thing about my dad, it was that he knew numbers. This man could do math with no calculator, just right off the top of his head. He was good with money, math, and he was street smart. Even behind bars, he was still trying to stay calm and take care of us. He wanted to manage everything at home by telling Mom step by step what to do. He was always aggressive, as usual, but he said what needed to be said.

My mom, on the other hand, decided to take us to Dallas, where her sister was living with my cousins. As a refresher this was the sister who had been married to my dad's brother, the one who passed away. These were the same cousins we were supposed to take that trip to Mexico with the trip Dad never picked us up for.

Mom had gotten closer to her sister by then, so we'd visit and sometimes go out to the lake or stay at their apartment. I loved my aunt so much. Sometimes, I felt more connected and attached to her than to my very own mom. She was loud, loved to dance and party, had long blonde hair, wore makeup, and was a complete extrovert. Mom, on the other hand, had always been an introvert. She had natural curly brunette hair and rarely wore makeup just eyeliner and mascara. She'd had permanent makeup done while Dad was out, so she really didn't need much. Mom had also never really been out before. Keep in mind, Mom hadn't even dated anyone before Dad. They were both practically kids when they got married.

So when we went to Dallas, Mom stepped out of her comfort zone more. She went dancing, shopping, doing things she never really had before. But let's be real at home everything was still a mess. Our home. Our lives. School. You name it. We stayed in Dallas only a few days before heading back home. By then, Mom had gotten rid of her good vehicles and so many things were gone from the house, the ranch, the business. By this point, Dad had already been taken into a "maximum security," "federal correctional complex," officially called the U.S.D. Pollock in Louisiana. This place was for males only and housed about 901 inmates total. It was a nine-hour drive, give or take, from our home and about four hours from Dallas where my aunt lived. Mom planned our visits carefully, selecting which days we'd leave and how long we'd be able to stay. Going to Dallas first, spending a day there, and leaving from there for visitation made sense it cut the drive down.

We were all still going to school except for my older brother, who had already graduated and just so happened to be expecting a baby with his girlfriend. Like I've said before, things changed so quickly when Dad was gone. My mother had bought a beat-up red car. It was small, ugly, and to be honest, I can't even remember if it had AC.

This place my dad was in Pollock was the first time in years that we were actually going to get a chance to see Dad in person. Nothing between us. A full-day visitation. No foggy glass, no plastic.

The facility itself was huge compared to the county prison. It had wired gates and security cameras on every corner you turned. It was way cleaner and much more organized than any other place I'd seen before. Massive, heavy metal doors would slide open to let you inside.

I remember that visitation like it was yesterday. We were totally new to this and didn't know what to expect. They had vending machines with food and snacks you could heat up while you were there since it was basically an all-day event.

When Dad walked into the visitation room, he looked different. He had a clean haircut. His uniform was brown. He had shiny black shoes and was wearing glasses the kind that go clear inside and switch to dark when the sun hits them. He looked so much better than before. He didn't come straight to us; he had to check in with the security table first, and then they sent him off to the section where we were seated.

I remember so clearly, as he walked toward us, he had this half smirk, half-frown. Like he was happy to see us but, deep down, he was in pain. It was like I could see right through him. When everyone got up to say hello and hug him, I stayed seated until the end. I let my mom and my brothers have their moment. Once he finished greeting them, he walked toward me, held out his hand for me to get up, and pulled me in for a hug.

I had a huge knot in my throat but swallowed it. I showed no signs of weakness but I didn't only do that for me. I did it for him. I wanted him to feel, to see, that I was strong enough to handle it all.

That first visitation, we ran out of change to buy snacks or food. We were all hungry, and I'm sure Dad was too. We didn't know the price of anything ahead of time, and although Mom had brought cash, she didn't bring any coins. No quarters and that's all the machines would take. We just weren't prepared. But for sure, by the next visitation, we would be. Dad caught a little bit of an attitude with Mom, and I quietly moved away from the group. I was beginning to feel upset not just at the situation, but because even though things at home were a mess, Mom was still doing everything she could. She was managing to send him money, pay for lawyers, and handle what she could with the house and ranch. Were all the decisions perfect? No. But she did what she knew how to do at the time. I was upset that Dad couldn't seem to see or appreciate that.

He noticed right away when I moved down, and suddenly the front security called him up. They got on to him. I don't think they could hear our conversations but they could definitely read body language. They could tell when tension was rising. Dad came back and apologized to me, quietly asking me to move back to my spot. And we finished out the rest of the visitation.

The following day, Mom went alone while we stayed behind in the hotel room. That became our routine. Throughout all of his visitations, we would either split the days or give Mom a full day with him alone so they could talk through things adult conversations, private matters without worrying about us overhearing.

In one of those visits, I can't remember if it was one of my brothers or someone else who came up behind Dad to pat him on the back or give him a casual hello. And Dad flinched hard. His whole face went pale for a second, and he reacted in such a way that it was almost scary. That's when I really realized the kind of environment he was living in. He had to be on guard all the time. You always had to watch your back because you didn't know who might come after you. It's crazy, because that's true in real life out here too but you don't think about it like that until you're in those types of circumstances.

Dad had also recently had surgery on his hand. I didn't know at the time what exactly had happened, just that he couldn't fully close it anymore. It looked bad. He didn't tell us the real story right away we were too young. But as the years passed, I came back to it. I was maybe 21 or 22 when I finally asked him, straight up, what had happened and why he needed that surgery.

He told me that when he was first sentenced and transferred to maximum security, there was an 18-year-old boy who had just arrived. The boy had been charged with something serious "grape." And apparently, about 13 older men planned to do the same thing to him inside. My dad said he couldn't let that happen not to a kid who was the same age as his own children.

He was in no way defending the boy's actions he told me flat out, "The punishment of him being here was already more than enough." But what those other men had planned was something else entirely. It was disgusting and cruel, and Dad said that boy wouldn't have survived. So my dad did what he felt was right. He jumped in. He told me, "I was already in here. What more could happen?"

The fight left him injured. His hand was never the same. He and the others involved were all sent to the hole for about a month after that. He said, "Most of us won't even make it out of here alive… but that's not a way to go."

I understood then why he didn't tell us when we were younger. But over time, I pushed for more open communication between us. I needed to know. And slowly, he started opening up.

Some visitations were canceled completely, and we wouldn't get to see him at all. Sometimes the phones would be taken away from them, and we wouldn't hear from him for weeks sometimes even months. Phone calls were always monitored, and we were only allowed a limited amount of time on the line.

Things started to shift a little when I turned… I don't know if it was 20 or 21… when we didn't have to write through regular mail anymore and could finally send messages through email. It was way more convenient for both of us. Dad had to learn quickly how to use the system because you had to pay per minute to use the computer.

His emails were always short, direct, and to the point. Mine were long, detailed, full of emotions until I realized he was getting charged per minute. After that, I started shortening mine too.

While inside, he started making things by hand leather bags and wallets, even paintings. I still have two of those bags. One of them even has my name engraved into the wallet. It's one of the coolest things I've ever owned, and I'm so glad I've kept it all these years. All handmade. Western style. It smells just like a brand-new pair of cowboy boots. And even after over a decade, the smell hasn't changed.

Dad also started taking classes parenting courses, typing, English, and even law. The more classes he completed, the more points he earned, and the more time could be taken off his sentence. So he was putting in work every single day staying busy, focused, trying to make the most of what he could in the worst of circumstances.

Chapter 13

Undecided, Unwanted, and

Disappointing Benson & Hedges

That year, everything shifted.

I had met so many new people and somehow ended up getting invited to all kinds of events birthday parties, kickbacks, late-night drives, even senior skip day at the beach, even though I wasn't technically a senior yet. I tagged along anyway. I craved that sense of freedom, that version of life that felt light.

By then, I had stopped working at the trucking company. My dad was locked up farther away now, and honestly, I didn't feel as safe without him nearby. As strange as it might sound, even when he was behind bars, I still felt protected. His presence lingered like a force field around me. And little by little, we were getting close again slowly, but surely.

I had my own cellphone by then, and Dad no longer had to call collect. He had picked up some jobs inside prison, doing small things to make a bit of cash. Whatever money he earned would go to his inmate account, along with whatever Mom deposited when she could. With that, he made sure to call me every other day at the very least, twice a week. Every time he called, it was like he already knew what was going on.

He always knew.

He knew we had traveled to Dallas and stayed at my aunt's. He knew Mom was going out more. He knew I was running around the streets with friends. I never really hid anything from him. At that point, I figured if I had nothing to lie about, there was nothing to be afraid of. Even if I told him something reckless or wrong, he couldn't and wouldn't hurt me anymore. That strange safety gave me so much space to be honest with him. I could vent to my dad without a filter. Even when I knew he wouldn't approve, I told him everything. And he'd talk to me like a teacher, breaking things down, explaining why certain choices might backfire.

It was the most consistent guidance I had.

Eventually, I got a job at Whataburger. LOL. I'm literally laughing as I write this because I only lasted about three days. I was just trying to make my own money. I liked nice things always had. Ever since I was little, it was easier to get what I wanted from Dad than from Mom. She would almost always say no, or take us shopping for hand-me-downs or no-name brands. And I get it there's nothing wrong with that at all. But there were certain things I wanted so badly, I knew I'd have to earn them myself.

Mom wasn't working at the time. She was still selling whatever she could to make ends meet, sometimes applying for government assistance to help cover the gaps. Things weren't the same without Dad.

So when I applied for Whataburger, some of my friends offered to help get me there and back. They knew the situation at home. They knew I didn't have a car to drive. Once I got hired, the manager told me I'd need black, closed-toe, closed-heel, restaurant-grade slip-resistant shoes. No tennis shoes. No regular footwear. They had to be safety-approved for restaurant work.

I was not happy about it. I had just started dressing more girly and finally felt like I was stepping into my style.

I asked my grandma P my mom's mom if she could help me buy the shoes. She loaned me $35 and told me to pay her back with my first check. I promised I would.

Orientation came first, and that went fine. But the moment I got assigned to a real store location, it was downhill from there. They made me wear my hair pulled tight into a slick ponytail, tucked into a hairnet, and then topped with the ugliest Whataburger cap or visor. I wanted to scream. The full uniform was hideous some stiff Dickies-style pants and a bright orange logo shirt. Oh my Lanta. I wanted to crawl under a rock.

Three days in, walking back and forth asking strangers if they needed extra ketchup, sweating in a hairnet and slipping on fry grease... I didn't just walk out of that job I ran. I paid my grandma back and threw those ugly shoes straight in the dumpster. I knew right then and there: I was never doing that again.

But of course... I went and applied at Starz next. Yes, another fast food job. As if I hadn't learned the first time.

This one turned out to be totally different though. I didn't have to cook or stand near the fryers. All I had to do was take orders, submit them to the kitchen, and run the food out to the cars. I kind of loved it. Starz had a whole different vibe. Families came in for ice cream nights, old couples pulled in for burgers and laughs it wasn't chaotic. It was sweet.

And I made money. I was walking out with a minimum of $60 in tips every day.

I would clock out, have friends scoop me up, and head out to get ready for the night. Sometimes I'd buy an outfit on the spot, or I'd carry clothes with me to change at their house. There was always a place to go always something happening. It's wild to think about how many spots were open, how easily I could just walk in no questions asked. I never even showed my check to my mom. I had a close friend who would take me to cash it, using the ID I'd gotten myself.

That friend was a guy who lived just a few blocks away. I had met him randomly one night while walking with friends. He was a little older probably around my brother's age and ran a business with his family. He had his life together, at least from what I could see. He helped me with a lot back then rides, advice, sometimes just hanging out when I needed space. He would invite me to parties and even his family's barbecues.

I'm sure some people assumed we were dating, but we weren't. He was just a really close friend someone who made that season of my life feel a little more stable.

One day we were headed to a family party out at a ranch. I had grabbed a last-minute dress, and before we even got there, my friend insisted on making sure I looked and felt my best. He paid a stylist $200 in cash just to stay after hours and blow-dry my hair. She had already locked the salon doors and was closing for the day, but when he asked her to stay just for me she did. I sat in that chair as she gave me a quick blowout, and then we headed to the event. And honestly? We had a really good time. He was super respectful, knew how to carry himself in public, and spoke the most proper Spanish the kind that made even strangers pause mid-conversation.

I remember another time when my mom needed to sell one of the last vehicles she had maybe it was the Tahoe… or a Suburban. I don't remember exactly. But I had casually mentioned it to him, just in passing, and asked if he knew anyone who might be interested. A few days later, without saying a word to me, he went straight to my mom, handed her $10,000 in cash, and bought the SUV just to help her out. I still don't know why she was selling it, or what the money was really for. I never asked. I never questioned her. I just stayed in my lane.

That friend of mine? He really helped with everything. He would even spoil my two baby brothers. They thought he was my boyfriend and were convinced he was some rich guy. I'd laugh every time they got excited to see him pull up. Over time, we grew closer. His parents started coming to events with us. It all felt easy until it didn't.

Eventually, he told me he wanted a relationship. But I couldn't give him that. I had never dated someone older, and I wasn't in a place where I even knew who I was yet. So I pulled back. I cut off communication completely. I felt bad, but I couldn't fake something I wasn't ready for. Part of me remembered what my dad always said that women should never be just friends with men. That line blurred, and in the end, it left me sad and distant. But I had to choose myself.

At the same time, the California guy was still in the background. We still talked "sometimes." It was inconsistent, unhealthy, but I wasn't ready to let go. I felt like I couldn't date anyone else because

I didn't know if I'd end up right back with him. Even though it was a mess, I liked him. And I wasn't ready to move on, not completely. I was just trying to survive trying to stay safe, hustle for my little brothers, and bring home food when I could. Sometimes I'd bring leftovers from Starz just to make sure they had something to snack on. I wish I remembered more from that time, but I don't. I don't know where Mom was most of the time. I don't know what was being sold, or what was being stolen. I just know I was doing what I could to keep my head above water. At some point, I heard that our house had been broken into too. All I know is, I tried to stay gone as much as I could. It didn't feel like home anymore.

And yet... the California guy never stopped popping up. He'd show up out of nowhere, talk to me for a few minutes, then disappear again for days. It was weird, inconsistent, and exhausting. But still I couldn't let go. It was like my heart didn't know what it wanted, only that it didn't want to lose him.

Meanwhile, our visits to Dad continued. And every time we went, I used those moments as a chance to reset. I'd pull him aside, take advantage of some one-on-one time, and tell him everything even the stuff I shouldn't. I'd snitch on myself like it was therapy.

One time, I remember he grabbed my hand and smelled it, then looked at me sideways and asked if I had been smoking. I nodded. I didn't even try to lie. Every time we'd go to Mexico, my friends and I would buy Benson & Hedges Premium always menthol. I was smoking more and more. Cigarettes became one of my heaviest vices. I'm not proud of it, but it's the truth. Dad was disappointed. I could see it in his eyes, but he didn't yell. He just looked... heart-broken.

On one of those visits to see Dad, we stopped in Dallas again and stayed with my aunt. My cousins wanted to take me out to cruise around Grand Prairie. They said there was a nice park and they wanted to show me around. While we were there, this guy walked up and asked for my name and number. I told him I wasn't from the area and gave him a vague answer just enough to make him go away. He told us there'd be a club that night, and my cousin mentioned maybe we'd stop by too.

That night, we got ready at my aunt's apartment. I don't think I mentioned this before, but I had a friend back home who got me a fake ID. I used it everywhere. So when we showed up at the club a packed Mexican nightclub that was probably over capacity I realized I had forgotten my ID. I ended up paying extra at the door to get in anyway. It was Fourth of July weekend, and the whole place was buzzing. Loud music, packed bodies, people dressed sharp. It wasn't like anything I was used to. Even the way they danced and spoke Spanish felt different.

And then, of course, the guy from the park was there.

He offered me a drink and a dance, but I wasn't interested. Plus, they had stamped a huge black "X" on my hand to mark me as a minor, so even if I had been interested, it would've been a no. I stayed near my cousins, danced a bit, and tried to have fun but the guy wouldn't leave us alone. He lingered nearby like I had come there with him. Like I owed him something. He didn't even pay for my entrance.

And to top it all off, the California boy was blowing up my phone the entire time.

Then, out of nowhere, this girl stormed toward me. I had no idea who she was or why she was coming at me, but before I could even react, the guy from the park stepped in front of me and covered me with his hands to "protect" me. I was caught off guard. Apparently, she was his ex and she was not happy. He told me not to worry, said she was crazy, that he'd handle it. But I didn't want anything to do with it. I backed away immediately and told him to back off. My cousins stepped in too and made it clear I was not with him, not on a date, and not interested. Later that night, another guy asked me to dance and surprisingly, we clicked right away. We danced like we had been partners in another life. He was tall, with a full dark black beard, and wore a perfectly steamed Tejana hat. I noticed the details right away. I knew western wear my dad raised me around that. He had on crisp black pants, polished boots, and a tan guayabera shirt the kind of linen button-up with pleats, popular in South Texas, Florida, and Caribbean Latino communities.

The man looked good. He was elegant, traditional, and clearly knew how to carry himself.

He offered to buy me a drink, and somehow already knew what I had ordered earlier. I laughed and joked, "You must've been stalking me." He smiled and played along. Funny enough, he didn't even drink but still, he bought me one. We ended up dancing the rest of the night together, floating from the dance floor to the pool tables where he hustled like a pro. I watched him line up his shots and win game after game. I could play too just not like that.

There was something captivating about him calm, collected, observant. He didn't try too hard. He just was.

And for the first time in a long time, I felt like I could breathe.

Once it was time to leave the club that night, he offered to walk me to the truck where my cousins and aunt were waiting. We talked the whole way there light conversation, soft smiles, that magnetic kind of curiosity that happens when someone's brand new but feels strangely familiar. He asked if he could see me again, and I told him I wasn't from Dallas. He looked a little surprised and said he thought I was from Fort Worth. I ended up giving him my number anyway. I didn't think much of it.

When we got back to my aunt's apartment, we all went straight to bed. The next day was the Fourth of July, and we were planning to spend it out at Joe Pool Lake one of the local hot spots for family barbecues and lake days.

The next morning, I woke up to a text from him. It was sweet. He said he had a really good time and wanted to see me again before I left town. I replied and told him we were heading to Joe Pool Lake for the day, and he said he and his family were going too. It felt like fate. He asked if he could pick me up, and when I asked my cousins, they said they all knew him from school. I told my mom I was riding with him to meet everyone there she didn't really ask many questions.

When he pulled into my aunt's complex, he was driving a white Dodge pickup truck with custom wheels, loud speakers, and bright blue LED lights glowing from the handles of the doors. We could hear him before we saw him. Classic. The kind of entrance that makes your stomach flip, even if you won't admit it.

The lake day was fun. I met his friends and their girlfriends, and everyone was hanging out and drinking. One of my aunt's friends had a boat and was giving rides around the water, and the vibe was light. I had a few drinks, and of course, my "smoking habit" came right along with me. At some point, his parents showed up and that's when the mood shifted. His stepmom gave me a hard side-eye the minute she saw me. She didn't even try to hide it. Later, I overheard people whispering that she had made comments about me calling me names, saying I looked like "trash" (to keep it polite here). I wasn't surprised. People always had something to say. They didn't know me, my story, or where I was from. I didn't even expect to see any of them again, so I let it roll off me. But still... it stung.

He tried to get us on the family jet skis, but his parents said no. They didn't want me riding. That part felt personal. Still, we made the best of it. After the sun started to set, he asked if I wanted to go out again that night. I said yes. I was leaving the next day, and I didn't mind soaking in one more adventure before heading home.

When I got back to my aunt's, my cousins and aunt were waiting with gossip. They told me his family owned the club we had been at the night before. Suddenly, everything made sense how he was able to get us drinks despite being underage, how comfortable he seemed walking around that packed place. And why his stepmom looked at me like I was a gold-digger and treated me like I didn't belong.

That night, we went out again. This time, it was more chill. We played pool and talked most of the time. When we left, we grabbed some food before he dropped me off. My phone kept ringing during the drive, and he asked if I needed to get it. It was the California guy again. I sighed and explained that it was someone from my past. That we had history. That we'd been on and off for a long time. He nodded, but I could tell he didn't love it. I couldn't blame him.

When he dropped me off, I didn't think I'd see him again. But just before I got out, he leaned over and gave me the tiniest kiss barely a brush of the lips. Just a quiet goodnight.

The next day we packed up and drove back home. He texted me the entire ride. And then the next day. And the next. It turned into a thing a routine. We'd stay on the phone for hours. I'd be rambling about everything and nothing, and he'd just listen. He was my complete opposite. I was loud; he was calm. I was extroverted and always going out; he was introverted and more of a homebody. I drank; he didn't. But somehow it worked. We balanced each other out in a weird way.

Back home, life fell back into its usual rhythm school, work, survival. I talked to my dad on one of our calls and told him all about the trip. About the guy I met. About how judgmental his family had been. Dad didn't interrupt or correct me. He just listened. I loved that about him. It was one of the few places I could speak freely and not feel shut down.

Mom, on the other hand, wasn't even taking me to school on time anymore. Some mornings she'd stop to grab herself breakfast, making me late again and I'd be so embarrassed walking into class with everyone staring. It was like no one cared whether I made it or not. Except for Dad. And maybe this boy from Dallas, who kept checking in every day.

A few weeks later, he planned a summer trip to the Valley. He and his siblings wanted to visit South Padre Island, which was only about 45 minutes from where I lived. He asked if I could come with them. Said his brother and stepsister would be coming too. I told him I'd check with my mom. When I finally said yes, they planned to drive down and even asked if they could stay the night at my house before heading to the beach. I said sure even though I had a feeling his family still didn't like me. I was polite anyway. That's how I was raised. When they arrived, I opened the gate and welcomed them in. My parents had always taught me to have manners, especially with elders so I was nothing but respectful even when his stepmom gave me that same cold look. Again.

His brother asked if I could hook him up with something to smoke, and of course, I could. I knew people. Plenty of people. You know, those kinds of people. I made it happen, and we all headed to the beach the next morning. The trip turned out to be amazing. We took tons of pictures, swam, laughed, and relaxed. His parents had booked a really nice condo we each had our own rooms. It was like a little vacation home, and it felt peaceful.

That might've been the first time I ever got high. I didn't even smoke myself, but the secondhand smoke from his brother had me lightheaded and giggly. I remember laughing so hard I couldn't stop. I still don't even know what I was laughing at just that I couldn't breathe from how much I was cracking up. His brother and he were total opposites. It made me laugh even more.

We stayed at the beach for what felt like a full week. When it was time to leave, they dropped me back off at home and headed back to Dallas. And just like before... I didn't think I'd ever see him again.

While he was back in Dallas, nothing changed between us. We still talked almost every day. He would check in with me in the mornings and again at night. Some nights, we'd fall asleep on the phone together the soft hum of each other's breathing becoming a comfort neither of us wanted to hang up on.

He asked me if I'd ever come back to Dallas again, and I told him maybe, whenever we made another trip to visit my dad. He seemed hopeful every time I said it.

Over the phone, I learned more about his life. He lived with his dad and stepmom, helped out at her salon, and sometimes worked next door at the little music store they also owned. Apparently, both businesses shared the same building. He also helped his dad with club-related things errands, equipment, cleaning. It was a family hustle. And even though he moved quietly through the world, I could tell he carried a lot of weight on his shoulders too.

Eventually, another trip to visit my dad came up, and just like before, we passed through Dallas.

I got to see him again and that feeling returned. That mix of calm and curiosity, like time hadn't moved at all. I asked my mom if I could stay behind and finish school in Dallas. I told her I wanted to stay with my aunt and keep dating him. She didn't say much. I don't think she had the energy to fight me on it.

When I brought it up to my aunt, she gave me a look half surprised, half-amused and said she had originally hoped he'd end up dating one of her daughters, my cousins. But then she added, "You're like a daughter to me too," so either way, she didn't seem to mind.

I stayed at her apartment with them, hopeful. But within a week, everything changed.

She started charging me rent. Out of nowhere, she said I needed to "make him responsible" and start asking him to give me money to pay her. That wasn't something I felt comfortable doing and definitely not something I expected from someone who claimed to see me like her own.

He would still pick me up to go out to eat, to hang out, to go swimming. But now, my aunt insisted I bring one of my cousins with me. Every time. Later, she started saying I needed to bring both of them. She said it wasn't fair to include one and not the other. Suddenly, my every move had rules.

To avoid the constant guilt-tripping and pressure, I started spending more time at his place. I felt safer there, even if it was temporary.

But eventually, his stepmom found out I had been staying over. And she was furious.

She pulled him aside and scolded him for letting me stay in her house. He told her I was only there because he wasn't feeling well said he had caught a stomach bug and I was just helping out while he rested. But she didn't care. She looked me dead in the eyes and told me I needed to leave.

It was humiliating. No matter how kind or respectful I was, she never gave me a chance.

Not long after that, he asked me to make things official to be his girlfriend, to move in, to stay. But everything around me felt like it was crumbling.

My aunt was still demanding rent. I didn't have a job anymore, and I hadn't even enrolled in school yet. I had no way of paying her the large sum she was asking for, and I wasn't about to start using someone else to cover it for me. I wasn't raised that way .

I didn't know what to do. I didn't know whether to call my mom and admit I needed to come back home or to push harder and try to make things work in Dallas. But the truth was, I didn't feel wanted in either place. I didn't want to go back home… but I didn't want to stay where I clearly wasn't welcome, either.

I felt stuck between two walls. Nowhere felt soft. Nowhere felt like mine.

Chapter 14

Monster-in-Law, Minor in Survival

Mom was finally taking another trip up to see my dad. She planned to head back to Oregon afterward, and on her way out, she stopped by to see me. My boyfriend and I sat her down and told her what we had been thinking that maybe it was time we moved in together and enrolled in school together. We asked if she thought it would be okay. She didn't love the idea. You could see it in her face. But we were persistent. We said we were serious. We wanted to do it the right way. Eventually, she just shrugged and said she wasn't going to tell me what to do.

So, I stayed.

When he and I moved in together, reality hit quick. The struggle showed up fast and loud. Looking back now, as an adult, I understand why it happened the way it did. I should've known it was coming. But I didn't not really. I was young, hopeful, trying to build a new life on a foundation that wasn't even finished.

The first blow came fast: Mom disconnected my phone. Just like that, I was left with nothing. No car, no phone, no real safety net. I had chosen this new path and she made sure I walked it alone.

His parents weren't thrilled either. Actually, it was mostly his stepmom. From the beginning, she had been cold, short, and sharp. Mean, really. She never made an effort to hide her dislike for me. His dad didn't say much. A man of few words. He never really addressed me directly not in front of her, anyway

We both enrolled in a local Private Christian academy so we could finish school and finally get our high school diplomas. That part, at least, I'm proud of. We followed through. We finished. His parents paid for his tuition. I paid for mine by working.

I lied about my age and told them I was 18 so I could get hired. I landed a job at a place called Silver Leaf Resort as a customer service rep. I used his phone to apply, to do interviews, to check in with my mom, to take return calls. I didn't have many ways to stay connected. I only got to talk to my dad when he called my aunt's house and even then, I had to be careful. There was always someone listening in. There was never enough privacy to really speak my mind.

At Silver Leaf, I actually did well. Really well. I learned my call script word for word within days and nailed every customer interaction like it was second nature. I hit my numbers, earned my bonuses, and even got sent home early with pay because I was outperforming everyone else. I remember holding that first real paycheck in my hand like it was gold. It felt like proof that I was capable. That I wasn't just surviving; I was doing something.

But without a car, getting home was always complicated. I had to call him to come pick me up after work and some days, I'd wait hours outside. Just sitting there. Watching the sky change color, thinking about how pointless it felt to clock out only to be stranded. More than once, I thought to myself, "I should've just stayed inside and kept working."

I think 16 and 17 were the years I became the most rebellious but not in the way people assume. It wasn't about sneaking out or chasing trouble. It was survival mode mixed with immaturity, clashing in real-time. I didn't know how life worked, but I was desperate to figure it out. Even if I had to fall on my face first.

Eventually, the pressure started building. His parents started complaining about the phone bill. His stepmom told him I was running up minutes by calling my mom too often. One day, he told me flatout: "They don't want you using my phone anymore."

I was humiliated.

But instead of breaking down, I turned that shame into fire. I walked into a Sprint store alone with no clue what I needed or if they'd even help me. I didn't have credit. I didn't even really know what credit was. But I told them I needed a phone, and I'd do whatever it took to get it.

And somehow, I qualified. I walked out of there with a phone that looked like a brick big, bulky, and ugly but it worked. I even got a second line and gave it to him. I was tired of asking. Tired of begging. Tired of being made to feel like a burden in a house I didn't belong in.

That moment changed something in me. The fire in my chest wasn't just frustration it was hunger. I had heard what his stepmom said about me. I heard it with my own ears. Heard her shouting that I was trash, a gold digger, a leech. Every ugly name she could come up with, she threw it my way.

And I took it personally.

But instead of shrinking, I swore to myself "I'm going to show her who's daughter I am."

I wasn't raised soft. I wasn't raised to stay silent while someone disrespected me. I was raised by survivors, by hustlers, by people who made something out of nothing. And if she wanted to see me as less I'd rise just to spite her.

I confronted him a few times. Asked him flat-out why he never defended me. Why he never stood up to his stepmom. Why he let me be humiliated in a house I was trying so hard to be accepted in.

All he said was, "I didn't know how."

I'm not going to lie that answer made my blood boil. I was already upset with him, but I was even more upset with myself. I started questioning everything every decision that led me to that moment. I felt so foolish for choosing to stay. For trying to build something real with someone who barely had a voice of his own.

He didn't have work ethic. He wasn't grounded. He came off like a mommy-and-daddy's boy quiet, dependent, soft-spoken to a fault. Turns out that one time I thought he had a stomach bug? It wasn't a one-time thing. He was just… always sick. Constant stomach issues. Constant excuses.

And then there was the fact that he'd never even left Dallas. Not once. He didn't know the world. Had never traveled, had never seen anything beyond his street, his circle, his comfort zone. He knew nothing outside of his parents' home. And here I was 16, exhausted, trying to work, trying to love, trying to find some version of freedom with a boy who couldn't stand on his own two feet. I felt trapped. Dumb. But I reminded myself: I brought myself here. So I'm going to ride it out.

I wrote to my dad. I kept the letter short and clean. I gave him my new number, but I left out everything I wanted so badly to say. All the pain. All the rejection. All the loneliness. I wanted to run to him. To lay my head on his chest and spill everything from day one to what I was currently living through. But I didn't want to worry him. So I told him I was okay. I asked for advice on work, kept the tone light, and kept pushing forward like everything was fine.

It wasn't long after that I got my second or maybe third paycheck from work and suddenly, everything shifted again. His stepmom pulled him aside and had a talk with him. She told him she'd buy him a brand new truck… if he left me.

Just like that. It was me or the truck.

I think it really got to him. Something changed. He started acting different. Distant. Cold. On my days off, he'd leave me home alone for hours and go out with his parents. He'd go out to eat with his dad, knowing I had no car and barely anything to eat. Knowing I didn't feel welcome in their kitchen. Knowing I had no other options. I tried everything I could to change her mind about me. I started deep cleaning her entire house. Every inch. Every drawer. Every floorboard. It was my silent way of saying, I'm not trash. I was raised right. I'm clean. I'm respectful. I'm not what you think I am. She never asked me to do any of it, I just did. I wanted her to like me.

The house was huge, so I worked in sections. They were all night owls late nights at the club, long hours at the salon so they slept during the day. I took full advantage of that quiet time. I scrubbed every bathroom, steamed the floors, organized closets, cleaned out drawers. I worked at my job, and I worked in that house all while carrying the weight of not knowing what came next.

Then one day, she came home in a good mood.

She looked around and said, "You did a great job," then handed me a hundred-dollar bill and told me to go shopping. I didn't even know how to respond. That might've been the only time she acknowledged my effort and even then, it felt more like a tip than a gesture of kindness. I took the money. But the ache stayed.

Later, his brother's girlfriend moved in. She was older than all of us, but she was kind. She never looked at me with judgment, never spoke down to me. For a moment, it felt like I had someone in the house I could actually talk to.

But it didn't take long to notice how differently she was treated.

The stepmom doted on her. Favored her. Gave her praise and respect I had never seen even though behind closed doors, she still spoke badly about her, too. But not to her face. Not like she did with me.

It hit me then: this wasn't just about me. She didn't like my boyfriend either because he wasn't her biological son. It was clear as day. She spoiled her own child and treated mine like an afterthought. All the puzzle pieces came together. It wasn't just personal it was petty. It was territorial.

Eventually, he and I had a fight. I don't even remember what triggered it, but I broke. I called one of my cousins and asked him to come pick me up. He did. I packed a bag and left.

But of course, my boyfriend called me that same night, crying. Begging. Telling me not to give up. That we could make it through this. That we could figure it out together. The next day, he came and picked me up, and I went back.

I kept working. Kept trying to be independent. Kept showing up for myself in all the quiet ways no one saw. I never asked them for anything not for a ride, not for food, not for money. I stayed in my lane. I kept my head down.

But the truth was I was tired.

Tired of proving myself in a house that wanted me gone.

Tired of being the girl no one believed in.

And still… I stayed.

A few days passed like nothing, and then one morning I woke up to a letter on the floor just outside the bedroom door. It was a handwritten note. From his stepmom.

It read:

"Grab one spoon and one fork from the kitchen and you have until the end of the day to move out."

That was it. No explanation. No conversation. No reason. Just a cheap piece of paper and a cold command. My heart sank. I didn't need context. I already knew she never liked me. Not once.

But to be fair… she didn't like him either.

It wasn't just me she disrespected. She belittled him, too. And his dad? Said nothing. Did nothing. He never stepped in. Never defended him. Never protected me. He just watched quiet and expressionless like we were strangers on the side of the road.

I showed him the note and asked if he could speak to his dad just to buy us some time. I didn't have anyone I could run to. Not my mom, and definitely not my aunt, who had already tried to charge me $800 after letting me stay at her apartment for two or three weeks when I was only 17. It was ridiculous. I felt completely stuck, but I told him I'd manage. I just needed time to figure it out.

After he spoke with his dad, they made us an offer if you could even call it that. They said we could move into a wooden house next door. It was old. Falling apart. No electricity. And it had rats.

I didn't hesitate.

I took it. No questions asked. Because in my head, I already had a plan. I picked my chin up, nodded, and told myself, "Let's go." It wasn't about pride anymore. It was survival. If no one else was going to take care of me, I'd do it myself.

He still wasn't working. Hadn't applied to a single job. Didn't even know how. So I told him to keep doing what he could do drive me to work. That was the deal. I covered the rest. I was paying for both phones, handling everything around the house, getting the electricity turned on, and making sure we had a bed to sleep in. I didn't ask him for much just not to get in my way.

Still, I hadn't told my dad anything. Every time he called, I swallowed the lump in my throat, smiled through the phone, and said I was doing fine. I told him work was good. I told him I was figuring things out.

He didn't know I had taken myself to Planned Parenthood to get on birth control.

He didn't know I was visiting a gas station every week just to look at job boards and apartment flyers.

He didn't know that at 17, I was out here making real-life decisions with no map, no support, and no backup plan.

But I had grit. I had instinct. I used my head, moved in silence, and fought for every little bit of peace I could find.

Eventually, my boyfriend took me to meet more of his family grandparents, aunts, uncles, his biological sister. But that didn't go well either. It was always something. A side-eye. A backhanded compliment. A cold silence that made my stomach twist.

His grandfather had started getting sick, so we were visiting more often. He'd sit in his old rocking chair while the family circled around him. I never said much to him. I'd sit next to him sometimes, just quietly, unsure of what to say. I was carrying so much so much regret, confusion, heaviness. I was tired.

Still, I felt for him.

He had never been rude to me. Never disrespectful. Honestly, he barely spoke at all. But his presence did something to me. Watching him in that chair aging, fragile, tired it stirred something deep. It made me think of my own dad. How much I missed him. How much I wished I could call him and tell him everything. How much I needed him, even after everything.

My dad had been harsh. Tempered. Abusive, even. And while I hated him for the pain he'd caused me, I was starting to understand what some of it came from. Not excusing it. But seeing it differently now that I was growing up. I wanted to give him credit but I couldn't. Not yet. I was still too hurt.

Then one day we got the call. His grandfather had been hospitalized. He wasn't doing well.

While I was at work, my boyfriend would go visit him. After work, he'd come pick me up and take me back home. Eventually, the doctors sent him home on hospice. His illness was terminal. Cancer.

One of his uncles opened up his home and made it available for hospice to come in so that family could visit, sit by his bedside, and say goodbye. His last days were spent surrounded by people. People who loved him. People who saw him.

And even though I didn't know him well, even though I had barely spoken a word to him, a part of me sat quietly with the realization:

That man had a place to die. I didn't even have a place to live.

Not long after, I went with my boyfriend to visit his grandfather again and that was the first time I officially met his biological sister. As soon as I walked into the house, the energy was off. The uncles were making jokes, loud enough for everyone to hear. They kept nudging her, saying things like, "So what do you think of your new sister-in-law?"

And she didn't hesitate.

"She's not my sister-in-law," she replied coldly.

The adults laughed like it was funny, but I felt the sting deep in my chest. It was an ugly feeling to be in a room full of adults who judged you, who dismissed you, who laughed at your pain like it was entertainment. I sat there quietly, my face blank, but inside… I was over it. So over it.

They kept making little comments to my boyfriend too about how nice it was that he finally had his own phone. I just blinked and let it slide. Deep down, I knew he hadn't done a damn thing to make that happen. I had paid for both phones. I had put both lines under my credit. But I didn't say a word. I let him pop his collar and enjoy the spotlight because, truthfully, I was still grateful. If he hadn't been driving me to work every day, I wouldn't have had the opportunity to make money at all. I showed appreciation where I could, and I carried the rest with grace.

His stepmom had canceled his original phone line because I was using it. And my mom had disconnected mine the second I decided to stay in Dallas. It felt like both sides of our lives had completely abandoned us financially, emotionally, and in every way that mattered.

He and I started arguing more. The fights were small but frequent. Always about the same thing: his lack of effort. His lack of work ethic. I was out here doing everything paying bills, job-hunting, planning our next steps and every time I told him I was done, that I was leaving, he'd swear he was going to change. "I'm going to start applying," he'd say. "I promise."

Then one day, in mid-November, I got pulled into the office at work. My manager sat me down with this serious look on his face. I had no idea what was going on. Then he said, "We found out you're 17. Not 18."

I froze.

He told me he was impressed by me my numbers were incredible, my performance was consistent, and my work ethic was better than most adults he'd hired. But legally, he couldn't keep me on payroll. Not yet. He said I could come back the moment I turned 18 and he meant it. He had heard bits and pieces about my life outside of work, and I could tell it genuinely hurt him to let me go. I didn't cry until I walked out the door.

That same day, I called my mom. She was still in Oregon. I begged her to let me come back just for a while. I told her I was homesick. That I had no support, no stability, and no one who truly cared. I didn't tell my dad. I didn't want to worry him. I kept it all inside, but my heart felt like it was breaking in slow motion.

My boyfriend spoke to his dad, and surprisingly, his dad agreed to buy me a plane ticket. But with one condition: the trip had to be permanent. I was either leaving for good, or not at all.

Fine, "I thought". I'll take the flight.

When I landed in Oregon, my mom picked me up and brought me back to the camper she was staying in. I stayed with her for a little while, still doing my online coursework and pushing to finish my high school diploma. I didn't plan to stay long and honestly, things hadn't changed much at home. I could already feel the same pressure building: the unspoken expectation that I'd watch my little brothers, stay quiet, take up less space. The tension. The rumors. The lack of peace.

I refused to shrink back into that version of myself.

While I was there, I took the opportunity to open up to my mom. Really open up. I told her everything how his family treated me, the way I felt cornered, belittled, unwanted. I told her I didn't want to tell my dad because I knew what he was capable of if he found out. The anger. The retaliation. The chaos it could stir.

One of my friends came to visit me during that time too. I vented to her told her everything. And I'll never forget what she said.

"Why are they even calling you a gold digger?" she asked.

"Do they even know anything about you? Do they know what kind of house your family lives in? Do they know who your dad is?"

She laughed in disbelief.

"Girl, if you really love him, then stop playing nice. Show them who you are."

I just smiled and shook it off. But something in me clicked.

That night, I took the longest shower I had taken in weeks. I washed my hair, straightened it, and sat in silence, letting my mind wander. I gave myself a full self-care moment not out of vanity, but out of grounding. I needed to feel like myself again. I needed to see myself clearly before I went back into the storm.

The next morning, I boarded a flight back to Texas.

During that trip, I had a long layover at some airport I can't remember where exactly, but I do remember sitting at a food court with a little money in my pocket from work, and some cash my mom had given me. I went to get something to eat and found a small table to sit at.

A man approached me and asked if he could sit down. I told him I didn't mind.

I was half-scrolling through my phone, half-journaling writing down goals, sketching out a game plan for what I needed to do once I got back to Dallas. I was deep in thought when he returned with a coffee and sat across from me. We started talking casual, surface level conversation. He asked where I was from. I kept my answers short. My dad always told me never to give out personal details to strangers. So I was careful.

But something about him was kind. Familiar. Gentle.

He introduced himself.

Charley Clark.

The Charley Clark.

Charley Clark Nissan.

LOL.

And that's how I met him. At a random airport, in the middle of one of the hardest moments of my life while I was quietly planning my next move, thinking no one saw me.

But somehow, the universe did.

He introduced himself. He was warm, kind, and super friendly. We ended up having lunch and talking for what felt like hours. He shared a little about his background and told me that if I was ever back in the Valley and needed anything anything at all I could call him. He gave me his number, shook my hand, and that was it.

Charley Clark.

Yes, that Charley Clark.

It was such a random moment in such a strange season of my life and somehow, that brief encounter left a mark. Like the universe was reminding me, You're still seen.

But when I got back to Dallas, it was like hitting a brick wall all over again. The nightmare picked up right where I left it. Only this time, I came back with a plan.

I had gone to a job interview right before the trip, and they called while I was away to offer me the position. I was scheduled to start that same week. My boyfriend and I were still spending time at his dad's club here and there, and I started seeing my cousins and my aunt more often, which gave me some sense of familiarity.

But in the quiet hours, when I was alone the cracks began to show.

I had started doing drugs occasionally. Nothing heavy, but it was enough to make me feel like I was escaping for a little while. It usually happened during those late nights, on weekends or my days off moments where I just didn't want to feel anything. His brother would come over and smoke, and I'd take shotgun hits from him. And even when I didn't, just being in the room meant I'd end up high. I never liked the feeling, but I hated the weight I was carrying even more.

Then one weekend, I got a call from back home in South Texas the Valley.

Our house had been broken into.

Mom was still in Oregon. There was no one else around to help. No one to check on the damage. I didn't even have a car. So I asked my aunt if I could borrow hers just long enough to drive down and file the police report. She hesitated, but eventually agreed. I loaded up with one of my cousins and hit the road in her white Tahoe.

Mid-trip, everything flipped literally.

There was a truck pulling a camper ahead of me, swerving in and out of lanes. The camper suddenly flipped, and in a split second, I tried to swerve around it. I lost control. My tires spun, and I slammed into the center cement divider. Then we spun again. And again.

We hit hard.

By the grace of God, we were okay. Other drivers stopped to check on us. Several other cars crashed too. The whole freeway turned into chaos. I didn't even have a license at the time and I knew that if police arrived, they'd tow my aunt's car. So I quickly moved it to a nearby dealership parking lot and waited.

My aunt showed up a few hours later. Thankfully, she had insurance and was able to report the accident. Somehow, she got it all handled but then she turned to me and asked for the deductible: $500.

I was stunned. I didn't even fully understand what a deductible was yet. I told my mom about it because my aunt kept pushing me to pay it. But the truth was I had just started working again. I was barely making ends meet. I was trying to stand on my own two feet.

After that, I didn't really see my family much anymore. And I decided that mom would have to figure out what to do about the house on her own. I was done trying to fix things that were never mine to carry. When I got back to Dallas, I tried to process everything. The accident. The guilt. The pressure. The silence. But it all boiled over one day while I was cooking lunch a huge rat ran across my food in the kitchen. That was my final straw.

I was done.

My boyfriend still wasn't doing much. He would leave me at the house for hours while he went out to eat with his dad. He knew I didn't have a car. He knew I couldn't leave. His stepmom, I'm sure, was entertained by it all like this was her twisted version of justice. And his sister? She started dropping her kids off at our door. Literally. She'd leave them on the steps of the old wooden house, and suddenly I was changing diapers, watching toddlers, and bringing them with us wherever we went.

I knew she was doing her best, too. But I didn't leave home to raise my siblings just to come here and do it all over again. I had things I wanted to do. I had goals. I wanted more.

By then, my boyfriend had opened up a little more. He told me more about how they were raised. About the way their stepmom treated them. About how their dad never stood up for them either. And as much as I wanted to hold space for that pain, I had to remind myself:

That's not my story to tell.

This is my life.

My book.

My truth.

And my truth was this: I was exhausted. I was done begging for decency.

So I made a move.

I applied for an apartment. I wanted out of that wooden house. Out of that yard. Out of that family dynamic. I wanted peace, silence, and space to rebuild.

That's when I found out my mom had used my credit while I was still living with her. There were power bills in collections and other utility accounts opened under my name now showing up as derogatory marks on my credit report. I was devastated.

Still... I was approved for the apartment. And I'm grateful, because if I hadn't taken that step, I would've never known. I kept working, and I kept job-hunting, too. I knew I could find something better-paying, but I wasn't about to let go of the opportunity I already had. I had also officially finished at the Christian academy. I took online classes to speed it up, got my transcripts, and had it all in hand. Diploma in check.

I had also enrolled in Business Fundamentals. Business management and ownership. I was buying money management books, studying during my breaks, and using every spare minute to build something smarter. Stronger. Mine.

I started picking up overtime. I was locked in. Focused. I saved every penny I could. And eventually, I saved enough to make a down payment on my own car.

On my day off, I told my boyfriend to take me to a few dealerships. I wasn't about to buy a junk car I needed something clean, reliable, and worth the work I'd put in. After a few stops, I found it. A small black Alero. Dainty. Cute. Mine.

I signed the papers. My credit was pulled. I drove off the lot.

I had done it. My first car. On my own.

That moment? That was freedom. I had my own job. My own car. My own phone. My own money. Finally, mine.

And for the first time…

I started sending my dad money from my paychecks just little bits here and there, to help with anything he needed. I told him to call me at least twice a week.

And this time, when he called…

I told him everything.

Chapter 15

I Am My Father's Shadow, The Untamable Lamb, Birthed by a Lion

Since I finally had my own everything my own job, my own car, and even my own place (okay, it was an apartment, but still, my apartment, I was finally able to sit in my own quiet space and talk to my dad. Really talk. I spilled everything. All the tea.

I had kept certain things from him before, mostly what happened between Mom and me when I still lived with her. Not because I was protecting her exactly, but because I knew how he'd react. I didn't want him blowing up or stressing from behind bars, not when there was nothing he could do about it. But everything else? He knew. The drugs. The parties. The work. The pain. The people. I held nothing back.

I sent my dad money from every paycheck like it was a bill I owed. Non-negotiable. I even sent extra when my little brother needed stuff for school. That was my responsibility too. I scheduled time off from work just to make the four-hour drive from Dallas to visit him. Just me and him one-on-one.

I had questions, and I needed answers. I was desperate for direction, craving something solid. Something safe. I was trying to rebuild my life, and every part of me kept gravitating toward my dad. We were alike in ways I was only just beginning to understand. The same fire. The same pride. The same hunger. We were both fighters and because of that, we fought each other hard. Always had. That part didn't stop just because I got older. One call would be calm and supportive. The next, a battlefield. Like pulling the pin on a grenade and waiting for the boom. We both wanted control. We both had something to prove. I think deep down, I was just tired of feeling dumb, used, and left out of every good thing in life. And he was tired of feeling powerless.

On one of those visits, we got into it. Again. He hated not being able to protect me. I told him everything how my boyfriend's family treated me, how my credit got ruined, how I was trying to fix everything on my own. His blood pressure practically rose through the phone. He was livid. Said he was going to "send people" to handle it. I believed him. His words were sharp, violent, full of heat. He meant it.

I begged him not to do anything reckless. "I'm strong enough," I told him. "I can handle this. I promise." He didn't like it, but he backed off for the moment.

"Remember whose daughter you are," he said. "I might not have been the best father, but over my dead body are they gonna treat you like that."

I told him that's exactly why I didn't say anything sooner because this was what I was afraid of. He needed to calm down. Eventually we cooled off. We sat side by side, eating honey buns and wings from the vending machines in the visitation room like nothing happened. That was our rhythm. Fire, then food. Fight, then pretend.

But something had shifted. I started realizing I held the power now. As awful as it sounds, I was the one on the outside. I had choices. I had freedom. And he didn't. I started putting my foot down more. Even caught a little attitude with him during visits. There was one time I told him I'd walk out of that room if he didn't calm down. He looked at me straight in the face and said, "Don't you dare embarrass me like that."

I looked right back and said, "Try me."

That's when it really hit me I am him. More than I ever admitted. More than I ever realized. The soft-hearted, rose-colored glasses were coming off. I was finally seeing things clearly. And I undertood something important: I didn't have to let that fire turn into destruction. I could flip it. I could use all of this pain this heat, this hunger, this generational weight and build something beautiful with it. I didn't know what yet. But there was a little spark in me that had finally caught flame.

My dad, for all his flaws, could still see parts of me that I didn't. He told me often that he hated the relationship I was in. He wanted more for me, someone who could provide, who could lead, who had real ambition. He didn't care much about education; to him, it was about hustle. About grind. About showing up and never folding. And he thought I was wasting my potential.

He apologized constantly told me he was sorry he failed me. Said it killed him to watch me struggle through life the way I was. I always shook it off. Told him not to say that. I defended my boyfriend, even when I knew he wasn't stepping up. I tried to make my dad understand told him about my boyfriend's upbringing, how his biological mom had sold him as a baby, how he was raised mostly by his grandparents, and how his dad was barely a father figure. I told him I believed in him. That I could help him become something. That maybe one day, he'd be so supportive and successful that I wouldn't even need to work anymore.

My dad didn't agree not for one second but he promised to be cool. To keep it light. To trust me. He didn't say it out loud, but I think he knew I needed to learn some lessons on my own.

A few months later, my boyfriend's grandfather passed away. It was a heavy time for their family, and even though I was already carrying a lot inside, I tried to be as supportive as I could. I showed up, stood by him, kept it together no matter how I really felt or everything that had already happened between us.

At this point, my boyfriend was still dragging his feet with everything in life. He kept saying he had job interviews lined up, but somehow, every time one came around, he'd get sick to his stomach again. Like clockwork. It felt like I had to monitor him, babysit him, make sure he was okay all the time. And honestly? I was exhausted. He was sick all the time. And I wasn't stupid I had already started crafting my exit strategy in my mind. I didn't have it all figured out, but I knew one thing: I'd rather struggle alone than keep struggling with someone who kept holding me down instead of lifting me up.

After the funeral, the family decided to go out to eat. It was a big group a whole crowd and they picked a well-known Mexican restaurant in town. We talked about it ahead of time and agreed we could afford it. I made sure we had the budget to go. When we got to the restaurant, they sat the whole family at one long party-style table in a private room. I already knew what it was giving and I wanted no part of it. I asked for a separate table right away.

I wasn't trying to be rude I just had boundaries now. I'd already gotten a taste of how his family moved, and I didn't want to pretend like everything was sweet. We could show up, be respectful, but keep our distance. That was fair.

When the waiter came, I made it very clear: "Separate tab, please." The waiter was a friendly older Mexican man, and he nodded like he understood completely. My boyfriend didn't see the point asked if it was really necessary. I looked him dead in the face and said, "Yes. It is."

I was the one working. I was the one paying. I was the one making the decisions.

When we finished eating, we closed our own tab, paid in full, and got up. I thanked the family for including us and let them know we were heading out. As we made our way to the door, one of his uncles stood up and called out, "Nah, nephew you can't leave. You gotta pay!"

I laughed. Loud. Because something in me already knew they were going to pull that. It was so predictable.

I stayed quiet and let my boyfriend speak for himself. "We paid our own," he said.

I nodded, calm but clear. "Ask the waiter. We handled our tab."

Silence hit that table like a slap. Nobody said a word. Not one person.

And we walked off.

As soon as we hit the outside doors, I jumped up so high and told my boyfriend, "Give me a high five!" I was hype. "Tell me that wasn't the best feeling ever!" I said. "To have your own. To hold your own. That's real power."

He nodded. He felt it too. And I told him, "Keep that energy. Step up. This is what grown life feels like."

It might have seemed like a small win to anyone else, but for me? It was a moment. A big one.

Meanwhile, my mom was dealing with her own chaos back in Oregon. She had finally returned home and said the house was completely destroyed. It had been broken into and torn apart. People stole so much. She even said there were human fetuses left in the middle of the living room. I couldn't even wrap my head around that part. The whole place had been violated. Photos were taken. Reports were made. Almost everything of value was gone.

I listened. I let her vent. But I didn't take it on. I couldn't. I had too much already. And deep down, I had always known their things were never mine. I never walked around saying we owned that house or we owned the businesses. It was always theirs. Their cars. Their companies. Their legacy. Not mine.

Even though Dad used to say, "You're never gonna have to worry about anything," it was clear by now that things weren't going to work out that way. If I wanted something, I had to get it myself.

That year I turned 18. Officially grown. I decided to stick with my job a little longer. I had the chance to go back to Silverleaf Resort, but I didn't take it. I was making good money with the advertising company I worked for. I got paid hourly plus commission, and I was killing it. My job was to create community calendars and get local businesses to buy ad space in them. Every company I signed? I got a cut. And depending on the size of their ad, that could be $800 off one deal. I was good at it naturally.

And even if I didn't land a sale, I still got paid hourly just for making calls. I loved the rhythm of it. The independence. The confidence it gave me. I decided to stay.

I built up PTO quickly, and my boss loved me. If I needed time off to visit Dad or study for school, it was approved. No questions asked.

I rarely went down to the Valley or saw my mom I was building my life now.

That Christmas was the first one I got to fully decorate my own tree. Buy the things I wanted. It felt magical. Music, lights, big gifts all mine. I finally bought myself that stereo system I had wanted since I was a kid. You remember the one? I even got a karaoke machine, and when I was home alone I would sing my lungs out like I was in Madison Square Garden.

One time, the complex manager was doing her walk of the property and heard the music blasting. She knocked on my door, and I opened it still holding the microphone in my hand. I was so embarrassed. But she just laughed and said, "Well, I can see you're having fun! I hate to interrupt, but do you mind turning it down just a little so we don't get any complaints?"

I laughed, apologized, and turned it down but I was still cracking up the whole time. That memory makes me laugh to this day.

That winter, it even snowed in Dallas. A soft, beautiful snow that just made everything feel extra magical. I was so happy. Things were finally feeling steady. I was handling business. Taking care of myself. Sending money to my dad. Watching over my little brothers from a distance the best I could.

I was young, but I was in it. Standing on my own two feet. Learning how to lead myself.

As the year rolled over, things felt steady for the first time in a long while. Work was flowing, my schedule was my own, and life had a rhythm I didn't want to disrupt. It wasn't perfect, but it was stable enough to feel almost like peace. My relationship with my boyfriend was still rocky always a little up and down but I kept making it work. We'd go out to eat here and there, and he would help his dad out with side work to bring in some money since he still didn't have a real job. I covered most of the bills and most of the meals, but truthfully? I didn't mind. I wasn't completely alone anymore, and I was proud of how well I was doing for myself. Even if I wasn't sure about our forever, I was sure about my right now, and I gave it my all.

Sometimes, though, I would drive myself crazy knowing I had complete control over my life my job, my home, my finances but I had no control over my love life. I knew exactly what I wanted from life except in romance. My dad had always drilled into my head that I'd be a lawyer or some kind of powerhouse professional a successful, single, rich aunt with no kids and no husband. And for a long time, I thought I wanted that too. So I'd laugh and tell myself, "This is my now. Make the best of it. Nothing's broken, so what is there to fix?" I genuinely cared for my boyfriend and didn't want to leave him, so I stayed. A huge part of me also wanted to push him so hard that he could become something great not just for him, but to leave his family speechless. That fire in me to prove people wrong never went out. It made me angry to see them treat him like he was nothing, and I wanted to show them they were wrong.

During the holidays, his family wasn't the kind that got together for big celebrations, so we mostly spent time with my side of the family at least those who were in Dallas. My grandma P (my mom's mom) would come visit, and I always loved when she did. She brought a warmth with her that felt like home. That year, in April right before Easter, my mom passed through Dallas on her way to see my dad he was still in Pollock, Louisiana and asked if I wanted to tag along. I said yes without even thinking. She let me drive part of the way, and we left around 4 a.m. so we could make it there by 8 and have a full-day visit. I remember it like it was yesterday. We even got stopped by a cop on a rest area exit and got a ticket for going over 45 mph. It was such a random moment, but it's burned into my memory. Later that morning, as we got closer to the prison, I told Mom I was starving. I was craving a biscuit with grape jelly. We stopped, grabbed food, and kept driving. When we finally arrived, the visit with Dad was calm almost tender. We talked, we caught up, and for once, there was no yelling. It felt like a good day. When we left and drove back to Dallas, we started getting everything ready for Easter Sunday. We did the egg hunt and everything. It was simple, but it was good. I sat next to my grandma the whole time because I had missed her so much, and we talked for what felt like forever.

At one point, Grandma looked at me closely and asked if I had been crying. I told her no, but she kept staring at my eyes. "They're glossy," she said. "I think you're pregnant." I laughed and told her there was no way. I'd been on birth control forever never missed a dose. I had always been firm that I didn't want kids, and my family made it a whole thing every time I said it because almost everyone else already had children. But for me, the thought still carried old trauma. Even though Dad and I had built a better relationship by now, I still remembered how harsh my childhood discipline had been. The spankings. The punishments. How we'd be made to kneel against the wall with our hands up until our arms burned. If we fell asleep, we'd have to start over. We were hit with whatever was nearby a shoe, a belt, a fly swatter. Anything. It wasn't always good. It left marks on my body and my spirit that didn't fade easily. So truthfully I didn't think I could conceive.

One time, at my cousin's house, I watched her try to give her baby medicine for a runny nose. The baby didn't want to take it, kept crying, and she snapped started slapping him out of frustration. I immediately stood up, walked out, and didn't say a word. I couldn't watch it. It was triggering. Even as an adult, I can't witness violence. My body remembers it. So when Easter was over, I went home, put myself together, and went to bed. I had work the next morning, and my routine was always to walk in with a smile, say hello to everyone at their cubicles, and start my day loud and cheerful, even if inside I was carrying things. Later that day, one of my coworkers an older woman who'd kind of taken me under her wing asked if I wanted to take lunch with her. She was sweet, funny, and even kept a "curse jar" for me on my desk. Every time I swore, she'd make me drop a dime in it. "You're too pretty to be cussing like that," she'd say.

That day at lunch, I stood up to join her and suddenly got super lightheaded. I almost fell. My knees went weak, the room tilted, and for a second I thought I was going to pass out. My coworker immediately rushed to help me and guided me back into my chair. I tried to brush it off, but she wasn't having it. She insisted we step outside to get some fresh air and something to eat. "Come on, little thing," she said, using the nickname she'd given me because of how small I was. At the time I couldn't have weighed more than 115 pounds. I still slipped into size-zero jeans my frame was naturally petite and toned from all my years on drill team in high school but this wasn't that kind of fit. This was weight loss from stress, from survival, from quietly carrying too much.

That night after work, my mind wouldn't settle. My grandma's words echoed in my head. The dizziness. The weight loss. I tried to convince myself it was just exhaustion. But something in me knew. On my way home, I stopped at the store and bought a Clearblue pregnancy test one of the "fancy" expensive ones with the digital screen. I remember clutching the box in my hands like it was a bomb and feeling my heart pound. I told myself I'd take it in the morning when I was calm.

The next morning, my little apartment felt quiet but heavy. It was a two-story with the master bedroom upstairs, and the master had its own bathroom. I had a pile of laundry waiting, so I tried to start the day normally. I got up, took the test, and set it down on the counter. I remember praying whispering under my breath that it would be negative. "Please God. Please, please no." I walked out and kept doing laundry, trying to distract myself.

I'd actually forgotten about it for a few minutes. I was putting clean towels away in the bathroom cabinet over the toilet when I glanced down and saw it blinking. One word. "PREGNANT."

My knees gave out. I dropped to the floor and let out a scream from somewhere deep inside me. It wasn't even a word it was a sound of shock and grief and fear all mixed together. My boyfriend came running. I hadn't told him I'd bought a test, hadn't even hinted that I suspected anything. My scream scared him.

He burst into the doorway, eyes wide, asking what happened. The little toilet room had its own door inside the bathroom and I swung it shut, locking it so quickly it almost caught my fingers. He knocked over and over, asking me to open up. His voice was panicked, but I couldn't answer. My whole body was trembling. My tears were hot, my chest tight, my breath shallow.

Please," he kept saying. "Open the door, tell me what's wrong."

I pressed my back to the door and tried to catch my breath, but the sobs kept coming. I wanted to disappear. I wanted time to rewind. I finally managed to choke out, "Give me a second. Please. Just give me a second."

I was still sitting on the tile floor, staring at that little blinking word. My whole life was about to change.

Chapter 16

Pregnant, I Refused to Suck as a Mother, Even If I Never Got the Wedding I Dreamed Of"

Finally, after taking a moment to gather myself, I opened the bathroom door with tears still streaming down my face and handed him the pregnancy test. I couldn't even say the words. I just held it out in silence. He looked down at the little digital screen, and his face lit up. I'll be honest he looked much happier than I did. It wasn't even close.

I snapped. Not in anger, but in panic. My chest felt tight. The tears turned heavier. "I didn't want to have kids," I said, my voice breaking. "I have so many plans." I shouted it out loud like I was trying to remind the universe or maybe myself that I was on a different path. That I had goals. That this wasn't supposed to happen. He tried to be supportive. He told me everything could still happen. That we'd figure it out together. That this didn't have to stop my dreams. But it didn't help. Not right then. I couldn't shake the feeling that I had failed. Not just myself, but my dad too.

I knew I had done plenty of things I wasn't supposed to do but being pregnant? That was something I had always sworn wouldn't happen. Not yet. Not like this. I had built so much for myself, worked so hard to stay focused and independent, and now everything felt like it was crashing down around me. The weight of the responsibility hit me hard.

Later that day, we met up with my side of the family. My grandma was there, and we decided to break the news. I remember letting a single tear fall when she walked up to me and gently held my face in her hands. She looked into my eyes with a kind of love only grandmothers have and said, "You're a fighter. You're going to be just fine." Everyone else lit up with excitement. They started gushing about how beautiful the baby would be because "look at the parents."

Compliments like that bounced around the room, but I was still in shock.

I tried to keep it together. I buried myself in work and finally told my coworkers. That same sweet lady who had helped me during lunch that day really stepped up. She walked me through what to do next. Doctor appointments. Resources. Questions I hadn't even thought to ask.

She asked me how I wanted to deliver, and I remember staring at her like she had asked me how I planned to land on the moon. I hadn't even had time to process being pregnant, much less imagine being a mother. The idea felt like it belonged to someone else's life.

Eventually, I got an appointment scheduled at a private midwife practice. I hated hospitals the smell, the feeling, the memories. I knew in my bones that I didn't want to deliver there, even if that was the "normal" thing to do.

The midwives ran tests and officially confirmed what I already knew. I wasn't just pregnant I was already three months in. I was stunned. I had walked around carrying life inside me without even knowing. They gave me my first ultrasound and sonogram. I walked out with grainy black-and-white pictures in my hand. For the first time, it started to feel real.

They talked me through my options. Water birth stood out to me natural, peaceful, strong. I wasn't sure yet, but it was something I tucked away to consider. They let me set up a payment plan so everything would be paid in full before my due date. I appreciated that. It gave me a sense of control in a situation that felt anything but controllable.

At home, I tried to focus on work and keep a positive mindset. I knew it was going to be hard, but I also knew I was built for hard. I pushed my boyfriend harder than ever. No more side gigs. No more half-in. I told him straight: helping his dad wasn't going to cut it. We were about to become parents. This wasn't a game. We had to become a team.

Even though I was trying to stay strong, I felt so ashamed. I asked everyone to please keep it from my dad. That was my responsibility. That was my conversation to have and I had no idea how I was going to do it.

He already didn't like my boyfriend. This was going to be gasoline on an already-burning fire. And it wasn't even just about the pregnancy. It was the implication. It meant he'd know I had been sexually active. That visual... me with a growing belly... it terrified me. My father had always been the center of my world, even when we fought, even behind bars. He had guided me from in there as best as he could. And now this?

I felt like I had disappointed him in the most personal way. I stopped visiting for a while. I couldn't face him. I didn't want him to see me like that.

Thankfully, my coworkers became a strong support system. My boss was kind, constantly reminding me to take breaks, stretch, walk around the building. They all treated me with care, like they could see I was fighting my own internal war while still showing up every day.

But then came the sickness. Not the emotional kind the physical kind. The kind that hit hard and didn't let up. I couldn't keep anything down. Food. Water. Even smells made me nauseous. I was constantly in the bathroom, holding my stomach and praying to just get through the day.

I lost weight instead of gaining it. I didn't even look pregnant yet. On the outside, I still looked like the same girl in size 0 jeans. But on the inside, everything had changed.

I started fainting often, sometimes out of nowhere. It got so bad that one of the times I collapsed, I fell flat onto the floor with nothing to catch me. My body was giving out. My boyfriend was constantly worried he didn't know what to do. Doctors had prescribed medication to help with the nausea, but it barely made a dent. I couldn't keep anything down, and the weight just kept dropping.

Eventually, he got a job with one of his uncles in aviation. It was an hour away, and even though he hesitated, we both knew we needed the money. I was missing more and more days at work. I tried to push through, tried to keep up with my projects and keep working like nothing was happening, but I just couldn't anymore. I was too thin, too weak, and constantly dizzy.

One day, he walked in from work and found me on the floor. I had fainted again. He panicked he thought something worse had happened. When I woke up the fear on his face made my stomach turn. I hated seeing him like that. I felt guilty and overwhelmed all at once. I looked at him through tired, swollen eyes and said, "Please forgive me, but I need to go home... I need to be with my mom and grandma." I said it as gently as I could, but it was the truth. I was alone all day, with no support system. His family wasn't close knit like mine, and I didn't feel like I had anyone to turn to over there. I needed to be around women. Around love. Around hands that knew what to do when life got heavy.

So I made the decision. I packed up my things and told my job I was leaving. They didn't argue. They had seen the physical toll the pregnancy had taken on me. My coworkers had tried everything bringing me snacks, suggesting remedies, checking on me constantly but it just wasn't enough anymore. The day I told them I was leaving, my boss handed me a letter of recommendation. She said if I ever wanted to come back, my position would always be waiting. That gesture stayed with me. It made me feel like I wasn't walking away empty-handed. To my surprise, my boyfriend decided to follow me back to the Valley. He quit his job on the spot even after I told him to stay, to keep working, to help us from where he was. But he refused. He wouldn't let me travel alone. I'm not even sure he gave his uncle a proper notice. All I know is that they never spoke again. His uncle told him he'd never help him get another job, and when I heard that, I felt responsible. I had begged him to stay behind... but he didn't listen.

When I arrived back home, my mom gave me back my old bedroom. But everything felt... different. The house felt smaller somehow, or maybe I just felt like I didn't belong anymore. I had left as one person and come back as someone else. What was I even thinking?

My boyfriend tried to settle in. He applied to local jobs and signed up with Workforce Solutions. My mom had just started working at the hospital and said she might be able to help him get in too. But when it came time to make decisions, fill out applications, or speak up, he leaned entirely on me. Every question was directed toward me. Every decision needed my approval. I was growing a whole human and trying to keep myself together, yet I still had to lead him like a child.

It was exhausting. My mom noticed it too. She'd make comments about how immature he was, how he needed to step up and carry his weight. And deep down, I agreed with her. I just didn't have the strength to argue anymore.

After a few months, my body started adjusting. I was still small, but at least I could keep some food down. I wasn't throwing up every hour. That alone felt like a blessing. But I wasn't working, and the frustration started to build. Money was tight. His paychecks barely covered anything, and jobs in the Valley didn't pay anywhere near what I made in Dallas.

I started applying for jobs myself, but the offers were insulting. $7 an hour? I had been making more than triple that before I left. I felt stuck. We couldn't survive on that income, and I wasn't going to break my back for scraps.

I sat my boyfriend down again and told him we needed to talk. We had to figure this out. I was getting bigger, and I couldn't carry all of this stress with me into labor. We were still in contact with his dad and decided to ask if we could come back to Dallas temporarily just for a few weeks so I could get my job back and we could get on our feet again.

His dad said he'd talk to his wife and get back to us. A few days later, they said yes.

We packed up again and made the trip back. When we arrived, things felt… different. His family was nicer to me. Maybe it was the belly. Maybe it was time. Maybe it was guilt. Either way, they were kinder. At least to my face.

His dad really stepped up and spoiled me sometimes. He'd buy me the fanciest, most expensive milk in the store to help with my heartburn. He started cooking more, asking if I needed anything. The family dynamic began to shift.

We all spent more time together his dad, his stepmom, the siblings. We'd hang out in the kitchen, making dinner together, laughing around the island. His stepmom even taught me how to make flour tortillas her way. I had learned differently growing up, but I took mental notes and picked up her version with care.

In return, I kept their house clean, helped with the laundry, stayed on top of the dishes. I wanted to show appreciation. I wanted to prove I wasn't some lazy pregnant girl freeloading off their space. I wanted to be helpful, valuable, respected. Here we were, back on square one.

For a moment, it felt like we were building something again. Not just a family, but maybe… a future.

One day I overheard my father-in-law talking to his daughter in a hushed tone. He just didn't realize I was within earshot. He told her she better not loan me any money from her income tax.

It hit me like a brick.

Especially because I had never not once asked them for anything. Not a dollar. Not a favor. Nothing. I had carried myself with respect, handled my own business, and contributed in every way I could.

Up until that moment, I really thought he liked me. I thought all the milk runs and meals he made for me were out of genuine care. But after hearing that… it was like a switch flipped.

It wasn't real. It was a performance.

I never said a word about it. Not to him. Not to my boyfriend. Not to anyone. I swallowed it down and let it settle in my gut like a cold stone. After that, I stayed guarded. I kept to myself. I didn't want to expose my heart to people who were smiling to my face but questioning my motives behind closed doors.

Not long after that, my boyfriend got a job at a furniture warehouse thanks to one of my cousins. He did him a solid recommended him, vouched for him, told him exactly what to do to get in. And it worked. He got the job.

I was so grateful. I still hadn't gone back to work, but at least we had something stable coming in.

Another cousin of mine helped me apply for medical insurance to cover the rest of my doctor visits and the delivery. I didn't have health insurance and wasn't employed, so the timing couldn't have been better. She sat with me, filled out paperwork, made calls she really came through for me.

During that time, I also finally went to the DMV and got my license. I had been putting it off for a while, but now that I was living at my in-laws' and had a bit of time, I made myself handle the things I'd been avoiding. Slowly, I was regaining pieces of my independence.

Eventually, I found a new doctor and stayed with him through the last weeks of my pregnancy. It was a huge relief to have consistency and care, even though so many other parts of my life still felt unstable.

Somewhere along the way, my boyfriend's truck got broken into completely destroyed. We were back to just one car between the two of us.

As I got further along in the pregnancy, sleep became a stranger. I couldn't find a comfortable position, my hips ached, and the heartburn was unbearable. I would toss and turn all night. And to top it off, my boyfriend snored like a bear in hibernation. I was already a light sleeper, but now it felt impossible to get rest.

I noticed he started acting different once he got that job. As my due date approached, he began spending more time with his family helping out at the club again. Everyone there already knew we were expecting his dad had told them and they'd greet me like a mascot. Some would stop by to rub my belly, say something sweet, and then go on with their day.

But there was a distance growing between us. Something I couldn't quite name yet.

Despite everything, my baby shower was incredible. One of the best parties I had ever had. We held it at the nightclub during the day, and I received an overwhelming amount of gifts. It took three car trips to get everything home. Everyone showed up, and for a moment, I let myself feel joy. For a moment, I felt celebrated.

But reality crept back in soon after.

One evening, I was taking a nap before everyone headed out to work at the club. I woke up groggy, slowly stretching, expecting to see my phone or my boyfriend beside me. Neither were there.

The house was quiet, but not in a peaceful way quiet like something was off. I wandered downstairs and passed one of the club employees in my brother-in-law's room. I asked him if he had seen my boyfriend, and he said no.

As the rest of the family left for the club, I realized the house had emptied out. I assumed I was alone.

But as I quietly stepped toward the stairs, I heard something. A voice. Low and muffled.

I slowed my steps, careful not to creak the wood beneath my feet. That's when I heard him. My boyfriend.

He was on the phone. And not just any phone call.

I heard him say, in a voice so soft it sent chills down my spine, "She's asleep… she won't know."

That was all I needed to hear.

I didn't make a sound. I calmly passed by and walked into the restroom. When I came out, we locked eyes. He knew I had heard him. And I knew he knew.

But I didn't explode. I didn't cry. I didn't even mention it.

I just walked past him. Back up the stairs. And in that moment, I started building the kind of silence that changes everything.

He came after me immediately as I walked up the stairs, and everything blew up. His face was pale, caught between guilt and panic. That night, I learned what I had already suspected for weeks he had been using my phone to talk to one of his stepmom's employees from the salon. He wasn't just talking to her; he had been planning to take her out to see my favorite band. The very band I'd once dreamed of seeing with him.

Deep down, I had already known something was going on. Weeks before, I started noticing the shift. He would only go to her for his haircuts, sitting in her chair laughing and giggling like a different person. It was a complete opposite of the cold, moody version of him I got in the car afterwards. Sometimes I'd just sit there waiting, looking through the salon window at them. I'd see them joking and leaning close to each other, and then a few minutes later he'd climb into the car, slam the door, and give me an attitude. The 180-degree switch burned.

Eventually, I saw the text messages. The calls. I didn't even need to look too hard; the betrayal was right there. It wasn't just the cheating it was everything I was carrying on my own while he was sneaking around. I was fat by then, swollen with pregnancy, hormonal, exhausted. My body felt like it wasn't even mine anymore. And to top it off, my heart was breaking.

I told him he was free to go. I told him he could date whoever he wanted. I didn't yell. I didn't beg. I simply told him I would be packing my things and leaving. It was the only power I felt I had left.

The next day, I sat down with his parents and told them what had happened. His stepmom said she was going to get rid of her employee immediately, and that they would speak to him directly. They had a serious conversation with him that same day. I'll never forget his dad's words. He looked at his son, shaking his head, and said, "If you didn't want to be with her, then why bring her here?" The weight of that landed hard. It was one of the rare times his father openly called him out.

I never told my dad any of this. Not a word. I carried it quietly, like I carried everything else. But during my last trimester, my dad started calling and practically begging me to come see him. He wanted to see me, to see me pregnant, to see this baby he knew was coming. Finally, I went.

I wasn't supposed to be traveling that late in my pregnancy, but guilt weighed heavier than fear. I couldn't stand the idea of him not seeing me like this at all. When he walked into that visitation room, his eyes immediately watered. He came straight to me, and the hug he gave me was the strongest I'd felt in years. He placed his hands gently on my belly, almost reverent, and waited for a kick. When he felt it, his entire face changed. He choked up. His voice cracked as he began to apologize.

He told me that for the longest time he had been afraid I wouldn't be able to have kids. He said the beatings he gave me as a child were something he'd regret until his last breath, and sometimes he wondered if the damage he'd done would follow me forever. Hearing him say that out loud cracked something open in me. He wasn't just my father in that moment he was a man looking at his own sins or wrong doings and wishing he could undo them.

It was one of the best visitations we ever had. Even with everything I was carrying, it felt like a small piece of healing. A moment of understanding between us.

Not long after that trip, the contractions started. The fighting, the stress, the emotional rollercoaster it all seemed to trigger something in my body. I sent a message to my mom and told her I thought I was going into labor. My family came into town right away. Sure enough, by the following morning I was dilating.

It was November 29th my dad's birthday. That morning, I was curled up in a ball with a pillow between my legs, not even speaking. My mom checked me and told me what I already feared: those were contractions. She wanted to rush me to the hospital, but I told her I had an appointment with my doctor scheduled for that morning anyway. I figured I'd just wait for my normal appointment and let my doctor tell me what to do next.

When I arrived at the doctor's office, I kept getting chills and goosebumps. The contractions were heavier than earlier that morning, and my body felt like it was shifting. A girl sitting across from me also visibly pregnant looked over and asked if I was getting contractions. I nodded and told her I thought I was. Without hesita-tion, she got up and walked to the front desk. She asked the nurse if they could put me ahead of her so I could be seen first. I'll never forget how sweet she was. A quiet kind of angel. I wish I would've exchanged numbers with her, but I never saw her again.

Once I was checked, the doctor told me I was already 3 centimeters dilated. Labor had officially begun. They told me to go home for a bit take a warm bath, eat something light, walk around, and relax until it was time.

Mom and I went to grab food, but I could barely eat. We walked for a while in the shade around the courthouse, just taking in the fresh air and trying to ease the pressure building inside me. When we got back home, I drew a warm bath and tried to soak in the stillness. Then I started packing.

I folded everything neatly my hospital bag, the baby's things, the going-home outfit. I had the cutest designer baby bag and a highend car seat all set up. I had planned my hospital outfits too. Nothing basic. I refused to be seen as average not now, not ever. Even in labor, I carried myself with pride.

My dad called while I was still at home. I told him I might be going into labor, and I could hear the electricity in his voice. He shouted through the phone, "¡Va a nacer en mi cumpleaños!" "He's going to be born on my birthday!" His joy was uncontainable. He gave me a whole pep talk, telling me I was the strongest woman he had ever known and that I was going to be just fine. He promised to call again before the night ended.

Once I was admitted to the hospital, the contractions intensified. I walked the halls for a while, trying to breathe through the pain. Time started to blur. The dilation was progressing quickly. Then, right in the middle of labor, one of the nurses walked in and said, "Your phone is ringing." It was my dad.

They handed me the phone mid-contraction, and I could barely speak. But his voice his voice steadied me. He was cheering me on from a prison phone line, whispering strength into me. "Breathe. You got this. You're going to be great." He kept saying, "Tú puedes, mi reina." That call even just hearing his voice carried me through those last moments. The line cut off eventually, but his words didn't leave me.

Just after midnight, I delivered. My firstborn was born on November 30th. Not quite my dad's birthday, but close enough that we all smiled about it.

I had a completely natural delivery. No epidural, no medication just me and my body doing the work. I was so proud. But I won't lie I went into a minor shock right after. I remember looking at my baby and thinking, Is this mine? I wondered if all new moms felt that. The disorientation, the awe, the disbelief.

Soon, visitors started pouring in. Family, friends, even people I hadn't expected. The woman from my mother-in-law's salon the same one my boyfriend had been secretly talking to sent roses to my hospital room. I had them thrown away without hesitation.

My in-laws came to see the baby, but the only one who thought of me was my boyfriend's stepmom. And that gesture meant the world. She had gone out to Dillard's and picked out the most beautiful robe, a few long sleeve turtlenecks, and a handful of stylish outfits for me to choose from when it was time to go home. Everything was exactly my taste extra, fancy, feminine. She really saw me in that moment. Everyone else was focused on the baby, but she thought of the woman who carried him for nine months. I'll never forget that kindness.

I left that hospital in full glam makeup done, hair curled, perfume on. I took care of myself. Nurses kept stopping by my room to tell me I didn't even look like I'd just given birth. My body bounced back almost instantly. My belly was gone, my skin was smooth, not a single stretch mark. I started breastfeeding right away and loved it. It kept my waist snatched, and honestly, I looked the best I ever had. But behind all of that, the reality at home was different.

Once everyone left and we settled back into the house, the real work began. The baby cried. A lot. I was up all night, breastfeeding, rocking, trying to soothe him. I was exhausted and raw. And my boyfriend he had the worst attitude. He'd get angry about the baby crying, yelling at me and snapping that he had to work the next day and couldn't lose sleep.

He was still working at the furniture warehouse with my cousin, and the second he got home, all he wanted to do was eat and go straight to bed. No help. No warmth. Just cold detachment.

It got to the point where I stopped sleeping in our room. I'd take the baby downstairs to the living room and breastfeed on the couch, just to keep the peace. Some nights I'd fall asleep there with the baby in my arms.

And oddly enough, the person who kept me company during those late-night breakdowns wasn't my boyfriend it was his younger brother. He'd walk in from the club at one, two, even three in the morning, and sit with me. No judgment, no awkwardness. He'd talk to me, ask how I was doing, even offer to hold the baby so I could close my eyes for a bit. He'd ask where his brother was, and I'd just shrug and say, "Sleeping." He'd nod, never pushing, just quietly stepping into the space that should've never been his responsibility.

His stepmom started acting different. Rude. Dismissive. The subtle digs turned into louder ones. Whenever I had a doctor's appointment, she'd tell me I could take one of their cars. But there was always a catch. One time, my stepbrother offered to let me borrow his truck it was snowing heavily and freezing cold and he knew the truck had working heat. But when his mom found out, she snatched the keys out of my hands and told me to take the Jeep instead. The Jeep had no heater, no AC, but I took it anyway. I didn't have the luxury to argue.

I'll never forget that visit to the doctor's office. It was the first one I went to completely alone. The baby had a diaper blowout all the way up to his neck. I panicked. I stood there in shock, unsure of what to do. Do I take him home like that? Do I wipe him down? Was there a place I could bathe him, even quickly? I didn't know. I was by myself and I felt clueless.

Believe me when I say: that was the first and last time I ever let that happen.

I ran into the public bathroom at the clinic, laid the baby down, and stripped him completely. I used every wipe I had. I dressed him in a fresh outfit and threw everything else away. The smell made me gag. I struggled. I had always said I didn't want kids not because I didn't love them, but because I was afraid I wouldn't be good at it. I had never even changed a diaper before. But I was already in it. This was real life. And I made a promise to myself that day: I refuse to suck as a mother.

Shortly after, I got a new job at the bank. It was a solid position well-paying, especially because I was bilingual and had a good education. My boyfriend's grandmother agreed to watch the baby while I worked. Of course, it wasn't free. We paid her it wasn't a favor. I'd wake up early every morning, bundle the baby up, load the car seat into the freezing vehicle, and head out into the snow.

I used to throw tantrums every morning quietly, to myself because every time I bent down to put the car seat in or take it out, I'd hit my head on the roof of the car. It became a daily frustration that ruined the start of almost every day. Still, I kept going.

The job came naturally. I hit my quotas, earned a raise fast, and moved up in rank quickly because we were one of the busiest branches. The bilingual pay helped. I started building credit. Got my first real credit cards. Paid my bills on time. I was getting into a rhythm.

Things were looking up. I found a small apartment called The Enclave in Arlington just a one-bedroom, but perfect for us. It had a cozy spot for a dining table and just enough space for two couches. The Walmart was walking distance. Right across the way, construction had begun on the new Cowboys stadium, so there was constant movement, noise, and energy. We even witnessed one of the tragic construction accidents the chaos of that day left an impression.

Still, it felt like a new beginning. My own place. My own income. Stability, for once. And somewhere in all that momentum, I brought up the idea of eloping. It was my idea not his.

I had always dreamed of a wedding. A real one. With flowers and a dress and a slow dance. But I knew that was never going to happen. His family didn't do tradition. There was no sense of formal values, no "ask for the father's blessing," no engagement talk, no ring. Just casual avoidance. Meanwhile, I came from a culture that honored ceremony, intention, and respect.

But I already had a child. And my mom kept telling me it was time to "do things right." She said I needed to make it official that I needed to submit and stick it out. That this was my life now, and I had to be a wife. Even if the fantasy didn't match the reality.

So I planned it. Quietly. I arranged a small courthouse wedding and decided to host a dinner at the apartment after. Nothing grand, but I still wanted it to feel special. I decorated. I bought a little cake. I tried to make it matter.

During the ceremony, his stepmom filmed us. His dad was there. A few of their nightclub employees stood off to the side, and on my side, only my aunt and cousins showed up. It was intimate, but heavy.

And then I heard it.

Members of his own family, whispering loud enough for me to hear "Don't do it." They were laughing and waving at him like it was a joke, but it wasn't funny. Not to me. It felt like a punch to the stomach. A private humiliation in a public moment.

Even now, that whisper still echoes in the back of my mind.

My cousins held the baby while we signed the papers and posed for pictures. Then we all went back to the apartment for dinner. It was quick and quiet. No fanfare. My mom told me I had done the right thing that I now had a husband and a child, and I needed to work hard and learn how to be submissive. She said it as if it were a badge of honor. As if submission was something noble.

But I've never been the type to just obey. No one told me what to do not even my dad, and especially not a man who couldn't show up the way I needed.

Still, I stepped into it. I made the choice.

This was going to be a whole different chapter for me.

Chapter 17

"He Lied and Cheated. The Next One Bruised Me."

From Me to You... Before You Continue:

This chapter is another one of the heaviest in my story. It contains real, painful memories involving betrayal, emotional trauma, physical violence, and moments where I didn't know if I would make it out.

If you've ever been hurt, abandoned, manipulated, or abused please take a breath before reading. I want you to protect your peace and honor your healing.

I'm not sharing these pages to shock you. I'm sharing them because someone out there needs to know they're not alone. That it's possible to live through hell and still rise.

If at any point it feels too heavy, it's okay to pause. To skip. To come back later. Or to never return to this chapter at all. I'll still be here. I'll still love you through the rest of the book.

Tómate tu tiempo. Tu corazón es sagrado.

With so much care,

Yesenia <3

If you or someone you love is experiencing abuse, you are not alone. Call or text the National Domestic Violence Hotline at 800-799-7233, texting "START" to 88788 or chat with someone 24/7 at the-hotline.org. It's confidential, free, and available any time.

Once we eloped, not much really changed. There was no magical shift, no newfound intimacy or transformation in our relationship. It was like crossing something off a checklist something we did because it felt like the "right" thing to do, not because it came from a place of mutual excitement or real desire. We still had good times, still got along, still went out together occasionally. Life kept moving forward in the same blur it always had.

My cousins were still a big part of our world. We'd hit up my in-laws' nightclub or other spots around town, IDs in hand, pretending adulthood came easy. Sometimes we pregamed at my aunt's place, and she would stay behind to watch my son. There was always music playing, laughter, the buzz of youth trying to stretch itself just a little bit further even when we were already carrying more weight than most people our age.

We spent holidays with his side of the family too. I played the role. Smiled in photos. Kept things light. I still kept in touch with my dad and sent him pictures from time to time trying to paint a prettier picture than what was real. I didn't want him to hate my husband any more than he already might've. He never said much, but I knew. Even so, he was never disrespectful. He was polite, kept it cordial, mostly because I always reminded him to. I didn't want more ten-sion than we already had.

One of my cousins was with me constantly my ride-or-die. She was the same one who had been with me in that accident when we were in her mom's Tahoe. We were inseparable. She had been there from the beginning through movie nights, food runs, swimming, all the early dates when I was still getting to know the Dallas boy I ended up marrying. She became more like a sister than a cousin, someone I leaned on without hesitation. She would come over, and we'd blast music, dance in the living room, laugh until our stomachs hurt. My husband would be there too, and I'd try to teach them both how to dance properly adding extra turns and dramatic moves, imagining us lighting up the dance floor when we went out. I wanted us to look fancy, to be that couple. But they just laughed at me. One time, they were sitting there cracking up, and I rolled my eyes and said, "Y'all are laughing, but still can't dance," and laughed too. I tried to make it fun, even when things felt off.

After a few months, we decided we needed more space. Our small apartment felt tight, especially with a baby and all the life changes stacking up. So I went to the leasing office and asked if they had any larger units available maybe a bigger one-bedroom, or even a two-bedroom. And they did.

I toured a few options and picked a beautiful place with a spacious layout and a patio that faced the Dallas Cowboys stadium. It felt like a real upgrade. The bedroom was bigger, the bathroom had more space, and the living room actually felt like a place we could breathe in. I decorated it with love and care, making it feel like home.

But with the move came a bump in rent. So I told my husband I planned to get a second job just something small, maybe weekends only, like a bar gig or something flexible that wouldn't clash with my main job at the bank.

By that time, I had built strong relationships with our bank clients. I was the only Spanish speaker at my branch, so I handled nearly all the customer service needs opening accounts, closing them, handling account audits, ordering checks. I didn't work the teller line much, which gave me time to connect more deeply with people.

I met so many interesting clients restaurateurs, salon owners, spa managers. Some of the wealthiest ones came in looking humble and lowkey, while others walked in dressed to the nines but were barely scraping by. It taught me not to judge anyone's financial status by their appearance. I even experienced my first bank robbery while working there. It was terrifying. Investigators came in and questioned everyone afterward. I remember feeling frozen violated, unsure, but still responsible. I couldn't afford to quit. I had bills. A child. A home. Fear wasn't going to pay my rent, so I kept showing up. One day, a client I had helped regularly walked in. While working on her account, I told her I was thinking about picking up a second job. She smiled and told me she owned a bar and asked if I'd be interested in helping out there. She also mentioned she did modeling.

projects for a magazine and needed women for events. She said she'd train me, show me the ropes.

I told her I'd think about it. A part of me was curious, but another part felt like I didn't belong. I was a mom now. I didn't want anything getting in the way of my momentum at the bank. I was killing it meeting monthly quotas, being recognized for my performance. I was so close to another promotion, either into the vault role or becoming a bi-district trainer. I was working for it.

But still, something about her offer lingered. I was balancing motherhood, marriage, bills, and a career already dancing in chaos. Part of me wondered: what's one more thing?

My husband wasn't making good money at his warehouse job and on top of that, his money management skills were all over the place. Let's just be real. I was the one holding it all down. I was paying the rent, my car note, insurance, daycare, sending money to my dad, helping out my brothers with little things here and there and still trying to keep up with my own standards. I've always loved nice things. I liked to look good, feel good, and have my space reflect the life I was working so hard to create. But the truth was, I couldn't keep carrying all of this on one income.

So, I called her the bar owner from the bank and said yes. I told her I was ready to take the opportunity she offered. I gave her my bank schedule, and during my off-hours, I worked with her. There was no rest. I was doing what I had to do.

My routine during this time? Insane. I'd wake up before the sun, rushing to get myself ready, then the baby packing bags, bottles, diapers, making sure his clothes were clean and folded just right. I'd drop him off at daycare, then hustle to the bank for my shift. Some days I opened, some days I closed. I was responsible for the branch operations, customer accounts, goals, training. On top of that, we had regional meetings big ones.

Those were some of my favorite days, even though they added to the chaos. I took them seriously. I always showed up sharp. Hair done. Clean, professional outfit. I'd drop the baby off extra early just to give myself enough time to look the part. I wanted to be seen. I wanted them to know I wasn't just surviving I was thriving.

At one of those meetings, we had our mystery shop results announced. That day, they called my name. I got a solid 100 on my evaluation. A perfect score. That rarely happened, and the whole room knew it. My branch manager looked so proud. It felt good to be recognized to know that even while juggling motherhood, marriage, and a second job, I was still dominating at work. Our customer service scores were posted, shoutouts were made, the top-performing branch was named. There were anniversaries celebrated, corporate updates, new products launched, and quarterly goals rolled out. And the best part? The environment. There were raffles, gift bags, team-building games, leadership talks, and catered lunch with coffee and snacks. Those meetings felt like a reminder: I'm capable. I'm powerful. I belong in these rooms.

Despite the madness, I kept in touch with my mom as much as I could. Sometimes I'd take a quick trip to see her, other times she'd come to me. She was always in my ear, reminding me not to burn out, not to carry more than I needed to.

But financially, I was doing well. I felt proud of how far I'd come. I even bought myself a beautiful parrot vibrant and loud with a massive gold cage I placed on the patio. He was wild, full of personality, and expensive. But I wanted him. He made the place feel alive. He made me feel like I could still enjoy something for me. Still, underneath all of that forward motion, there was tension building. I had a really hard time stepping back and letting my husband take the lead because deep down, I knew he wouldn't. My mom would tell me, "Mija, you need to stop doing everything. Let him figure it out. You need to slow down." But I didn't want to slow down. I didn't want to lower my standards or lose momentum waiting on someone who wasn't ready to carry that weight.

That's when she told me something I'll never forget: "You have to learn to live with only what he can give you." That hit me. Hard. But I couldn't accept that. I didn't want to settle. I didn't want to pretend less was enough when I had already tasted more.

I was working crazy hours. I barely had time to sit and breathe, let alone spend quality time with my baby. There were days when I felt the exhaustion in my bones but I didn't stop. I couldn't. I told myself this was temporary. That the grind would be worth it. That I just had to stay focused, stay disciplined, and keep my eyes on the prize. Because even when I was running on fumes, deep down I knew I wasn't just working to survive. I was building something. I was fighting for a future that had room for all of me. There was one month in particular where I completely overdid it. I spent more than I should have way more. Bought things I didn't even need. I was feeling drained and restless, and instead of slowing down, I distracted myself with spending. I bought clothes, little home decor, some makeup... and even splurged on the newest BlackBerry smartphone. That thing was expensive, but I convinced myself I needed it for work and the life I was juggling. Deep down, I just wanted something that made me feel caught up like I wasn't always sacrificing while everyone else got to enjoy the extras.

But then rent hit. And I didn't have enough.

So I turned to my husband and asked him to cover the rent or at least part of it. I was the one holding down everything, and I was tired. By that point, I was about 20 years old, and I had been carrying this weight alone since I was 16. Four years of responsibility, and now a whole child later, and I still felt like I was doing it by myself. He said he'd take care of it.

He didn't.

A few days passed, and just like that, an eviction notice was taped to our door. I was livid. My heart dropped when I saw it. Not because I didn't know we were behind but because I had hoped, for once, I wouldn't be the one to fix everything. I told him we needed to come up with the money now. I was already thinking about asking for extra shifts at the bar, even though I was bone tired. I needed rest. My body was running on fumes. I was still my normal goofy, high-energy self on the outside talkative, bubbly, always in good spirits but inside, I was craving stillness. I needed to breathe.

But breathing wasn't an option when your name is the only one on the lease.

The apartment was under my name, which meant if we got evicted, my credit would take the hit. And if that happened, I could lose my job at the bank. People don't realize this, but credit matters in banking. Most financial institutions won't even hire you if your credit is bad, and if you're already working there and they find out your financial profile is a risk, it could jeopardize everything.

I wasn't about to let that happen.

So, I reached out to the woman from the bar the one who had become a mentor in a way. I told her exactly what was going on. Without hesitation, she offered me $1,500 to fly with her to Tulsa, Oklahoma. She was organizing a huge photoshoot that week and had been asking me to come for a while. I always said no because of the baby. But this time, I said yes. I had to.

That trip changed something in me. From the moment we left, it was like I was transported into another world. She let me ride with her, and we went to all these upscale restaurants and meetings. I'm talking cloth napkins, dim lighting, crystal glassware, the kind of places where everyone spoke softly and carried themselves like they were somebody important. For those two days, I let myself fully lean into it.

I did the photo shoot too and whew, I had no idea how much physical work that would be. Holding poses with my core tight, wearing high heels, keeping my face soft and composed it was intense. By the next day, my body was sore all over. But the pictures turned out incredible. I looked strong. Confident. Like a woman who could walk through fire and still strike a pose.

She paid me and even drove me to the airport herself. She made sure I was good before dropping me off and asked me to check in when I got home. That kind of care meant something to me. She didn't just give me a handout she gave me a chance. She opened a door and trusted me to walk through it.

When I got back to Dallas, I was excited. I wanted to surprise my husband and my son, so I didn't tell them when I'd be landing. I caught a ride home instead. At the airport, I bought my son a little toy airplane and tucked it into a cute gift bag. I couldn't wait to give it to him, to kiss his little face and hold him close. I was proud of myself. I had gone out and handled business. I had made more than enough to cover rent and get us back on track.

It was a lesson learned. A hard one, but I got the message loud and clear.

But nothing could've prepared me for what I walked into next.

Turns out, while I had been grinding working my ass off to keep us afloat my husband had been entertaining other women behind my back. I didn't see the signs. Not because they weren't there, but because I genuinely believed he wouldn't do that to me. I thought I was doing everything right. I wasn't out partying. I wasn't out doing God knows what. I was working, building, mothering, sacrificing, hustling.

I kept myself looking good. I always dressed up. Home was spotless. I made sure he had packed lunches. I took care of my skin. I was fun to be around, high-energy, always trying to make life beautiful even in chaos. I even used to brag and say, "He doesn't have eyes for anyone but me."

And if I'm being brutally honest I'll be transparent now I used to say I was one of the best-looking cousins in the family. Not because I thought I was better, but because I was putting in the work. I knew I looked good because I made the effort. I took pride in it. My work outfits? Fire. Pencil skirts, pantyhose, clean pressed suits, closed-toe heels. Hair always done. And after giving birth, my hair had grown so much long, healthy, full. I took care of myself.

So no, betrayal wasn't even on my radar.

But it happened. And when it did, it shook something in me.

Because when you give everything your body, your time, your energy, your loyalty and someone still looks elsewhere, it cuts deep. It makes you question your worth, even when deep down you know your value.

That chapter of my life hurt. But it also revealed what I was made of.

Because no matter how broken I felt I didn't crumble.

Well, he did. And this time, it was with my very own cousin. Even now, I don't like to touch this part of my life for too long because it's one of the deepest cuts I've ever felt. When I arrived home from the airport, happy and proud of myself, I asked him straight out what he was doing with her. He stumbled for an answer. Apparently, she had called him to ask for a ride from school, and he had left work during his lunch break to go pick her up.

I swallowed every sign, every suspicion, every knot in my stomach, and I stayed cool. I told her to get in the car and that I would be the one to take her home. I told him to go back to work. He tried to tell me that I needed to rest since I had just landed, that he could handle it, but I wasn't hearing it. My face stayed calm, my voice steady, but my insides were screaming. "I said what I said," was all I told him.

I walked in front of them both, their shadows stretched behind me like a reflection of a betrayal I didn't want to see. Side by side, whispering, walking a little too close. She got in the car with me, and I could see her hands tremble. She said softly, "I have something to tell you." Without looking at her, I said, "I know." Nothing else. I needed a minute to process.

Then she told me he had been holding her hand while they were walking behind me. The sting of it burned in my chest, but I kept my composure. I drove her home anyway. Dropped her off. Picked up my son. And then I lost it.

I drove straight to his job at the furniture warehouse where he worked with my cousins, shaking with rage. I had tried so hard to play it off, but the dam broke. How dare he play me like this. I had already let the first time slide when I was pregnant, and now this with my own family. It was like a double betrayal. The man I had built my life with, and the girl I treated like a sister.

That's the moment I had my first panic attack. It felt like my chest was caving in and my heart was being squeezed. All my life I had fought for happiness, clawed my way out of chaos, tried to build something solid and it seemed like every time I reached a new level, life yanked me back down. I felt like I couldn't breathe.

When I got to his job, I wanted to smash every piece of his truck with my bare hands. People there knew who I was. They called him out fast, and he stormed outside, knowing I'd found out. I locked the car doors and screamed at him through the window. He kept denying it, which made me even more furious.

"She already told me!" I shouted. My voice cracked with fury and heartbreak. After that, it's a blur. All I know is I kicked him out of the car. He tried to open the doors, saying he wanted to see his son, saying I couldn't just drive away. I refused. I told him, "I'm done. I want a divorce." I was exhausted, betrayed, and emptied out.

I had done everything to hold us together worked, mothered, cleaned, cooked, hustled, even defended him to my father and now this. It felt like being betrayed by my best friend. I told him he was going to be responsible for paying for the divorce and that I wanted nothing from him. Thank God the truck was in his name and my car was in mine; at least that part would be clean. I even told him I didn't want child support and that I didn't need him in my son's life. I wanted to be free.

I drove back to my apartment complex, paid the rent, and ordered an emergency lock change from maintenance. I sat there in silence, trying to breathe. The tears wouldn't stop. My chest felt like it had a boulder on it. Did you read that", I finally cried. I never did till now. I'd always been so prideful.

My phone blew up with calls from my cousins telling me I was "overreacting" and that I should work things out because he was the father of my son and she was family. I ignored everyone. How on earth could they say I was overreacting? We were on the brink of eviction, and I was working myself to exhaustion trying to keep our life afloat while he was sneaking around. That's not overreacting. That's betrayal.

What cut even deeper was when my dad called. I told him what happened, expecting him to be furious on my behalf. Instead, he said, "Well, what did you do wrong?" My heart sank. I couldn't believe it. Was he siding with him? Why would he even ask me that? Did he think I deserved this? That moment broke something in me. For the first time, I felt truly alone.

Even his family tried to get us to reconcile. They said I should forgive, that it was just a mistake, that I shouldn't ruin everything. But I was done. I wasn't going to let this slide like the first time. Something inside me turned cold. I shut everyone out my family, his family, friends. I stopped going places. I stopped talking. I clocked into work, took care of my son, and kept moving. I felt betrayed, angry, and empty all at once.

My dad was also pushing my mom to sell the trucks in Oregon and divide the money between my brothers and me. He wanted each of us to either sell or put them to work. Mom said he wasn't dead and didn't need to do that, but he insisted. When it came to me, I told her to sell mine and just send me the money so I could buy a house or do something useful with it.

When she sold the trucks, she sent me only $2,000. I asked what they had sold for, and she told me she used the rest of the money to buy a car for her brother. I didn't say a word. I don't even remember telling Dad. I was already drowning and didn't have the energy to fight over it. My mindset was simple: I've been doing it alone this long, I can keep doing it.

Mom herself was going through bankruptcy, and the house was being repossessed. I didn't even know the full story of what was happening back home. I was too busy trying to hold my own life together.

I started working more nights at the club, partly for extra cash and partly to keep busy. One night, while I was on the clock, someone put something in my drink. It knocked me out cold. My coworkers tried to help and even contacted my husband to come pick me up.

He didn't.

Later that night, I forced myself to shake it off. I guzzled water and tried to stay awake as my coworkers whispered around me. They later found out there had been men at the bar slipping pills into women's drinks that night. It chilled me to my core. That was the moment I realized that my husband truly didn't have my back. Not even when it mattered. Not even when my safety was on the line. He knew exactly where I worked, he knew how dangerous the nightlife could be, he knew I had no one else to call and yet he stayed home. He didn't check in. He didn't come. He left me out there in the dark to fend for myself.

Over time, I began talking to a man I'd met through the bank. He was a longtime client, always polite, and he'd ask me questions while I handled his accounts. I casually mentioned I also worked at a bar at night, and he always laughed at the contrast how I looked so professional during the day, polished in suits and heels, like someone who would never even set foot in a bar. I'd shrug and say, "A girl's gotta do what a girl's gotta do. I like nice things, and I have to work."

Eventually, I opened up about my marriage, my heartbreak, and the betrayal I had just gone through. He said he liked me a lot, told me I didn't deserve what had happened, even offered to help pay for my divorce. He made me feel seen at a time when I felt invisible. But the truth is, I wasn't ready for any of it. My heart was still in pieces, my head still spinning. He wasn't my type. He was kind, but not what I wanted. Part of me even saw him as a form of revenge, my "perfect payback moment" for what my ex had done to me. It was toxic, and I knew it.

One day he called and asked me to step outside to his truck. He had a gift for me a massive Louis Vuitton bag with a custom tag engraved with my name. It was gorgeous, expensive, thoughtful. But I couldn't react. My face stayed blank. Not because I didn't appreciate it, but because expensive things have never impressed me. Maybe he expected me to cry or jump into his arms. Instead, my numbness probably looked like ungratefulness, and I could tell it irritated him.

While I was still working through the divorce, my ex started threatening me for dating someone else. I reminded him calmly that he had cheated on me twice. If anyone was going to get hit with adultery charges, it would be him. I had done my research. I knew I was walking a fine line, but at that point, I didn't care. Something in me had flipped. I was numb, reckless, running on fumes. I made stupid decisions and barely recognized myself. I started drinking more, smoking too, spiraling deeper into a version of myself I'd promised I would never become.

The man I was seeing would take me out on the weekends when my son was with his dad. Sometimes I'd even stay at his place. I never fully knew what he did for a living; he just said "business" and left it at that. Months passed like this, a blur of high-end dinners and low-end emotions. One day he saw me texting my ex about something related to our son and snapped. It was the first time he hit me. Just one strike, quick, a flash of rage followed by a flood of apologies. He swore he'd never do it again. My dumb heart forgave him. Things seemed to get better after that.

Then came my 21st birthday. He had promised to take me out, told me to grab cash from his closet and go shopping for something to wear. I opened the closet and saw stacks of cash wads of it. I only took what he said to take and left the rest alone. I was excited, hopeful even. Maybe the night would be a turning point. Maybe things would finally feel good again.

But something in him snapped that night. I don't even know what triggered it. All I know is that instead of celebrating, I was being beaten. On my very own 21st birthday. The memory is still a blur, like a film with missing frames. I remember trying to fight back, my body in survival mode. I remember seeing a Corona beer bottle sitting on the bathroom sink while he hit me, and my brain telling me to grab it, smash it, and fight my way out. But I didn't get the chance.

At one point, I ran to the closet to hide. He came in after me, pulled me out by my hair, and kept going. He was under the influence, completely unhinged. And there I was twenty-one, bruised, bleeding inside and out, holding all the weight of a life that felt like it was collapsing in slow motion.

I took a few days to recover and even longer to step outside. He wouldn't let me leave. Wouldn't let me be seen. So I kept quiet and stayed put. Not because I wanted to but because, for the first time, I was genuinely afraid. The kind of fear that paralyzes your throat, clouds your thoughts, and makes you question everything you thought you knew about yourself.

The rest of that year passed like a blur. I walked through it emotionally numb, trying to piece together a way out. I knew I didn't feel the same anymore. I wasn't the same. I couldn't look at him without remembering what he did. And how small I felt. How powerless. I started dreaming of going back home, of disappearing, of escaping all of it.

I never told my ex-husband what had happened. But I think he knew something was off. My spark was gone, my light was dimmed. A few weeks after the assault, the man I was living with promised to take me out to dinner said he wanted to make things up to me. I got dressed. I did my hair and makeup. I sat on the edge of the bed waiting like a fool, but he never showed up. I remember falling asleep in my outfit, the perfume I'd sprayed for him still clinging to my collarbone.

He came home late. Woke me up like nothing had happened. I could tell he'd done something he was off. He muttered a half-hearted apology and climbed into bed. The next morning, I found weed under his bathroom sink.

That was it. I knew I had to go. I was already planning my exit in secret. I didn't want to see him again. I didn't want my son around that energy, around drugs, around violence. But he was controlling, calculated, and he could smell it on me the readiness to run.

So when I left my son in a safe place and returned to his house to grab my things, he sensed something was up. He told me to come upstairs. I tried to play it cool. Act like everything was normal. But the joke was on me.

He sat me on the edge of the bed and asked why I didn't have my son with me. Then, he stepped back, turned off the light and began to hit me. Again.

This time it was different. I genuinely didn't think I was going to make it out alive. I thought about the window, wondered if I could jump, escape, survive the fall but we were three stories up. It would have killed me. So I stayed. I endured. My body trembling, heart pounding.

He took my car keys and made sure I couldn't leave.

His cousin was downstairs the entire time. Heard everything. Did nothing. That silence hurt too.

The next morning, he left for work. I could hear his truck rumble out of the driveway. His cousin was still asleep in the guest room downstairs. I knew this was my only chance. I quietly called my mom and gave her a brief rundown. My voice was shaking, but I kept it together. I told her I was going to run. That I'd figure something out.

I searched the house from top to bottom looking for my car keys. Nothing. I started to panic. I didn't want to alert anyone, but I could feel the clock ticking in my chest.

And then call it instinct, call it intuition, call it God I went down to the garage. I stood there, staring at a neatly stacked pile of tires. Something inside me told me to reach up and check. I don't know how or why I just knew.

I reached up, slipped my hand between two tires... and felt metal.

My keys.

Only God could've led me there. There's no other way to explain it. I grabbed a few of my son's things, shoved them into the car, my hands shaking the whole time. I was sweating. My mouth dry. My mind racing. I heard movement inside the house. His cousin was waking up. I knew he'd heard me. Knew he was going to tell him.

But I didn't stop. I left everything behind. All my clothes, all my shoes brand new, still with tags my makeup, my accessories, all of it. I didn't care. I grabbed my purse, nothing more, and ran.

As I got on the highway, I saw it his truck. Headed toward the house.

My heart dropped. His cousin had told him I was leaving.

But it was too late. I was already gone. I was on the opposite side of the freeway, and this time, I wasn't looking back.

I made it out alive.

Chapter 18

My Escape Wasn't My Freedom

The only thing running through my mind as I drove off was calling my mom and getting out of Dallas. I didn't have a plan just a burning instinct to get far away. I picked up my son and called his dad, who was already staying with one of his uncles. He had moved on, dating someone new. I didn't care. I wasn't calling to argue or make things messy. I just needed him to understand what was happening. I briefly explained what had occurred, told him I was scared, and made it clear: I was leaving with our son.

Telling him wouldn't change anything, but I didn't want to vanish without communicating. One thing about my ex we always managed to communicate clearly. We'd argue, sure, but at the end of the day, we'd find a middle ground, settle things, and maintain peace for the sake of our son.

I didn't care about the apartment, the furniture, the clothes, my makeup, or the things with tags still on them. None of that mattered. My safety mattered. My baby mattered. I felt helpless, terrified, and completely alone. He gave me $100 cash for gas, and I drove away from Dallas with my hands shaking and my heart heavy. I called my mom. She was crying when she picked up. She said she had been on her knees praying the whole night, waiting to hear that I made it out alive. I told her I did.

Then I tossed my phone out the window. I didn't want to be reachable. I didn't want to explain myself to anyone. I just drove.

But when I got to my mom's house, I didn't feel any safer inside. I felt even more unhappy confused, disconnected, angry. Why was I back here? Why had I returned to the place I swore I'd never live in again?

I hated the Valley. Always had. There was no future for me there no inspiration, no opportunity. The jobs were underpaying, the area was small and dry, and everything about it felt like a dead end. But I needed safety, so I swallowed the discomfort. I told myself I'd rest. I told myself I'd figure it out.

My mom was relieved to have me home, but there was still tension in the air between us. She kept trying to tell me how to live my life. She insisted I get back with my ex. She said everything had happened for a reason that it was my duty to return to the man I had married, that it was the right thing to do now that we had a child. That I needed to submit, to let him lead, to make the marriage work no matter what had happened.

I didn't agree, and I stopped responding altogether. It wasn't worth the argument. She couldn't see how exhausted I was. How broken I felt. She didn't understand that I had just clawed my way out of something I wasn't sure I'd survive.

She started throwing jabs. Saying I was just like my dad. That I ate like him, talked like him, moved like him. She'd point to my hands and say they were his. The way I rolled my eyes, the way I sighed, the way I shut down when things got loud "just like your father," she'd say. I stayed quiet, but it stung.

I was holding onto so much resentment toward her, too. Things I didn't know how to talk about back then. Maybe I still don't. But I couldn't understand how she went from being a woman with homes, cars, businesses, and luxury to barely getting by. I was too young to fully grasp what was happening at the time, maybe 15 or 16, but even then, it blew my mind how everything just disappeared. It was like one day we had it all, and the next, it was gone. Just like that. Blink, and it was over. I didn't have the words, the resources, or the power to help then. But even years later, I couldn't wrap my head around it. I wasn't angry that it ended I was angry that it felt like no one fought for it to last.

That lifestyle left a mark on me. It showed me what was possible. It showed me what I wanted but not in a shallow way. I knew now that I wanted to rebuild, to hustle, to find a way to create something even better… and to do it legally. With pride. With power. With purpose.

But not yet. I was too emotionally wrecked to chase anything. I didn't even have the energy to cry, let alone build a new life.

Still, being home was a wake-up call. I hadn't spent real time with my mom in so long. Being back, I started noticing everything the differences, the decline. The way she lived now compared to the life she had with my dad was night and day.

I drove by the old ranch. By the house. My heart ached. I remember asking myself, How can I get back there? What will it take? What do I need to do, who do I need to become, to reclaim a version of that life on my terms?

Everything around me felt like a reminder. My mom had changed so much. The way she dressed, the way she talked, the car she drove it was all so different. She had gained weight. Her energy had shifted. She didn't seem to care about her appearance anymore. And while that isn't what defines a person, it was jarring to see such a dramatic difference. My mom used to be effortlessly beautiful. Her curly hair didn't need styling, her skin glowed, and she never wore much makeup but she always looked put together. Now it was like she had stopped trying. Or maybe she was just tired, too.

The house was a mess. And that wasn't like her. She used to be obsessive about cleaning. Floors mopped, counters wiped, not a speck of dust in sight. Now I was walking into clutter, into chaos, and it hit me like a cold wind. What happened? How did everything spiral like this? And why was I the only one who seemed to notice?

I didn't want to judge her. I really didn't. But it was so hard to ignore what was right in front of me.

My mom, by this point, had already been baptized and saved. She had become a Christian. I wasn't there when it happened, but I knew she was deeply involved in church, always surrounded by her church family, attending services, and volunteering for events. She even donated almost everything she had to the church. I didn't always understand it, but I could see it gave her a sense of belonging and purpose.

She was also working at an adult daycare when she had an accident. I believe she was carrying someone extremely heavy and injured her back badly enough to need surgery. The recovery changed her life. She moved slower, her energy was different, and even her spirit seemed a little dimmer. I think that accident and the surgery that followed shaped the way she was living. She was fighting her own battles while I was fighting mine, but at the time I couldn't see it clearly.

I had been so focused on my own survival, so caught up in my own pain, that I'd lost track of everything happening at home. I didn't really know what was happening with my brothers either. My older brother had stopped speaking to us completely after getting together with his girlfriend and having a baby. The family dynamics shifted overnight. But that's not my story to tell, and it wasn't my place to judge.

While all of this was happening, my own personal life was still a disaster. From the outside, it probably looked like I was resting at my mom's, but in reality I was hiding. I had run away from all my problems and planted myself back in the one place I swore I'd never return to. It wasn't safety it was escape.

And as much as I wanted to pretend I'd left it all behind, the truth was following me. The man I had been seeing the one who hit me had gone through some of my personal belongings. Because I left in such a rush, everything I owned was still there. He found my dad's address. He read my letters. Years' worth of letters. Letters I had kept carefully in shoe boxes, organized by date, every single one from the very first day my dad got locked up. Pictures. Gifts my dad had sent me. Pieces of my heart. My history. He violated all of it.He even wrote to my dad in prison. To this day, I don't know exactly what he said. I never found out word for word. But based on what happened next, I believe he confessed to my dad that he had hit me. Not long after, I got a call from my dad. His voice was low and steady. He said, "I'm gonna handle it." He also asked me why I had never told him. And I remember this moment so clearlyI was filled with anger and shame. I told him, "It's not like you could do anything about it." In my head, I felt like I deserved what had happened to me, like this was some twisted karma for trying to get back at my ex.

It was a dark moment for me. Everyone around me kept saying I was overreacting, that I should work things out, that it wasn't as bad as it seemed. And when you hear that enough, it starts to settle into your bones. You start to believe maybe you are overreacting. Maybe it really is your fault. I was full of hate, full of pain, and I was angry at everyone including myself.

He tried calling my mom's house phone to talk to me. He tried convincing me to come back. He even sent roses. But it was over. I trashed them. I didn't care how beautiful they were or what they meant. I wasn't going back. Not this time.

Game over forever.

I had been dumb enough to stay before, but I wasn't going to make that mistake again. I could have been killed. Now, looking back, I know I should have left the very first day he put his hands on me. But I didn't. And there's nothing I can do to change that now.

During that season, I tried stepping out with my mom here and there, showing up at church functions or family gatherings, but no one really knew what I was carrying inside me. A lot of my family didn't even know I had gone through a divorce. They just saw me with my little boy and assumed life was steady. My aunts and uncles would smile and ask the same question over and over: "When are you going to have another kid?" They'd say it like small talk, like a normal thing to ask. I'd smile and nod always smile and nod but inside I was screaming. My son was already turning two. He was my only one and, to me, that was perfect. I didn't want more kids. I couldn't even imagine bringing another life into what felt like constant chaos. But nobody needed to know my reasons.

Mom encouraged me to get more involved with her church, so I did. At first, it was just to help her out, but in some ways it started helping me too. I began volunteering with the kids' classes, bringing coloring books and simple stories to read with them. It was healing in its own quiet way there was so much about the Bible I didn't know. Growing up Catholic, this was a whole different experience.

I even went on a church mission trip to Mexico with them. We helped cook, served meals, and spent time with families who had no shoes, no power, sometimes no homes at all. I'd thought I knew what "struggling" looked like, but this was something else entirely. The kids were barefoot and smiling. The parents shared what little they had. It was humbling and bittersweet heartbreaking but heart-warming all at once. We even did a chicken cook-off that turned out to be one of the messiest things I've ever done, but it stripped me down in a good way. It made me grateful for every small thing back home. Even a cup of soup felt like luxury compared to what these families had.

Meanwhile, my ex-husband was still in touch. I'd gotten a new phone by then, and he would call to check if I was okay. He begged me for another chance. He offered to move down to the Valley, or have me move back to Dallas. I stood my ground. I told him things might change one day, but right now, I had nothing left to give. I was still processing too much.

Mom, however, had her own old-school beliefs. She'd tell me over and over that because I had married him even if it was an elopement it was my duty to go back, to make it work, to let him lead, to submit. I was exhausted by the constant pressure.

And then, without asking, he came down to the Valley. He said he was working with his dad again, helping at the club, and despite my protests, he showed up. Mom opened the door for him. She let him stay at the house.

At night, when everything was quiet, I'd lay awake crying. I'd cry myself to sleep on the couch or in the bed, then wake up startled, my heart racing. Sometimes I'd jump in my sleep. Trauma does that. It lingers in your body like an echo. But I never told anyone. In front of people, I was strong, smiling, holding it together. Alone, I was unraveling.

I was angry too. Angry that I'd always been the one working, the one paying bills, the one carrying everything while he couldn't even plan a simple dinner or hold a job consistently. In my eyes, I had no future with a man who couldn't even make small plans, let alone big ones. So yes, I know I was going through a lot, and yes, I made choices I shouldn't have but I refused to settle. I was hurting, but I wasn't going to surrender my standards.

We started sharing a bed again, but it wasn't the same. I'd lay there crying quietly, trying not to wake my son. He'd look at me sometimes and tell me softly, "Stop crying. Everything's going to be okay." His voice was gentle, but my heart was numb. I'd already stopped caring. My energy was gone. My voice was gone. My spark the fire that had always driven me was gone. I felt like an empty shell, completely shut down. I was only doing what everyone said was right, including mom.

Then, a few months later, my son got sick and needed to be rushed to the children's hospital. We alternated staying with him me one night, his dad the next. It was exhausting but necessary.

One afternoon, on one of my breaks, I went to Chili's for lunch alone. I was drained and needed a moment for myself. And that's where it happened I bumped into my old sixth-grade boyfriend, "California Boy." The Valley was small. Everybody knew everybody, so I wasn't exactly surprised. But still, seeing him was like a strange jolt from another life, another version of me that had existed before all the chaos.

He came up to me and started talking, like no time had passed. He sat on the stool next to me at the bar, the same boy I'd known in middle school but now older, with a man's face and calloused hands. He told me he'd grown up, that he had a real blue-collar job now, and that he couldn't believe I was back in the Valley. I kept the conversation short. I told him I had a son who was currently at the hospital. I didn't share the whole story. I didn't have the energy to.

Then he said the words that hit me in the chest: "My dream girl is back. This has to be a sign." He leaned in a little, like he was offering a lifeline. "I actually have a really good job now. I make good money. I can take care of you." His words should've made me feel something hope, nostalgia, anything but my body felt heavy, disconnected. My mind was somewhere else. Spiritually, emotionally, I wasn't sitting on that barstool at all. I was still inside my own chaos. I hugged him, told him it was nice to see him, and left to go back to the hospital. *261*

As I walked out, he followed me into the parking lot and pressed his number into my hand. He told me to call if I ever needed anything, if I'd ever consider giving him another chance. He promised he'd be there. But I didn't feel worthy of any promises. I didn't feel like I deserved anything good from anyone. I felt small. Invisible. Hopeless. Like a nobody.

And then, almost immediately after, I found out I was pregnant again. This time, the first thought in my mind was abortion. I was terrified. There was no way I could handle another child. Even though I'd been on birth control, my life had been so chaotic pills missed, schedules thrown off that my body must have given up on me. When I saw the positive test, I cried and cried. It felt like life kept piling weight on me and I kept standing there letting it crush me.

The abortion didn't happen. And now I have my two boys. But that pregnancy nearly broke me. It was harder, riskier, sicker.

After my first delivery, my doctor had explained my rare Rh-negative blood type. He'd warned me: "The first pregnancy is a freebie. After that, every pregnancy is high risk. You'll get very sick." He'd given me a book with my blood type and told me to keep it in my purse at all times. If something happened, it would be hard to find a match to save me. This second pregnancy proved his point. I was ill, drained, and scared the whole time.

One morning at Mom's, we were having breakfast. My ex was at the table flipping through the newspaper, job hunting. Out of nowhere he said, "Oh look your ex from high school. Says he passed away." And then he laughed. A small, ugly laugh.

I snatched the paper. My heart dropped. Sure enough, it was him. California Boy. We were so young. He had a whole life ahead of him. And I had just seen him, just heard him call me his dream girl again. Now he was gone.

Mom heard my ex laugh and was furious. She said nothing but her eyes were sharp, her jaw tight. I couldn't even form words.

I got the information for the service, borrowed Mom's car, and went to pay my respects. When I arrived, his mother wrapped me in the tightest, longest hug. I hadn't been held like that in years. I could feel her pain pressing into me. She sat me next to her for the service. Everyone knew who I was we'd all grown up together. After the service she told me he had spoken about me recently, that seeing me at Chili's had made him happy, that he said I was the love of his life and that we'd end up together no matter what.

I couldn't speak. I was too emotional. I was there only to show respect.

Then she asked, almost begging, if my pregnancy could be her son's child. He hadn't had any children. Her eyes were pleading, looking for a piece of him to live on. I told her firmly no. We had only bumped into each other. That was all.

After that day, my head spun. I couldn't stop thinking about it. I couldn't stop seeing my ex's smirk over the obituary. I was disgusted, disappointed. I knew then with absolute clarity I didn't want to be with him.

This pregnancy was already brutal, my health fragile, my emotions frayed. And then, one morning, we were all in the car Mom, my ex, my brother son our way to a restaurant. Mom and I got into an argument. In a flash, she reached over and slapped me across the face.

In that moment, something inside me shifted. My chest burned, but not from shame. From resolve. It was my breaking point. I remember thinking, I'm not going to go through this anymore. This ends here. I talked to my dad and told him everything. I let it pour out. The pregnancy, the depression, the constant fighting, the disappointment, the fear. I begged him literally begged him to tell me what to do. I wasn't looking for a rescue, I was searching for answers. For peace. For a way forward. I told him I already had one child and now I was pregnant again, and I didn't want this cycle to repeat anymore. I asked him if there was anything anything he could recommend so I could make sure this never happened again. I told him I didn't want any more kids. That I was tired of struggling, tired of giving everything I had and still coming up empty.

I asked him for relationship advice, for parenting advice, even for business ideas. I just wanted a plan. I told him that even though I didn't love the man I was with, I felt like I had no choice but to make it work. I said, I already have two kids now who's going to want someone like me? I didn't believe I had any options, so I told him I was willing to stay. I was going to give it my all and try to build something out of nothing. That was the plan I had settled on. Even if it killed my spirit. It was so bad I didn't even laugh the same anymore.

Things only got worse. My car got repossessed. I had been trying so hard to keep things together, but the truth was, I couldn't even keep up with work. My body was shutting down. My mind was a mess. My spirit had already left the room. I remember standing at my mom's window watching them tow my car away like it was just another Tuesday. That car had been a symbol of my independence, my hustle, my progress. And just like that, it was gone. Another piece of me, taken.

Eventually I moved out of Mom's house. I couldn't take the tension anymore. I stayed with my older brother for a while. His apartment had stairs, and with how risky the pregnancy was, going up and down became dangerous. So I left. I moved in with my grandma Mom's mom. She lived just down the street from my brother. That move changed something in me.

This was the first time in my life I truly got close to her. She took care of me. And I helped take care of her. I cleaned up her house the way I used to help my ex's parents when I lived with them I just needed to feel useful again. I scrubbed and organized and tidied every room, making her space feel loved. She noticed every time. Her eyes would light up when she saw the changes, and I could tell she liked having someone around. But I always stayed out of her way unless she called me. I didn't want to be a burden. If she invited me to sit with her, I did. If she told me to come eat breakfast or drink coffee, I did. Otherwise, I stayed in the room. Quiet. Healing. During this time, my ex finally got a new job working at a furniture warehouse as a wood tech. It gave me more space more time alone with my grandma. We'd water plants outside and just sit, talking. She made coffee throughout the day, and every cup felt like medicine for the soul. We'd talk about everything her childhood, her relationship with my grandfather, why she was the way she was with her kids, including my mom. I'd never had conversations like this with her before. And for the first time in my life, I opened up too.

I told her everything. The truth. I told her why I left, why I filed for divorce, what I had been through. She hadn't known any of it. She listened without judgment. She looked me in the eyes and said, "If you know deep in your heart that you can't forgive him, then you need to stand on that. You're not me. I didn't leave. But that doesn't mean you shouldn't." She told me she was proud of me. That I had strength. That I just needed to believe in it. Then she said something that stuck with me forever: "Tú no necesitas un hombre." Meaning, "You don't need a man". It hit me so hard. She liked him, sure. But now that she knew the truth, she didn't try to convince me to stay. She just wanted me to believe in myself again. Still, I went through that entire pregnancy the same way I had the first without seeing my dad. We only spoke on the phone, sent emails, and mailed letters back and forth. He checked on me often, sometimes daily. I kept myself hidden, again. I don't know why. Maybe I didn't want him to see me like that. Maybe I didn't want anyone to see me like that.

Eventually, I knew I had to try to get back up. I started job hunting again. I wasn't picky I just needed something. Anything. A short term gig, something to hold me over while I figured out what I really wanted to do with my life. My dad guided me as best as he could, giving me steps to start from behind those prison walls. Even from there, he was still trying to lead me out. While all of this was happening, my dad got news that he was being transferred. He had been in the same facility for years, and finally, they were moving him to a medium-security prison closer to home. He called to tell me the news himself, and I remember the sound of hope in his voice. He said I'd be able to come visit more often now. He knew I was struggling, and even though he couldn't be out here with me, he wanted me to know he was still my anchor. Still my safe place.

And he always had been.

Even in the darkest moments, my dad never made me feel ashamed of where I was. He only wanted me to find my way out and he believed I could. I think in some strange way, knowing he was getting moved closer made me feel like maybe I was getting closer too. Closer to healing. Closer to myself. Closer to something better.

Eventually, I made it to the final trimester. I was exhausted, drained in every possible way, but I still wanted to create a moment of joy even if it was small. I threw a little baby shower, nothing fancy, just something to celebrate this new life. I knew none of what I was going through was the baby's fault, and I wanted to do at least one thing that reminded me there was still beauty happening in the middle of everything falling apart. That pregnancy had taken everything out of me. I was in and out of the hospital for all nine months. It was the most physically demanding, emotionally exhausting thing I had ever been through. And still, I kept going.

After I gave birth, my grandma stepped in and really took care of me. She made sure I was eating, bathing, healing. She cooked for me, held the baby when I needed a moment, and made sure I wore body shapers to help my body bounce back. She wasn't doing it out of vanity it was her way of showing love, of helping me feel strong again. That postpartum period was rough, but she was there through it all. Quietly, consistently. I'll never forget that.

Eventually, I landed a job working the front desk at a hotel. It wasn't glamorous, but it was something. I finally started making some money, enough to start thinking about leaving my grandma's house. Around the same time, some of my cousins moved in with her, and once they did, I knew it was time for me to go. I found a small apartment that offered a month-to-month lease. It wasn't much, but I didn't want to commit to anything long-term. I needed flexibility. I needed options.

Little by little, things started to shift. My finances were still tight, but slightly more stable. I even had a little bit of money saved some from the job, some from what my dad had sent me. I hadn't done anything for myself in a long time, so I decided to treat myself and get my nails done. I reached out to an old friend I'd seen on Facebook back when I still had one. She was doing nails now, and from the photos she posted, she looked legit. I messaged her and made an appointment for a simple sport-short French tip set.

The second I walked into her setup, I was amazed. Her space was beautiful. Cozy, feminine, professional. It was clear she took pride in it. And honestly, I know it sounds silly now, but I had no idea that anyone could just learn to do nails and make a business out of it. I didn't know this was even possible for someone like me. I asked her so many questions during the appointment and she didn't gate-keep. Not one bit. She told me everything about licensing, the programs, different schools, even options for art colleges. I left her place feeling something I hadn't felt in a long time: inspired.

The second I got home, I went down a rabbit hole on my phone, looking up local schools. That's when I found it University of Cosmetology Arts & Sciences (UCAS). I picked up the phone and scheduled an appointment immediately. I didn't even wait. Some-thing in me had woken up, and I wasn't going to let that fire die. Later, when I spoke to my dad, I told him about the school and how excited I was and he thought I was out of my mind. He told me I had already done enough schooling and hadn't used the degrees I had. He wasn't wrong. I had the paperwork but no real results to show for it. He asked why I didn't just go back to banking or customer service something "safe." I explained to him that I could always return to those fields. My old jobs had told me I was welcome back anytime. But none of those opportunities were in the Valley they were in Dallas. And with a car repossession now sitting on my credit, I wouldn't even pass the background check for a bank job. That door had quietly closed behind me. I told him this new path gave me a little hope. The school had flexible hours, help with childcare, financial aid, and even payment plans. I could keep working my night shift at the hotel and attend school parttime during the day. It was going to stretch me, yes. But long term, I knew it would be worth it. I just needed someone to believe in me and at that moment, that someone had to be me. When I showed up to UCAS for my appointment, I was so nervous. The front desk signed me in and gave me a tour. I walked past students working on real clients and others listening intently in classrooms.

I felt completely out of place. I was a mom now, with two kids. Could I really do this? Could I start all over again? My thoughts were racing the entire time. What was the plan? How much money could I make? Would it be enough to build a real future? Would it even work?

But still I stayed. I went through the whole tour and sat down to review course schedules, options, financial plans, graduation timelines all of it. They asked me if I wanted to think about it, and I said no. I didn't need to think about it. I needed to do something. I signed up that same day. I filled out my financial aid paperwork, paid my deposit, and locked in my start date.

The money I used came from my parents from the trucks. It was their hard-earned money, and even though things had been messy, I felt like I was finally doing something good with it. I owed it to them to try.

While juggling school paperwork, night shifts at the hotel, and taking care of the baby, I also kept searching for a better place to live. That apartment I'd rushed into was too small, too temporary. It didn't feel like home. I was in transition but at least now, I was transitioning forward.

Chapter 19

Daughter of the Grind, Not the Game. I was raised by the hustle but I refused the blueprint.

I gave my parents the news I was going back to school again! I was excited, nervous, and ready to do something for myself. But when I told them, they both kind of brushed it off. No big reaction, no proud moment. They didn't even ask any follow-up questions. My dad didn't hold back either he straight up said it wasn't a "real career" and that it wouldn't take me anywhere meaningful. According to him, it lacked potential. But that was just my dad being my dad always chasing money, structure, and status. He didn't understand anything that looked different from what he was used to.

My mom and grandma had a different kind of reaction. They weren't necessarily supportive, but they weren't surprised. They both kind of smirked and said, "We always knew you'd end up in the beauty industry." My grandma reminded me how I used to carry a paraffin wax bowl around the house, pretending to give her manicures and pedicures when I was just a kid. My mom laughed, saying it made sense because growing up I was always obsessed with nails and beauty but also pointed out how ironic it was because when I was a toddler, I was more of a tomboy. She said I used to cut the hair off all my Barbies and would rather play outside with my brothers and their Hot Wheels or bikes than touch anything remotely "girly." And now here I was nails, lashes, gloss, and all. Girly as hell. Life's funny like that. Around this time, my dad had just been transferred again this time to FCI Bastrop, a low-security federal prison in Texas. It held around 793 inmates, and I think the housing unit had about 1300 guys total on the yard. He finally got moved closer to us, which made communication a little easier in theory, but every transfer was the same mess. For the first couple of weeks, we wouldn't hear from him at all because it always took time for his phone and account access to be reactivated. No emails, no phone calls. Just silence until he got resettled, which was always hard. But thankfully, those transfers didn't happen often.

So, life continued. I started juggling school, my hotel job, and applying for something better because even while I was studying, I was still determined to find more stable income. And of course, I was also full-time momming it. Life moved fast. I barely had time to think between early mornings, daycare pickups, assignments, and bills. I constantly felt like I was running behind, trying to catch up to something invisible. Like peace was always just out of reach.

One weekend morning, we actually had a rare pocket of calm. I wasn't at work, and nothing was urgently due. He was in the kitchen making breakfast, and I was tidying up the bedroom, fluffing pillows, straightening blankets just trying to bring some order into the chaos. I can't remember exactly what I was reaching for or what triggered it, but I randomly picked up his phone. I wasn't snooping or going through it intentionally I think I was going to open the browser or look something up but the screen lit up right into a thread of messages.

And just like that, my stomach dropped. Again.

It was another woman. A girl he had gone to high school with back in Dallas. I knew who she was and she knew who I was. That made it worse. They were messaging back and forth like two teenagers sneaking behind lockers. Talking about getting lunch together, casually throwing in flirty emojis, winks, and suggestive jokes. One message even said, "No one needs to know". I'm pretty sure she was married too.

I didn't say anything. I just rolled my eyes, set the phone down right on the counter, and left the message thread open. I didn't feel like arguing. I didn't even feel shocked anymore. It was like my body already knew how to absorb disappointment. I was just… tired.

When he noticed I had read the messages, he immediately came over, wrapped his arms around me, and tried to act sweet. The same old tactic hug me, kiss me on the forehead, act like nothing happened. This time, it didn't even faze me. I was livid. My hands were shaking, but my voice was steady when I told him I was going to message her husband and let him know what was happening. I said I hoped he'd get his ass beat for disrespecting our marriage. I was so angry I could feel the heat in my face. He just stood there, quiet like always, eyes lowered. He never said much in moments like these. That was his pattern silence. And that silence made me look like the bad one every time. It painted me as the dramatic wife, the loud one, the extroverted, flirty, sassy troublemaker. People on the out-side probably thought I was the one causing chaos, but they didn't see what I was reacting to. They didn't see the betrayals. They only saw my fire, not the sparks that lit it.

I forced myself to shake that whole situation off and focus on what really mattered school and work. Around that time, I finally landed a job in an office an insurance and tax office. The pay wasn't great, nowhere near what I used to make in Dallas, but it was a step up from the hotel front desk. I took it without hesitation. The hours were grueling, especially when stacked against my school schedule, but I made it work because I had to. There were nights when I honestly thought about quitting school altogether. It was so much to handle nail anatomy, health and sanitation, sterilization, artificial nail techniques, business and professional skills for management and customer service. People think beauty school is just painting nails or doing hair, but it's not. It's studying the human body, safety protocols, and science behind every service. My mom would tease me, "Are you studying to be a doctor or to paint nails?" She had no idea how deep the coursework actually went. We had to learn about skin and nail types, nail health, treat-ment safety, recognizing health problems, all while practicing tech-niques. It was intense far more than most people ever imagine. On top of that, I was juggling tests, long hours, my boys, the house, and the stress of just keeping everything afloat. Even my car started giving me trouble. I had bought a little Beetle from a buy-here-pay-here lot. It looked cute at first, but maintenance was a nightmare. Then I got into an accident someone hit me and it never worked the same after that. I filed the insurance, dropped it off at the collision shop they sent me to, but even after repairs, the car kept giving me issues.

It felt like one more thing on an endless list of problems.

Finally, a little light showed up at the end of the tunnel. I found a small, cute house not too far from my job at a decent price. The landlord told me that if we rented for a year, we'd have the option to purchase. It had three bedrooms, a small but cozy living room, a nice kitchen, and even a garage. The backyard was just the right size not too big, not too small. I remember thinking, Thank God, I don't have time for yard work anyway. So we moved in. My ex bought some furniture, and so did I. Because he worked for a furniture company, we got high-end pieces at a steep discount. The house came together beautifully gorgeous, really. Everyone who visited complimented it, and for a moment, it felt like we'd built a little slice of stability.

But stability never lasted long for me. Not too long after we moved in, my dad called with news. He was being transferred again. By then, I was almost done with my school course, so hearing him say he was moving one more time hit me like déjà vu. This time, he was transferred to FCI Three Rivers in Texas, a medium-security prison for men with a satellite camp. It housed around 1,244 inmates 1,066 in the FCI and 178 at the camp. This was the closest he had ever been to us only two hours away. I asked him why he'd been moved from a low-security to a medium, and he ex-plained it was the only option to get closer to us. He wanted me to visit. He said he needed to discuss some things with me. His voice was calm but serious, and I could tell he really wanted that time. So I arranged the visit. I packed up the kids and took them with me so he could see them, especially my youngest. The moment he saw them, his entire face softened. I had never seen that side of him so gentle, so openly affectionate. He adored them. Even though he didn't approve of my ex-husband, he kept it respectful. He even asked my ex to take the kids and step away so he and I could talk privately. I stayed in Three Rivers for two days straight, visiting him both days. Those visits were heavy but also eye-opening like getting a glimpse at a version of my father I never knew existed.

That weekend, everything shifted. My dad opened up to me completely more than he ever had before. It was like he had finally accepted that I wasn't a little girl anymore, that I could handle the truth. He told me everything. The full rundown. Trips to Mexico, quick stops in Houston, deals in Dallas, even Oregon. He didn't hold back. I sat there listening, heart pounding, mind racing, as he gave me a play-by-play of everything he'd been involved in while he was out. It was surreal. Part of me already knew deep down, but hearing it confirmed out loud made it all too real. He was calm when he talked about it, almost casual, like we were discussing a business plan.

He also told me that even inside, he hadn't stopped hustling. He was running a little store from within the prison walls handling business for other inmates. Canteen stuff, commissary, favors. A full-blown operation. I remember sitting across from him thinking, He really never learns. But the truth is, he didn't want to stop. Hustling wasn't just what he did it was who he was. And deep down, he didn't want to be idle. He needed to feel like he still had control. Still had something of his own.

After that visit, I made it a habit to see him almost every weekend. It became our new routine. We'd talk for hours about everything work, school, the boys, the house, my job, his ideas. He'd ask questions, give advice, tell stories. There was something healing about those visits, even with all the heaviness in between.

Then one day, he asked me for a favor.

He said someone owed him money, and he wanted me to pick it up. He promised I wouldn't have to get out of the car. All I had to do was pull up, and they would walk it over to me. If it wasn't the full amount, he said they'd be handing over a car instead, to make up the difference. I went silent. My stomach turned. I didn't know how to respond. He went on explaining that I'd need to send him a portion to his inmate account, keep a small percentage for myself, and take the rest to his mother my grandma for safekeeping until he got out. It was all mapped out like a business transaction. I told him I would.

But the moment I got back in the car, I started talking to my ex about it. He didn't seem surprised. He just nodded and said, "Okay." No opinion, no reaction just passive, like always.

Later that night, my dad called. That's when I told him the truth I wasn't going to do it. I told him I loved him, but I loved my kids more. I told him we didn't know how something like that could go, no matter how "sure" he was. I told him I was trying to build something for myself, for my children, and I couldn't risk everything. I reminded him that he made a choice that left us behind once already, and I wasn't about to leave my kids the same way. I told him kindly but firmly that if he ever tried to involve me again, I'd stop visiting him. It was the hardest boundary I'd ever had to set with my father.

He apologized.

But just like always, he found a way to do things on his own. He had someone bring the money to me anyway without telling me beforehand. The person didn't even know what it was for. Dad was always one step ahead. He called afterward and told me to deposit it as we had initially planned. Turns out, he even had a cellphone smuggled in somehow. I don't know how he pulled it off, but he gave me all the details of how it happened. It was wild to hear. My dad was back in the game dealing again, from inside a federal prison. He had one of his best friends dropping off money to me regularly, both for him and for me. He said he was tired of seeing me struggle. He told me he'd do whatever it took to help. And I let him. I didn't stop him. As much as I wanted to live clean and do things the right way, I also knew how hard I was fighting to survive. That extra money kept the lights on. It kept gas in the car. And I told myself I wasn't asking for it. I told myself he was going to do it anyway. Meanwhile, my job started shifting, too. The owner of the office saw potential in me and wanted to invest in my growth. She told me to get certified with a county mutual license and offered to help me with training in tax preparation, too. She paid half of my tuition, and I paid the rest. I went to Dallas for a few days to take the classes and tests. I failed one of them and had to pay for a retake, but I didn't quit. When I got back to the Valley, I passed everything and was officially licensed. Around the same time, graduation for my UCAS beauty school program was coming up. I had signed my kids up for daycare and school right next door to my job so everything could stay as close and manageable as possible.

Graduation day finally came. I had done it. I had pushed through the hardest season of my life and came out the other side with a diploma in my hand. Not only did I graduate, I graduated at the top of my class and was selected to give the student speech during the ceremony. Standing on that stage, I felt proud of myself in a way I hadn't felt in years. It was like I had finally proven something not to anyone else, but to me. I took tons of pictures that day. I sent them all to my dad. He congratulated me, but I could tell he still didn't believe the beauty industry was the smartest choice. That was just who he was old-school, skeptical, always chasing bigger moves.

But to me? That moment was everything.

I had finally taken the time to really research the beauty industry and what it would take to build something of my own. I started taking clients from home during my time off from the office, little by little. I didn't just want to do nails I wanted to run a full business. I started building a client base, documenting everything, and writing out my business plan with actual structure. I knew I didn't want to work in a salon. I didn't want to clock in for anyone. I wanted my own suite, my own brand, my own hours. Total independence. That was the dream.

Thankfully, the school I attended wasn't just about textbook learning they let us work on real clients and practice the daily tasks of running a salon. It gave me so much hands-on experience. And even though this wasn't the same type of business my parents had run, I had grown up watching them hustle, watching them manage their operations, their books, their customers. The foundation was in me. I had taken business management as part of my course too, and I knew enough to take the first step forward. So I started with location. I drove all over town, checking out different suite rentals and store-fronts, writing down addresses, prices, square footage, and terms. Some of the pricing was outrageous. Unbelievable, honestly. There were days I sat in my car and thought, Am I insane? Everyone around me thought I was. Even I questioned myself. But I had a written business plan. I had a savings jar. And I had a fire in me that I couldn't explain. I was determined to follow through, no matter how crazy it looked from the outside.

At one point, my dad tried to get involved again. He had a friend reach out and offer to help me financially, but I turned it down. I didn't want anyone's money if it meant being tangled up in something that could compromise me. I was trying to stay clean. Trying to prove that I could build something on my own terms. And meanwhile, I was still working full-time in the insurance and tax office though that job was draining me more than helping. The owner was arrogant, petty, and constantly on a power trip. She piled tasks on me that weren't even in my job description, treated me like I was disposable, and talked down to me as if I didn't have goals of my own. I was getting fed up. Now, you're probably wondering how I was even thinking about opening a salon while holding down a 9 to 5. I wondered too. But the answer was simple I was stacking every single dollar I made from nails. I wasn't touching that money. I used it for supplies, equipment, tools, and marketing. I ran specials constantly. I did $20 full sets sometimes even less just to get my name out there. I wanted people to try me out, talk about me, come back, and bring their friends. That's how I built momentum. That's how I built trust. But behind the scenes, my relationship with my dad was getting more tense. We were arguing constantly. He kept insisting on me running errands for him or sending more money from whatever side hustles he had going on. I told him over and over I wasn't making Dallas money anymore. I was doing my best, but I wasn't in the same place financially. He didn't want to hear that. He was so desperate to help that he kept pushing me to listen, convinced his way was the answer. I started ignoring some of his calls.

One visit, we got into it so bad I stood up and walked out on him.

His face turned blood red. He looked stunned like he couldn't believe I'd actually done it. But I was done folding for everyone else. Done people pleasing. Done getting pushed around and guilt tripped and manipulated. That day, I chose myself. I finally, fully, chose me. And for the first time in my life, I stopped explaining it to anyone.

I even started going to the gym. Just a small local spot with a $10/ month membership. I had never been inside a gym before. I didn't even know how to turn on a treadmill at first. I hired a trainer once a week to show me how to move, how to lift, how to take care of my body. I was learning everything from scratch, just like I was with business. But it felt good. It felt like I was coming home to myself, one rep at a time.

Months passed and eventually, my dad helped me get a new car. A silver Chrysler 300. Sleek, comfortable, grown. I loved that car. He told me to take the money he'd been saving and just use it. He said it was part of my reward for everything I'd been doing on my own. He made me promise that when he got out, if he ever needed help, I'd return the favor. I told him I would—but only if it was legal. That was the deal.

The new car gave me more freedom to travel and visit him again. But of course, people started talking. I remember one person's face when she found out about the car. She gave me the dirtiest look and snapped, "How is it even possible that your dad is in there and got you a car?" She was livid. Furious that someone like me could have something nice without her understanding the full story.

And that—that was exactly why I kept to myself.

Why I distanced myself from family.

Why I stayed quiet about what I was building.

People were always ready to judge, always ready to assume the worst. No one ever asked how hard I was working. No one ever asked what I'd sacrificed to get here. They just saw the result and rolled their eyes. But I was over it. I was done explaining my blessings. I had earned them.

And I wasn't slowing down for anyone.

I had finally started diving deeper into the beauty industry not just the art of nails, but the actual business behind it. I spent late nights doing research, watching videos, reading articles, and mapping out what success could look like. On my days off from the insurance office, I started taking clients at home. I rearranged a corner of the house, sanitized everything like we were taught, and gave every client the most professional experience I could offer. Slowly but surely, I began building a client base. I tracked their preferences, wrote down their names, kept notes in a little notebook, and began drafting a real business plan. I already knew I didn't want to work under anyone. Not in someone else's salon. Not by someone else's rules. I wanted ownership. Autonomy. I wanted to build something that was fully mine.

Thankfully, the school I had attended gave me more than just theory. We were able to work on real clients. They showed us what it meant to run a full salon not just nails, but operations. Booking, customer service, sanitation, merchandising, professionalism, even conflict resolution. It was a full picture, and it gave me confidence. Plus, I had also taken business management, and I had the muscle memory of watching my parents run their companies for years. Even if it wasn't in the same industry, the foundation was there. I understood the grind. I understood the structure.

So I started with location.

I drove around town sometimes for hours checking out different suites, storefronts, and buildings that were available. I'd pull into random plazas, peek into empty windows, jot down leasing company phone numbers, and do the math on what I could afford. Some of the prices were absolutely ridiculous. Laughably high. There were moments I sat behind the wheel staring at the numbers, thinking, Maybe they're right.

Maybe I am crazy. Everyone around me seemed to think so. They'd make little comments or try to bring me back down to earth. But I had a written business plan and a spark I wasn't about to smother. I was determined to follow through with or without anyone's approval.

At one point, my dad had a friend reach out to me, offering to help with startup money. But I turned it down. As tempting as it was, I couldn't risk getting pulled into something that felt off. My gut said no. I had already drawn my line. I knew how quickly one favor could turn into a mess.

So I said thank you but no. I was still clocking in every day at the insurance and tax office anyway, even though the job was starting to wear on me. The owner treated me like I was lucky to be there. She was condescending, nit picky, and constantly assigning me tasks that weren't even part of my role. I was exhausted and frustrated, but I kept my head down and did what I had to do for now.

You're probably wondering how I even planned on opening a salon while juggling a 9 to 5 job and everything else. The answer was simple: I stacked every single dollar I made from nails. I didn't touch it. I used it to buy equipment, order products, restock supplies, and fund my dream little by little. I ran crazy specials just to get clients in the door $20 sets, referral discounts, anything to build momentum. That's how I started getting my name out there. Word of mouth was everything, and I made sure every client left satisfied.

Meanwhile, the tension with my dad had started rising again. He kept trying to involve me in errands and money drops. He wanted me to send more cash or coordinate favors like before. I kept telling him I wasn't making as much as I had in Dallas.

I was stretching every dollar just to stay afloat. But he was relentless. He said it would benefit him and it would benefit me too. That it was a win-win. I started ignoring some of his calls, especially when I knew I didn't have the mental energy to argue. On one of my visits to see him, we got into it again. Bad. I stood up, looked him in the eye, and walked out mid conversation.

His face turned blood red, and he stared at me like he couldn't believe what just happened. But I meant it. I wasn't going to let anyone push me around anymore. Not even my father. I had spent so much of my life people-pleasing, trying to keep the peace, making sure everyone else was okay even when I wasn't. I was done with that. That season was over.

I started choosing me, unapologetically.

I was over it.

I wasn't just trying to survive anymore.

I was building something with or without their approval.

If I ever needed money, my dad would tell me to swing by my grandma's house to pick up fifty or a hundred dollars, especially on the days when I was traveling to see him with the kids.

It was his way of making sure we were taken care of, even from inside. He would tell me exactly where to go, what time to stop by, or to bring Grandma along so she could visit too. It was routine by then. His voice on the phone saying,

"Ve a la casa de tu abuela, ella tiene algo para ti."

That was his love language making sure we had gas money, snacks for the road, or a little something for the boys. Our relationship was complicated, always a roller coaster, but even with the arguments and disappointments, I couldn't deny how deep our bond was. At the end of the day, he was my best friend. No matter how ugly the fight, one of us always broke the ice.

Either he'd call and act like nothing happened, or I'd show up to see him, pretending I wasn't mad anymore. Somehow, we always found our way back to each other.

Around that time, something in me shifted. I started going to church again faithfully, every week. Twice a week, actually. Sunday morning service and Wednesday night Bible study.

On the outside, things were moving. I was doing well at work. I had finished school. I was building my client base. But on the inside, I still felt broken.

There was a hollowness I couldn't fill with money, hustle, or achievements. I needed something deeper. That's when I made the decision to get baptized and give my life to Christ. I didn't tell many people. I didn't want to be labeled as one of those people who act holier than thou. That wasn't me. I wasn't trying to pretend I had it all together. I was still a mess. I still had questions, pain, and patterns I hadn't broken yet. But I just wanted peace. I wanted clarity. And every time I walked into that sanctuary and heard the worship music play, I felt it. That stillness. That softness. Like I could breathe again, even if just for a few minutes.

My mom was proud of me for taking that step. She had already been a Christian for some time. My dad, on the other hand, had different beliefs and didn't really understand why I felt the need to change. But he didn't argue with me about it. He just stayed quiet and let me do my thing. At home, things with my ex stayed... quiet. That's the best way I can describe it. It wasn't good, it wasn't terrible it just was.

We coexisted. Polite. Calm. Present, but not connected. Like two people living under the same roof, raising kids, going through motions, but no longer building anything together. It was there but it wasn't.One afternoon, I went in for a routine check-up at the doctor's office, and they found something abnormal during my pap smear. I was scheduled for a bio freeze treatment. My ex wasn't planning on coming with me at first, and honestly, I didn't expect him to. But someone from his job overheard and told him he should go, and surprisingly, he did. I didn't say much, but deep down, I appreciated it. I was nervous and didn't want to go alone. And I'm glad he came because right after the appointment, as I walked out of the building, I fainted. Everything went black. I don't know if it was the stress, the procedure, or just my body crashing from everything I had been holding in but I passed out cold. He caught me and helped me back into the car. In that moment, all the complicated feelings between us didn't matter. I was just grateful someone was there.

Not long after that, I borrowed my brother's truck to pick up a new mattress from the warehouse where my ex worked. I remember that day with crystal clarity. My phone would not stop ringing. I ignored it a few times, thinking it was just clients or spam, but something in me finally said, Pick it up. When I answered, it was one of my dad's old friends. He didn't greet me or make small talk. Instead, he asked, "Where's your brother?" I paused, confused. "Why?" I asked cautiously. And then he told me.

My older brother had been arrested.

I felt the blood drain from my face. My hands went cold. My throat tightened. I went pale and froze right there in the parking lot. I don't even remember if I put the mattress in the truck. I just stood there, trying to breathe. I yelled at the man on the other end of the phone said things that came from a place of rage and betrayal. Things I can't take back. But I meant every word in that moment. How could this be happening? How did we get here?

I hung up and started calling my brother over and over. Straight to voicemail. I panicked and started digging, trying to figure out where he was, what had happened, and what the charges were. I finally found what I needed and met up with my dad's friend to give him all the information. He looked at me like he wanted me to fix it. Like it was my responsibility to tell everyone. And just like that, the weight of this whole mess was dumped onto my shoulders.

I had to be the one to call his girlfriend. I had to be the one to tell my mom. I had to be the one to deliver bad news that shattered people's hearts. I felt like I couldn't breathe again. The pressure was unbearable.

Not long after that, my phone rang again. It was a call from prison. I knew it was my dad. As soon as I accepted the call, he didn't even say hello. His voice cracked through the receiver: "Tell me it isn't true." That was all he said.

And I broke.

I burst into tears and yelled at him through the phone. "How dare you?" I screamed. "How dare you involve my brother in this mess?

How dare you put him in that position?" My chest was heaving, my voice shaking with rage. There was silence on the other end. A long, painful pause. He didn't argue. He didn't yell back. He just said, "Let me fix this."

Then, as calmly as he could, he gave me instructions. What to do. Who to call. How to handle things from that point forward.

And I did it.

Because that's what I always did.

I talked to my brother's girlfriend first, and she was absolutely livid. I expected shock, maybe some confusion but what I got was pure rage. She was furious at my dad, at the situation, at the fact that no one had warned her. I couldn't blame her. I had barely wrapped my own head around it. Not long after that, I sat my mom down and told her I needed to talk to her about something important. I could feel my heart pounding the entire time. When I finally told her the truth that my brother had been arrested her reaction mirrored mine. She was enraged. Her voice trembled with disbelief and anger. She immediately demanded to know if I had been involved. My stomach sank. I told her no, that I hadn't been part of it, and that I didn't know all the details. I didn't tell her how many times Dad had tried to pull me into things, or how close I had come to being caught in the crossfire. She didn't need that weight. I made sure to gather every piece of information I could. I tracked down court dates, locations, timelines anything that would help us stay ahead of what was coming. I updated everyone. My dad's friend stayed in contact too and eventually asked if I could help take my brother's wife to some of the hearings. He gave her some money to hold her over for a bit while they figured out what came next. We were all in crisis mode, trying to stay afloat. I arranged another visit with my dad to confront him face-to-face. I needed answers. He sat across from me and swore that he had never instructed my brother to do any of what had happened. He looked almost as confused as I felt. But I couldn't shake the disappointment. Whether he meant to or not, it had happened on his watch through his circle, his lifestyle, his shadow. I couldn't pretend it didn't trace back to him.

Meanwhile, my brother's case moved fast faster than my dad's ever had. He got transferred almost immediately, and before we knew it, he was sentenced. His girlfriend and I made the drive to visit him regularly. It became a rhythm, a routine we didn't ask for but had to adapt to. My mom and I took the kids to see him too. I wanted to keep the kids connected to their dad, even if it was through glass and visitation hours.

I started writing him letters weekly. Long ones, sometimes pages and pages, where I'd update him on life, send him pictures of the boys and his kids, tell him silly stories, or remind him of things from our childhood. We had always been goofy together, and I tried to keep that spirit alive. Even in those dark places, I wanted to give him some light. Something to hold onto. A little normalcy.

The place he was in wasn't too bad compared to others. It almost looked like a small camp, quiet and calm. They even held family days, kind of like outdoor field day events where the inmates could interact more with their loved ones. We took the kids to one of those events once, and it was beautiful to see them laughing and playing together. For a few hours, it didn't feel like prison. It felt like family again.

I visited my brother a few times on my own too, just me and the road. But now I had two men behind bars to visit my dad and my brother. And to be honest, my relationship with Dad had taken a major hit. Those few months were hard between us. I still visited when I could, but there was distance. Emotionally and mentally. He knew I was hurt.

Still, I kept him updated. I told him how close I was to graduating and how I wanted to open up a salon right after. I told him I had already started scouting locations and working on my plan. And in true Dad fashion, he listened, gave advice, and promised support in his own way.

But something about him had changed. My siblings and I all felt it. We found ourselves getting into arguments with him more frequently. He was moodier, more demanding, more secretive. Ever since he had been moved to Three Rivers, Texas, something was just...off. At first, everything had seemed fine. He was excited to be closer to us. But being near familiar faces, familiar habits, and familiar temptations started to bring out the old version of him again. The one we had all tried so hard to forget. The one he had claimed was gone.

We did our best to keep him in check, but he was stubborn. Always had been. And even though his release was finally getting closer, it felt like we were losing him again. He was almost done with his sentence. He had completed the required courses, taken the rehab programs, and earned two years off his original ten year sentence. He was so close to being out. To being free. But I didn't know if he was truly ready. Or if we were ready for what would come next.

Chapter 20

You Don't Get to Fund My Future. "Business Minded, Heartbroken Daughter".

♥ *This chapter includes emotionally sensitive themes such as parental betrayal, family tension, isolation, and references to a serious accident. Please take care while reading.*

While I was going to school, I started bringing in my own clients to the campus so I could get more hands on practice. At the time, the long, dramatic, blinged-out sets were all the rage especially duck nails, which were making a huge comeback. Our school was constantly on us to pull in people from the outside to help us complete our salon hours. It wasn't just encouraged it was required in order to graduate. I was hustling both inside and outside those school walls, networking and exchanging numbers with every client I could. I knew I needed those contacts when I graduated, so I could start building up my clientele from the ground up. Every single interaction counted.

At one point, the school announced a nail art competition, and it was a pretty big deal. Each student had to participate it counted toward our grade and we were allowed to use any nail products we wanted. Acrylic, gel, polish, rhinestones, 3D art, glitter anything and everything was fair game. We were encouraged to be as creative and bold as possible.

Some of the girls used practice mannequin hands and built out these insanely long, intricate nails with full 3D sets. There were butterfly themes, pirate themes, cartoon designs, you name it. Some of them looked straight out of a museum display case. My design? A full blown Dallas Cowboys theme. I went all out. I decided to build a football helmet out of acrylic yes, actual sculpted acrylic. I started by blowing up a balloon to use as my base. Once I laid the acrylic over it and let it fully dry, I popped the balloon and began shaping and carving out the rest of the details. I molded a star from acrylic too and hand-painted everything using nail polish. I mounted the finished helmet on top of a plastic practice hand and, of course, added a full nail set to the hand silver and blue nails to match the team colors. Then I used even more acrylic to anchor the helmet to the hand for display. The entire piece was bold, detailed, and over-the-top just the way I like it. Listen if there's one thing about me, it's that I love everything extra. My goal is always to go above and beyond, to leave a mark that nobody forgets. And I did exactly that. I passed with flying colors, and everyone students, staff, even visitors loved it. Truthfully though, the whole competition was a vibe. Everyone showed up with their own twist, and the creativity in that room was something special.

By this point in the course, I was already doing almost every girl's nails in my class and even some from the other classes too. But to be honest, the school itself was a mess when it came to structure. We had so many different instructors rotating in and out during my time there. That was one of the hardest parts: no consistency, no rhythm. But then, midway through the program, we got an instructor who finally changed everything and I loved her.

She was Mexican, from Monterrey, Nuevo León. A total powerhouse. Elegant, sharp, and incredibly skilled. Her English wasn't perfect she had an accent but she carried herself with such class and grace. She brought fun and professionalism into the classroom. She made things interesting again. She didn't just teach nails she talked to us about the business side too, about what it takes to run your own salon and be your own boss. Her presence was magnetic. She taught us how to create 3D art, sculpt roses, draw intricate characters things I never imagined I'd be able to do. But beyond technique, one of the most valuable things she gave me was language. She taught me how to speak nail Spanish. I learned how to name every finger and explain every step of the nail process en Espanol. She made me bilingual in my craft and that became such a powerful tool for my future clients and my confidence.

I opened up to her about my business ideas. Sometimes I'd even talk to her after hours to get her input. I would share things my dad had suggested, too because even then, I was still bouncing ideas off him, telling him every move I planned to make. But I always ran it by her for a second opinion. She had owned a salon herself once, so she understood both the dream and the reality.

I told her I didn't want to work for anyone. I had a vision. I wanted to create something of my own something bigger than just nails. I wanted to build a space where women could work, grow, and win. I had this dream that one day my team would come to work and tell me they just bought their first house, or paid for their college, or finally got a car all because they had steady work, good pay, and respect in a salon I created. I wanted to be the opposite of every boss I'd ever worked for. Because truthfully? I'd had so many jobs where the owner or manager acted superior, constantly looked down on employees, and created toxic environments. I was done with that. I wanted to change the game.

That was my real goal not just nails. Not just business. Impact.

One late evening, I was finally home and everything was quiet. The boys were asleep in their rooms, the kitchen was cleaned and sparkling, the lights were off except for the soft glow of my dimmed bedroom lamp. The whole house smelled fresh and warm like Fabuloso and candles and for the first time in what felt like forever, there was nothing left to do. No dishes, no toys, no chaos. Just silence. It felt like the ocean after a storm: still, glassy, and calm. I could breathe. I stood in front of the mirror washing my face, doing my skincare routine, and for a moment I thought, maybe things are finally settling down. Maybe this is my new normal. The house looked beautiful. The furniture was exactly how I had dreamed, my side hustle was thriving, school was going well, and thanks to Mary Kay my skin had never looked better. I felt like I was learning not only a new craft for my future but also learning myself all over again. I was becoming a better mother, a better granddaughter, a better sister. I was taking care of my brothers' kids, being present for my Grammy, and pouring into my boys. I was cleaning up my image, my heart, my habits. All of me. For a second there, I felt a fragile but real sense of peace.

But that calm didn't last long.

My phone rang. It was my dad. At first, the call felt normal his voice was light and chatty, joking around like he always did when he was trying to ease into something. He asked how the boys were, how school was going. He told me to sit down because he had something to tell me. Immediately my stomach dropped. He said, "Don't get mad at me..." which is never how you want a conversation to start.

Then he dropped the bomb. He said he was "talking" to someone having a "relationship," as he called it. I froze but stayed quiet, waiting for him to finish. And then he said it: it was with one of my aunts. One of my aunts.

I remember every detail of that moment. The dim room. My wet hands still dripping from my skincare routine. The sound of my heartbeat in my ears. He kept talking, explaining, and then said it was my mom's sister. That she had been visiting him and now they were "serious."

Something in me snapped. It was like every buried feeling about betrayal, humiliation, and broken trust came back all at once. My mind immediately flashed to my own marriage to the betrayal with my cousin. Out of all the people in the world, how dare he? How dare my father put me in this position?

I went off on him. I cursed at him something I had never done before, not even at my worst with him. I had walked out on my dad before. I had slammed phones and refused visits. But cursing at him? That was a line I'd never crossed. He threatened me in anger, and I went off even harder. I told him I didn't ever want to speak to him again.

Then he said something that made my stomach turn even more. He said, "I thought this would make you happy since you've always loved her like a mother." I couldn't believe the words coming out of his mouth. It felt surreal, like I was listening to a stranger. I hung up on him mid-sentence, crying hysterically.

He called me back over and over. I ignored every call. I ignored his emails. I shut him out. For days I couldn't eat. I lost my appetite, my focus. I just wanted to lie in bed and disappear. It felt like depression slammed into me out of nowhere. This wasn't just about him "talking" to someone. It was about the flood of memories it triggered betrayal, infidelity, family secrets. The feeling of being blindsided all over again.

I had always known men could break my heart. But my father? That was a kind of pain I never prepared for. And I kept thinking about my mom. Even though she and my dad weren't married anymore, I hated the idea of her finding out. I hated the thought of her feeling the same kind of gut-punch heartbreak I felt. On top of that, my aunt had once been married to my dad's own brother. It was like betrayal layered on top of betrayal.

By then, my dad was spiraling inside the prison. He had gotten multiple cell phones, was running a store inside, making money however he could. All the progress he'd made, all the steps he'd taken to be better it felt like he was undoing it in front of me.

Eventually, I answered one of his calls. He was furious with me for ignoring him, but even then, he didn't want to hear my side. I threatened to hang up again. He begged me not to. I told him flatly that I needed time. He asked me to come see him in person, to talk it through face-to-face. But I told him I had nothing to say. I needed distance.

And for once, I chose myself.

He knew I was never going to be okay with it. Deep down, he knew. But what offended me even more was what came after he called again and brought up my schooling. He mentioned how I was going to beauty school and casually said he could help me open a few salons. Then, as if that wasn't already tone-deaf enough, he said he could open the salons for me and my aunt. That the two of us could own them together. That was the moment I nearly lost it. The suggestion alone triggered something in me I didn't even know was still raw.

I told him flat out I didn't need him, and I definitely didn't need her. How could he even say something like that to me? Nobody in our family had ever gone to college. No other woman in our family had pursued school or built something of their own like this. I was the only one who had pushed through not just dreaming, but doing. And now he wanted to hand my dream to someone who didn't earn it, didn't build it, and definitely didn't deserve to benefit from my work? It was infuriating.

In the middle of all this chaos, I had also signed up for Mary Kay. So I was juggling school, doing nails, working a job, and running my Mary Kay hustle. I made it work by blending them all cross-selling like a one man brand machine. Anytime I had nail clients, I handed out Mary Kay business cards too. I started hosting little skincare parties or kept products displayed at my nail station. If a client needed moisturizer, foundation, eye cream I had it on hand, ready to go. That's how I began stacking more money and building up my confidence as a businesswoman.

Then came the visit.

A few weeks after the fight with my dad, I finally agreed to go see him in person. What I didn't know was that she would be there too. My aunt. She had driven down from Dallas to Three Rivers, and I had driven up from the Valley. When I arrived and signed in at the visitation desk, I saw her sitting there, and everything in me went cold. She barely acknowledged me, no hello, no eye contact, just tension you could cut with a knife.

When my dad came out, he sat her on his right and me on his left. I'll never forget the moment she looked at him and said, loud enough for everyone to hear, "How do you expect us to get along when she won't even say hi to me? Look at her." She pointed at me like I was a problem, a child, a nuisance. I clenched my fists under the table. My blood boiled. That was lower than low.

The guards who worked visitation already knew who I was. They'd seen me visit with my mom before. They knew the dynamic. And now here I was, forced to sit beside this woman while pretending not to break down or explode. That entire visit was awkward, painful, and emotionally exhausting. I couldn't wait to get out of there. I remember thinking to myself over and over: Please let this be a bad dream. Please let me just wake up.

After that, I kept my distance from my dad. We still spoke, but it wasn't the same. I didn't visit as often, and when we did talk, I kept it short. I had too much going on in my own world to keep getting pulled into his. I was focused laser focused. I knew that if I didn't commit 110% to what I was building, I'd get distracted or derailed. And I had worked too hard for that. The only real comfort I had during that time came from my grandmother my mom's mom. She became my safe space. Most mornings, I would stop by her house. We'd drink coffee together, water her plants, fold laundry, or just sit on the couch and talk. That slow, quiet time with her became one of my most cherished routines.

Before all this, my grandma and I didn't have a particularly close relationship. We were always kind and respectful to each other, but we weren't emotionally close. That changed during this season. If I didn't show up one morning, she'd notice right away and call to check on me. She'd ask why I didn't come drink coffee, and something about her asking always made me feel seen. Loved.

She had helped me so much during my second pregnancy, and now she was helping me again just in a different way. I opened up to her about everything. Even the mess with my dad and the woman he chose. I don't remember her having a strong reaction. I don't think she wanted to say anything bad about her daughter, and I respected that. We both tiptoed carefully around each other's emotions, but somehow it worked. We spoke like women who understood the weight of complicated family history. I told her how I felt, and she accepted it without judgment. She didn't try to change my mind or fix it. She just listened. That was enough. That was everything. Whenever I'd start to spiral or lose my cool, she knew exactly how to calm me down. Like she could reach inside all the chaos and smooth it back down with noth-ing but a soft word or a second cup of coffee.

That connection with her it grounded me. When everything else felt out of control, my mornings with Grandma reminded me that healing didn't always come in big dramatic moments. Sometimes, it was found in quiet conversations, in fresh coffee, and in someone simply choosing to sit beside you without trying to fix or judge.

A few weeks after everything blew up, word reached me that my aunt had been in a serious accident on her way to see my dad. The details were vague, but I knew enough to understand it was bad severe enough to cause damage to her face. I didn't ask for specifics. I didn't know if she had surgery, how she was recovering, or what the full outcome was. And honestly, I didn't want to know.

What I did know was that, even though I couldn't support what they were doing, I didn't wish bad on her. Not then, not ever. I stayed in my lane, didn't gossip, didn't make jokes, didn't even comment on it beyond a few words to my dad. I just...kept quiet. But inside, I was angry at him all over again. Angry because he had dragged everyone into this chaos. Angry because he had created a situation where even accidents felt like part of some dark karmic ripple. I went off on him again after the accident, not because I was glad it happened I wasn't but because I couldn't wrap my head around why he had chosen this path in the first place.

The thing about my dad and me is that our relationship wasn't something most people would understand. We were extremely close closer than we had ever been in my entire life especially during his time in prison. We thought alike. We'd finish each other's sentences. We could read each other's moods without even trying. When we talked business, it felt like we were two halves of the same mind. He was pure street smarts; I was pure book smarts. Together, when we brainstormed, it was like building something unstoppable ideas, plans, dreams.

For nine years behind bars, our conversations had been some of the best of my life. We had built this father-daughter connection from scratch, and in some ways it was deeper than anything we had when he was free. But I had to remind myself when he went away, I was just a girl. Fourteen, maybe fifteen. All my memories of him on the outside were from childhood, which had been a rollercoaster: highs, lows, good days, scary days. The consistency, ironically, had only come with his incarceration. Prison forced routine. Prison forced letters, calls, visits. Prison had built our bond.

By the time my boys came along, he had slid effortlessly into the role of grandfather. If anything, he was a better grandpa than he had ever been a father. It softened him. Every time I visited with the boys, his face would light up. He'd scoop them into his lap, teach them little tricks like sipping soda without spilling or eating neatly without a mess. He loved to pose for pictures with them, like he wanted proof of every moment he was missing. He would talk for hours about the things he planned to show them when he got out farming, ranching, how to raise animals, how to live off the land.

Even his style had shifted. He'd tell me how, when he got out, he wanted a simple white BMW SUV clean, classy, comfortable, nothing flashy. Enough room for the grandbabies, enough space for a life without chaos. He would tell me, with regret in his voice, how he wished he had stopped the old life earlier, how he could have simply stayed with his trucks and his business and had a steady, comfortable life. I took in every word. It stuck with me because it sounded like a man reflecting on the life he could have had.

That's why this whole situation with my aunt broke me the way it did. It wasn't just betrayal; it was like watching everything we had built all that trust, all that progress go up in smoke. I felt like I'd lost my best friend. I'd lost my dad. I'd lost the version of him I had started to believe in again. I still spoke to him from time to time, but nothing like before. The calls felt forced. The warmth was gone. I couldn't understand why he would do this. I had held him up in my heart as someone who, despite all his flaws, was trying to be better. And now it felt like I'd been wrong all along. This was the man who had helped people get their first car, their first home, their first job, who had protected so many people and poured into them. I knew there was good in him. I had seen it with my own eyes. And yet, here he was making choices that felt like the ultimate step backward. It broke something in me that I still don't know if I've ever fully gotten back.

I even told him once in full confidence that I was going to be so damn successful that when the time came and he got sent to Mexico after his sentence, I'd help him rebuild a life out there. I meant it. I told him he didn't need to worry. I'd take care of it. I had it all mapped out in my head.

But being "Dad," he didn't like that idea not because he didn't believe in me, but because he didn't want his daughter grinding the way I was. He supported my dream of building a business, owning something of my own, creating a career. But he didn't like that I had to work so hard just to stay afloat. In his mind, it was a man's job to build a life where a woman could be soft. Where she didn't have to hustle to survive, but instead had the freedom to nurture a passion or a craft she loved not because she had to, but because she wanted to.

That was his philosophy. He used to say, "It's a man's job to make the woman soft." To create a space where she could rest, feel safe, and thrive. A space where she could move with grace, not stress. "Women are the roses in the garden," he'd say. "Men are the gardeners. It's their job to water the roses, to feed them, protect them, and keep the garden in order." He believed that real men set the tone through actions, consistency, discipline and that women, in return, mirrored that tone.

It was traditional. It was old-school. But it was how he thought.

And because of that, I think deep down he could sense just how shattered I was. He knew that after what happened after he told me about his relationship with my aunt everything we had built was suddenly fragile. The calls. The trust. The bond. It had all shifted. He could hear it in my tone. Feel it in my absence. The daughter who once ran to him with every new idea, every problem, every decision, had gone quiet. Cold. Distant.

And I hated that. I hated that it turned me into someone I didn't recognize. I said things I wish I could take back, but I was caught off guard and grieving a version of my father I thought I knew. This wasn't the man I expected betrayal from especially not in that way. So I told him I'd be stepping back. That I wouldn't visit him as often, not while he was still talking to her.

I didn't make a scene. I didn't yell. I just shut off.

Instead, I poured myself into everything else. I worked my 9-to-5 job. I kept attending my Mary Kay meetings. I showed up to school every day, did nails at night and on weekends, and saved every extra dollar to invest in my future salon. I was raising my boys, managing my home, helping my mom with my older brother's kids, writing letters to my younger brother, and visiting him when I could.

All while holding back a storm I couldn't talk about.

I didn't tell anyone not my friends, not even my mom. And maybe that was the hardest part. Because even though my parents were no longer married, I still carried the weight of what this would do to her. I could feel the pain it would cause if she ever found out. And the truth is, I knew she never would've done something like that to him. So how could I bring myself to tell her what he had done to us?

So I stayed focused. It was all I could do.

I missed him. God, I missed him. He had become the first person I turned to for everything my mentor, my business advisor, my emotional support. And now I had to grieve that relationship while still pretending I was okay. I used to jump in my car and drive hours to see him without hesitation. If I had a problem, I'd hop on a flight or send him an email asking him to call. But after this, all of that faded. The connection was severed.

I was hurt. And I wasn't the only one.

Even though my brothers didn't speak on it, I could tell it rocked them too. They were men, sure tough, stoic but I knew deep down this whole situation disappointed them. It shook our whole family. Whether they admitted it or not, we were all trying to make sense of it.

Not long after that, my dad got transferred one final time this time to Big Spring, Texas. It was his last stop.

He went from being just two hours away to a full eight-hour drive.

Big Spring was a low-security, all-male facility with around 595 inmates in the main FCI unit and just over 100 in the camp portion. It was a smaller facility, more structured. And this we hoped would be where he'd finish his sentence for good.

But for me, it wasn't just the distance that changed. It was everything.

The man who once sat at the center of so many of my plans the one I wanted to succeed for, the one I wanted to help rebuild after prison now felt like a ghost in my life. Present, but unreachable. Alive, but changed.

And that broke something in me that I'm still learning how to live with.

Chapter 21
Terminal Illness and Bachata on Chains

TRIGGER WARNING:

This chapter contains graphic and emotionally intense descriptions of terminal illness, including physical deterioration, hospital confinement, and dehumanizing treatment of a patient during end of life care. It includes vivid imagery of medical restraints that may be distressing to those who have experienced medical trauma or loss. Please read gently and take care of your emotional space.

While Dad was now in Big Springs, Texas, I didn't go see him as much. He had also requested fewer visits, saying it would help him get through this last stretch easier and faster. He always said that the more we visited, the more it stretched time out like taffy, making the days drag on; if we visited less, time would just flow faster and he could mentally push through. I never knew if that was true or just his way of protecting himself from the pain of goodbyes, but I honored it.

He started asking for money all over again to start another store at the new facility. Every transfer wiped him clean he'd lose almost all his belongings, his setup, his routine. He told me he would hand down his things to other men to help them make some money for their commissary or just have something of their own. He said he liked helping those whose families wouldn't come visit, who didn't have the resources to be successful inside. Sometimes it was hard to believe him after everything we'd been through, but part of me still wanted to believe he was trying to be better, even in there.

I only took a few trips to see him, and when I did, I tried to turn it into a mini vacation. I would book a nice hotel with a jacuzzi tub in the room, order good room service, and shut the world out.

I've never been much of a go-anywhere kind of girl, so having a place with good amenities was always a win in my eyes. A good bar downstairs was a bonus a girl loves her whiskey and it helped calm the nerves, soften the edge of wanting to fight my dad. I was still so feisty with him back then. I'd tell him on our visits how much I loved the drive to Big Springs because it took me through San Antonio, how I fell in love with the city each time I passed through. I'd tell him one day I'd move there, to the far west side where it was green and open. "If you want it, go for it," he'd always tell me, adding that the city had more opportunities to grow.

Oh, how I wish he were still here to tell you about the real conversations we had our huge fights, our stubbornness colliding like two storms. He would sometimes look at me and say, "Don't forget who I am," like it was supposed to scare me. And I would shoot back without hesitation, "Well, don't forget who birthed me and whose daughter I am." I don't know why, but that line always disarmed him. He would either go completely silent or break into a smile. Me, on the other hand, I never knew how to stay quiet. Anytime he wanted to say or do something, I fired right back.

There were so many times he tried threatening my mother. And even though my relationship with her wasn't and still isn't the best, I defended her fiercely. I'd threaten him right back if he crossed the line. The same went for my brothers. I warned him more than once about dragging them into his mess, telling him that if he did, he'd have to deal with me. He had awakened a side of me I hadn't yet learned how to control. I'd always been controlling not in a malicious way, but in that driven way that comes from needing things to be perfect, on track, ahead of schedule. Maybe it was an old wound, being overlooked, misunderstood, or underestimated for so long. But somewhere deep down I knew I could turn struggle into strength, confusion into clarity, and pain into power. It was at 23 and 24 that my voice truly sharpened. I'd always had it, but now it came from a deeper, more personal place fueled with fire and anger. No matter how much I wanted to be soft, I just couldn't.

By then Dad had more connections outside of prison than ever before. As his release date crept closer, he'd constantly send his friends to check on me, to make sure I was taken care of. They all knew I wasn't on the best terms with him, but he never stopped watching after me, even from behind bars. Somehow Dad always knew my every move mine, my mom's, my brothers'. My older brother was on house arrest at the time, waiting for his court case to finish. He was granted that privilege because he had no record. None. My older brother had always been a hard worker, and I was so damn proud of him. In fact, all of my brothers inherited that trait the grit, the hustle and I loved that for them. I loved it for me too.

Every time Dad called, he somehow already knew what I was up to. He'd ask questions in that way he always did, as if he'd been watching from a distance. Sometimes it felt like he had eyes everywhere. For a while, I was short with him. I had so much on my plate, and his calls no matter how much I loved him felt like extra weight I wasn't sure I could carry. Someone once told me, "Don't sweat or stress the small stuff." I tried to hold onto that advice, but some days it felt like everything was big stuff. I had told him about the situation with the lady whose house I was renting. She'd changed her mind about selling, and I was tired of feeling like I was throwing my money away. Deep down, I'd always wanted something of my own a place to invest in, something stable, something I could build a future on. With my new project of wanting to open up a salon after graduation, I knew my time, energy, and money were about to be stretched even thinner. I either needed to size down or find a home I could actually buy, so that all my hard earned money wasn't just slipping through my fingers into someone else's pocket. Every week I picked up the paper and magazines at the gas stations, flipping through them like a ritual. My eyes scanned for salon suites, available spaces, anything that could hold my dream. But the prices scared me. Two thousand dollars or more a month before a single customer walked through the door. And if the building was unfinished? That was on me too: flooring, paint, lighting, plumb-ing, licensing, permits. All of it would cost an arm and a leg, and rent would still be due from day one whether I opened or not. The numbers swirled in my head like an endless math problem, and yet,

I couldn't let go of the dream.

I told my dad I needed to start building a team even before I found a building. If I knew which girls or guys wanted to work with me, at least I'd have backup and stability. So I began spreading the word at school. Everyone thought I was bluffing, but I knew exactly what I was doing. I could see the vision even when no one else could.

My days at school started getting pushed back a little because I missed hours leaving to talk to Dad in person. Despite our differences, I still went to see him. I wanted his help with this project—if not financial, at least guidance. I also knew the next few months we wouldn't be seeing each other as much. He'd asked for fewer visits, and I was going to respect that. I would lock in on my goals while he locked in on finishing his time. It felt like a win-win situation: we both had work to do and needed to keep our eyes on the prize.

But time has a way of revealing things you're not ready to hear. I found out Dad was still talking to my aunt. On one of my last visits to see him, she showed up too. That moment still sits heavy in my chest; it was my last time seeing Dad in a visitation room, my last time seeing him in that setting. We took our final pictures together, and he even took some with my kids. I didn't know then how much I'd replay that moment later.

After learning about my aunt, I told Dad I was stepping aside. He looked so hurt, but I couldn't side with him on this one. I'd been his ride-or-die so many times before, but not for this. Not for anything illegal. That was a line I wasn't willing to cross, no matter how much I loved him.

Even after I stepped back, Dad still tried to watch over me. He'd have his friends bring me money to make sure I was doing okay. He'd even given them orders to help me find a house I liked, with strict instructions that if I didn't like it, they had to respect my decision. It was his way of still trying to take care of me from the inside. I looked around at the houses. I thought over everything. But I never decided on anything. My pride wouldn't let me. I didn't want my dad to one day throw it in my face, to say I wouldn't be where I am without his help. Just imagining that future fight haunted me. The thought of having something so important tied to his power over me felt unbearable. So I finally denied his help, even though a part of me wanted to say yes.

I had decided to move in one more time with my mom and put all my nice furniture into storage. It wasn't an easy decision, but it was the smartest one. This move was going to help me get closer to the area where I wanted to open the salon and still be close to the city. The Valley may be small, but I wanted to be right where the growth was, where the movement and opportunities lived. Somewhere with visibility. My mom cleared out a room for me, and I told myself this was only temporary. Not a step backward just a stepping stone. A "later" to get to where I was meant to be. And I reminded myself of that every single day.

I started taking nail clients from my mom's house, just to keep momentum going. I wasn't about to sit around waiting for the perfect timing. I knew I needed to keep building my client base and stacking that side money for the salon. Everything I was doing was out of pocket. Not a single dime came from a bank loan. I had everything written down my vision, my numbers, my plan. I even printed and laminated it. I had documents for my business plan, financial goals, and personal home planning. All I had to do was stick to it.

Writing things down has always helped me stay focused. I'm a very visual person. If I can see it, I can do it. I need reminders in front of me. I write everything down and leave it where I can see it, where it stares me in the face until I make it happen.

While I was already doing nails from my mom's place, I started hunting even harder for a permanent salon location. I set a date in my mind a goalpost for when I wanted to be up and running. I had just wrapped up my hours at school and completed most of my salon time. All that was left was studying for my state exam and getting it scheduled so I could be fully licensed. By November 2011, I had officially completed my entire course. Some of the other girls were still working on their hours, so our graduation ceremony was going to be pushed a bit so we could all finish and celebrate together. Then one day, completely out of nowhere, I was driving around and saw ita salon set up for rent. It felt like divine timing. Like a literal sign from God. The building already had manicure tables, pedicure chairs, and everything inside. The owner was renting out the building and selling all the equipment inside with it. Nothing needed to be installed. It was already there, already ready. I bought everything from her in cash, right then and there, and secured the building too.

I already had the clients lined up, so I knew I could cover rent. The salon was located right between the heart of the city and the outskirts a perfect middle ground with great accessibility. The building itself was a little older and needed some love. The inside was functional, but not quite my vision. It had good bones, but I wanted it to reflect me. So I was willing to wait and renovate before opening the doors. This also bought me time to finish my exam and get all the licenses and permits lined up properly.

I hired someone to design the name of the salon and create signage for both the front entrance and a larger sign that would face Main Street. I was intentional about placement and branding. I wanted people to see it and feel something. Parking was great, too, which was a big deal in our area.

I chose paint colors that felt clean and warm. I bought cleaning supplies and started working on giving the space a fresh, soft touch. The two pedicure chairs that were already installed came with plumbing and all they were black with a grey base. Simple, but elegant. There were three manicure tables already set up too. Honestly, it was the perfect way to start. Just enough to grow into, not too over whelming to manage alone.

I bought everything else myself microfiber towels, a sterilizer, tools, professional products, gel polishes, a cash register, and the register system. I even had a landline installed specifically for business use. I was determined to set boundaries this time.

I had a terrible habit of booking clients through my personal phone no matter where I was or what time it was. It made me feel like I was constantly working, constantly reachable. I could be at a party, having dinner, or spending time with my family, and I'd be glued to my phone booking appointments. That kind of hustle sounds admirable, but it drained me. I never had a real break.

One night, I got a text from a client while I was out enjoying happy hour. I replied instantly, out of habit. The next day, I re-read the message I had sent her and it was filled with typos. I was so embarrassed. That moment taught me a lesson I never forgot: I had to start respecting my own time.

I couldn't keep mixing business with my personal life like that. I needed to learn when to reply, and when not to. I needed to be more than a businesswoman I needed to be a woman with boundaries. And this salon? It wasn't just a dream come true. It was my first real chance to build that kind of balance.

By this time, I was no longer working at the insurance and tax office. I hadn't left because I wanted to or because I felt ready; I left because I simply couldn't tolerate the owner any longer. She had started treating me like her personal assistant instead of her employee, sending me on errands for her kids completely outside my job description and walking in with an attitude as if she had the right to speak to me however she pleased. I reached a point where the disrespect became louder than the paycheck. One day I simply handed her my keys and walked out.

After that, I doubled down on working out of my mom's house. I pushed sales harder than ever. I booked myself at all hours and all days. I had something to prove to myself, to everyone that I could do this on my own terms.

One late evening, while I was doing nails on one of my absolute favorite clients, my cell phone rang. It was the kind of call that makes your stomach drop before you even answer. They had already called twice. I hated answering the phone while working my clients were paying for my time, and I always tried to respect that but this felt different. I asked my client if it was okay to take the call, and she immediately said yes. She was so understanding.

It was a call from FCI Big Spring, Texas. My heart started racing as soon as the man on the line spoke. He asked for me directly and then asked, "Are you Felix's daughter?"

I froze but said, "I sure am."

Apparently, Dad had given them my number as an emergency contact. Out of everyone, he gave them mine. Even now, I still feel the weight of that choice.

The officer told me I needed to head that way immediately because my dad was very ill. My hands went numb. I already knew Dad hadn't been feeling well he had been calling me and my mom asking us to call the front desk at the facility to pressure them to take him seriously. He'd told the staff himself that he wasn't feeling well, but nothing was being done. It felt like shouting into a void. So he turned to us, hoping our voices would matter.

I remember my mom calling the facility, her voice sharp with urgency. I remember her arguing with the officers on the phone, warning them that if something happened to my dad, they would be held responsible. I think that's what finally made them send him to get checked.

Now, hearing this officer on the phone, I felt like my chest was caving in. I asked him how bad it was because I had my kids, and I couldn't just leave. His voice was steady but heavy as he said, "It's really bad. I don't think your dad is going to make it."

At that exact moment, my acrylic brush slipped from my fingers and clattered onto the floor. It was like my whole body went cold. I was in shock, crying before I could even process what was happening. My client's eyes widened as she watched me break right there in front of her.

Even as I write this now, I'm in tears. It was one of the worst days of my life.

Amanda if you ever read this I'm so sorry you had to witness that moment. I will always love you and be grateful for how supportive you were during that time.

I told the officer to give me everything I needed names, numbers, location anything that would help. I said I would be on my way immediately. I explained that I was eight hours away and would need time to get there, but I was coming. No hesitation. He gave me his direct contact information and told me to reach out if I needed anything during the drive.

I swallowed my tears, blinked hard, and somehow pushed through to finish my client's nails. There was no way I could leave her half done, not with her hand in mine and her eyes looking back at me full of concern. She didn't even know what to say. She tried to leave right then and there, insisting that I didn't owe her anything and that I needed to go take care of my dad. But I couldn't let her walk out like that unfinished, uneven, not polished. That wasn't how I worked. I told her gently, "Let me finish what I started."

The second she walked out the door, I broke. I walked straight into the kitchen, and before I could even get the words out, I collapsed into my mother's arms. I told her everything what the officer said, how bad it sounded, that I needed to go now. She immediately panicked. I could feel her chest heaving beneath me as she started to cry and then switched into prayer like second nature. She called the church, asked for prayers, and started a prayer chain on the spot. She told me she was going with me there was no discussion. She wasn't going to let me drive eight hours in that kind of state, and especially not by myself.

I called my ex-husband and begged him to help me watch the boys. I explained what was happening, voice trembling, heart breaking. At first, he said it would be hard to miss work, but when he heard the desperation in my voice, he didn't hesitate again. He said yes. I told him I could ask my brothers or family for help if needed, but I just needed him to help right now.

It was one of the hardest things I'd ever done leaving my boys behind. I had never left them before, not for a trip, not for a break, not for anything. The guilt hit me like a wave. The grief of what I was heading into, the weight of watching my mother cry, the strength I was trying to hold onto for my dad it all hit me at once.

I packed what I could and we got on the road that very night. My mom and I drove through the entire night. She kept me awake with conversation, music, and her quiet presence. She cried with me. She held the silence when I needed silence. And she kept talking when I couldn't talk. She made sure I didn't fall asleep at the wheel. I owe her so much for that drive for staying awake and being strong

306

when I couldn't.

When we arrived, they checked my documents at the hospital and confirmed my identity. The officers told me that my dad had left specific instructions: no one else could see him, receive updates, or sign anything on his behalf except for me. If paperwork needed to be filled out power of attorney, medical forms, anything it would go through me only.

I knew the weight of that was going to cause problems. I already knew some people in the family would take issue with it. But in that moment, it didn't matter. I agreed to everything. It wasn't time to fight with my dad or anyone else about what he wanted. He made his choice clear, and I honored it.

Once the paperwork was complete, they finally walked me into the hospital room where he was. Nothing could have prepared me for what I saw.

He looked like a different man. He had lost so much weight. His face was sunken, his skin pale. He looked frail, exhausted, and weak. He had already undergone one surgery before I even arrived. His body was chained to the hospital bed hands and ankles as if he could run anywhere in the condition he was in. It was heartbreaking.

For the first time ever, the officers didn't stop me from walking in with my purse or my cell phone. They didn't separate us, didn't bark instructions. They just stepped back and let me be a daughter. I fought the tears, forced a little laugh, and pulled a joke on him as I walked in. I said, "Oh no, is that my old man? You better chin up, sir. You look kinda bad."

He let out a laugh. It was weak, but it was real.

And just like that, I fell into him into his arms, into his chest and I cried. Cried like a daughter who had tried to be strong for too long. He held me, told me to stop crying, told me everything was going to be fine. He said it over and over like he could will it into existence. Then the doctor came in and told me the truth. They had done surgery, but my dad had Stage 4 colon cancer. And after the surgery, the cancer had already started spreading to his lungs. Fast. Aggressively.

It was only going to keep spreading.

And nothing has ever felt the same since that moment.

My dad's birthday was coming up the following week. He was 47 years old and just days away from turning 48. That number felt so young. Too young. Especially for someone like him he had always been athletic, strong, and tall with a frame that looked unshakable. Health and image were everything to him. He carried himself with pride, always focused on how he looked and how he moved. That's why hearing he had cancer stage four, and already spreading was like being told the sky had fallen. It didn't make sense. How could someone who looked like that be sick on the inside?

The hospital allowed me to stay in his room with him. The nurses brought in extra pillows and blankets so I could sleep next to him. It wasn't much, but it made all the difference. I didn't want to be anywhere else. Dad couldn't get up on his own anymore, so I helped him when he needed to go to the bathroom. I can still hear the sound of the chains dragging on the floor as he shifted off the hospital bed, trying his best to move with dignity even in pain. The nurses helped when they could, but sometimes he couldn't hold it and when that happened, I was there. I didn't flinch. I didn't hesitate. I just helped.

I would step out from time to time to make quick phone calls and keep the family updated, since no one else was allowed to see him. I also needed those small moments to call and check on my babies. I missed them so much. My mom was so patient during this timeshe'd wait outside or in the waiting area, never rushing me, just quietly supporting. Even while I was there physically and emotionally over-whelmed I still studied for my licensing exams. I'd sit on the side of my dad's bed while he slept, going over my notes and trying to focus in between waves of emotion. I was also still working toward opening the salon. Even though I was hours away and everything felt like it was on pause, I didn't want to let it fall apart. During this time, the officers at Big Spring helped me with something

I'll never forget. They encouraged me and gave me the steps to write formal letters to the warden, the governor, the vice president, and even the president of the United States to request a compassionate transfer for my dad to MD Anderson in Houston. They believed in what I was trying to do. They knew how serious his condition was and didn't stand in my way. Without their help, I wouldn't have even known where to start. I still carry so much gratitude for that.

When Dad's birthday arrived, I was still there with him in Big Spring. I couldn't let him be alone on his day. I asked my ex-husband if he could bring our kids to visit. I needed to see them to hug them, even for a little while. They stayed for a bit, and just having them nearby brought me back to life for a moment.

That day, I stepped out and bought a small cake. I asked Dad what he wanted to eat anything in the world and told him I would get it, no matter what. I got permission from the officers, and they granted it without hesitation. I'll never forget what he asked for. A brisket taco and a regular vanilla ice cream cake. Nothing fancy. Just simple comfort food. And so, that's what he got.

He could barely eat, if I'm being honest. But he tried. He took a few bites, and we sang happy birthday. I watched him smile through it, even in pain. I would've given anything to freeze that moment.

The very next day was my firstborn son's birthday. But we didn't get to celebrate that year. There was just too much going on. Too much emotion, too much weight. That was a moment I quietly stored away in my heart one I knew I'd make up for later.

I ended up staying with my dad through the rest of December. Eventually, they moved us into a room on the tallest floor of the hospital. It had the biggest window and the prettiest view of the town. It felt symbolic, like they knew how much we needed peace, even if it was just in the form of sunlight and a view.

I played music on my phone while Dad rested. Some days he would hum along quietly. Other days he slept in silence while I sat on the couch nearby, still studying, still pushing toward the goals I promised myself I wouldn't give up on.

There were always one or two officers stationed in the room with us. Dad still wasn't allowed to be left alone, even in this condition. But by then, it was always the same ones, rotating shifts. We got to know them. I got used to their presence, and they got used to mine. They gave us space but were still part of those long, quiet days. In a strange way, they became part of the memory too witnesses to one of the most sacred, fragile seasons of my life.

While my dad was asleep, the officers assigned to our room would often start small conversations with me. I think they just wanted to make the time feel more human, less heavy. They'd ask me what I was studying, what I was planning to do after I got licensed, and where I wanted to take my career. I'd answer in pieces, distracted but grateful for the company.

Then, little by little, they started sharing things with me about my dad things I'd never heard before. They told me what he was like during his time at that facility. They said he was deeply respected, that he treated everyone with dignity and carried himself with quiet authority. They told me he was respectable toward the staff and the inmates alike, that he wasn't just known he was admired.

One of them admitted that they'd wanted to meet me for a long time. They said my dad always talked about me. Always. I hadn't been able to visit as often as I wanted to I had school, my kids, work, life but apparently, it never stopped him from speaking about me with so much pride.

They told me that every time I stepped out of the room, whether to grab food or take a call, my dad would turn to them and talk about me. He'd point out the window and say, "You see that car she's driving? I helped her get that. She deserves that and so much more." That sentence never left me. It sat in the back of my chest like a whisper I'd always wanted to hear out loud.

The officers were always kind to me. Always respectful. They didn't treat me like just another visitor they treated me like a daughter who mattered.We got to spend Christmas of 2011 together. It was quiet, simple, but full of warmth. And then, just a few days later, it was my birthday.

December 30, 2011. I turned 25 years old in that hospital room. It would be the last birthday I ever spent with my dad.

That day, the officers all stepped out for a moment and came back in with a cake and birthday gifts. They had pulled together what they could to make the day feel special and it worked. Even the nurses surprised me with something small and sweet. One of them told me, "Out of all the daughters we've seen come through this hospital, you're one of the most caring. Your dad is blessed to have you here." Maybe they were just being kind. But it meant the world to hear those words. I had helped a lot. Even when it wasn't pretty. I helped change the bedsheets when accidents happened. I got him out of bed slowly so the nurses could clean. I helped him shower and stretch his arms while he leaned on me. He could barely walk anymore. The cancer was moving fast so fast, it felt like he was fading right in front of me, day by day.

That night, when they brought out my birthday cake, he could barely hold the fork. It was strawberry with white icing. He took two small bites and smiled at me like he wanted to eat the whole thing but just didn't have the strength.

That same day, since the guards had already allowed me to use my phone for work, I pulled up Pandora and played some bachata. I reached for him and got him to stand up just a little, and we swayed to a song or two right there in the room. It wasn't a dance—it was a memory. A last one. I caught one of the guards wiping away a tear.

The next day, that same officer didn't return. He had requested to be taken off shift. He sent a handwritten note with the other guard that said the situation was affecting him emotionally, and he respectfully apologized. I didn't take it personally. I understood. Some moments are just too heavy to witness, even from the sidelines. On the night of New Year's Eve, Dad and I stayed up and crossed into midnight together. We stood next to each other, looking out the window from the highest floor of the hospital, watching fireworks scatter across the sky. We held hands as the night changed years.

I had spoken to the rest of the family on the phone. They were all celebrating, having drinks, trying to keep the mood light. I think my brothers were still in denial at the time. They didn't want to believe that Dad was actually sick. That it was cancer. That it was real. They clung to the idea that maybe, just maybe, there would be a miracle. That someone would walk in and say the diagnosis was wrong, or the surgery worked, or that he was going to heal.

But I couldn't judge anyone for how they processed what was happening. I was living it right in front of me, and I could barely handle it myself.

That night, we didn't say much. We just stood there, hand in hand, watching the fireworks burst above the town from that big hospital window. It was quiet, sacred, and still. It was our New Year. And it became one of the most unforgettable moments of my entire life.

Author's Added Note: Now that I look back, it's crazy how vividly I can still see everything. I remember the smell of the hospital room, the soft beeping of machines, the drag of the chains when he tried to stand, and the way the guards would quietly step out when they saw we needed a moment. I can still picture the exact way the fireworks lit up the sky that night on New Year's Eve, his hand in mine. It's like that whole month lives in a little glass box in my memory painful, but sacred.

What's even more surreal is that some of the officers I met back then still reach out from time to time. One of them added me on social media years ago, and every now and then, he'll send a message just to say he's proud of me or that if my dad were still here, he'd be proud too. One day, he messaged me out of nowhere after seeing a bouquet of soft white and yellow flowers simple, peaceful ones that reminded him of the ones I had asked to be placed in the hospital room while we were there. I had asked for those because we were in the middle of fall and winter, and they gave a nature feeling to the room. I wanted to add life to such a heavy moment. He said seeing them again brought him right back to that time, to the love I had shown my dad, and to the quiet strength I carried.

We didn't stay in close contact, but I think they remembered how I never left my dad's side. How I tried to bring even just a little softness into that room, even when everything felt so hard. I don't think they'll ever fully understand how much those little messages mean to me. Somehow, it feels like a small piece of my dad still finds a way to speak to me through them. Like he's still watching... just quietly now, from somewhere I can't see.

Chapter 22

The Strongest Goodbye That No One Respected

This was supposed to be the final goodbye. A sacred one. A moment of peace after a decade of chaos. But even in death, my father's life and mine were surrounded by whispers, tension, and eyes that didn't see the full picture. This chapter isn't about the drama. It's about the strength it takes to stand tall while your heart is breaking, to protect dignity in the middle of noise, and to honor someone you love even when no one else understands.

When the holidays were over and the year crossed into January, the warden at the facility where my dad was being held finally made the decision to release him. His condition had worsened rapidly. Because his illness was now terminal, there was no reason left to keep him behind bars. He was no longer a threat to anyone just a dying man trying to hold on a little longer. I remember getting the call that it was official, and everything after that felt like a blur I had no choice but to walk through.

During that time, one of my uncles my dad's brother, who I'll call Uncle B—stepped in and became one of my biggest sources of strength. I honestly don't know what I would've done without him. He guided me through every single step, every phone call, every legal form. I was emotionally drained and exhausted, so I just followed his directions like it was a checklist for survival.

He asked me to get in contact with MD Anderson Cancer Center in Houston, and I did. But sadly, they let us know that they couldn't take my dad's case. His cancer was too advanced too far along for their treatments to make any real difference. That news crushed me. I had been holding on to that tiny sliver of hope, praying maybe Houston could help us. But hearing the word "too late" just echoed the finality of it all.

By the time we were making arrangements to bring Dad home, he had already had visitors at the hospital his mother, a few cousins, some uncles. People came to say goodbye in their own way. It was bittersweet seeing so many faces show up for him, especially knowing how things had played out over the years.

Uncle B didn't hold back. He paid for everything flights for me, my grandma, and my dad. He wanted to make it as smooth and painless as possible, especially since the drive would've been long and uncomfortable for Dad. I kept thinking about what this experience must have been like for him. He had been locked up for over a decade. And now he was out, not with freedom in his hands, but with sickness in his body and limited time in front of him. Everything must've felt so strange. The airport. The noise. The cell phones. The people. The stares. The cold air. The screens. The wheelchair. It all had to be jarring. My heart broke for him in a hundred different ways that day.

At the airport, I tried to make things as normal as I could. I ordered us food something simple for my grandma, my dad, and myself, so we could have a small meal on the plane. Dad barely touched his food. Grandma didn't eat much either. I think we were all anxious, afraid to say too much, afraid of what was coming. I asked my grandma if she wanted to take my seat next to Dad so they could sit together, but she gently declined and told me to stay with him. She knew he needed a lot of help standing and moving, and I was stron-ger and quicker to assist him. That moment stayed with me. I didn't know it then, but I would treasure those hours sitting next to him on that flight for the rest of my life.

When we finally landed in South Texas and made our way to the hospital, it felt like everything started moving in fast forward. The hospital filled with family. My cousins came. My kids arrived. My mom showed up. My brothers were there. For a second, it felt like a family reunion but the kind you pray never happens under these kinds of circumstances.

And as much as I hate to even bring this part up, it wouldn't be real if I didn't. The family drama started almost immediately.

Every time the doctor came into the room to give updates or discuss options, they would pull me out. Always me. They'd ask me to step into the hallway, or into a quiet room, and go over everything directly with me. Paperwork. Medical reports. Final wishes. And every time it happened, I felt a mix of emotions mostly sadness, but also a little frustration with my dad.

You remember how I said that he was the one who instructed all communication go through me only? That he told the doctors I was the only person allowed to receive information or make decisions on his behalf? Yeah... well, I didn't ask for that. I didn't sign up for this kind of pressure or authority. I wasn't trying to be the one in charge I was just trying to hold it together and be a daughter.

My brothers were pretty neutral during this time. There was no tension between us. But outside of that, chaos started brewing. One of my sister-in-laws in particular got upset. She didn't like that the doctors weren't speaking to my brother directly. She told him that he needed to "step up and demand answers" because he was a son too and she wasn't wrong. She was just saying what everyone else was thinking.

But the thing is... I wasn't the one making the rules. I wasn't deciding who got to know what, or who got to stay, or who got to sign what. All of this was based on my dad's wishes. But that didn't stop the tension. That didn't stop the passive-aggressive comments, the eye rolls, or the unspoken accusations. It felt like I was doing everything I could to keep things afloat, but still being met with side-eyes and whispers like I was trying to control the narrative.

And I hated it.

Because deep down, all I wanted was for everyone to come together, love my dad, and give him peace during his final days. Before all of this, my dad had a one-on-one conversation with me. It was one of those moments that etch themselves into your soul because you know, even as it's happening, that it's going to change you forever. He knew his illness was terminal. He knew he wasn't going to make it. And in his quiet but steady voice, he told me that if something happened if his heart stopped he did not want to be brought back to life. He signed the paperwork for it right there in front of me. "This was his decision."

It was one of the heaviest moments of my life. I didn't realize then that this conversation would stir up so much conflict later. I don't know if my family thought I was the one making that decision or pushing for it, but I wasn't. Not at all. This wasn't my choice. It was strictly, specifically, my dad's request. But still, I had to sit there and listen to everyone argue about how they wanted him resuscitated if something happened. I had to listen to their wishes knowing mine didn't matter, because this wasn't about me. I was just the one holding the paperwork.

As painful as it was, I agreed with my dad. I knew the doctor wasn't exaggerating when he explained what resuscitation would mean at that stage. He said if they tried to bring him back, his ribs would almost certainly break. My dad's cancer had spread so aggressively during November and December that by the time we reached the new year, it had already covered his lungs and even reached his brain. His body was shutting down. He couldn't speak well anymore. He couldn't walk. He couldn't do most of the things that had made him who he was. In just weeks, he had become almost unrecognizable.

He was losing his memory too. I remember testing him gently, asking if he knew who I was, just to make sure his mind was still there. Because he couldn't talk anymore, he'd just put both hands together and rock them like a cradle, showing me that I was still his baby. That small gesture broke me into pieces, but I smiled and nodded and said, "YES! See, you know who I am!" as if I could convince both of us to believe it.

While he was still in the hospital, I asked the nurses if I could bring in my nail equipment. I wanted to do something anything that would make him feel human again. My dad had been in prison for almost a decade and had never had a manicure or pedicure. His nails and toenails were so long they hurt him under his socks. So I packed up my travel kit, my portable pedicure bowl, and set everything up right there in the hospital room. I gave my dad a full manicure and pedicure, trimmed his toenails, filed them down, scrubbed his feet, massaged his hands, even shaved his face. It was my way of saying, I see you. I'm still your daughter. You're still my dad. The whole time I wanted to cry, but I didn't shed a single tear in front of him. I didn't want him to feel like a burden or like I was afraid.

When my dad was finally released through hospice, things got even harder. Early in his sickness, he had asked me that when the time came, he wanted to come home with me. I think, because he was so sick and because I hadn't been visiting him as much before, he must have forgotten that I no longer had my own home I was staying at my mom's. He kept insisting, saying he wanted to go to hospice but in my home. That request sat on my chest like a stone. I've carried that weight for years, feeling like I failed him by not giving him what he wanted. I wasn't able to provide a home for my dad during the most important days of his life, a place where he could just sleep, worry less, rest, and enjoy being loved by his grandchildren while we read to him or watched TV together.

But the hospice paperwork had been signed, and my dad was sent to my grandmother's house instead. That's where everyone my aunts, uncles, cousins, friends came to visit him. I still went to see him there, but I felt like I was being pushed to the side. Maybe it was all in my head. Maybe it wasn't. But my heart felt it just the same. My siblings and my mother would probably agree the atmosphere was tense.

After my dad got locked up all those years ago, I had slowly lost connection with my extended family. They didn't push me away; I removed myself. I was young, the house was a mess, and I had to do what was best for me at the time. So during this period, when everything was happening, I was seeing faces I hadn't seen in years. It was family, yes, but it didn't feel like home. It felt foreign, like I was stepping into a place where I used to belong but no longer did.

And through all of that tension, my dad was struggling to breathe. Sometimes he'd choke or stop breathing for a few seconds, and every time it happened, my heart seized up. I thought each one might be the last. I tried so hard to pull myself together, but there were moments I just couldn't. I would step out of the room, call my mom, or simply let out silent tears in the hallway where no one could see me. Then I'd walk back into the room, put my face back on, and sit down like nothing had happened. It was one of the worst feelings a person can ever experience watching someone you love slip away, while trying to stay strong enough to make it to the next moment.

I was in daily communication with my uncle "B." He never left my side family drama or not, he stayed locked in with me the entire time. It was like he made it his personal mission to make sure I wasn't alone. He knew how much I was holding, how heavy everything felt on my shoulders, because I kept him updated constantly step by step, sometimes multiple times a day. There were moments when I'd call him, and the pain in my chest made it hard to even breathe. The kind of pain that sits in your throat and makes your voice shake before the tears even come. And even though I refused to let anyone else see me cry not my family, not even my dad somehow I always found myself crying on the phone with Uncle B. I'd break, and he would catch me every time with his words of encouragement and calmness. He held space for me when I couldn't hold it for myself.

The hospice team was also incredibly kind. They called and texted often just to make sure we were managing everything okay. They offered counseling, therapy, any resources they had to help soften the weight of what we were going through. You could feel their compassion, even through a phone line. They didn't just treat my dad like a patient they treated all of us like humans, like grieving family trying to do our best.

My mom brought in her pastor and his wife to pray over my dad. She wanted to be sure that, no matter what happened, his soul was saved. I watched as they held his hand and prayed over him and he followed along. Even though he was weak, he pushed through and got the words out. He finished the prayer. And something about that moment brought a sense of peace into the room, even if just for a few minutes.

But my dad didn't last long. He passed away on February 4th just a couple of days after making it home. I think deep down, he was just holding on long enough to come home one last time. Once he made it, his body started shutting down almost immediately. He couldn't drink water anymore. We had to use little sponge swabs dipped in water to wet his mouth. He couldn't eat. Even his teeth had vanished I don't know how else to explain it. They were just.. gone.

It was one of the strangest and most heartbreaking things I had ever seen in my life.

I was there when my dad took his final breath. I was holding his hand, crying in front of him for the first time. And even in that final moment when he had nothing left to give he used what little energy he had to comfort me. He reached up with his trembling hand, ran his finger down his own cheek like a tear, and then gently moved it as if to say, no more. He was trying to tell me not to cry. Even in his last moments, he was still trying to protect me. Still trying to be my dad.

He was exhausted. I don't blame him. Even before we left the hospital, he was telling me, "Just tell them to stop already. Tell them to leave me alone." He was tired of being poked with needles, tired of the tests, the machines, the pain. He was ready to rest. When he passed, a lot of family members were in the room with us or standing just outside. And even in that moment of deep loss, we could still hear the whispers behind our backs. Comments being made. Judgments. Quiet criticisms. It was heartbreaking. We were already shattered and to feel that kind of coldness from the people around us only made it worse. I'll never forget the way it felt, standing there with my mother and my brothers, completely gutted, and still somehow made to feel like we didn't belong.

My mother had been married to my dad since she was just a kid. Say what you will about them, but their history ran deep. And even though their relationship was far from perfect, her grief was real. It wouldn't have been normal not to grieve after decades of shared life. She hurt. We all did. Thankfully, Uncle B had already taken care of everything. The funeral, the church service, the cemetery it was all arranged ahead of time. And while I was grateful for that, I can't lie those days moved like a blur. My body was there, but my spirit wasn't. I was operating on autopilot. I remember being at the funeral home, sitting at the front row with my brothers. We were his children, but no one knew that. Not a single person acknowledged us as his kids. They walked right past us as if we weren't there. Only a few came up to offer their condolences. It wasn't until much later that it really hit me how invisible we were in a moment where we should've been held.

My mom was disrespected at the service too, and that stung. I don't care what had happened in the past she was the mother of his children, the woman who had shared a lifetime with him. We were all grieving. And she deserved kindness, not coldness.

And when it came time to show a slideshow of photos, I wasn't allowed to put it together. That hurt more than I let on. But instead of fighting it, I made my own. I gathered all the photos the ones from Oregon, our Christmases, our road trips, the rare sweet moments he spent with his grandbabies and I put them all into a video. I didn't exclude anyone. I made sure everyone was represented because I wasn't trying to prove a point. I just wanted to honor the full story.

The funeral home allowed me to use a separate room with a TV to show the video, and anyone who wanted to come see it could step over. And they did. People watched, and smiled, and cried. They saw memories they hadn't seen in years. They saw the version of him that we grew up with. The one who taught us to be strong. The one who danced. The one who laughed. My brothers and I didn't pay for the funeral, so we didn't get a say in how things were done. But I didn't make it about that. I simply asked for permission to share my video in the other room, and that was enough. And honestly, watching everyone's faces light up when they saw their photos come up next to my dad it made everything worth it. Because for a moment, it wasn't about drama or distance. It was just about him. About us. About all the pieces of a life that was complicated, painful, beautiful, and real.

The church service was held at the same church where my parents got married. I hadn't stepped foot inside since that day. As soon as I walked through the doors, the memories hit me all at once. The same walls that once held laughter and new beginnings now echoed with grief and final goodbyes. It was too much, too symbolic, too emotional to process all at once but I took it all in anyway. When the service began, the preacher opened with, "Wow, you all are an extremely beautiful family." And for a moment, it was like time stood still. We were all dressed in white my brothers, my mom, me. My brothers carried the casket with so much care and strength. As my dad's only daughter, I didn't walk beside them carrying it but I held his memory just as tightly in my hands. I carried something invisible, but just as heavy.

My ex-husband's work family sent one of the most stunning floral arrangements I've ever seen. That gesture meant more to me than I can even explain. In a time where I felt so isolated, so unsure of who was really there for me, they showed up with open arms and full hearts. They didn't have to but they did. And I'll be forever grateful. After the service, many of them came up to greet me, hug me, tell me they were proud of how strong I was. I'll never forget that.

And neither will I forget what my ex-husband did for me in one of the most delicate moments of my life. As the service ended and everyone began walking out, my father's casket was being carried out to the hearse. I was somewhere in the crowd, just going through the motions, completely outside of myself. And that's when he stepped in, gently pulling me to the front of the line. He told everyone that I was the daughter that I deserved to walk behind the casket, not be lost in the crowd. And just like that, they made space for me. It's wild when I think about it how I never got to walk down a church aisle in a wedding dress, never had that grand romantic moment people dream about. And yet here I was, finally walking down the center of the aisle… following the casket of my father. Everything around me felt like it was moving in slow motion. I looked up and locked eyes with so many people. Some stared with confusion, others with pain. It was written all over their faces, in ways words couldn't explain. I don't wish that kind of sorrow on anyone. After the service, I got into my own car to follow the limo carrying my family. Again, my ex stepped in. He made sure the escorting team knew I was the daughter. They repositioned the cars so I could drive directly behind the limo, instead of being buried in the line of vehicles behind us. That gesture small to some meant everything to me. Because in a moment where I felt overlooked, forgotten, maybe even invisible, someone made sure I was seen.

At the cemetery, I held myself together as best as I could. I've never been one to show too much emotion in front of others, but burying a parent there's just no preparing for that. It rips you wide open, silently and violently. My mom's pastor, his wife, and several church members came to show support. That kindness wrapped around me like a blanket. The pastor even purchased the wooden cross that was placed over my dad's casket and gave it to me as a gift. He didn't have to do that. But he did. I keep that cross safe. It's stored in a box with our last flight tickets mine, my dad's, and my grandma's from the trip that brought him home. I hold onto that memory like it's sacred.

There's no denying that I wasn't given the space or recognition I probably deserved throughout the process. But to be completely honest with you I don't care. I didn't care then, and I certainly don't now. Maybe back then it stung more, maybe I was still in a place where things like that mattered. But now, with age, with healing, with maturity I've let that go. What matters to me now is knowing I was there. Knowing I showed up. Knowing I loved him. Knowing I did right by him.

And knowing that through everything, my bond with my brothers has only deepened. I love them in a way that's hard to explain. If I ever lost one of them, I know I'd completely lose it. But even with that closeness, I've always known where my place is. I would never, ever try to take up the space that belongs to their children. That's not my role. That's not my right. No matter how much I love my brothers, I respect the role of a child grieving a parent. I could never stand in that place, nor would I want to.

But I do see myself as more than just an aunt. I'm a second mother. A second father, too, if they ever needed one. I'd be their shield, their safety net, their biggest protector. I'd help, guide, love, and educate them not because I'm older, not because I think I know everything, but because I genuinely love them. I love them the way I wish someone would've loved me through all of this.

And that, more than anything, brings peace to my heart.

When I got home, the phone started ringing nonstop. Family. Friends. People checking in. But I felt completely muted. Hollow.

I didn't want to talk to anyone. I couldn't. My ex took over all the calls for me. He became my voice when I had none. If someone insisted on speaking to me directly, he'd gently hand me the phone, but he shielded me from the bulk of it. I'll never forget that.

I remember one call in particular his stepmother called and said, "Poor T," meaning my ex. He immediately snapped back, "What do you mean? She just lost her father. She's the one grieving." That moment stuck with me. He had my back when I needed it most. And I ignored what anyone else had to say.

But then, like pouring salt into an open wound, I got a call from one of my cousins. She called me just to curse me out. No compassion, no check-in. Just drama. She accused me of being the reason her mom couldn't attend the funeral and blamed me for an arrangement that had been removed from my dad's grave an arrangement she claimed belonged to her mother. I calmly told her I had absolutely nothing to do with it. I already had the weight of the world on my shoulders, trying to hold myself together after the most devastating loss of my life and now this? It was disgraceful. Disrespectful. And above all, unnecessary. I was the daughter who had just lost her father and instead of honoring that they tried to diminish my grief and drag me into drama. It's inhumane and in a moment where grace and love should've been the only thing in the room. I refused to entertain the chaos, but that doesn't mean it didn't hurt. I had also gotten into a heated text argument with one of my aunts not long before. There was just too much happening, too many people projecting their pain in the worst possible ways. And I'll admit it I might've even lost it and gone off on a few people. I'm human. And my pain had reached its limit. But things only got worse. Some cousins actually showed up at my brother's house after the funeral, ready to fistfight. After the funeral. We had just buried our father. And here we were, facing chaos upon chaos. That moment was another line in the sand for me. That was when I truly began pulling away. I knew I needed to protect my peace, because every time things felt like they were starting to get better something always came along to ruin it.

And I didn't give myself much time to grieve. I jumped right back into work almost immediately. I had a salon to open, bills to pay, goals to reach. I had no choice but to keep going. Just 37 days after losing my father, I hosted the grand opening of my salon. I had been building it from scratch, and even though my heart was still shattered, I showed up with everything I had.

It takes some finesse to keep moving forward when your soul is grieving. There are moments where I catch myself thinking: What if there's no tomorrow? What if there's no next week, no next month, no next year? What if there's not even a next hour? And because of that because I've tasted that uncertainty I've learned to live differently. I live with urgency now. Presence. Gratitude. I don't wait anymore. I do everything I want to do today, because tomorrow isn't promised.

That kind of mindset tends to offend people. They don't always get it when I say, "Why wait? Do it now." But I'm not trying to be morbid. I'm not saying something bad is going to happen. I'm just saying: life is unpredictable. Life is life. You can walk out the door and not return. You can work out today and never step foot in a gym again tomorrow. You just don't know.

So I don't see anything as an obligation anymore. I don't have to go to the gym. I get to. I'm privileged to move my body. I'm blessed to have a membership. I don't have to go to work. I'm blessed to have work. I'm blessed to have plans. To be busy. To have problems worth solving. Every trial and tribulation I've been through has reshaped my perspective, and I see the world through a whole different lens now.

But back to the story.

When I first signed the lease for the salon, one of the very first things I did was reach out to my church family. I asked them to come pray over the space. I wanted to cover it in peace, protection, and purpose. Everyone came. They anointed the doors and walls and prayed with me and for me.

On March 11th, I hosted a grand opening celebration. Balloons, a beautiful cake, a ribbon cutting the whole nine. And I know this might sound wild, but on that first day alone, I made more than enough to cover the salon's rent for the entire month. I was so damn proud of myself. It felt like a divine confirmation that I was exactly where I needed to be.

From that point forward, I was fully self-employed. No more clocking in anywhere else. I worked at the salon every single day and ran service specials twice a week. I invested in paid ads and promoted my work like crazy on social media. I was everywhere. And yeah, I know some people were probably sick of seeing me post so much but I didn't care. Social media is free marketing. Why not use it?

I had worked so hard. Grieved so quietly. And risen so powerfully.

And this? This was only the beginning.

I kept my Facebook page open just a little longer, mainly for work. That's where I posted everything photos of the salon, updates on my services, hiring notices, any little detail I thought might help the business grow. It became more than just a platform it was a journal of my hustle, my healing, and my progress.

Around that same time, my brothers pulled my ex aside and had a heart-to-heart with him. They told him straight up that if he even wanted a chance to stay in my life, he had to grow up. Mature. Evolve. Because I was no longer the same woman I used to be, and I was only going forward from here. They didn't sugarcoat it. One of my brothers even offered him a lifeline an opportunity to work in the refinery. He had been stuck at a local job making the bare minimum, and there was no future there. No benefits. No real stability. This new job would be hard and dangerous, but it would offer real growth.

He took the opportunity.

His first project landed him in Oklahoma. He came to me and explained the situation. I listened. I understood. He's the father of my children, and if he was willing to make real changes, I wanted to support that. Not for us as a couple but for him, and for our kids. Watching their father succeed would make them proud. So I told him I'd help where I could. What I didn't expect was how quickly I'd become part of that journey.

Soon after he left, I found myself sending money to help cover hotel expenses, tests, certifications, gas everything. Starting over isn't easy, and he didn't have savings. My brothers helped him too. Every time a new project came up, it felt like we were all pitching in to help him stay afloat. He had started at one of the lowest paying and most dangerous positions in the refinery: scaffold builder. But even then, I appreciated that for the first time, he was pushing himself out of his comfort zone. Trying. That mattered. My brothers often reminded him: "She's always evolving. She doesn't wait around. You've got to get it together."

At one point, I took a trip to Oklahoma with my sister-in-law to visit him. The refinery was only a few miles away from WinStar Casino, and since the guys were working all day, we made the most of the time. I'll never forget putting $20 into a slot machine and winning $2,000. I panicked and cashed out immediately I wasn't about to push my luck! That trip meant a lot to me. It wasn't just about seeing where he was working. It was about proving to myself that I could create joy even in the middle of rebuilding. That win was how I bought myself my very first Michael Kors crossbody bag. I was so excited. It might've been small to others, but to me, it was a milestone. A reward for all I had endured and overcome. When I got back home, I had to start preparing for my graduation ceremony. It was happening in just a few weeks, and I had to write my speech. I was nervous. Overwhelmed. I had been processing so much emotionally losing my father, stepping into independence, running my business and I didn't want to seem weak. I was just being hard on myself, something I tend to do more often than I should. But deep down, I wanted to be proud of how I carried myself. I wanted to walk that stage with my head high.

Around that time, I also started going to the gym and taking it more seriously. I began eating healthier too. It wasn't just about physical fitness it was a promise. One that I made to my father in that hospital room. I remember him asking me, plain and simple, "Promise me you'll take care of yourself. Stay healthy. Drink water. Exercise." And I kept that promise. I bought a treadmill, weights, and workout equipment, and set it all up in the spare room of the house

I was staying at. The room used to be a garage, so it had plenty of space. That house became my little sanctuary for a full year while I ran my salon and saved for a second one.

It was all work and no play for the next few months. The salon took off from day one. I advertised in local magazines, used social media every day, and eventually hired help to keep up with the demand. Friends from high school started coming in to get their nails done. Even girls I had once been close with during those wild days on the ranch riding four-wheelers, laughing under the Texas sun started supporting me. It felt full circle in the best way.

And remember that childhood friend? The one who lived behind our little white house? The one I'd sit with on top of the brick fence just to talk for hours? The same girl I got into a fight with on the bus in sixth grade? She became my client too. And now she brings her daughter to me. To support my business. To show love. To show up.

How beautiful is that?

After all the loss, the chaos, the heartbreak, the silence, the grief things were slowly starting to feel good again. Not perfect. But peaceful.

And that kind of peace?

That's everything.

Chapter 23

"3 B's: Business, Blue-Collar, and a Boob Jar"

Like I mentioned in the last chapter yes, things were finally starting to feel good again. Balanced, even. I had stayed focused, and the salon was thriving. I hired help almost immediately, and the girls I started with were amazing. We built something special in that little, But if there's one thing about me it's that I never stay too comfortable. Especially when it comes to business or education, I'm always asking myself, "What's next?" I've never wanted to feel stagnant. I've worked too hard to get here to let myself get stuck now.

The salon I had at the time wasn't brand new, and it wasn't located in the city either. It was small cozy, yes but limited. I didn't have the space to add more pedicure chairs, or extra manicure tables. Which meant I couldn't hire more technicians. And if I couldn't bring in more people, I couldn't serve more clients. I couldn't grow. I couldn't scale. The business was already profitable, don't get me wrong. But once you start making money, your mind automatically wonders how to make more. And then the more you earn, the more you spend. It's just the reality of business and life. There's always room for improvement, always a new level to reach and I've always been hungry for that next level.

So I started researching again. Driving through different parts of town and into the city, scouting new possible locations. I looked up equipment costs online and started comparing prices for everything I'd need: new pedicure chairs, extra manicure tables, LED lamps, front desk setups, decor ideas, towel colors, client menus, even bar options. I had it all written down again on paper, just like I did when I first dreamed up my first salon. Every price, every vision, every note. I needed to see it all in front of me so I could stay motivated. That's how I work best visually, tangibly. I have to hold the dream in my hands before I bring it to life.

And in the middle of all that hustling and planning, life was still happening. I made more friends through the salon two amazing women who became regulars and close confidants. I even reconnected with some old high school friends and made time for little lunch outings. Stepping outside of the salon, even for a few hours, felt good. It was a chance to breathe. A chance to feel normal again. A chance to momentarily put aside the grief and the overwhelming responsibility of rebuilding.

Some months were harder than others. I was still playing every role at once full-time mom, entrepreneur, taxi driver, school activity volunteer, and everything in between. I was still going to the gym, still working on my health, still trying to keep my promise to my dad. And yes, I was still helping my ex-husband navigate his new career path and all the traveling that came with it. I always believed that if I helped him get to a place of stability, then one day he could return the favor. Maybe I'd finally get the chance to take a breather. That had been the hope for so long.

But let me be clear my motivation wasn't selfish. Whether we ended up back together or not, I wanted to see both of us succeed. Because at the end of the day, we have kids. Kids who are watching us. Kids who are learning how to survive, how to cope, how to build. I wanted to give them everything I never had emotional intelligence, confidence, book smarts, street smarts, all of it. I wanted peace in our home. I wanted calm. I wanted healing. I wanted to break every single generational chain I could, especially the ones built with violence and chaos. And yeah, I still yelled around the house sometimes I mean, if you know me, you already know my voice is loud. Now just imagine me upset! Loud would be an understatement. LOL.

But the hustle didn't stop. Promos kept running. The salon kept thriving. And I was so proud so damn proud of my very first baby:

Luxurious Nails #1.

I also started focusing on my credit and finances. I was determined to get everything in order once and for all. I hired a credit recovery company to help clean up the mess that had followed me for years things my ex had put under my name, and even accounts from when I was a kid or a teen. I had no idea how half of that stuff even ended up on there. I mean seriously, how was that even possible? But it was. And it was weighing me down. The company I worked with was really good they handled everything professionally, and I had zero issues with them. They even got the repossession from that old car off my report. I didn't run my credit for anything during that entire two-year period while everything was getting cleared. I stayed patient, and eventually, it paid off. Things were finally starting to fall into place.

Around that time, I got really close with one of my old high school friends the same girl who used to come hang out at my parents' ranch. She was a regular at my salon, and I did her nails all the time. She had a habit of biting them down, so I suggested she keep acrylics on consistently to help her grow her natural nails underneath. She trusted me with the process and came in often for infills, designs, or even simple sets anything to keep her hands out of her mouth and give her nails a fighting chance. We'd go out for lunch, dinner, and just hang out. Our bond grew quickly. For this book, I'll call her Eve. She didn't work her husband was the sole provider but she was such a sweetheart. A total doll. Funny, kind, and just good energy to be around.

I also became close with another woman who was around my age, maybe just a little older. Like me, she had young kids, so we had a lot in common from the start. I'll call her E in this book. E and I did just about everything together work, clubbing, errands, kids' activities, projects you name it. She was with me for the grind and the good times. She was also one of my best salon clients! She loved her long, creative sets, always wanting a different design on each nail. I loved doing her nails because it challenged my creativity, and she always hyped me up. E had been divorced too, and she'd gone through her own season of struggle, even having to live with her parents for a while like I once did. She had a great job and carried herself with ambition. I admired that in her. We stayed close for a while, and I still look back at our friendship with gratitude.

There was also another friend, older than me, who I'll name M in this book. M had her own job, a beautiful family, and a great heart.

She was such an amazing woman still is. A solid mom, a devoted wife, and just the type of person who brings peace when she walks into a room. I'm so thankful our paths crossed.

Eventually, the guys my ex and the crew ended up getting sent out to Louisiana for work. I decided to take some time off from the salon, and my sister-in-law and I would drive out to visit them. None of my sister-in-laws worked at the time, so it was always easy to get up and go when the opportunity came up. And it was always a good time. The guys were staying in a single-wide trailer not fancy, but familiar. It reminded us of home, so we were comfortable while we stayed.

During those visits, the girls and I would go shopping, run errands, and of course I brought my travel nail equipment. I never missed a beat. Wherever I went, I could work. That's one thing about being in the beauty industry I can carry my hustle with me. Some of the women working in the refinery with the guys heard I was in town, and word of mouth started spreading fast. I started doing their nails too. These women loved bold, exotic sets full design, long lengths, bright colors so I was making over $100 per set. I also posted that I was traveling on social media, and without fail, I'd always have people from the area follow me and book appointments. That's the beauty of building a brand people start to look for you, even when you're miles away. Social media really is free marketing when you know how to use it.

Even though it looked like I was having time off, I was still working. Because of that travel setup my manicure table, lamp, tools I was still making money wherever I went. But I didn't stop there. I started thinking outside the box.

I came up with an idea to make homemade flour tortillas and prep breakfast tacos for the guys to take with them to the refinery. I figured if I could make at least 100 tacos a day and sell them for $1 or $2 each, that would be an easy $100 to $200 per day. And let's be honest most of those men didn't have wives traveling with them, and many were eating plain sandwiches for lunch. A warm, home-made flour tortilla filled with love? That hit the spot. They were grateful. And it worked.

The real reason behind all of this the travel nails, the taco hustle was to fund my second salon. I didn't want to touch the income from my first salon. I wanted to build the second one from the ground up, independently, and without the stress of a loan hanging over my head. The idea of getting a loan always made me nervous. What if it didn't go as planned? What if the second salon didn't bring in the income I hoped for? I didn't want to live with that kind of pressure. My dad always told me that business was a gamble some days you win, some days you lose. And truthfully, you never know how any given month is going to go. I would rather take baby steps and build slow, than carry a giant weight of debt on my back.

I was already dealing with enough raising kids, managing school responsibilities, being a present friend, maintaining my health, and hitting my personal goals. Financial stress? No thank you. I didn't need that too. So I pitched the tortilla idea to the guys, and they were all in. Every night, I prepped the flour from scratch and rolled out every single tortilla by hand. I'd wake up at 4 a.m. to finish cooking, then make a variety of breakfast options wrapping each one in foil to keep them warm. And sure enough, they sold out every single day. A hun-dred tacos at $2 each? That was $200 daily. Just like that, I had a whole new income stream.

It was exhausting but it was working.

During the days I'd do the refinery girls' nails, that was my hustle. That was the day money. I made sure to take photos and film every set I did even if I wasn't at home because I needed content to keep my social media presence alive. I knew how important it was to stay visible, to show consistency, and to keep my work in front of my clients' eyes. Whether I was in Texas or Louisiana, I made sure to keep posting, editing, sharing, and connecting.At the same time I was making money, I never stopped researching and shopping for new salon equipment. I would be up late scrolling through websites, comparing prices, watching reviews, and figuring out what pieces I could afford next. I ordered everything one by one—one manicure table at a time, one client chair at a time, one nail tech chair at a time. I was literally building my second salon before I even had the space for it. Slowly but surely, the boxes started showing up at home. Every delivery felt like a step closer to the next chapter.

Eventually I came back home, and just like clockwork, things got busy. I had been away for a few days, and my clients were always eager to book a new set the moment I returned. My calendar stayed full. But I didn't complain I loved my job. I loved the creativity, the detail, the challenge. I loved watching my clients light up when they saw their nails. And I loved that I could take art workshops and nail design classes to keep growing. That's where the real money was in the design work. The more I expanded my creativity, the more valuable my services became.

If you're wondering where things stood between me and my kids' father, well we had reached a crossroads. I told him we couldn't even think about trying again unless we both worked on ourselves first. He needed to focus on his career, and I needed to keep building mine. We stayed cordial and got along well. I've always carried the role of both mom and dad, to be honest. And as he started traveling more for work, the time he had to spend with the boys grew shorter. He wasn't always able to visit, so I became the one to travel, making the effort so our boys could still see him and feel connected.

Thankfully, he always covered the full cost of my travel flights, gas, food, whatever was needed. But even still, after a while it became emotionally and physically exhausting. Long drives. Disrupted routines. A lot of effort for something that never felt equal. I started to feel bad for my boys. They deserved more. They deserved someone who would meet them halfway. As for me, I had already made peace with the fact that I wasn't going to date or get into a relationship until my kids were either done or almost done with school. I wasn't going to bring anyone around who could hurt them or disrupt their peace. I had already been through enough, and I would never gamble with their hearts.

So I kept going. Running the salon, being a full-time mom, managing the household, staying present in school activities, keeping up with friendships, going to the gym, traveling when needed and still setting personal goals for myself.

Remember how I told you they used to call me "Limones" in school? Yeah, that stayed with me. For years. So one of the personal goals I set was finally getting a breast augmentation. Something I had quietly wanted for years not for anyone else, but for me. I scheduled my first consultation with a local surgeon, but the moment I walked in, I hated the vibe. It just didn't feel right. So I booked a second appointment at a different place, but that one felt even worse. They tried to pressure me into getting 450cc or 500cc implants massive. I was flat-chested, and there was no way I was going that extreme. I wanted a boost, not a transformation.

Then I found Dr. Rodriguez Ayala from Monterrey, Mexico. Everything about that appointment felt different. He listened. He under-stood my vision. He agreed with me. He didn't try to push me into something big or over-the-top. He just wanted to give me that subtle confidence boost I had always craved. I left his office feeling heard and respected, and I told him I'd be in touch when I was ready.

Back at the salon, I created a tip jar and labeled it "The Boob Jar" yep, you read that right. It was where I'd save every single tip and every bit of extra cash toward my surgery. That was the plan: pay for it in cash, no loans, no credit, no stress. Just me and my grind. Some of my clients found out about the jar and would joke around and throw in extra, saying "Tips for the tits!" every time they added a few bucks. It made me laugh, but it also reminded me why I was doing this. It was for me. Not for a man. Not for attention. Not for anyone else's validation. I had talked to my mom about it, and of course, no one really agreed with the decision but I was grown. I didn't need permission. This was a self-love investment. An act of reclaiming my body and how I felt in it. That jar motivated the hell out of me. It made me want to work harder. I didn't want to touch any money from the salon's profits or from my future second salon fund. That tip jar became sacred. Every time I saw it, it reminded me that I could give to others and still pour into myself.

At this point, the salon was running smoothly. The girls knew what to do, and I trusted them to hold things down while I stepped away here and there. I'd plan trips to take the boys to spend time with their dad. On one of those drives, I found a butterfly necklace that caught my eye. I can't remember if I said anything out loud, but something about it stuck with me. Lately, I had started writing everything down, journaling more, taking pictures of moments, and saying things out loud so I could remember. My memory wasn't always the best I've always said I have a bird brain so that helped me hold on to things that mattered.

Even as life moved forward, I found myself crying randomly. Grief hits in waves. During that first Father's Day after my dad passed, I actually fell asleep on the cemetery bench. I had walked up to his grave and just sat there, and I could almost hear his voice. I could see him standing up with open arms, greeting me the same way he always did. That same hug. That same warmth. That same safe place. I lost so much weight during that time, too. I was borderline anemic. It was part of the reason I was trying so hard to stay consistent with the gym and rebuild my strength. I started taking iron pills, and my grandma even injected me with iron shots that she and my mom brought from Mexico. They'd take me to get the shots when I was feeling really weak.

So behind the scenes of the salon, the travel, the friendships, the tacos, the tips, the gym behind all of it I was still struggling. Quietly. Silently. In ways no one really saw. But I kept going anyway. Oh, and mom life? Yeah… it was kicking my ass. Every single day felt like I was running a marathon with no finish line in sight. I was dropping the boys off at school, rushing to make it to teacher meetings, doing pickups, making sure they were fed, helping with home-work, running the salon, and trying to keep some type of order in the house. And just when I thought I had a rhythm going, life would throw in one of those chaotic mom moments. Like the time the boys locked the house with the keys inside. And another time? They did the same thing… but with my car. I remember just falling to my knees outside in the driveway and bursting into tears. Not the quiet kind either this was loud, ugly, baby-crying. Exhausted crying. It all hit me in that moment.

Doing everything on my own had its wins, sure, but it had so many heavy moments too. Some days were just harder than others. I had to call a locksmith that day to get the car open and of course, it cost me $200. I wiped my tears, faked a smile for the boys like everything was fine, and handled it. That's the job you don't get to pause when you're both mom and dad. You just do what needs to be done. And if you know what it's like to live in survival mode or if you're a blue-collar wife or single mom, you feel me. That kind of tired doesn't go away with one night of sleep.

Some time later, I came across a warehouse that was selling pre-owned pedicure chairs. Now if you know this industry, then you know how big of a deal that is. Pedicure chairs can go for $2,500 each and up. And I needed multiple. This warehouse would buy them, remodel them, and resell them for way less. It was a solid opportunity, and I wasn't about to pass it up. I did my research on them and decided to make the trip out. I asked my mom and one of my aunts to go with me it was about a two hour drive, and we needed a flatbed trailer to load the chairs. Thankfully, my aunt knew how to drive one.

My plan was to buy as many as I could, store them at home, and slowly build my inventory until I was ready to open the second salon. I was also assembling every manicure table myself as they arrived at the house. One by one. Every delivery felt like another brick in the foundation of my next dream. That same warehouse also had a gorgeous matching front desk and reception area piece. The moment I saw it, I knew it belonged in my next space. I had to get my hands on it. I pictured it all in my head so clearly how the space would look, how the towels would match, the smell of new products, the playlists playing in the background.

So I kept taking little trips to the beauty supply store to buy towels in bulk, along with all the tools and products I'd need to keep the future salon stocked for a few months. I didn't want to take any risks with running out of anything during the early days. I had a vision of what I wanted the menu to look like, what services I wanted to offer, and how I wanted everything to feel. It wasn't just about nails. It was about experience, atmosphere, and elevation. This was all in the same year too. There was no slowing down. The vision was alive.

Eventually, I found a location I liked for the new salon. And when

I say it was bigger I mean it was at least three or four times the size of my first one. The rent reflected that too ouch. But I wasn't afraid of it anymore. I had lost that fear. I had proof I could do this. I knew what it took. But getting this new space open was going to require major work. Plumbing. Flooring. Electrical. Equipment. The whole setup. I was prepared for it. And thankfully, my social media presence had grown strong enough that I wasn't too worried about advertising. I already had the clientele. I just needed the place.

I scheduled a tour of the space and got the ball rolling. The process was a headache from the start. The closer you got to the city, the harder it got to get permits and approvals. But I was used to red tape and obstacles by now. I signed the lease and got to work immediately. I hired a company to create my custom salon sign. They handled everything design, production, installation and offered financing. That was actually the first thing I ever financed. Well, that and my new credit card processing machine. I'd been using one of those old-school ones you had to batch out every night, and it was finally time for an upgrade.

We polished the floors, started bringing in and setting up the equipment, plugging things in, and doing the final touches. I had a goal of opening within a month or so. That was the vision. It was ambitious, but possible.

When the day came to open, we didn't do anything huge. It was small. Simple. But so meaningful. A cute celebration, some balloons, champagne, and a little cake. My very first paying client in the new salon was my grandma my mom's mom, Grandma P. She was so proud of me. She refused to get her services done for free, even though I would've done them gladly. She insisted on paying and loved her pedicures. Her support meant everything to me. From the moment we opened, the salon was packed. The waiting area stayed full. We were booked until late. It got busy fast. Once I had the systems running smoothly, I registered my salon with a few supply stores so I could call in orders and do quick pickups. That saved me time and kept us stocked.

But with the new salon open and most of the extra rooms in my house now empty from moving out inventory, I realized I was coming to the end of my lease at home too. I needed to start looking for a new place to live. It was exhausting another thing to juggle but I wasn't going to rush into buying a home I wasn't sure about. That's a huge commitment. I gave myself about three months to plan and prepare for the move. I've always been the type to stay one step ahead. Last-minute scrambling gives me anxiety. I can't operate like that.

As all of this was happening, my surgery date started approaching too. I had already paid half of it, locked in my date, and was preparing to pay the rest in full on the day of. The surgery was going to be in Mexico, and I needed help with the boys. I spoke to my mom about it and asked if she could take the trip with me. I also talked to my ex about possibly helping with the boys or joining me for the procedure, but he couldn't. So I asked my stepdad instead.

Oh and I just realized I hadn't mentioned yet: my mom had remarried. So my stepdad stepped in to help, and he watched the boys while my mom came with me to Monterrey.

It was all happening at once home, salon, body, motherhood, healing. It was a whirlwind. But somehow, even through the tears and the chaos, it still felt like I was stepping into a new version of myself. When I arrived for my surgery, I was two seconds from backing out. No lie I told the surgeon I couldn't do it. I was already processed, in the back, changed into the gown, and all I could feel was fear washing over me like a wave. I'd never had surgery before. Not even close. My heart was pounding, and all I could think was "What the hell am I doing?" This wasn't something I needed. It wasn't life or death. It was something I chose. Something I wanted to look and feel better, to finally feel more confident in my own skin. But in that moment, all I could think about was my boys. I remember staring at the floor and whispering in my head, "What if I don't wake up? What if I die just because I wanted boobs? What kind of mom does that?" I kept thinking about losing my dad not too long ago and how that grief still lived so heavy in me. I didn't want to do that to my kids. I didn't want to risk them losing me over something like this. That's when the surgeon came into the room. He must've seen it on my face. He walked up, looked me in the eyes, and pulled me into a hug. He told me gently, "You're in good hands. Trust me. Just breathe and relax." I nodded, still scared, but I went through with it.

When they wheeled me into the surgery room, I noticed everything. The big bright lights, the stainless steel tables, the mirrors on the ceiling and the walls. It was cold. Sterile. Intimidating. A nurse walked in, smiled, and started talking to me. She asked about my kids how many I had, their names, their ages. I was answering her casually, and the moment I got to my second born's name, I was out like a light. Lights out. She did that on purpose to distract me and calm me before the anesthesia kicked in. Smart move, huh? I appreciated that little kindness so much more later.

A few hours later, I woke up groggy and in pain more pain than I expected, honestly. I could barely open my eyes, but when I did, I saw my mom sitting on the couch in the corner of the recovery room, crying. She looked exhausted and relieved all at once. She told me the surgery took three hours longer than they originally said, and she had been terrified the entire time. Hearing that crushed me. I didn't mean to put her through that kind of worry, and I felt so guilty, but she was there for me, every step of the way.

The doctor came in shortly after and checked on me, explaining what the healing process would look like, what meds I'd need, and what kind of help I'd need at home. I nodded and tried to absorb it all, still foggy from the meds. And let me just say the hospital food in Mexico? Way better than anything I'd ever had in the U.S. They brought me a hot bowl of fideo soup and a plate for my mom too. It hit the spot, especially after surgery. That hospital stay was cleaner, kinder, and more comforting than both of my U.S. hospital stays for childbirth combined. No shade just facts. You could tell they cared.

When it was time to head home, I realized quickly that recovery wasn't going to be as easy as I'd hoped. I was in so much pain. My body felt foreign to me, sore in ways I couldn't even describe. My stepdad looked alarmed when he saw me he said I looked pale and weak. He and my mom helped me out of the car, walked me into the house, and got me settled. They also helped take care of the boys during those first few days, which was such a blessing. My best friend "M" showed up soon after with a sweet gift and hugs, just to check on me. That visit meant so much to me. I'll never forget it.

I told myself I'd take a full two weeks off from the salon to rest, but by the end of the second week, I was crawling out of my skin. I asked someone to drive me just to check on the salon and peek inside. I thought I was ready. Bad idea. If you've ever stepped into a nail salon, you know the chemical smell from the monomer hits you hard. With fresh wounds, that smell went straight to my blood-stream or at least that's what it felt like. I ended up getting an in-fection from that visit alone, and it pushed back my recovery a little longer. Lesson learned: rest actually means rest.

A few weeks after the surgery, we took a family trip to Oklahoma to visit my brother while he was serving his time. That was the first trip I took after healing, and I pushed through the soreness because I didn't want to miss the visit. I was able to get back to working full-time at the salon about a month after surgery, but the gym? That took way longer. It was at least five months before I even felt okay enough to start light weights again.

Looking back, that whole season of life feels like a blur a mix of ambition, exhaustion, beauty, pain, and healing. I was building, growing, dreaming, and grieving all at once. I was putting in work on the outside through salons, travel, social media, and surgeries but I was also putting in work within. Quietly. Alone. In the still moments between the chaos. It was a lot. But I made it through.

Chapter 24

"New Keys, New Staff, Live-in Nanny and Still a Soft Spot for Him"

"Welcome back to work, Yesenia."

I had never been so genuinely happy to hear those words. I missed the routine, the hustle, the sound of nail drills humming while music played in the background, and the feeling of walking into a space that I built with my bare hands. My girls had done an amazing job while I was out recovering. I was proud of them, and I made sure to let them know. While I was gone, we actually got hit with two surprise inspections from TDLR. Someone must've called the state on us probably a nearby salon or a bitter soul who just couldn't stand to see us doing well. But guess what? We passed. Both times. With flying colors. Everything was documented, clean, compliant, and handled professionally. I had built this place to be solid, and that's exactly what it was. I had enough licensed girls doing pedicures, enough nail techs handling acrylics and designs, and business was steady.

But with growth... came problems.

As the salon got busier, the cracks started to show. Some of the girls I had hired started slacking. No call, no shows. Clocking in and out as they pleased. And even worse when new clients found the salon online and saw that I was the owner, they all wanted to book with me directly. The pressure was nonstop. I was already running off appointments only, but I still had women calling me because they didn't like the set they got from another tech and I would either issue a refund or fix it myself. It was exhausting, physically and emotionally. It felt like I was managing chaos on top of my regular workload, constantly cleaning up messes I didn't make.

A lot of the women I had hired were refinery wives. If you know, you know they didn't really need the job. If their husbands were in town, they were ghosts. They wouldn't show up for shifts. Some of them treated it like a part-time hobby instead of a professional business. I understood to a degree I'm not heartless but as a business owner, it was draining.

Around that time, one of my friends expressed interest in learning nails. You might remember her we'll call her "Eve," like I did in an earlier chapter. I offered to help. I told her if she enrolled in school, I would help cover her license costs, and she could come work for me. She was excited, and she actually followed through. She enrolled in a quick manicure course to finish faster, got certified, and joined the team.

And let me pause right here to say something I wish I would've listened to back then: don't mix business with friendship or family. I learned the hard way. And yes, it ended badly.

Let me break something down for those who may not be familiar with the beauty industry. When you're a nail artist, esthetician, or cosmetologist, you usually work one of three ways:

You rent a booth or chair at a salon and pay a weekly or monthly fee.

You work on commission usually split 50/50 or 60/40 depend-ing on your experience.

(Rarely) you get paid hourly, but even then, you're usually responsible for building your own clientele.

Most of us, especially nail techs, bring our clients with us wherever we go. Walk-ins help, but we never rely on them completely. I always had a solid client base, and any salon I worked in knew I was going to pull numbers.

So when I hired Eve, I offered her a commission-based setup. She didn't have experience, but I still gave her 50%. I was trying to help, trying to lift up someone I cared about. I remember one day in particular she hadn't taken a single client, but I still handed her a crisp $100 bill. I didn't owe her that. I wasn't obligated to pay anything if she didn't work. But I did it out of love.

Things started shifting around summer, as they always do. Business slows down when clients leave town with their kids or travel for the season. One of my other girls had left the salon because of it. It happens. But then one day, I asked Eve if I could borrow her phone to find mine. She handed it over without thinking. While I was swiping through to clear a text, a message from that same girl who left popped up.

What I saw made my heart sink.

A whole thread of messages… talking about me. Dragging my name. Calling me every name in the book. Laughing, judging, twisting things that weren't true. It wasn't even about the words it was the betrayal. This was someone I brought into my business. My friend. Someone I had supported financially and emotionally. I never said a word. I just looked at her and told her she could leave. And she did. I never told her I saw the messages. I never even confronted her. To this day, we haven't spoken again.

It hurt. It really did. Because I wasn't just losing an employee I was losing someone I considered a sister.

But here's what I've learned in business, and in life: not every client is a good client, not every dollar is worth earning, and not every person deserves access to your space even if they once had your heart.

I will never apologize for protecting my peace. I built this salon from nothing. And I refuse to let bitterness, drama, or disrespect live inside the walls of something I bled for.

I stand on that. Always.

After that situation, I went back to the drawing board and hired new people. I reached out to local beauty schools and asked them to send me any recent graduates looking for salon work. I figured if I could catch them early, I could train them my way with structure, professionalism, and respect. I started hosting weekly team meetings, just once a week, to make sure we were all aligned. It gave us a chance to speak openly, address any issues, and reinforce the standard. Working in a space full of women can be beautiful but let's be real, it can also be chaotic and full of drama if not kept in check. We needed peace in that building. The salon had to be a space of growth, not tension.

And guess what? Life has a funny way of circling back.

Remember the owner from that tax and insurance job I used to have? The one who treated me like I was less than, who always had something rude to say? Well… her salon was right next door to mine now. Can you believe that? One year later, the same girl she probably thought would never "make it" ended up becoming her neighbor as a business owner. That's why I always say: you never know who you're sitting next to, and where they're headed. Always treat people with kindness and respect. Titles mean nothing when your spirit lacks character.

In my personal life, things were shifting too in the best way.

I had finally found the most gorgeous two-story townhouse. It had the tiniest little gated yard in the back just enough space to feel cozy and safe and it was perfect for me and the boys. Three bedrooms, three bathrooms (one downstairs and two upstairs), a garage, and it was in a secure gated community with a stunning pool. And the best part? I was the first person to ever live there. Everything was brand new. Fresh walls. Clean carpet. A blank canvas that felt like a reward for everything I had pushed through.

All of my furniture fit perfectly inside. I can still remember the day I moved in standing in the living room, just smiling, feeling proud. It was in the heart of the city too, only two blocks away from the university. Starbucks was around the corner, all my favorite shopping centers were within a few minutes, and the gym was literally just one light away. I had everything I needed at my fingertips. There was even a big ranch-style home across the street, and I'll never forget how the branches of one of their tall trees bent inward and naturally formed a heart shape. During sunset, the light would hit it just right, and I'd find myself taking pictures or short videos completely mesmerized. It felt like God left that heart-shaped tree there just for me.

And then... came the live-in nanny. My angel.

Hiring her changed everything. She moved in and helped me with everything. From the house to the kids, the laundry, ironing, cooking, groceries, morning drop-offs, errands all of it. She could see how exhausted I was, even when I tried to hide it. Before she came into our lives, I used to have my boys wait in the back break room of the salon. They'd watch movies, munch on snacks, sometimes finish homework... and other times, just sit there bored out of their minds. If we had a late night which we often did they'd fall asleep on the front lobby couch, waiting for me to close up.

I'd be the last one out. After sanitizing everything, closing the box, locking up, and taking cash home to deposit the next morning it wasn't unusual for us to leave after midnight. Me carrying bags, tired feet, and two sleepy boys. That wasn't safe. It wasn't fair. It wasn't healthy. But I didn't have another choice at the time. I was doing my best with what I had.

So when my nanny came into our world, it felt like God had placed her directly in our path.

She would pull cute dresses out of my closet still with tags on them and tell me, "You need to go out. You need to live a little." She wasn't just helping around the house; she was speaking life into me. She reminded me that I was still young, still vibrant, and still worthy of enjoying the life I was building. She even taught my kids a bit of Spanish while I was at work. And they adored her. They truly did.

Looking back now, that season was so layered. I had never felt more pulled in different directions building a business, running a home, raising two little boys, and trying not to lose myself in the shuffle. But the help... the home... and the love that surrounded me during that time made it all bearable. It reminded me that no matter how much I carried, I was never carrying it alone.

During this season, my presence on social media began to skyrocket. I was growing across every platform, especially on Periscope back when that app was still a thing. I remember the day I hit a million views like it was yesterday. I would sit in my car and talk for what felt like hours, just being real, unfiltered, and connecting with people. Sometimes I'd even go live from the gym, sweaty and out of breath, but people still watched. They listened. They related. I started putting more effort into Instagram and slowly leaned away from Facebook, which had started to feel stale to me. I used all my platforms to promote both my nail business and my fitness content. It was a double-win I was showing up in people's feeds and turning that attention into clients and leads. Social media became a part of my hustle.

Eventually, the work I was doing online started catching the attention of companies and organizations. I had adult daycares for the elderly reaching out, asking me to provide onsite services. I would go with one of my girls and offer gentle water manicures no tools, no risks just polish, soft scrubs, light hand massages, and a little love. Especially for clients with diabetes or sensitive skin, it was all about safety and comfort. It became something I looked forward to. Watching their eyes light up over something as simple as having their nails done reminded me why I loved what I did.

And then... the calls kept coming. Funeral homes began reaching out for delicate end-of-life grooming services a final, beautiful act of love for families saying goodbye. It was emotional and deeply personal, but I treated it with the care and grace it deserved. That same week, bars, lounges, and even clubs started contacting me too asking if I'd do pop-up nail services at their events. Some did "Manicure & Martini" nights, and let me tell you... those were always a vibe. Loud music, pretty cocktails, and tips flying left and right. They paid well, and it brought my work into spaces where nails had never really been part of the scene before.

Back at the salon, business didn't slow down either. We became known for our pedicures and our signature 3D nail art. It got to the point where people would drive in from two hours away just for our designs. My girls used to joke and say we should rename the shop "3D Heaven" or "The Pedicure Palace," because that's all anyone came in asking for. We laughed, but it was true and that kind of word-of-mouth is priceless.

Outside of work, I started taking more time for myself. I was waking up earlier, hitting the gym consistently, and actually tracking my macros and calories. I was determined. Not just physically, but mentally. I wanted to feel strong again. I wanted to feel good again.

And on the nights I wasn't working? Oh, I was out living.

Me and my girl "E" would hit the town downtown bars, clubs, lounges you name it. We even found this one spot that played nothing but oldies and freestyle music. That place? Pure magic. It was giving "Take Me in Your Arms" by Lil Suzy, "In a Dream" freestyle mix by Rockwell, "Diamond Girl" by Nice & Wild, and "I Can't Wait" by Nu Shooz. We danced the entire night away, heels off, blisters on our feet, not a care in the world. Just two girls living like life owed us a good time.

Sometimes, after a wild night, we'd spontaneously hit the beach. The drive was less than an hour from where I lived. We'd roll down the windows, blast Latin reggaetón and old-school Mexican hits Calor by Nicky Jam, Gasolina by Daddy Yankee and vibe the whole way there, singing and laughing and just being free. Those drives healed parts of me that therapy never could. And of course, she'd tease me about my habits. "You're so damn picky," she'd say. "Were you raised fancy or what?" Because I refused to eat off paper plates. Mozzarella sticks? Always eaten with a fork. No double dipping, ever. And I never and I mean never put my elbows on the table. She wasn't wrong. My parents raised us old-school. You didn't grab your utensils with your whole fist. You didn't slouch or slurp or reach. You ate properly or you didn't eat at all. Elbows on the table? That was basically a sin. My dad would go off if we even tried. So yeah I kept some of those manners with me. And she loved to tease me about it.

"E" and I did everything together back then. There was never a dull moment with her, and even though she was one of my closest friends, she was still a loyal client too. That's when I really started learning the delicate art of separating business from friendship. During work hours, I was her nail tech her boss even. After hours? We could vibe like always. That balance was key. And for once, I was starting to figure it out.

My relationship status at this point? Pretty much non-existent if we're being real. I wasn't dating, I wasn't entertaining anyone new. I was focused on my kids, my business, my body, and my peace. But of course, the relationship with my ex always managed to hover in that gray area. We weren't together, but the door didn't feel all the way shut either.

He had moved up from the position he started in no longer working scaffolding. I can't remember exactly if he was officially a boilermaker or a journeyman by this point, but either way, his paychecks had definitely leveled up. And with that came the gifts. He started showering me with thoughtful things "just because" flowers, name-brand bags, and luxury luggage sets. He even paid my hairstylist directly, so when I showed up for my appointment, everything was already covered. No questions, no swiping cards just "You're good, girl." He knew when I had those long hair days too especially when I was getting my micro extensions put in. I used 22 to 24-inch bundles because I've always loved my hair long, thick, and full of volume. But it's not cheap, and it's not easy to maintain either. Still, he looked out.

On those salon days, I'd get random Uber Eats deliveries or snacks brought to me he just wanted to make sure I had food in my stomach. That's one thing I'll always say about him: he's always been thoughtful in his own way. He never forgot to pay attention to the details.

Mother's Day? He went all out. He started sending massive gifts not just one bouquet, but three. One from each of the boys, and one from him. Huge flower arrangements, boxes of perfume, accessories, gift bags stacked on top of each other he never did the bare minimum. And yeah, I'm not gonna lie, that was cute. I felt seen. He knew I was running around non-stop, juggling the weight of my world. He even had groceries delivered to my door just to take something off my plate. My nanny would unpack them and put everything away. He was helping quietly and behind the scenes in a way that lightened my load and gave me back small pieces of time. I appreciated that.

But of course, the peace was never perfect. We still argued sometimes for no reason, sometimes for good reason. And what always bothered me is that when he did do something nice, he'd throw it in my face during the next fight. As if I had begged for help. I never did. I never asked. It was the kind of cycle I had grown used to highs and lows, sweetness and tension, showing up one minute and shutting down the next. A rollercoaster, always.

Everyone around me had something to say. Friends, family, even strangers who only knew the Instagram version of our story they all swore up and down that he loved me more than anything, and that I was crazy for not taking him back. They'd say things like, "No one else will ever treat you that good," or "He's changed, can't you see that?" And deep down, I never once said I wouldn't take him back. It was just that he always knew exactly what to say when he didn't have me. But the second I gave him another chance, everything would crumble all over again.

But that wasn't anybody else's business. So for years, I took the criticism. I let them talk. I stayed quiet and just did what worked for me for us. We had figured out a rhythm that allowed us to coparent in peace. When we hung out as a family, it was actually really nice. We laughed, we shared meals, we had good moments. I think we've always worked better as friends than lovers. That dynamic just made more sense. It took me years to accept that not everyone would understand it and that's okay. They don't need to.

I also don't really believe in staying friends with exes at least, not in most cases. I don't think men and women who've shared a romantic past can always transition into platonic friendship without complications. But he's different. He's the father of my kids. That bond, that shared responsibility, makes it different. He'll always be in my life, no matter what chapter I'm in.

I tried, more than once, to sit down and have deep, meaningful conversations with him. I'd open up about my dreams, my business goals, my next moves but I always felt like I was talking to a wall. He never had much to say in return. His comprehension just wasn't where mine was. Not in a mean or belittling way that's just how he is. And I've learned to accept it. I don't need him to understand everything about me. I just need him to keep being a good dad and show up when it matters most.

This year felt like the year I really leveled up quietly, without the noise or the chaos. I saw progress in so many areas. I was balancing life with more grace than ever before. Kids, friendships, business, employees, meetings, content, and my own health I was managing it all. Not perfectly. Not without hard days. But with heart. And a kind of maturity I hadn't known in years past.

I was deeply invested in church during this time. I had finally found a place of my own, a church that truly felt like home and I had been attending the same one faithfully for a few years by now. But this season was different. I wasn't missing a single service. Just like how I never missed a workout for my body, I treated church as my heart and soul's workout. It was my sanctuary. A place where I could breathe. A place where my heart could rest. I was chasing peace and trying to build a balanced life not perfect, not flawless, but grounded and steady.

Not to get overly religious, because that's never really been my style, but I found so much healing through worship. Still, I was never the type to switch up who I was completely. I still listened to regular music. I still do to this day. Music and dancing are parts of me that will never change. I dance with my kids around the house all the time. At family parties or events, we're always the ones laughing, moving, living. That joy is part of our culture, part of our heartbeat. Both my boys were involved in church, too. We loved the worship team. The way they sang, the way it felt it moved us. It became a ritual that bonded us. The music there, just like the music we danced to at home, stirred something in me. It reminded me who I was, what I'd survived, and who I was becoming.

The church services? So many times they spoke directly to me, like God Himself knew exactly what I needed to hear that day. And this continued up until we moved. (But we'll get to that in a few chapters.)

And if you think I stopped at just two salons you clearly don't know me well enough yet. Because no, baby, I wasn't done.

I had noticed a new building going up just a few blocks from my current salon. And not just any building this one had a luxury vibe. Brand-new construction, high ceilings, glossy white tile floors that shimmered under the light, elegant finishes it was beautiful inside and out. It looked like something out of a dream. I didn't tell anyone about it. I just made a quiet mental note. I wanted it. I didn't know how, but I knew I'd figure it out.

On top of everything else, I decided why not take another course? I mean, what was one more thing, right? I signed up for my NASM certification to become a personal trainer. That's right another title, another layer. Another door I could open if I ever needed to pivot. I've always believed that education any kind of license or certification is a safety net. Something you can fall back on if your current path ever collapses or you simply fall out of love with it. I never wanted to feel stuck, and I definitely never wanted to feel powerless. So I signed up. It was an online, self-paced course challenging, but doable on my own time.

I had already gone through three different personal trainers at the gym, and each time I found myself frustrated. Most of them seemed more interested in the paycheck than in actually helping people. It rubbed me the wrong way. I was showing up, I was serious, and I didn't feel like I was being poured into the way I deserved. So I took matters into my own hands again. I started studying. I wanted to understand my own body and health better, and maybe even help others down the line.

During the late evenings at home or on quiet Sundays, I'd sit down with my laptop and study materials, and I'd read. I'd underline, highlight, take notes. It gave me a different kind of focus one that wasn't about the salon or social media or clients or being a mom. It was just for me.

Friday and Saturday nights, I'd try to be social when I could. I'd step out with friends but only if I didn't leave the salon too late. If you know, you know some days we'd close late, and I'd barely have time to shower before bed. But when I could sneak in a girls' night, I did.

Even my drinking habits had changed. I had started cutting back a lot. If I did drink, it was low-calorie and light. Vodka with water or club soda. Sometimes just whiskey. No sugary drinks, no mixers with tons of calories. I've actually kept that habit to this day.

But just when things were starting to feel good like I had created this solid, beautiful rhythm my salon started to fall apart, literally. The building was older, and between hurricane season, rain-storms, and bad weather, we started having leaks in the ceiling. Tiles were falling. Water damage. And that was just the beginning. I made call after call to the landlord, requesting repairs, submitting service forms but nothing ever got fixed. It was frustrating. Because the missing ceiling tiles meant the AC and heater were working over-time. My electricity bills were outrageous. It was a complete mess.

I even offered to hire a repair team myself and just deduct it from my rent or get reimbursed. Still, nothing. And anytime I showed up in person to the leasing office, they gave me the runaround. Delays, excuses, empty promises.

You know what I've noticed over the years? Some businesspeople especially landlords or contractors don't take women seriously. Especially if they know you're single. If you don't have a man next to you, they treat you like a little girl playing dress-up in business. And I hated that. That's actually why I started wearing a ring even after my divorce. Not because I was trying to fool anyone, but because I felt like people respected me more when they assumed I had a husband backing me. It's a sad truth, but it's how I learned to navigate certain rooms.

Eventually, I called my ex. I told him what was going on and asked if he could step in. I figured that maybe his tone, his voice, his presence would make them take things seriously. And you know what? It worked. He made the calls. He said the right things. And finally finally stuff got fixed.

Sometimes you just need a firm voice and a little pressure in the right places. And if that meant swallowing a little pride to get what my business needed, then so be it. I'd do anything to protect what I'd built.

I had slowly begun to soften toward my ex again. Not in a fairytale kind of way, but in a real, grown, we've both been through some things kind of way. He was doing well on his own. And I was thriving on mine. It felt like, finally, we were both evolving in our own corners of the world. Our careers were solid, our priorities had matured, and the lens we saw life through had shifted just enough to let a little more understanding in. We weren't the same people anymore and that wasn't a bad thing.

So yes, I started to travel more to see him. I wanted the boys to spend quality time with their dad, and I no longer felt the need to control everything or protect my energy the way I used to. I had worked through a lot of my own inner healing by this point. And part of that growth meant I was finally okay with saying "yes" to help especially when it came from him.

Let me be clear, that was big for me. I've always been incredibly prideful. If you know me, you know that when I decide I'm done, I mean it. And when we divorced, I didn't ask for anything. No child support. No financial help. Not because I didn't need it but because I wanted freedom more than anything. Freedom to raise my boys my way. Freedom to make my own money. Freedom to rebuild from scratch without owing anyone anything.

It was never about proving I didn't need him it was about proving to myself that I could survive, thrive, and protect my peace without sacrificing it for stability. But now that time had passed, and I'd built a strong foundation, I was open to receiving again. Slowly. Cautiously. But it was happening.

He even brought up the idea of me moving with him. He told me I could work less, travel with him, or even settle in Houston since it was more central easier for him to travel to and from. It was one of those conversations where everything sounds easy and sweet in theory. We didn't make a decision right away. We just... floated the idea. Entertained the fantasy. But I'm glad I didn't jump.

Because not long after, I got that message. The kind of "hey girl" message that comes in when you're finally starting to feel peace again. My social media pages had been booming. My following was growing quickly, and more people were watching my moves including women I didn't even know. One of them messaged me directly, screenshots and all. Pictures. Conversations. Proof that he'd been reaching out to her, flirting, playing his usual game all while still trying to wine and dine me, still texting me, still asking me to come see him, still treating me like I was the one.

And I didn't even respond. Not to her. Not to him. I saw it. I read it. I sat with it. And I moved on. I didn't have the energy to fight over someone who couldn't see my value not with words, not with receipts, and certainly not with more heartbreak. There was a time I would've cried, argued, spiraled. But not this time. I just... chose me instead.

Around this same time, something beautiful started to bloom. I hosted my first full Thanksgiving at my home. I took care of everything. The fall decorations, the food, the desserts, the little details that make a house feel like a hug. I told my mom she didn't need to bring anything just herself. I wanted her to rest. I wanted her to feel loved and honored. I had it covered.

My family came over. We took pictures, watched movies, laughed, ate and for a moment, it felt like those old days when my dad was still with us. When the house would be filled with noise and food and joy. When he would light up just seeing everyone under one roof. That's what this felt like. Hosting made me feel close to him again. Like I was picking up where he left off. Like I was becoming the kind of woman he'd be proud of one who takes care of her people and fills a room with warmth.

Then came Christmas, and I wanted to do more. I started getting involved with the community for real. My business began donating toys and contributing part of our service sales toward local causes. Even if it wasn't thousands of dollars, it felt good to give. Whether it was toys for kids or a warm gesture to a stranger, giving back made my heart feel full. And honestly? That's what mattered most. I knew what it felt like to be the one in need. So now that I was in a place to help, I wanted to pour it forward.

No matter how complicated my love life was... no matter how many roles I juggled... I was finally showing up as the woman I always dreamed of becoming. I was steady. I was soft. I was strong. And I was home in every sense of the word.

Chapter 25

Luxurious Nail Salon, Mother, Lawsuits and Life Threats The Real Cost of the Dream

I built a beauty empire from the ground up, but no one ever talks about what it costs to keep it standing. Between broken water heaters, lawsuits, school calls, and real-life threats, success demanded everything from me. This was the chapter that tested me as a mother, a businesswoman, and a survivor. Once the new year rolled in and the boys went back to school, it was game time all over again. That quiet holiday breath had passed, and now it was back to the grind. But the salon? It was driving me insane. The maintenance issues were nonstop leaking ceilings, poor insulation, busted lights and all of it made the salon look bad. And when the salon looks bad, I look bad. My name, my brand, my standards they were all tied into that space. I had my stepdad come by and help me patch things up the best we could. We managed to temporarily fix a few things, but the landlord was completely useless. No follow through, no effort, not even a response sometimes. It had gone from frustrating to flat-out embarrassing. I had weathered every season summer, fall, winter with these problems, and nothing had changed. I was done.

Instead of throwing more money into a place that was crumbling around me, I made a different kind of business decision: relocate, not reinvest. I had found another building I liked even more, and the second I felt peace in my gut about it, I signed the deal.

I didn't buy more equipment. I didn't go into more debt. I worked with what I had and made a plan to move smart, not move fast. I started prepping early for a smooth transition and made the announcement publicly to give my clients enough time to adjust.

I promoted one of my girls the nail tech I had the longest relationship with to head nail tech, and she truly showed up for me. She not only helped organize the move but also stepped into leadership and ran the salon for me when needed.

My mom, with all the good intentions in the world, had suggested I hire a family member who was planning to go into nails. She thought it could be a win-win to bring her on board at the new location. But I stood firm on that boundary. I didn't want friends or family mixed in with my business. I had learned enough by now to know that when you blur the lines, things get messy and I had too much riding on this move to risk it.

The new building was stunning. It was a U-shaped plaza, and my suite was right in the center, holding the spotlight. It had a high peak where we mounted a beautiful LED sign, and I hired a professional team to install a full vinyl window design with salon branding, beauty images, and service listings. Not only did it catch the eye it also helped with privacy and climate control. You couldn't see in, but we could see out. It was sleek, it was polished, it was elegant.

That was the very first step before we moved anything major in, we made sure the vision was in place. The space had previously been used as a dance studio, so there were mirrors on every wall. Once they were deep-cleaned and steamed, they opened up the room and made it feel even more spacious. I upgraded the lighting and added statement fixtures. A sparkling chandelier greeted clients at the entrance, and I even had a customized art canvas created a photo of me with the salon name beside it, bold and beautiful. The vibe? Elegance, crystals, and bold black tones. We moved in phases, intentionally. All the small things first decor, plumbing prep, electrical checks so that when it came time to roll in the big salon equipment, it would be quick and smooth. My stepdad helped the most. Truly. That man probably rolled his eyes every time my name popped up on his phone, but he never said no. He lifted, loaded, fixed, and showed up. Every time.

Having my head nail tech beside me made all the difference too mentally, emotionally, physically. She was in it with me, and I think that's what made this transition feel like a fresh start for all of us.

We went from falling ceiling tiles and chaos to boujee, high-end, and polished perfection. This location wasn't just a glow-up it was a complete reset.

I even had a sound bar system installed so there was always music playing while we worked, and mounted TVs in the waiting area and around the workstations. It created an experience. And just like the last time, my grandma P — my mom's mom was the very first to visit. She showed up with the same soft pride in her eyes as she walked through the door. She came often, even just to say hi. Her presence blessed that space just like she did the last one.

And the plaza itself? It had great energy. A cellphone company was at the end, with a makeup tattoo artist, a barbershop, a boutique, and a small tax office filling the other suites. The vibe was a solid mix of services and believe it or not, couples would come together, the man would hit up the barber, and then his girl would walk right into our salon for a set. We were surrounded by traffic and community, and we thrived in it.

This salon had to be the smoothest things had ever run for me in a long time. It felt like everything just clicked. Even the power bill was significantly lower than the old building and I mean way lower. At one point, my previous location had me paying over $1,000 a month just to keep the lights and AC running. That alone was what finally pushed me into taking the leap. The numbers made the decision obvious: change wasn't just a desire, it was necessary. And once I made it, I had no regrets. I was satisfied, proud, and at peace with my choice. That kind of alignment? Priceless.

The shop stayed busy. Constant flow. We had girls coming in for quinceañeras, bridal parties, birthdays you name it. Whether it was soft glam for a sweet sixteen or a full luxury set for a bride-to-be, we were booked and we were thriving.

Around this time, I finally completed my NASM certification. I had been quietly chipping away at it during my downtime, and the day I passed the test, I was so proud. I went out to celebrate with a few friends and gym buddies who had been cheering me on throughout the journey. It wasn't just about the certificate it was about proving to myself that I could finish what I started. That I could grow beyond nails. That I could expand who I was.

But while I was winning in one area, another was starting to fall apart my car.

The Chrysler my dad had gotten me had been acting up for months. It was roomy and had always been a reliable ride, but lately it would randomly turn off while I was driving, and it scared the hell out of me. I kept trying to make it work because the car was paid off no monthly payment was a blessing in business. The salon income always fluctuated. Some months were incredible. Others? Not so much. The last thing I wanted was a car note breathing down my neck.

Still, I hit my breaking point.

One day, without telling anyone, I just got up and took myself to the dealership. The salesman tried to guide me toward a four-door mom car or a basic sedan. I smiled and politely declined. I wasn't about to make a big purchase and not love what I was driving. I kept circling back to one car a shiny red Camaro. Something about her called to me. She was bold, sleek, fast, and loud in the best way. So I bought her.

They took the Chrysler as a trade-in and I drove off the lot in my first real "me" car. I knew my dad probably wouldn't have approved he always said he didn't want me in a sports car because of how small and risky they were. He used to joke that if I bought a Jeep, it'd flip with the first turn I made. But even knowing all that, I couldn't help but smile. It was my choice. And for once, I didn't let fear or someone else's voice drown out mine.

The Camaro was everything. Reliable, new, clean, and red as hell. She turned heads everywhere I went.

It didn't take long before people around town noticed. I'd catch random photos of my car posted on social media girls tagging me like, "Yesenia really out here living!" A few whispers started going around that business must be booming if I was making moves like this. What they didn't know was that I was just tired of stalling at red lights and praying my car wouldn't shut off in traffic. LOL.

Sometimes success is just solving a headache you've been putting off.

My boys loved the new car too. I made sure we created memories in it. We started doing trampoline park dates, pizza runs, and we even started a weekly tradition: every Tuesday was our movie night. No late appointments. No salon emergencies. Just the three of us. We'd head to the bistro theater, order food, and eat while watching a movie together. I always ordered the chicken wraps. My nanny would tag along sometimes she knew how much I treasured that time with my kids and would let us have our space, but she was always there to help if I needed an extra hand in public.

This was also the year I dove headfirst into bodybuilding and competing. I started clean meal prepping in the spring, and before I knew it, I was stepping onto my first stage for a local fitness competition. The nerves? Real. But the adrenaline? Even more powerful.

And guess what?

YES — LUXURIOUS NAILS SALON CLOSED FOR THAT. LOL.

My girls came out in full support. They showed up for me the same way I always tried to show up for them. Watching them cheer from the audience while I stood under stage lights in my first competition suit made me emotional in a way I can't describe. I felt supported, seen, and celebrated. That moment like so many others that year reminded me that I was building more than a business... I was building a life I loved.

The reason I stepped into the world of bodybuilding in the first place was simple: the gym had always been my sanctuary my version of a playground. I needed a challenge to keep me motivated, not just to look good, but to feel good too. And to be honest? The cash prize for first place was pretty tempting. That kind of money could go toward anything a future investment, a well earned vacation, or even just a little cushion to fall back on during slow business months.

But it wasn't just about the money. It was a bucket list thing. I wanted to earn my pro card, and I wanted the satisfaction of knowing that

I set a goal, saw it through, and could say I did that. I never planned to compete forever, but I knew that accomplishing this, even just once, would be something I could hold on to with pride for the rest of my life.

The gym itself was lit with energy back then it was during the time when "Black Beatles" by Rae Sremmurd and Gucci Mane was going viral. Everyone was hopping on the mannequin challenge trend, and our gym got in on the fun. We froze mid-lifts, mid-jumps, mid-pose for the video it was so funny. That moment in time felt electric. Life was hard, yes, but it was fun too.

And that night? I took first place.

Winning that first show was surreal. That one trophy opened the doors to so much more than I expected. Suddenly I had supplement companies and gym gear brands reaching out. I started making my own workout plans, tailoring them to help the women around me my friends, my salon girls, even some clients. It felt good to be in a position where I could inspire others through my own transformation.

I created a profile on a fitness site called BodySpace I'm not even sure if it still exists now, but back then it was the go-to hub for fitness enthusiasts. I tracked my workouts, shared updates, posted videos, and connected with others who were just as committed to the process. That platform gave me an outlet to share my journey, and it felt empowering.

At the same time, I launched a Snapchat page, uploaded content to YouTube, and promoted myself across all my social platforms. I wasn't trying to be famous I was trying to build something. I used everything I could to pick up leads, promote my programs, connect with women, and grow my brand. And it worked. Slowly, but surely, it worked.

But not everyone was supportive.

Criticism came in heavy. Random comments from people I didn't even know judgment, assumptions, insults. Keyboard warriors who had nothing better to do. And I'll admit, at the beginning, it got to me. I'd log off for a few days, sit with it, and try to shake it off. It took time to build a thick skin. To understand that not everyone deserved access to my energy especially not strangers behind screens.

Still, I kept going.

After my first show, I competed in two more competitions, back-to-back. One was held in Houston, Texas, and the third one took me all the way to Sacramento, California. And yes I earned my pro card that year. A huge milestone. Something I had only dreamed about just months before.

After the third show, my coach encouraged me to take a break. He told me I had leaned out so much that my body needed time to rest. To reset. To just be human again. He wanted me to enjoy food. To taste life again the things I had been deprived of during strict prep. So, I did just that.

I let myself breathe.

During this season, I met someone at the gym a guy we'll call "Salads." (My friends are going to laugh when they read this because it's such an inside joke!) Salads and I became really good friends. We trained together, had deep convos, shared macros, meal prepped, and held each other accountable in and out of the gym. There was no pressure. No expectations. Just a genuine connection rooted in health, respect, and routine.

We'd meet for workouts, grab food after, and vibe in a way that felt easy and safe. But I was cautious. Very cautious.

At the time, my boys were still really young, and I wasn't ready emotionally or mentally to bring anyone around them. I didn't want to confuse them. I didn't want to rush into anything. Most of all, I didn't want to put myself in a position where I could be hurt again. I'd been through too much. I had come too far.

So I let it be what it was. A friendship. A few dates. A breath of fresh air. A reminder that I was still capable of connection even if I wasn't ready to take it further.

Part of me still held hope that maybe just maybe things would one day work out with the father of my children. Even though I had no guarantees, a piece of my heart still lived in that space. Quietly. Softly. Waiting.

I know what you might be thinking that I was crazy or even dumb for still holding on, especially after everything that had already happened. But the truth is, I just didn't want to start life all over again with someone new. The thought of opening up to another man, of learning someone all over again, trusting someone all over again? That terrified me. I was still carrying so much trauma, and I couldn't imagine ever stepping foot into another man's home, much less defending on one.

Even when I'd get asked out randomly dinner, a movie, just something casual I never accepted rides. I always insisted, "I'll meet you there. I'm bringing my own car." I couldn't shake the discomfort of being in someone else's vehicle, especially a man's. It wasn't about being difficult or high maintenance. It was about pro-tecting myself emotionally, mentally, physically.

And for a while, things really did seem to be flowing beautifully. Business was steady. My social media pages were growing fast. I was getting brand deals and paid promotions companies reaching out to collaborate, asking me to make videos to promote their products or services. I even created a gift link, and people would send me things constantly nail supplies, gifts for my kids, clothes, beauty products anything from my Amazon wish list. Some came from women who followed me and supported my journey, and yes, some came from men too. It felt surreal that people I didn't even know wanted to support me just because they believed in me.

But while the businesswoman in me was thriving, the mother in me… was drowning.

There's only so much one woman even with help can carry.

My nanny did all she could, but there were so many things only I could do. I'd be in the middle of working on a client in the salon, and out of nowhere, my phone would ring: the school. The principal, the vice principal, a teacher someone calling to tell me there was an issue with one of my boys. It was always something. And the worst part? They expected me to drop everything and come right away.

I couldn't just walk out on a client with nails half-done, hands wrapped in foil, soaking, mid-process. But I also couldn't ignore the call. That's when the pressure of being both a mother and a father truly hit me. I was holding it all alone.

For almost a year, I tried to tough it out. I didn't ask for help. I told myself I could handle it. But eventually, the emotional weight caught up to me. I found myself sitting in a doctor's office, asking if something might be wrong. Was there something off with my son's behavior? Was it a developmental issue? Was I doing something wrong? Was I failing them?

I started to doubt myself in ways I never had before. I questioned my motherhood. I questioned my patience. I questioned whether I was even doing enough even though deep down, I knew I was giving everything I had.

The school journey became a roller coaster. Some weeks were calm, others were absolute chaos. Things would go really bad, and then randomly smooth out. It felt like I was holding my breath all year. I even made the decision to switch them from public school to private school hoping a different environment might help. But the challenges followed us for nearly three years straight. It was exhausting.

There was one incident that still makes my stomach turn.

My oldest got jumped at school. A group of kids for no real reason ganged up on him, hit him hard enough to open his scalp. I rushed him to the ER, heart pounding the entire way. I had to shut down the salon that day, of course, just like I did the day he got injured playing sports. I was also a sports mom practices, games, team events I never missed a beat. But every time I started to find balance, something else would come up.

My youngest had his own set of struggles, too. He was younger, but bold. The rebel. He'd square up with anybody, even teachers. I got a call once because he had kicked a teacher in class. I didn't know whether to cry or scream I just remember feeling helpless.

What made it more confusing was that at home, they were calm. Respectful. Loving. My nanny couldn't figure it out either she was with them often, and she said they were sweet and polite with her. And I'd never had major issues at home either. It didn't make sense. I've always believed in talking to my kids first. I wasn't the type to spank or hit them. I didn't want to parent through fear. I grew up with spankings, punishments, groundings all of it. And I remember how much I hated it. I swore I would never repeat that cycle. So I found other ways. If they misbehaved, we skipped movie night. I'd take their bike away. Or cut back on things they loved. But never my love, never my presence. I think I only ever raised my hand at them once and I carried that guilt for days. It crushed me. That moment was enough to know I never wanted to feel that way again.

So I had to get creative.

That's when I came up with the idea of giving them ownership a little taste of responsibility and reward. I helped them start a small snack business at home. I went to Sam's Club, bought boxes of chips, sodas, candy, and got organizing bins and a display cabinet. I set it all up like a mini corner store. Then I taught them how to run it.

I even used a chore calendar system. Each task came with a different dollar amount. Five dollars for taking out the trash, five for mopping the floors, five for cleaning the bathroom, a dollar for dishes. They earned their way. And then they had to restock, reinvest they learned that not all money made was money they could spend. That some of it had to go back into the business. And most importantly? They knew these privileges came with boundaries. If they acted up, the business shut down. If they disrespected me, no sales, no snacks, no exceptions.

It worked. It actually worked. It gave them structure, a sense of pride, and something to focus on. And it reminded me even in the middle of the chaos, I was doing something right.

I had started volunteering at the school and signing up as a chaperon one for their field trips. I wanted to be as present as I could in my boys' lives, even if it meant stretching myself thinner than ever. But every hour I gave away from the salon meant another hole opening somewhere else. Around the same time, my nanny needed time off to go see her family. She wasn't sure if she was even coming back after her trip, and that uncertainty alone was enough to keep me up at night. I could feel the walls closing in. The help I relied on was slipping, my youngest was giving me a hard time again, and I was back to juggling everything on my own. My stress and anxiety were through the roof.

The more my kids needed me, the less I could tend to the business. And without me being there, things just didn't run the same. My staff did what they could, but at the end of the day, I was the face and heartbeat of the salon. People didn't care that I had staff. They wanted me. They wanted the Yesenia experience they had seen on social media.

To make things worse, issues with the building kept popping up. I'll never forget the day the water heater, which had been installed in the ceiling, burst. Hot water splashed everywhere. I had to get on the phone immediately and shut the water off until it could be fixed. It felt like no matter how hard I tried, I couldn't catch a break.

As the salon grew busier, clients started getting upset that I wasn't around as much. They didn't understand that I was running a business, raising two boys alone, and managing staff. I had worked so hard to build this place, to create something beautiful and professional, and yet people acted like I had abandoned it if I wasn't personally doing their nails. I even went out of my way to take house calls for regular clients women who had just had surgeries, mothers without childcare, or clients who simply couldn't make it in. I'd show up at their homes after hours with my travel kit because I never wanted anyone to feel neglected.

I tried to adjust my hours, cutting mornings and working mostly evenings so I could handle the kids and school calls during the day. But the problems with my staff didn't stop. Girls wouldn't show up on time. Some wouldn't open the salon at all until I got there. It felt like I was constantly putting out fires. Between my boys, my employees, school emergencies, salon maintenance, and my clients,

I had too much on my plate.

I almost wanted to quit. There were days I'd sit in my car and think about walking away from it all. But then I'd remember my "why." The boys. The life I was trying to build. The independence I fought so hard for. I couldn't just let it go.

I tried changing the system. I signed up for online booking something I thought would be a lifesaver. Clients could book appointments while I was asleep or busy, especially those working night shifts who wanted to secure their spot first thing in the morning. It was seamless and efficient. For me, it was freedom. I've never been a texter I hate going back and forth through messages, DMs, emails, comments. I prefer calls or FaceTime. So online booking felt like the perfect solution.

But of course, the town didn't like it. Clients criticized me for it. They wanted the old way. They didn't understand that I was drowning and trying to keep up with demand. They saw change as inconvenience.

And then the chaos really started.

I had a client who somehow hurt her foot with the door while walking in. None of us saw what happened the shop was busy, everyone had their heads down working but she called the cops to make a report and tried to sue me over it. I couldn't believe it. In the middle of building my dream, here I was dealing with legal threats for something out of my control.

I also started noticing a shift in behavior from clients. Some would walk out without paying. Others would take polishes from the racks like they were souvenirs. It was shocking, frustrating, and humiliating. But what really broke me was one afternoon when a client, after paying for her own set, her sister's set, and her mother's set, decided she didn't like the total at checkout. She started shouting at me across the salon, from the front desk to the table where I was designing another client's nails. She threatened me, yelling loud enough for everyone to hear. I felt my face flush with anger and em-barrassment. This was my business. My safe place. And it was being violated in front of my eyes.

But nothing compared to what happened at the mall.

One weekend, I was out with my boys just a simple day out, trying to make memories and escape the stress for a while when a man approached me. I didn't know him. But he said he knew who my father was. His voice was low, threatening. He said if he saw me again, I'd "end up like him." Meaning unalived.

It chilled me to my core. For a moment, time froze. My boys were right there. I didn't know what he meant, who he was, or if the threat was real. But I refused to show fear. I kept my face steady, my body calm. Inside, though, my heart was racing.

All of it the business issues, the school calls, the clients, the threats it weighed on me like a boulder. Every night, I'd get home and collapse into bed. And still, I'd pick up the phone and call my ex. Not because we were back together but because I needed someone familiar. Someone who knew me, who knew the boys. He wasn't dating anyone, and I was on and off with "Salads," so our communication stayed open. Sometimes I just needed to vent. Sometimes I needed advice. Sometimes I just needed to hear another voice say, "You're going to be okay."

That was my life at that point a mix of power and fragility, triumph and exhaustion. Running a business, raising two boys, and trying to hold myself together while the world kept pulling at every seam.

Chapter 26

The Beginning of the End, Prada to Nada.

As my ex and I started getting closer again, he kept encouraging me to take a break to unplug from the chaos of my world and just come visit him. To breathe. Reset. Unwind. He'd say things like, "Just come see me. Get away from all that stress for a little while." And to be honest, I needed it. I was unraveling mentally, emotionally, physically. I had been carrying too much for too long. My body was starting to feel it. My mind was shutting down in moments I needed to be present. And my spirit? My spirit was tired.

So, I said yes.

I let go of the reins just a little. I asked the girls at the salon to step in more and hold it down while I was gone. I even leaned on my mom a bit more than I usually would. I finally gave myself permission to pause, to breathe differently, and to try to salvage something that once felt like home even if I wasn't sure what that meant anymore.

And then there was "Salads." Remember him?

That chapter quietly closed, without drama, without flames. Just a soft ending. We had been in each other's lives for nearly five years. Five years of blurred lines, late-night calls, gym sessions, birthdays, parties, inside jokes, emotional convenience, and a familiarity that almost felt like comfort but never commitment. We weren't in a relationship, not really. But we played the part when it was convenient, when we were lonely, or when we didn't know how to be alone. For a long time, I mistook that for something deeper. His presence in my life filled a void. But now?

Now I can answer his calls or not and feel nothing. Not because I hate him or because something bad happened. But because

I've healed past needing him. That's the difference. I loved him once, sure. But I was loving him from a version of me that didn't know better. A version of me that just wanted to feel seen, protected, wanted. These days, I know better. These days, I know peace.

And peace doesn't need his voice in my ear. Peace doesn't look like scrolling through my contacts and stopping at his name. Peace is silence and not missing the noise. The truth is, it wasn't ever really that deep. Not for either of us. There was never a true emotional connection. We just existed in the same space, for a season. And while we shared time, memories, and a strange kind of mutual understanding, we both knew it wasn't forever.

When I told him I "just might" be getting back with my ex though at the time, I wasn't even sure if that would actually happen he didn't protest. He didn't fight for me or ask for details. He simply said he wouldn't get in the way. That if I ever needed him, he'd still be there.

And that was it.

I never called him again. I never explained. I changed my number shortly after and never looked back. We left it in silence. In peace. And that was probably the most honest ending we could've had.

When I'd return from those trips and jump right back into work, I still had my people. My friends "E" and "M" would come around, hang out with me, keep me company, and try to pull me back to life when I felt like I was fading. They gave me little pockets of normalcy. But even that eventually started to crack.

"E" and I had a massive fallout one that left a sting. She couldn't understand why I refused to get back with my ex-husband. She'd raise her voice at me, call me stupid, say things like, "Any woman would kill to have a man who provides. You don't know how lucky you are." Maybe she wasn't entirely wrong in her eyes. Maybe it sounded good on paper. But she never lived through my pain. She didn't see the nights I spent crying in silence or how hard it was to hold everything together alone. She didn't carry the same scars or memories. She didn't know what it cost me to survive those years. She didn't know how much of myself I'd already lost trying to love him right. I couldn't just wipe the slate clean and pretend none of it happened. I couldn't unfeel what my body remembered. Forgiveness wasn't easy anymore, not when I was finally learning to listen to my own intuition and not silence it again. She didn't get it. Worse, she didn't try to. Her words cut me deeply. The tone, the judgment, the dismissal of everything I'd endured.

Eventually, I let her go. No dramatic goodbye. No final argument. Just distance. Just peace. And from that moment on, I stopped letting people too far into my personal life. I started keeping things to myself. Not because it was the healthiest thing to do, but because it felt safer. Silence became my boundary. And in that quiet, I started reading more again.

One of the books that landed in my lap during that time was Why Men Love Bitches by Sherry Argov. That book? Whew. It was full of unapologetic one-liners that slapped me back into a mindset I didn't even know I needed. I wouldn't say it was the most emotionally grounded advice but it was empowering. And it hit. Hard. I devoured that book like medicine and took notes like I was in a masterclass on reclaiming my voice.

A few quotes stayed with me: "He must feel that you choose to be with him, not that you need to be with him. Neediness is what turns a man off. Independence is what keeps him interested."

And another that had me laughing but also lowkey nodding in agreement: "A bitch gives a man plenty of space so he doesn't fear being trapped in a cage... then she locks the door behind him."

LOL. Like I said... maybe not the healthiest doctrine, but it helped rewire some of my thinking.

See, I'm a sapiosexual. I need to be mentally stimulated. I'm deeply attracted to intelligence minds that stretch mine. It's not just about how you treat me. It's how you see me. How you meet me. And my ex? While he eventually started contributing financially finally he was never fully present. Not emotionally. Not mentally. Not spiritually.

When my car broke down? I figured it out.

When I got locked out, when the power got shut off, when I needed new tires or surgery recovery help it was always on me. After giving birth? Alone. That list is long, and I've memorized it. Even beyond the physical support, I just wanted real conversations. I wanted us to grow together. I'd talk to him about business ideas, future dreams, the kind of legacy we could build, and he'd look at me like I was speaking another language. It was like trying to plant seeds in concrete. He just wasn't there. He couldn't meet me where I stood. And I wasn't trying to mother my man. I didn't want to raise him. I wanted to build with him. I wanted to be a wife not a replacement for the things he never healed from.

Still, I kept trying.

I tried to communicate better. I expressed what I needed. I spelled it out. And to his credit, he made some effort. He did try but life kept hitting us. The layoffs came again. They always did. Two or three times a year, like clockwork. And each time, I went right back into survival mode. Not just for me. For both of us. I took on more. I picked up the slack. I carried the load even when I was already breaking under the weight of my own. I even helped him apply for a higher position one that intimidated him. He didn't want the responsibility. He doubted himself. But I told him he had to grow. Not just for me. For himself. For our kids. For his own legacy.

And for a little while… he did.

But it never felt solid. It never felt sustainable. It felt like I was building a house of cards in a windstorm, praying it wouldn't all collapse with the next gust.

Meanwhile, I started noticing money going missing from my business cash from my box, deposits from the bank, just… gone. Slipping through cracks I didn't even know existed. And the worst part? I didn't have the time or energy to track it all because I was too busy surviving. Too busy helping him. Too busy trying to be everything for everyone. I was pouring myself out like water and before I realized it, I was bone dry. I gave and gave and gave, and my own life started unraveling behind the scenes.

My mom, always in my ear with her old-school wisdom, would say things like, "You have to stay. You have to try. You have to hold it together for your family." And I know she meant well she always does but that's the generational script. That's the ride-or-die narrative we were handed as women. That belief that love means endurance. That staying is the prize. That sacrifice is the badge. But I was bleeding out while trying to wear that badge with pride.

I was doing too much.

I was the one managing the books, keeping track of every payment, every credit pull, every overdue balance and everything was under my name. I was the one filing taxes, calculating income, shifting funds, stretching every dollar like elastic. The cars? In my name. The bills? In my name. Every move? On me. I scheduled payments, ran the business, ran the household, kept the kids afloat, kept the peace, kept the mask on. I was the mom. The dad. The wife. The right-hand woman. The backbone.

But even bones break when the weight gets heavy enough.

I didn't even realize how deep into people-pleasing I had fallen until I couldn't hear my own needs anymore. I was trying so hard to keep everyone else happy my kids, my staff, my man, my family that I forgot what it felt like to make decisions just for me. I forgot what it meant to protect my own peace. It took me a long time to admit that. And even longer to unlearn it. But I promise you we're getting there.

The salon, the place that once felt like mine... like my pride and peace... started feeling like a cage. I hated being there. I hated designing nails. The passion I once had that spark that used to wake me up excited it was gone. Burned out. After six years of grinding nonstop, I had nothing left to give. Walk-ins became anxiety triggers. The online booking system I worked so hard to implement? People ignored it like it was optional. Small town mentality. Everyone still wanted to text, to pop in unannounced, to demand their way. I was outgrowing all of it, and fast.

I wanted more systems, structure, real growth. I wanted to run the salon like a true business, not just a hustle. But no matter how much

I upgraded the tools or tried to elevate the process, I couldn't keep the team together. No matter how much I cared, coached, or poured into them I couldn't fix everyone's life. And everyone was going through something. Some of the girls had kids, partners, personal battles. Call-outs were constant. Cancellations, no-shows, late arrivals the salon slowly started to unravel. Some days, we'd all have to leave at the same time to pick up our kids or handle emergencies. And it showed. The business looked scattered. The clients could feel the chaos.

And deep down, I knew I couldn't build what I envisioned in that space anymore. That version of the dream no longer fit the woman I was becoming.

Everything was catching up to me the betrayal, the burnout, the heartbreak, the pressure. And still… I kept pushing. I pushed through every red flag, every breaking point, every sleepless night. I tried to save the salon. I tried to save the relationship. I tried to save the version of life I swore I wanted the family dream I had envisioned since I was a little girl.

I was clinging to everything all at once, gripping the rope with both hands, holding up two entire lives mine and his while silently watching both of them sink.

Failure wasn't an option. I refused to be the girl who gave up. I couldn't stomach being labeled a failure, not after how hard I worked. Not after everything I'd sacrificed.

But the truth? I was drowning.

The town I lived in felt too small. The conversations were too small. The mindset was too small. And no matter how hard I worked to modernize the business, to teach structure, to get clients to respect the boundaries and systems I had built they just wouldn't budge. It felt like dragging dead weight. Everyone wanted things the old way. And I couldn't be at the salon as often as I needed to be anyway. Between the boys, the stress, the emotional wear and tear the guilt started eating at me. I was spread too thin.

The burnout wasn't just physical. It was emotional. It was spiritual.

And the scariest part?

I didn't even recognize myself anymore.

I even tried to reignite the fire by attending nail and beauty shows in San Antonio the Armstrong McCall expos, educational workshops, nail competitions. I was even invited as a guest speaker at local beauty schools. I took little trips whenever I could manage them, hoping they'd breathe some new life into what I had once built from scratch with so much love. That business was more than just a salon it was my dream. And for a moment… it worked. A small part of me came back to life. Not necessarily because of the nails, or the products, or the new trends but because of the city. The energy. The movement. The feeling of being somewhere that didn't feel so small.

Being away from that tiny town reminded me of the woman I used to be the one who wasn't constantly bending, folding, or break-ing herself to keep everyone else comfortable. I realized I needed more. Not just more income or clients, but more life. More options. More room to breathe. For myself. And for my kids. I didn't want them to grow up boxed in by small-town thinking. I wanted them to be surrounded by people who chased dreams out loud. I wanted them to see success in color not just in the shades of survival I was used to.

But I didn't know how to fully walk away. I had worked so hard for what I had. I couldn't just abandon it. I had memories in that space. Nights where I fell asleep at my manicure table, eyes heavy, brush still in hand, dreaming up new designs, new collections, new ideas for the shop. I wanted to spark that same fire in my team I really did. I would try to motivate them to join me in workshops, to come along to shows, to dream bigger with me. But no one ever followed through. Not one of them. Even my family I'd push content ideas, I'd ask for support, reposts, something anything. But it was like silence. And I don't think I've ever said this before, but I can't even recall a single time a family member walked into my salon and supported me as a paying client.

I always did everything alone.

I would take the girls out to Olive Garden just to break bread together and create space for honest team conversations to ask what we could do differently, how I could better support them, how we could grow together. I even started ordering lunch to the salon, just so we could share a meal and talk. Still… nothing shifted. It felt like trying to breathe life into a balloon that had already popped. And I don't think I ever felt weaker than I did during those final months. I felt like a failure in ways I never expected.

I don't even think I've mentioned this part before, but I provided everything for my nail techs. Every lamp, every brush, every tool, every supply. In most salons, you're expected to bring your own. But not with me. If someone walked in and said, "I want to work but I don't have anything," I made sure that wasn't a problem. I would get them set up. I made it easy because I wanted to remove every barrier between women and financial independence. That was my whole vision to create a space where they didn't have to rely on a man, or anyone else, just to build a life.

That's when the idea of moving first entered my mind. It was one of the hardest decisions I ever made. Because it wasn't just about me leaving it meant my girls would be left without a job. My clients, some of whom had been with me since I was a baby tech fresh out of cosmetology school, would have to find someone new. These weren't just customers. They were loyal women who watched me grow, who rooted for me, who believed in my hands. It broke me to even think about saying goodbye.

Another thing I never really spoke about I used to take long drives alone just to spark something in myself again. I'd stop by dealerships, mostly Range Rover, and sit inside the white SUV I knew I wanted one day. I'd run my hands across the leather, inhale the scent of possibility. I'd visualize my next chapter and ask myself not if I'd get it, but how. How can I make this happen? How can I earn it? I'd try to shake off the scarcity mindset. I'd say things like "This is mine. I'm going to get this." Even if I didn't fully believe myself, I kept saying it until I did. That "fake it till you make it" was all I had to hold onto some days.

Truthfully though, I didn't even want the car just for the flex. I needed something that made business travel easier. Something with enough space for my manicure kits, for weddings, for mobile services. But even then, my main focus wasn't myself. It never had been. My goal was always to provide for my team to give them steady jobs, a space where they could thrive, have income, shop for their kids, fix their cars, get what they needed. My vision wasn't self centered. It was community-centered. I just wanted to give what I never had.

While I was sitting in that transition space debating whether to sell the salon and start fresh I'd take weekend trips to San Antonio, sometimes even weekdays. I'd book hotels, drive around neighborhoods, apply to jobs, walk into other salons just to ask how they operated, what they paid, what systems they used. I did all of this research on my own. Quietly. Carefully. I was preparing for my own exit plan, even if I didn't fully admit it yet. And to be honest, I didn't even know if I wanted to stay in Texas. A part of me was pulled back toward Oregon… or maybe Washington. Somewhere smaller, calmer. I knew things were better paid up north, but I also knew the cost of living was higher. I just didn't know what I wanted. All I did know with absolute clarity was that I didn't want to stay where I was.

I couldn't.

I randomly asked a salon in the city if they needed help with nails. I was actually getting my own pedicure done that day not even planning anything serious but when they saw my work and I mentioned I had my brush and UV lamp in the car, they hired me on the spot. That same morning, I took my first client. She tipped me $50 on top of the service, and I remember just sitting there stunned. Like… what? After just one week of helping the salon, the front desk receptionist told me I was fully booked for the rest of the week. Not only that most of the clients I had seen had already rebooked their next appointment in the system before even leaving. And every single client who sat in my chair tipped generously never below $20. It was wild to me because where I came from? Most people tipped two, maybe five dollars max. And don't get me wrong I appreciated every tip. Two dollars, five, twenty, fifty, or none at all. I've always respected the hustle and understood that tips are not mandatory. But it was a huge difference an eye-opener. This city valued what I offered. And more than that, they wanted bigger, bolder, more creative nail sets. That lit me up. I couldn't get that kind of energy back home.

And remember how I told Dad I wanted to move to San Antonio before he passed? Well... this felt like my chance. My moment. It was all starting to align.

I just had to plan the move the right way because I had a lot to lose. This wasn't some local relocation. I was about to uproot my entire life, move cities, and start over. That meant coordinating U-Haul rentals, deciding what to take and what to leave, figuring out how to make this transition permanent... because once I left, I didn't want to look back.

One thing I knew for sure: I wasn't renting an apartment. That was off the table. I had it in my heart that I would buy a home even if it was small, even if it wasn't my dream house. I wanted something that was mine. I didn't want to throw money into someone else's pocket anymore. The home I had in the Valley was beautiful. And even though I knew I might have to downsize, I was okay with that... as long as the downsizing meant ownership. Something I could eventually rent out in the future. That was my mindset.

I didn't think it would be too difficult to find something more basic. In fact, that's what I wanted a smaller place, minimal yard, easy maintenance. It was just me and my boys, after all. I couldn't do it all work, motherhood, business, and now landscaping too? No, thank you. Truthfully, one of my biggest dreams was to raise my boys into good men, help them graduate, go to college or find careers they love, and support them in building the kind of life I never had growing up. And once they were settled? Maybe I'd finally exhale. Maybe I'd finally get to live. I used to daydream about doing nails in a quiet little beach town, or some hidden gem where no one knew me. Maybe somewhere in Mexico, where I could speak both languages freely and build a slower life. Or even a tiny farm in Oregon, or a peaceful island where I could unwind and finally stop having to lead all the time.

I prayed for that. Prayed for something soft.

I wanted real love the Hallmark kind. The kind where a man would take the lead, sweep me off my feet, build me a tiny home or let me make his feel like mine. Someone who would just say, "I got you. I got us." A safe space where I could finally rest, be held, be protected. A home where I could breathe.

And part of me used to hold back from buying a home because I had always imagined that my person would be the one to do that with me. I thought I'd wait. I thought maybe that's what he'd do surprise me, plan something, build something with me. But life kept reminding me: it's okay to want that, but you also have to be willing to build it for yourself.

I still craved that "soft girl life"… just with a side of hustle. But how would any of that ever happen when all I ever did was work?

My life was my kids. My business. My clients. My gym time. That was it. And whenever I let myself drift off into those kinds of thoughts, I'd shake them off. Because deep down, some part of me didn't believe it was possible. I thought… maybe I'm just meant to be alone. Like my grandmother. Strong. Independent. Alone. And I convinced myself that I would rather be alone forever than ever get hurt again.

Still, I started to lean more seriously into the decision to move. And the first people I talked to about it were my boys. They were sad… not angry, just hesitant. They didn't love the idea of starting over new city, new school, new friends. It was scary for them. I didn't blame them. But I promised them it would be a transition. I told them this might not happen right away maybe in a year, maybe longer it was just something I was thinking about. Exploring.

To prepare, I started downsizing. Selling things little by little. I made the decision that I'd go back to doing nails from home while I prepared for the transition it would give me more flexibility, and also help save money for when the time came. I didn't want to wait until the last minute to sell everything. I knew that cash could serve as part of my investment once I landed in San Antonio. I had to be smart about every step.

This was the beginning of a new chapter... I could feel it. But I also knew the end had to come first.

I had also asked my mom to come with me to San Antonio on a few occasions to go house hunting. Sometimes we looked at townhomes, sometimes brand new construction. I scheduled showings in advance and researched everything beforehand I didn't want to rush anything. I needed to be sure. The boys and I even turned some of the trips into little staycations. We'd stay at nice hotels, go out to eat, and I'd sneak in job interviews or home tours in between. I was trying to make the process feel less scary for them and more like an adventure a new chapter, not just a hard goodbye. I was doing everything I could to make the best decision for all of us. I was careful. I was thoughtful. I wasn't running away I was moving forward. Slowly. Intentionally.

My ex-husband was disappointed when he found out I was planning to move. Not because he was angry but because, in his words, "this might actually be the time you move on for good." And deep down, I think he knew I meant it this time. But we were still on good terms, and surprisingly, he eventually started helping me brainstorm ideas and gave his input on things like the job market, neighbor-hoods, and what to look out for. I told him I'd go back to corporate temporarily, just to create stability while I built up a new client base. I had done it before from nothing. But this time, I wasn't starting from scratch. I was starting from experience. And I mean real experience. I had grit, wisdom, lessons I'd bled for. I had built something once from pure hustle, and I could do it again.

Okay... now this is the part where I'm about to shock you.

In the middle of all the chaos the move, the business shifts, the growth, the healing I made the wild decision to give my ex another chance. Yep. DON'T COME FOR ME. Or do. Whatever. LOL. I can't go back and change it now. I've made peace with it.

The truth is, there's always been a version of me the 17-year-old me, the young mom version of me who just wanted it to work. Who wanted the love story. Who wanted the full-circle redemption. And maybe, just maybe, we were finally ready.

We talked. We planned. We told ourselves it would be different this time. And we made the impulsive, reckless, hopeful decision to elope. Again. We were living in separate places, figuring it out, and terrified but also a little excited. It felt like maybe this was the reset we needed. We weren't kids anymore. We weren't 16 and 17. We had grown. We had healed. And to be honest? Part of me loved the idea of skipping the awkwardness of dating someone new. He already knew the little things like the fact I hated touching a sweaty drink cup, so he'd always wrap it in a napkin before handing it to me. Or how I liked my eggs cooked. Or how I'd zone out when I was overwhelmed and needed someone to gently bring me back to center. We knew each other. And that comfort is hard to find in this world.

And now, combining what we had? Two homes, two careers, two beautiful boys it sounded like the perfect second chance. Plus, I had helped him level up. He was finally a boss like, officially. He had stepped into a position that once terrified him. He was now overseeing a whole team of men at the refinery, and I had pushed him hard to apply. He didn't think he was ready, but I knew he was. I believed in him. I always had. His pay had shot up. It was one of the highest rates in the industry and he even invited me on a project he was considering in Alaska. Don't quote me, but the offer was something like $40–$50 an hour, working 12-hour shifts, seven days a week, with $150 per diem daily. I didn't go, obviously I had my own life and business to focus on but I was so proud of him. I had known him since we were broke teenagers sleeping on air mattresses. Seeing him step into his power was emotional for me.

But then… three weeks in.

Three. Weeks. I found out he was cheating.

He was living a double life while working out of town. And the other woman? A young, pretty, 22-year-old blonde from my hometown.

No kids. No history. No strings. She was one of his coworkers and while I was planning our future, packing his lunches, being soft, excited, present he was building a whole other life with someone else.

And the worst part? I didn't even see it coming.

We had just come back from Vegas. We were taking shots at Tacos El Gordo on the strip. Laughing. Vibing. Loving. I thought we were good. I thought I was safe. I had opened my heart again. I had become the softest, most loving version of me... all over again.

This broke me.

Like really, broke me.

Out of everything I've survived and I've survived a lot this was the moment I felt the weakest. I had no strength left to fake it. No energy to explain myself. No more breath to carry the pain in silence. I didn't recognize the woman staring back at me. I had gone from Prada to nada just like that. But somehow... in the middle of all that heartbreak and humiliation, I finally felt something I hadn't felt in years.

Freedom.

Because for the first time, there was nothing left to save. Nothing left to fight for. No illusion left to chase. The fog had cleared. The fantasy had died. And all that was left was me.

Raw. Bruised. Exhausted. But finally... awake.

I know it probably doesn't make sense to most people. But when you've spent years pouring yourself into someone trying, sacrificing, fixing there's something strangely liberating about the moment it all collapses. Because in that collapse, you're released. You can finally say, "This isn't my burden to carry anymore."

And that?

That was the beginning of my freedom. I knew I had tried my very best over and over and over again.

And this time… it really felt different. At least to me. I genuinely believed that because we were older, more mature, and had already made our share of painful mistakes, we wouldn't let it happen again. I thought we had both learned. I thought we'd both grown. I thought this was our redemption arc.

If you're wondering how I found out, here it is.

At this point, I had finally started transitioning to San Antonio. The move was happening. And he and I were doing great or so I thought. He was taking time off from work to visit me, and I told him I'd do the same. I was soft again. I let my walls come down. I was doing all the "wifey" things, trusting that we were finally on the same page. He had been working close enough to come see me every week or two, and I welcomed him with open arms every time.

But then… I noticed something shift.

It was subtle at first. But I felt it. It started around Valentine's Day. I had never gone all-out for Valentine's before not really so I decided to surprise him. I bought him a brand-new Apple Watch, some thoughtful gifts from the boys, and even splurged on the new Creed cologne, which smelled divine. I wanted him to feel special, seen, celebrated.

When he opened everything… he barely reacted.

The boys were bouncing with excitement, eager to watch him unwrap their gifts but he just sat there, cold and nonchalant, like none of it meant anything. It was so unlike him. At first, I convinced myself he was just tired from work. But deep down, something felt off. Something had shifted.

Then he told me he probably wouldn't be able to come visit as often anymore. After all his nonstop talk about seeing me every weekend how the drive was no big deal, how he missed me the moment he left now, suddenly, he was too tired. Too busy. Work was picking up, he said. I told him I understood. I didn't want to come off clingy or insecure. But the calls and texts slowed down too. The sweet good morning messages stopped. The mid-day check-ins disappeared. He told me the refineries had stricter rules now, that he couldn't have his phone on him as much. And while that could be true, I also knew that people in his position general foremen, project managers, directors they needed their phones. I didn't push it. I didn't accuse. I just stayed quiet. But the knot in my stomach grew heavier.

And then came the moment that shattered me.

One weekend when he came to see me, he woke up early and left. No goodbye. No forehead kiss. No "see you later, babe." Nothing.

It might sound small, but that? That was everything.

He always kissed me goodbye even when we were on bad terms. It was second nature. And that morning, he just walked out. I stood in the silence of the house, unsure if I had imagined it. But I felt it in my bones. Something was wrong.

I pushed through my day, stayed busy with clients, organizing, anything to distract myself. But out of nowhere, I just broke down. I burst into tears not even soft ones. I sobbed. My throat had a knot I couldn't swallow, and no matter how hard I tried to shake it off, the feeling wouldn't go away. I couldn't sleep. I couldn't think.

I finally called one of my friends to vent I just needed a safe space to let it out. She told me to breathe and said she'd check in on me later. She asked me what was making me feel like something was going on. I told her about the gift, the lack of affection, the weird energy. And then, after hanging up… something told me to check the phone bill. I had never done that before. Never felt the need to. But this time, my gut wouldn't let it go.

So I looked. And there it was.

Everything.

He had been calling the same number repeatedly. During his lunch breaks. After work. On the weekends. Even while driving away from my house, not even ten minutes after pulling away, he'd already be on the phone with her. Hours of talk time. Dozens of texts. Constant communication. I felt sick. Physically sick.

I didn't want to jump to conclusions, so I paused. I took a breath. Then I called the number.

A girl answered.

I hung up.

She called back.

This time, I answered and asked calmly if she had been talking to someone by his name. She said yes. She told me she had no idea he was married. She said she'd answer any questions I had. I didn't ask a single one. I just thanked her for her honesty and hung up.

I sat there in disbelief. My heart thudding so loud I could barely hear my own thoughts.

I called him.

He picked up.

And I lost it.

I screamed. I yelled. I cried. I told him how disgusted I was. I told him I couldn't believe he did this to me again. That he had the nerve to smile in my face, to make me believe in something real, to lie with such ease. To elope with me while secretly entertaining someone else?

And what did he say?

"I don't think I told you guys."

That's what he said. As if that made it better.

He made excuses. He dodged. He lied. Again.

He had just bought me a $12,000 ring as if that was supposed to make it all okay. As if money could patch the hole he ripped through my chest. As if a shiny band could fix betrayal.

I didn't care.

I was beyond rage. I was numb.

And worst of all… I was embarrassed. I felt so stupid. I felt like a fool for believing. For hoping. For trying so damn hard again.

Right then and there, I told him I was filing for divorce.

AGAIN.

I was done. I had nothing left to give. No more fight. No more softness. No more second chances.

Just me, staring at the broken pieces of a dream I tried to piece back together one last time… and watching it fall apart in my hands.

I didn't want a single thing from him. Not a dollar. Not an apology. Not a promise. I didn't want his help, his excuses, or his gifts. I was done. I told him if he ever came back into town to see me, he could meet me at the police station and I wasn't bluffing. I meant it. I was ready to file a report before he even tried to come near me. That wasn't a threat; it was a boundary. A line in the sand. I wasn't the same little teenage girl he once knew. That girl was gone. If he had the guts to cheat, then he needed to have the guts to face what came next.

And just like that, I went back to doing everything on my own. Again. In a heartbeat. The autopilot survival mode I hated so much kicked in because it had to. It was muscle memory at this point being my own safety net, my own backup plan. But what cut the deepest wasn't the logistics or the finances. It wasn't the loss of help or the loss of a future I thought we'd have.

It was the loss of trust.

That was what broke me the most. Not the cheating, but the betrayal of my belief. The betrayal of me. After everything we had been through, after all the mistakes we had supposedly learned from, after all the years of building and rebuilding I had trusted him with my heart one last time. I had let him back into the softest, most vulnerable parts of me. And he broke it again.

Why did I keep believing this man would change? Why did I keep thinking that maybe, just maybe, I was finally safe? He had seen me at my lowest. He knew my scars. He knew my pain. I had given him chance after chance. I had loved him with everything I had left. And still… I was the one left holding the pieces.

I remember walking into my room that night, my whole body trembling. My hands were shaking so hard I could barely grip my phone. My chest felt heavy, like there was no oxygen in the room. I dropped everything. I threw myself onto the bed. I threw my phone across the room. I yanked every framed picture of us off the walls and nightstand and hurled them to the floor. I didn't care if the glass shattered, if it cut my hands, if the noise woke the whole world. I just wanted it gone. All of it.

I fell to my knees and cried like I did the first time all over again the same guttural cry that escapes you when grief finally pushes past your throat and leaves your body shaking. My palms pressed to the carpet, my hair falling around my face, my tears soaking into my clothes. I couldn't stop.

That night was the first time in my life I felt depression so heavy, it scared me. The first time the thought of not wanting to live crept into my mind not because I didn't love my kids, not because I didn't have reasons to stay, but because I was just so exhausted. So drained. So ready for something, anything, to finally break in my favor.

I lost my appetite. My sense of humor. My spark. My fight. All of it was gone.

I went to sleep crying.

I woke up crying.

I didn't know how to move forward. I didn't even know where to start. All I knew was that I was a mess a woman who had given everything, tried everything, and still ended up here.

And yet, even in that darkness, something in me was still alive a tiny, flickering ember under the ashes. I didn't know it then, but that ember would become the fire that rebuilt me.

Authors note: " That night, I thought it was the end of me. I thought there was nothing left to give, nothing left to rebuild. But what I didn't know then was that endings have a strange way of being beginnings in disguise. I wasn't just breaking I was being cleared. Stripped down to the rawest version of myself so I could finally rise as her. This was the night everything shattered, but it was also the night my freedom and my comeback quietly began."

Chapter 27

The Turn Around

I didn't know it then, but I was already halfway across the bridge out of survival mode. Life hadn't gotten easier let's be clear about that but something inside of me had shifted. I stopped waiting for a rescue. I stopped looking around hoping someone would notice the weight I was carrying. Nobody was coming to save me, and strangely, that realization didn't break me it built me. I became my own safety net. My own therapist. My own source of stability. And no, it wasn't glamorous. It wasn't some overnight glow-up. It looked like quiet mornings with a half made bed and a full to-do list. It was budgeting every dollar to the cent, planning grocery trips around digital coupons, filming gym content in between clock-ins, and sending out emails for job leads and new goals while reheating coffee for the third time. I was starting all over again, brick by brick, from the bottom up but the chaos that had once ruled my life had finally started to slow.

And in that unfamiliar quiet, I found something I hadn't felt in years: space. Space to think. To breathe. To hear my own thoughts without panic. That silence? It was terrifying, yes but it was also healing. It was mine. Every raw inch of it. And that solitude didn't feel lonely it felt sacred.

After years of crash-and-burn cycles, betrayals, toxic loyalty, and desperate rebuilding, this season felt like a reclaiming. It was about proving myself right. I had crossed over into something new. I had made it through the fire, and though I still had ash in my lungs and bruises on my heart, I was still standing. Scared, sure. But stronger. Smarter. More rooted than I had ever been. This wasn't about proving anything to anyone anymore. This was about my boys and me. And I was determined to move forward, even if I had to wear one of those funnel cones like horses do, the kind that forces them to look straight ahead. That was going to be me focused, unbothered, eyes only on the road in front of me. This was my chance to create a new life for us. Not for family. Not for friends. Not for old coworkers or followers online. Just us.

I still had my contract with Universal Animal Pak. That was something I was proud of. I loved working with that company. I don't even know if I mentioned it in earlier chapters, but they reached out to me after I had consistently posted my competition prep and fitness journey on Instagram. I had done the hard work, stayed disciplined, and stayed visible even when I didn't feel like I was being seen. That partnership had been one of those moments where it felt like life whispered, "Keep going." So of course, keeping that contract meant the gym content had to continue. And I was serious about that. The first thing I did once I got to San Antonio was get my gym membership set up. Priorities.

Before I even moved, I had already started looking at homes. There was this neighborhood called Lucky Ranch Homes, and it seemed perfect on paper. I had even gone as far as doing the paperwork to purchase a home there. It was tucked just enough outside the city limits to feel peaceful, but still close enough to everything that mattered Six Flags, SeaWorld, shopping centers, and only about a ten-minute drive to downtown. I took the kids to go see the area and started to picture our life there. But something didn't sit right with me. These houses, they were beautiful but they were cookie cutter. Perfect little boxes in neat rows. And I don't say that in a judgmental way, but I knew deep down that wasn't where I wanted to plant roots long-term. I couldn't bring myself to lock into a $400,000 mortgage just because it looked good on paper. So I let it go. And I'm proud of that decision. Instead, I looked into nearby lots with modular and manufactured homes. Some people turn their noses up at those, but I've never cared much about what people think. The prices were shockingly low, and I figured why not buy something outright with cash and give myself some breathing room? I was in a transitional phase anyway. My goal was to stay put for about 13 to 16 weeks, get grounded again, and then decide what came next. It gave me space to figure out if I even liked San Antonio. At that point, I couldn't drive around the city without a GPS I didn't know the area at all. This was my way of easing into something new without rushing it. A soft landing

Once I got somewhat settled, I started layering in little joys for the boys and me. I bought us memberships to SeaWorld, Aquatica, and Six Flags. We lived just minutes from all three. It was one of the best decisions I made that year. It gave us something to look forward to on weekends and summer nights without breaking the bank. The boys had a blast swimming, going on rides, and floating down the lazy river while I sat in the shade with my refillable member cup, hydrating and finally, finally breathing. Just the three of us. No chaos. No pressure. Just peace.

Enrolling them in school was surprisingly easy. There were no road-blocks or major issues something that felt like a small miracle after all the battles we'd fought just to get here. It may not have seemed like a big deal to anyone else, but for me, getting my boys enrolled smoothly was a win I held close. It meant we were doing it. We were settling in. We were safe.

At the same time, I was letting go of the "dream life" I used to cling to—the one that I thought had to look a certain way. I was rewriting the vision, one choice at a time. I stopped chasing what looked good and started creating what felt right. And I don't care what anyone says: it's never too late. You are never too far gone to begin again. You can always change your mind. You can shift your path as many times as you need, as long as you stay aligned with what truly brings you joy. There is no shame in that. None.

I believe that deeply. I've made mistakes. I've learned lessons the hard way. But the truth is, we're always evolving. The things I wanted at 18 are not the things I want now. I'm not ashamed of that. I honor it. I embrace it.

I saw a post once that stuck with me:

I'll never hate on the old me… I love her.

I understand her. I know exactly why she did the things she did.

She was surviving with the tools she had at the time.

And honestly, she carried me through seasons I didn't think I'd survive.

Nobody can use that version of me against me,

because without her, there wouldn't even be a present me.

Every mistake. Every wrong turn. Every heartbreak.

It all shaped who I am now.

I don't disown her I thank her.

That's my growth. That's my story. And I stand on it.

Isn't that beautiful?

That version of me deserved a thank you. Because she got me here.

I had lined up a few job interviews before my move. Most of them were for corporate roles, including one at a bank. It seemed logical I had experience. I knew what the job would require. But when I thought about it, I was flooded with memories of the robbery that happened when I worked in Dallas. It still haunted me. The trauma was real. On top of that, the bank's location here was honestly in a rough area, and everything in my gut told me it wasn't worth it. I turned down the offer.

And just like that, another version of me one who used to say yes out of fear or desperation took a bow and stepped aside. I was stepping into something different now.

I got the job behind a desk in corporate at Goldman Sachs. It felt like a turning point, but not in the way movies make it seem. It wasn't a celebration moment. It was strategic. My mindset was the same as when I was house hunting: 13 to 16 months. That was the window I gave myself to get everything in motion to stack, to stabilize, to heal, and to build. The plan was clear, even if the process wasn't always easy.

I was assigned the night schedule. I clocked in at 8 p.m. and clocked out at 5 a.m. I'd drive home in the dark, exhausted but commit-ted, drop the boys off at school with a tired smile, then crash for a nap before noon. I'd wake up around midday, wipe the sleep from my eyes, and dive straight into nail appointments until about 3 p.m. Then I'd try to squeeze in a little time with the boys dinner, homework, play, cuddles before heading right back into the grind. Same routine, day after day, for a little over a year.

It was exhausting. But it was mine.

There were still quiet moments where I'd question it all moments that didn't get posted, recorded, or spoken out loud. I'd sit in the car after drop-off with the radio off, the air still, and I'd stare at the sky like it might have answers. Is this what rebuilding really looks like? I'd ask myself that. Because it wasn't pretty. It wasn't exciting. It wasn't some glamorous transformation arc. It was early alarms that came too fast. It was tears in the shower I'd wipe away before the boys ever saw. It was juggling nail clients in between login calls and figuring out how to stay awake long enough to cook dinner.

It was reheating chicken and rice while playing pretend with super heroes in the living room. It was being a mother, an employee, a business owner, a friend, a motivator, a teacher and feeling like I was barely keeping any of those roles afloat. But I kept going. I kept trying.

And even though it still felt heavy, something was different now.

I didn't panic when things didn't go to plan. I didn't spiral at the first sign of change. I didn't catastrophize. I took life piece by piece, day by day. Quietly. Gently. My nervous system, after years of running on caffeine, trauma, and fight-or-flight, was finally starting to trust me again. I was no longer addicted to chaos. I wasn't chasing instability just because it felt familiar. I wanted peace. I wanted predictability. I wanted the boring, beautiful, consistent kind of life I used to roll my eyes at. And for the first time, I was the one writing the script.

Even our first Christmas in San Antonio felt special. It wasn't over the top. It was cozy. We put up our tree together and had our little family dinner. It felt like we were settling into a new chapter. I had joined a local fitness team too, and we'd do little activities together. We even had matching holiday T-shirts and crop tops, laughing and showing up for each other in a way I hadn't experienced in a while.

San Antonio was showing me softness. It was being kind to me.

Going back to corporate wasn't unfamiliar I had worn that hat before. I remember ordering a few new things from Fashion Nova, piecing together cute but comfy work fits, and putting effort into showing up polished. It mattered to me. And one of the most freeing things about living in a new city was that no one knew me. No exes. No old friends. No family. No pressure to play a role I had outgrown. I was free to reinvent myself completely, and I did.

I started making new friends. I started over. I liked clocking in and clocking out, knowing that part of my life had structure. I even made it a little personal challenge to always be the first one on the floor. I'd be up, dressed, and out the door on time and apparently my manager noticed. He lived near me and joked that he'd see me flying down the highway, speeding toward the site like it was a race. He wasn't wrong. I was racing toward a future I hadn't yet seen, but one I was determined to reach.

Not everything was smooth though. There was one manager in the office Crystal. Her name is hard to forget even if the details of the issue blur. All I remember is her loud voice, her condescending tone, and how she humiliated me in front of the entire floor. I felt that sting the one where your blood runs hot and your dignity tries to rise and defend itself. I wanted to snap. I really did. But I didn't. I walked over to my manager, calmly asked if I could step outside, and took a moment. I breathed. I processed. And I walked back in with grace. I knew what I was working toward. I wasn't about to risk everything I had built for a petty argument or someone who thought belittling others made her powerful. Later, my manager apologized to me. He admitted he should've spoken up. Should've said something. And honestly, he should've. I should've reported her to HR. But I didn't. I stayed cool. I stayed focused. My mind was on bigger things. After everything I had survived, this was barely a bump in the road.

What kept me grounded? The gym. Prayer. My kids. And getting dressed every day with intention. I know it might sound silly, but those things reminded me who I was and what I was building. They anchored me when nothing else did.

Some people at the site loved my energy. They'd compliment my outfits, ask where I shopped, or tell me they admired how I carried myself. Others weren't so kind. I saw the side-eyes. I heard the whispers. The passive-aggressive comments. But that was high school behavior and I wasn't in high school. I was a grown woman with real goals, real responsibilities, and no time for anything that didn't feed my peace.

And the truth is, I liked who I was becoming.

After a few months of working there, my manager started asking me to help on the floor from time to time. Sometimes I'd assist with floor watching, other times I'd help coach new hires or support coworkers who were struggling. They gave me this bright orange vest to wear like the kind construction workers or traffic signalers wear and I couldn't help but laugh every time I put it on. I felt like I belonged in the middle of a highway waving down cars instead of answering phone calls. But I wore it with pride. It meant I was trusted. It meant I had earned a level of respect in the building, even if I wasn't shouting for it.

One of my favorite things about that job oddly enough were the themed days and silly corporate potlucks. We had "casino day," "beach day," and all kinds of random themes that gave us a little break from the monotony. It was refreshing to be a part of something where I wasn't the boss. I didn't have to lead or manage anyone. I just had to show up, do my part, and clock out. There was peace in that. A strange kind of freedom. I could be quiet. I could just exist without carrying the weight of everyone else's expectations. I kept to myself for the most part. I was friendly, of course but private. I didn't really talk about my social media, my businesses, or the things I had built outside of that office. I wasn't there to impress anyone. I was on a mission: earn a stable paycheck, save up, move into a nicer home, rebuild my nail business from scratch, and most importantly, keep my boys happy and secure. That was it. Get paid, get out. Simple. Focused.

That said, there were a few coworkers I genuinely vibed with. We had our little inside jokes and morning banter. Some days, we'd clock out at 5 a.m. and take a spontaneous drive to Buc-ee's thirty minutes away just for snacks and laughs. It was a small thing, but it gave me something to look forward to. In those early hours, driving under the stars with tired eyes and music playing low, I remembered how good it felt to just be.

Unfortunately, not every connection at work was a positive one. There were two women who sat behind me that eventually started causing issues. They whispered behind my back, made side comments, and I did my best to ignore it. I stayed in my lane until one day, I overheard them call me "Lord Farquaad." They said I looked like a man. The words hit harder than I expected. It wasn't just the insult it was the cruelty of it. The intention. And the fact that it happened so publicly.

That was my limit.

I finally reported it. I brought it up to my direct manager, and soon after, I was called in to speak with the Operations Manager. I told her everything. She handled it immediately and took it seriously. I appreciated that. Because even though I was strong and composed, I still deserved respect. I wasn't going to allow anyone to dim my light or bully me into silence. Not anymore.

At home, I was finally making space for rest, too. I'd lay on the couch with my boys, watching movies with bowls of snacks and blankets all around us. And if I fell asleep halfway through the movie? They didn't mind. They'd tuck in next to me. That was something I hadn't had time for in the past. I cherished those simple nights more than anything.

On my off days, I started driving around to drop off business cards and flyers for my nail services. I'd walk into stores and quietly place my cards near checkout counters or community boards. I made new Instagram pages from scratch deleting everything old and only keeping my fitness account alive. I needed a clean slate. A true reset. I began posting my work again pictures of sets, designs, before-and-afters. I joined every local Facebook group and online community to promote my services. That's how the real client base started to grow.

Before I knew it, I was getting booked up quickly. Word-of-mouth spread fast. People were sharing their results and tagging me. I was grateful but cautious. I didn't want to leave corporate too soon. I wasn't sure yet if these new clients were one-time visits or if they'd become loyal, returning customers. I needed to be sure I could sustain this. At the same time, I was getting closer to paying off my Camaro. That car held weight. My ex had promised me that when we got back together, I could relax a little. He said he'd cover the payments and help ease my load. And just like before, he didn't follow through. The payment was small but it was the principle. Once again, I stepped up and handled it myself. I worked harder, hustled smarter, and by the end of that year I paid it off. On my own. That moment meant more to me than just owning a vehicle. It was a symbol. A quiet victory. It said: "I don't wait on anyone. I've got me." And that was a new era of self-respect I had stepped into.

The gym helped, too. It wasn't just a physical outlet it was community. Word started to spread there that I did nails, and soon, I was picking up even more clients through that space. My reputation grew because I had experience, delivered quality, used high-end products, and gave people long-lasting, professional results. I wasn't new to this I was just reintroducing myself. Eventually, some of the girls in my dance class started coming to me for their nails, too. One connection led to another, and before I knew it, I was asked to be on Fox 4 for a friend's feature. I showed up, and that one opportunity opened doors to more. I met girls through social media, events, and workshops. Networking became second nature. I always kept my business cards on me. You never know who's watching or where one conversation might lead. Whenever I had a shoot, an event, or anything beauty or fitness related, I'd tell my manager. He was the only one who knew everything I was juggling my dreams, my healing, my businesses, my kids. He never judged me. In fact, I think he admired how much I was doing. I stayed busy not just for success, but to protect my mental health. If I stopped moving, the weight of everything I'd survived might catch up to me. So I kept pushing but not in chaos. Not in panic.

This time, I was doing it calmly, peacefully, and with full intention.

No more racing other people. No more proving myself to anyone. This was me vs. me. Quietly evolving. Silently stacking. Softly winning.

I had already started looking around for a house again and finally decided I wanted to customize a modular home just for me and the boys. I needed the extra space not just for us to live, but for me to work from home in peace. I dreamed of having my own studio, a designated room where I could do nails, film content, and create without being squeezed into corners or converting small spaces. I knew exactly what I wanted: no carpet, all hard flooring, white kitchen cabinets, and clean lines. Nothing too fancy, just functional, light, and mine. It was actually kind of fun, shopping around and looking at floor plans. And compared to traditional houses, it wasn't going to cost a fortune either.

I visited different places and ended up choosing Clayton Homes, mostly because their floor plans made sense for what I needed. A lot of the homes I had seen in newer subdivisions were only about 1500 square feet and that included the garage. That didn't sit well with me. The homes felt cramped, cookie-cutter, and didn't offer the space I knew I'd need if I was going to grow my business again from home. Clayton had homes ranging from 1,950 to 2,400 square feet or more. That felt right. It was more spacious, better laid out, and gave me flexibility for the future I was building.

Another reason I loved the location I was currently in was the accessibility. When clients came to see me, they didn't have to drive through confusing neighborhoods or get lost in traffic heavy side streets. It was right off the highway easy in, easy out. And in a city like San Antonio, that mattered. I was thinking about my life, but I was also thinking about my clients' experiences. I was building something functional for everyone, not just pretty for pictures. I even purchased my dream washer and dryer a beautiful white front-loading set as a Mother's Day gift to myself. I didn't have them installed right away. Nope. I kept them boxed and ready, untouched, because I already knew exactly where they were going. I could see them in the laundry room of my future home. I used that vision as motivation. They were a reminder that I was close, that I was getting there.

And the best part? I got them on sale. A win is a win, if I may say so myself. My oldest had started sports around that time too, and I made a promise to myself I was not going to miss practices, and I was definitely not going to miss games. I finally had a schedule that allowed me to be present. Since I didn't start work until 8 p.m., I had time to be a mom first. Even when I was tired, I showed up. I cheered. I clapped. I filmed. I loved every second of it. My youngest was doing amazing in school too, and seeing both of them thriving was such a personal win. It felt like a reset for all of us.

But just as we were getting into a rhythm just a few weeks into our new normal COVID hit.

The city shut down. Lockdowns were announced. Curfews were put in place. Schools closed, and everything began to shift. Our office scrambled to get ahead of it and send people home. Emotions were already running high for me. I had been on and off crying in private, still processing so much that had happened before the pandemic ever even arrived. The stress would come in waves. Some days, I was fine. Other days, I felt like I was dragging my soul through molasses. My boss saw it. He knew I was carrying a lot. So he chose me as one of the first employees to be sent home with equipment. I still remember that day like it was yesterday. I packed up my things, hugged the box with my monitor and headset like it was some kind of emotional trophy, and rode the elevator down to the parking lot with a lump in my throat. I genuinely loved being on-site. I know some people dreaded going into the office, but for me, it was a break. It gave me interaction, energy, structure. I've always been a homebody, but working at home while raising two boys, rebuilding my life, and running a business? That wasn't easy. Going into work gave me a reason to get dressed, to socialize a little, and to get out of my head. It wasn't perfect, but it was mine and I was grateful for it.

When I got home, it was chaos. I didn't even know where to set up. I was this close to closing on the new home, so boxes were already everywhere. It was cramped and overwhelming. My boys had been sent home from school too, so now we were all suddenly in the same space, trying to log into our devices and stay productive. It felt like we were all bumping elbows and stepping on each other's routines, but surprisingly, it worked. My youngest was still in elementary, but he didn't give me much trouble. He kept himself busy and followed instructions. Our little home was calm, even in the middle of all the confusion.

Since the house was so full and everything was in transition, I paused nail appointments for a while. There was no space to work, and honestly? I needed the rest. For once, I could sleep during the day. I didn't have to do drop-offs or run errands constantly. I'd clock out of work in the morning, close my laptop, and crawl into bed guilt-free. COVID was messy. It brought fear and uncertainty. But in some strange way, it also gave me a pause. A breather I hadn't realized I desperately needed. As a mother, I never had the luxury of slowing down. Now, for the first time, I did.

But with that quiet came another kind of heaviness. My depression started creeping in again this time, deeper. Being isolated, packing up old memories, coming across photo albums, handwritten notes, and things from my past... it all hit me at once. I had moments where I'd open a box and have to sit down because the grief came on like a wave. Memories of my ex. Everything we had gone through all over again. It was hard to stomach. I tried to keep it private. I tried not to cry in front of my boys. But somehow, they knew.

Kids are more intuitive than we give them credit for. Mine always were.

No matter how much I smiled, distracted, or kept things moving, they could feel the shifts. They overheard things. They saw the tears I thought I had hidden. And they began to carry their own emotions about it. Both of them were heartbroken by their dad. Angry, confused, disappointed. I tried to tell them it was nothing, tried to minimize it, but their energy shifted. Their moods changed. They knew the truth. They could feel it in the silence, in the tension, in the way my voice sometimes cracked when I said I was "fine." That part broke me more than anything.

Because when you're a mom, you want to shield your kids from

Everything especially the heartbreaks they didn't cause and can't fix. But no matter how hard I tried, they were hurting too.

I would get on FaceTime, Zoom, and Teams video chats with my coworkers and my boss just to help each other out, stay awake, and honestly keep each other company. The late nights could feel heavy sometimes, and those small windows of connection really helped. We'd share tips on how to get through the work, laugh about things that happened on the floor, or just vent. It was more than just clocking in; it was a reminder that I wasn't alone.

It was during one of those video calls that my boss and a few team members gently encouraged me to start therapy. They could see it my depression had gotten pretty bad. I was functioning, showing up, smiling even but underneath it, I was heavy. They weren't trying to pry. It came from love. So I finally did it. I signed up for therapy for the very first time in my life. I'm not gonna lie it felt a little weird at first, like I was opening doors I had kept locked tight for years. But I also felt like I needed it. And the truth is... it helped. A lot. It helped me release things I didn't even realize I was carrying. It helped me process, untangle, and begin to truly heal.

Around that time, my new home was finally ready and the official move-in day had finally arrived. The excitement in our house was unmatched. We had even purchased bikes to ride outside when we didn't have much to do. Sometimes we'd hop on them just to go check on the new place, feeling like kids again. The only reason we didn't move in right away was because I had a checklist to go through first. I needed to get the ADT security system installed, the power turned on, the washer and dryer hooked up, water and WiFi connected, and everything cleaned top to bottom even though it was brand new, I still wanted to wipe it all down myself. I'm just that type of person.

Thankfully, the setup process went quickly. Everything was done within the same week. That whole process made me even more grateful because getting to that point hadn't been easy. I had declined the home three times because things weren't exactly how I wanted. I had been specific I needed extra windows because I loved natural light (who doesn't?), and I didn't want a single square inch of carpet in the house. I also requested an extra room that would serve as my personal nail studio, my creative space. Every time something came back off, I'd say no. And I'm glad I stood firm. It was worth it.

We had started moving things from the old shed into the new, larger one behind the house. I even bought a brand-new outdoor rug and placed it right in front of the door even before we moved in. I would sometimes take my lunch break at midnight, hop in the car, and drive to the new place just to sit out front. I guess I just wanted to feel the presence of what was coming. I was so excited to finally have a place I could settle into and not worry about moving again unless I chose to.

Then one night, I decided to stay in instead. I didn't take the drive. I knew that the following day was our official move-in day. I was ready.

But the next day, when I arrived to start moving... the house had been broken into.

It was brand new, so there wasn't much to steal inside but they tried. What they did take was everything we had stored in the shed: boxes, clothes, bikes, outdoor decor, even the rug I had lovingly placed by the front door. They broke into the shed and completely emptied it out. They tried to break into the house, too windows had been picked at, most likely with tools or knives, and the sliding door in the back showed signs of being tampered with. The Ring camera I had installed? Gone. Even that small outdoor welcome mat had disappeared. The violation felt deeply personal.

Clayton Homes immediately launched a case and started working on repairs. They replaced everything that had been damaged. We had to wait a little longer to move in, again but once everything was fixed, I doubled down on protection. The security cameras were reinstalled, outdoor motion lights were added, and ADT came in to install sensors on every window and door. If anything opened, an alarm would go off. I wasn't playing around with safety. Not anymore.

Still, moving in felt a little strange. It was the first time in my life I was walking into a brand-new home that no one else had ever lived in and yet it had already been invaded. I didn't want to carry fear with me, so I held myself in prayer. I fasted for a few days. I prayed over the home, over the walls, the doors, the air, my children, myself. I prayed for safety, peace, and protection. We were the only ones on that street. My house was the very last one on a cul-de-sac, and at the time, it stood completely alone. No neighbors. No traffic. Just silence and open road. I'd be lying if I said I wasn't scared but the security system helped. The cameras gave me peace. And the vision of everything I had built gave me strength.

I finally moved all the furniture in, set up my work area, and got to breathe again. The upgrade felt like a long exhale I had been holding in for years. I even gave my coworkers a little house tour on Face-Time! I showed them my piano and joked that I'd play during lunch breaks. They laughed and cheered for me. That small gesture made me feel seen. My boss was unbelievably sweet during this time. He knew I was going through a lot, even if I masked it well. He would send me flowers or have McDonald's breakfast delivered to my porch just to make sure I ate something. No words. Just kindness. Those mo-ments of thoughtfulness reminded me how much goodness still existed in the world.

That same year, I decided to join TikTok for the first time ever. I had people in my life constantly telling me to get on there, but I had always stuck to what I knew Instagram, Pinterest, YouTube, Snapchat. Those were my go-tos for work and content. I didn't really understand TikTok at first. I honestly didn't even like the idea of starting over on another platform. But I'm glad I gave it a chance. My coworkers used to love scrolling through the DMs on my fitness page and laugh at the stuff people sent me. I never responded to any-one, but we'd laugh about it during downtime. It was a weird kind of comic relief.

So when I finally downloaded TikTok, I decided to learn the platform before diving in. I studied what made videos work, watched trends, and tried to understand what people liked. Then one day, I posted my very first nail video and it instantly went viral. Within hours. I was shocked. It was weird, but also kind of exciting. So I kept going.

I didn't stick to just nails either. I made funny videos with my kids, dancing clips, gym routines, supplement reviews, unboxings, and little slices of mom life. I shared it all. I didn't try to fit into a box I was the box. And the page took off. It grew like wildfire.

After a few months of working from home, my boss told us that a few of us would be allowed back on-site. Man, I was so excited. I had missed being around people. I had seen my coworkers daily on FaceTime, but nothing compares to that in-person energy. I missed the inside jokes, the vending machine chats, the real-life laughter. Walking back into that building felt like stepping into a hug.

During that summer, I had been so excited at the thought of seeing my grandparents. Even though COVID was still raging, I held onto a quiet hope that things might ease up soon that maybe, just maybe, it would be safe enough for my grandma to finally come visit me and see the new place I had worked so hard for. She had already visited my first home the tiny single-wide trailer I started in. She never judged me. Not once. She didn't care about the size or finishes. She was just proud of me. Genuinely proud. That alone meant the world.

But in July, everything changed. Both my grandma and grandpa contracted COVID and were taken to the hospital. The updates were terrifying, vague, and full of unknowns. I remember praying. Hoping. Pacing around my room trying to make sense of it. But despite everything, despite the machines and medicine and hospital efforts my grandmother didn't make it out. Only my grandfather survived. The grief came in a strange, heavy wave. It was made worse by the fact that everything took longer. Because of the pandemic, arranging a funeral wasn't as straightforward as it used to be. Many families weren't even having proper services. It was heartbreaking. No gathering. No hugging of loved ones. No shared moments of remembrance. Just distance.

At that time, San Antonio was still under curfew. The city was quiet at night, almost eerie. No one was allowed to be out past a certain hour, and leaving town especially for a gathering was completely out of the question. I don't even know who ended up attending her funeral. I didn't go. I couldn't.

As much as I loved her and I loved her deeply I had to think about my boys. About our safety. About staying healthy and staying home. I carried guilt for that decision, but I also knew I was doing what I believed was right in that moment. I was protecting my household. My peace. My children.

My mom was hurt. She let us know. She told me that all her siblings had their kids with them, and that she was the only one who didn't. That stuck with her. I could hear the pain in her voice. But what she didn't fully see was that we all lived far. We all had businesses and responsibilities pulling at us from every angle. It wasn't that we didn't care. It was that we were trying to survive, too. And truthfully it wasn't just hard emotionally; it was against the lockdown rules. That was the reality.

Still, she held it against us for quite a while.

They ended up live-streaming the funeral, and the family sent photos and videos in our group chat. I remember watching the service from my living room, tears streaming silently down my face. It didn't feel real. It didn't feel like enough. I had dreamed of her walking through the door of my new home, smiling at how far I'd come. Instead, I said goodbye through a screen.

Work gave me bereavement leave so I could take some time off, and I used that time to retreat into myself. I didn't go out. I didn't socialize. I isolated in my nail room and quietly filmed content. I created as a way to cope. The camera couldn't see my grief, but it helped me keep moving. I had gotten so close to her over the years, and not being able to say goodbye in person not being able to hold her hand one last time cut deep. There was a kind of ache that words couldn't soothe.

COVID took so much from so many. And I was over it. We all were.

The isolation. The fear. The unpredictability. The stolen moments and altered goodbyes. It changed things forever.

But even in the midst of all that loss, I kept going. I kept showing up. I kept healing one quiet breath at a time.

Chapter 28

Three Streams. Two Camaros. One Soft Mom.

And No to Comedy Dates.

Grief doesn't leave just because the week is over.

But life doesn't pause either. It keeps moving fast and indifferent. And somehow, we have to find the strength to move with it.

I came back to work and logged into Zoom after my bereavement leave, still aching from the loss of my grandma. I was holding the kind of sorrow that settles in your chest and doesn't let up. But alongside the ache was something new something sharper, steadier. I was more determined. I had cried until there was nothing left. I had journaled pages that bled my soul. I had created in silence, filmed through pain, and kept myself moving to avoid the stillness that grief demands. I did everything but fall apart. And even through the heartbreak I was building.

I didn't even realize it yet, but the seeds I had planted in my quietest moments had already begun to bloom.

By the time I logged back into corporate, something unexpected happened.

I went viral.

And not just one lucky video. My entire page blew up.

A few of my TikToks just me being me, showing off my pressons, sharing behind-the-scenes moments of my nail life, and mixing in glimpses of motherhood caught fire. Thousands of comments. Shares. Follows overnight. Notifications pouring in like rain. And with it, my Etsy store exploded. Orders started rolling in without pause. My phone buzzed with back-to-back sales, Etsy receipts, and TikTok Creator Fund earnings. Custom sets were selling out. DMs were flooding in. It was surreal.

Between Etsy, corporate, and content I had more income streams than I ever imagined.

For once, I wasn't just surviving anymore.

I was stacking.

I was thriving.

The weeks that followed felt like a dream, but one I had worked damn hard for.

I still had my corporate job, but the rest of my schedule? It was mine. No more asking for permission to take a day off. No more adjusting my life around someone else's business needs. I was the business now. I decided when I took clients. When I filmed. When I rested. When I mothered. When I created. My time was finally mine again.

And in that freedom I carved out space for joy.

Real joy.

The kind that feels light and earned.

I took the boys to Six Flags and SeaWorld regularly. We had mem-berships, and with the parks mostly empty because of COVID, it felt like we had the city to ourselves. We'd ride rollercoasters until we couldn't scream anymore. Laugh until our bellies hurt. I'd film little TikToks of our adventures capturing the soft life I used to only dream about.

Because in a way, I was living the dream.

A different kind of dream. One I built with my own hands.

I adapted fast. I added a clear hard-plastic divider to my manicure table, upgraded all my sanitation protocols, and earned my Barbicide COVID-19 Certification before most people were even thinking about it. I didn't wait for the world to give me the green light. I kept building. Kept flowing. Kept adjusting. With no full salon or staff to manage, everything I earned from nails was either profit or reinvested directly back into the dream.

I ran lean.

I ran clean.

I ran smart.

And most of all I was just so damn happy to be designing again.

My days finally had rhythm. I'd clock in for corporate, squeeze in content creation between Zoom calls, and take clients when I wanted to. And I still showed up fully as a mom, a woman, a friend, a daughter, and the CEO of my own life. I wasn't running on fumes anymore. I was running on intention.

It wasn't just productivity.

It was peace.

It was power.

It was happiness.

And then came the cherry on top

I bought a brand-new 2021 white sport Camaro.

Black wheels. Zero miles. Clean AF.

It was mine.

I was literally in bed, scrolling on my laptop, and clicked "custom order." Just like that. A few days later, it was delivered right to my home like a manifestation on wheels.

Everywhere I went, heads turned.

People stared. Asked questions.

They couldn't believe I pulled it off especially not during COVID.

But it wasn't just about the car.

It was who was driving it now.

Because they remembered the old me the version barely surviving in South Texas.

The girl who was grieving, broke, overwhelmed, and drowning in responsibility.

The one with circles under her eyes and too many dreams she had no time to chase.

And now?

Now, I was her but rebuilt.

Viral.

Vital.

And absolutely unbothered.

They didn't expect the comeback.

But I didn't just come back I reinvented myself.

And the wildest part? I still had my red Camaro completely paid off.

Now, I had two.

Two Camaros.

Three income streams.

And one woman who finally believed in her own power.

I filmed everything. No niche. No box to fit into. Just vibes. That was me.

Day-in-the-life vlogs

Nail designs, tutorials, pedicures, and product reviews

Restocks, packaging hauls, and label printing

GRWM (get ready with me) videos

Travel content

Humorous skits

Christmas transitions and themed sets

Iconic Grinch nails

Best friend videos

Home décor updates

Furniture unboxings

Chill, soft life moments, business content, mom content all of it

If I could film it, I did.

If I could create it, I posted it.

And if it was my life, I shared it unapologetically.

Not for clout.

Not to chase validation.

But to prove something to myself:

That I was really living.

That I was out of survival mode.

That I was walking fully into a life I built from the ashes of grief, from pure grit, and from ground zero.

When I returned to corporate, still working from home, something shifted. I saw the value in the margins the cracks in the routine where freedom lived. I took advantage of every spare minute. Every break. Every lunch hour. Every pause between Zoom calls. I moved a small travel size manicure table right next to my computer desk so I could work on Etsy while clocked in. It was a tight space, but I made it work.

My workspace became a hybrid of hustle and hope spreadsheets on one side, sculpted nails on the other.

At the time, I was prepping for a major press-on nail launch. And when I say prepping, I don't mean casually posting about it I mean living and breathing that launch. I spent hours every day designing new sets, packaging them with care, taking product photos in natural lighting, filming promo content, and uploading listings to Etsy. I worked deep into the night sometimes until 5 a.m. tweaking every detail until it was perfect.

Because this wasn't just about press-ons.

It was about creating an experience.

I teased the launch across every social platform. I hyped it for weeks. And when launch day finally came 5 a.m. on a Saturday I was nervous, pacing, hopeful... and ready.

By noon, every single set was sold out. Gone.

I stared at the screen in disbelief then smiled.

Because I had believed.

I planned for this.

I worked for this.

I manifested this.

And in that moment, I realized something important: launch days were the move. Instead of constantly restocking, I started treating every drop like a limited-edition event something people would look forward to, something worth the wait. And with each new release, the momentum kept growing. Each one sold out faster than the last.

With the extra income, I reinvested immediately. That's always been my mindset: feed the dream, fuel the fire. I bought a brand new desktop computer, a sleek white printer, and a label printer so I could fulfill orders faster and more professionally. No more handwritten labels. No more last-minute post office runs. I streamlined everything linking Etsy to my shipping dashboard and even syncing it with my nail client booking site.

Then, I upgraded my whole setup. I made a trip to IKEA and bought a beautiful white desk and matching shelves. I wanted the entire space to feel cohesive, calm, and creative. White has always been my favorite color it feels clean, fresh, and full of possibility. A blank canvas with unlimited potential.

My studio was becoming everything I had envisioned.

Peaceful.

Elegant.

Mine.

I created a safe, beautiful workspace that reflected the woman I was becoming. I didn't need a busy salon or a full team. I didn't need noise or chaos or constant validation. I just needed me.

I was the only nail tech in that room.

It was intimate.

It was intentional.

And every single detail from the lighting to the layout was chosen by me, for me.

My San Antonio clients loved the new setup especially the fact that I had a full booking website. It was a total shift from when I ran my old salon. Back then, it was non-stop back-and-forth: Instagram DMs, missed messages, last-minute cancellations, and no-shows that drained my time and my patience. I used to spend hours just trying to manage people's expectations. Now? I simplified everything.

Clients could book online 24/7. They could see my real-time availability, know exactly what services were offered, check pricing, and even browse pictures of my space before ever stepping foot inside. I didn't have to chase anyone down. I didn't have to explain policies ten times. My site spoke for me and it said everything with clarity and professionalism.

I kept it detailed and clean because truthfully? I suck at checking messages. And I'm okay with that. The website became my boundary, my buffer between the art I loved and the admin side I didn't. It created space for me to protect my time, my energy, and my creativity. And it worked. My clients respected it, loved the transparency, and I finally had breathing room to focus on what I was best at the work itself.

Despite juggling corporate duties, Etsy orders, and a growing client list, life felt lighter than it ever had.

I wasn't managing a full staff anymore.

I wasn't bending to someone else's vision.

I wasn't surviving paycheck to paycheck.

I was doing this for me.

And for my boys. Always for them.

They were my motivation in everything, but this time around I didn't forget me either. I wasn't waiting for permission to enjoy the life I was building. I wasn't watering everyone else's garden while mine sat dry. I was finally able to give myself the things I wanted without guilt. Without apology. With love, intention, and a little bit of well-deserved luxury.

Around that time, I moved into my new home and one of my sister-in-laws had just moved into hers too. We were both so hyped. Like two big kids with Pinterest boards and dreams of cozy lighting. We started swapping home décor ideas, sending each other Amazon finds, changing out light fixtures, putting up wreaths, and turning our homes into full-blown seasonal wonderlands. It had been so long since I felt that excited to "nest." It was healing. Fun. Femine.

Safe.

Every extra dollar of profit I made? I poured it right into my space. I bought a high-end coffee machine that had all the bells and whistles, because I deserved a moment every morning. I added cute farm-house-style bathroom signs, clean all-white dishes and cookware, glass straws, wooden accents, and themed decorations for every holiday. I had inflatables and banners and table décor for New Year's, Valentine's Day, Easter, Fourth of July, St. Patrick's, Halloween, Thanksgiving you name it. Everything boxed, labeled, and ready to be pulled out like magic. It wasn't about showing off it was about curating joy. I had created a space that felt like a warm hug.

That's when I really embraced being a homebody.

I'd always loved being home, but post-COVID? Yeah outside wasn't calling my name at all. You couldn't catch me out in the streets if you tried. I was living my soft life through Amazon Prime, Etsy orders, Pinterest inspiration, and home delivery everything. My peace had become a priority. Non-negotiable.

And social media? That wasn't just a hobby anymore.

It was my business partner.

It was my money-maker. My marketing machine. My content bank. My digital resume. I became intentional with it. I only kept the plat-forms that paid me, inspired me, or helped me grow:

Pinterest fed my creativity and fired up every vision board.

Instagram started paying for Reels and expanded my reach.

TikTok became the holy grail the place where I built real connection, real traction, and told my story in my voice. YouTube wasn't my favorite, but I kept it in rotation. I used it for longevity and tapped into a different kind of audience. It taught me consistency and helped me grow more comfortable on camera.

Each platform had a purpose.

Everything I posted had a plan.

And every single dollar earned went back into building a life that finally felt like mine.

Of course, I took care of my priorities first. Always.

The first month I received a major payout from TikTok, I didn't spend a single dollar on myself. I used it to clear all of my debt. I wiped my credit cards clean, caught up on every bill, and was left with only the essentials: car note, electricity, water. The basics.

For the first time in a long time, I wasn't drowning.

I was rising.

And with that extra breathing room, I started investing in my business like never before. I bought bulk orders of supplies every gel color I could find, a rainbow of acrylic powders, every kind of glue, gallons of acetone, monomer, and polymer. I restocked like I was preparing for war but really, I was preparing to win. I wasn't just building a business. I was building an empire.

And my gym routine? That made a comeback too.

But this time, it was different.

I wasn't training for competitions. I wasn't chasing abs or trophies or someone else's approval. I wasn't starving myself or bulking for show. I wasn't squeezing into meal plans that didn't make me happy. I was working out for me in my natural body, at my own pace, with normal meals, a clear mind, and a healed heart.

I'll never forget the first time I sipped a Coke again after who knows-how-long. I actually coughed. I had gone so long without soda so long being overly disciplined, overly hard on myself. But now? I was just living. Fully. Joyfully. Guilt-free.

My squats were solid, my deadlifts were strong, and for the first time in a long time... I felt good.

I felt grounded.

Of course, people kept sliding into my DMs on Instagram asking if I'd ever compete again. It was flattering, and part of me smiled at the idea. I had so much love for that version of me the discipline, the drive, the way I held it down on stage. But that chapter had closed. I had bigger things to focus on. That kind of grind didn't align with my new vision. I had other plans now plans rooted in balance, in peace, in expansion.

And since I was constantly filming, my nails were always fresh. My toes, too. Pedicures always on point. I took pride in the details. I even ordered more mobile equipment so I could start offering luxury in-home services when requested. Everything I did was elevated. Every part of my business had a system streamlined, intentional, and rooted in care.

That year, I dropped my first line of merch.

It was more than just products it was me, printed and packaged.

I partnered with a talented local woman in San Antonio who helped bring my cartoon logo to life. We printed it on hoodies, tees, mugs, and stickers in a variety of colors. I launched everything on Etsy, and the response was incredible. Orders came in from cities I'd never been to people I'd never met, supporting a brand that I built from my own story. I especially loved that Etsy offered a "buy now, pay later" option. My clients and followers could split payments into two or four, making it easier for everyone to shop comfortably. Accessibility mattered to me.

I upgraded my packaging too bigger bags, branded tissue paper, bubble wrap, little handwritten thank-you notes because I wanted the unboxing experience to feel special. Personal. Everything had my touch on it. I wanted people to feel the love when they opened something from me. I wasn't just mailing out orders I was delivering a piece of my journey.

That summer, the boys and I finally stepped out into the world again.

After being cooped up for so long during quarantine, we took a trip to Falcon Lake our very first time there. It felt like freedom. We rented tubes and floated lazily across the water, sun on our faces, breeze in our hair. It felt like peace... right up until the moment it didn't.

My kids were having the time of their lives jumping off cliffs, swinging from ropes into the water with no fear at all. They were bold, wild, free. And then, in a stubborn mom-moment, I decided to jump in too... completely forgetting one small but important detail.

I didn't know how to swim.

Mid-air, my heart dropped. The second I hit the water, I panicked. I thrashed. I couldn't find the float. And all I could think about was my kids my babies watching me panic and trying to help. They rushed toward me without hesitation, trying to push my float back under me, trying to guide me to safety. But in my panic, I almost pulled them down with me.

That was one of the scariest moments of my life.

I wasn't worried about myself I was terrified for them. But they were so calm, so strong, even in the chaos. They handled the situation better than I did. They pushed my float all the way to the edge of the lake and didn't let go until we were back on dry land. I cried afterward quiet tears of fear, of gratitude, of realization.

That moment changed me.

I promised myself I'd never jump into water again without a life jacket.

Ever.

Because I love my boys way too much to take that kind of risk again.

But even with that scary moment, that year was still one of joy.

Joy I hadn't felt in years.

We filmed silly videos together. We laughed constantly. I created content simply because it brought me joy. For once, I wasn't documenting to chase a number I was creating to remember. I was learning how to exist, not just survive.

I got into daily affirmations and manifestation practices. I spoke life into my mornings. I wrote down goals and celebrated small wins. I took care of my skin, my hair, my teeth every part of me that had been neglected during my darker seasons. I bought myself the Kenzzi laser hair removal machine and gave myself full at home treatments during quarantine. And let me tell you game changer. My legs were smooth, ingrowns were gone, and I finally said good-bye to daily shaving. A win is a win, and Kenzzi was definitely one of my best self-care investments.

That year belonged to me and my kids.

No one else.

Sure, my inbox was still full men from the past checking in, new ones trying to shoot their shot, admirers I didn't ask for. But I didn't entertain any of it. I was too focused. Too intentional. I had already been disappointed before. I had already opened myself up and watched it break. I wasn't doing that again at least not until I was ready.

If I ever did go on a date, I made it clear from the jump: I wasn't looking for a relationship. Not until my kids graduated. Not until my personal goals were met. That was my mindset. Unapologetic. Non-negotiable.

Because sometimes, healing doesn't look like rest.

Sometimes, it looks like momentum like rebuilding a whole life from the ashes of the one that broke you.

And that's exactly what I was doing.

Every nail set, every video, every carefully packaged order was part of my grief in motion.

It wasn't just work it was therapy. It was healing. It was my quiet way of saying:

"I'm still here."

I was finding myself again.

Piece by piece.

Design by design.

Moment by moment.

I was reclaiming joy.

Redefining what happiness looked like on my terms. Not anyone else's.

My heart was still tender. Some nights still felt heavy. Grief didn't just disappear; it lingered like soft static in the background of my brightest days. But still, I was proud. So proud.

Proud of the woman I was becoming.

Proud of the peace I was finally protecting.

Proud of the power I had stepped into with both hands.

I had taken pain and shaped it into purpose.

I was no longer just surviving I was living.

And life felt lighter. Not because everything was perfect. But because for the first time...

I had chosen me.

I had my kids.

My career.

My goals.

My routines.

My store.

My peace.

But even in the calm, a quiet question began to form:

Could I trust again?

Could I love again this version of me?

I didn't know it yet, but the next chapter would test me in ways I never saw coming.

Because I had cracked the code.

Not just in business, but in life.

For the first time ever, I wasn't chasing survival I was designing my days.

I had built something out of nothing and turned it into everything I needed.

And no, I didn't have all the answers yet

But I knew this with certainty:

I was no longer waiting for life to happen to me.

I was building it one bold move at a time.

Grief never really left me.

But neither did my fire.

I entered this chapter still aching...

But also still dreaming.

I cried. I hustled. I created.

And somehow through the chaos

I bloomed.

They thought I disappeared.

But really, I was just getting quiet... while I made magic.

They didn't expect the comeback.

They definitely didn't expect the reinvention.

But I did.

And I did it with grief in one hand and purpose in the other.

I didn't need a soft launch.

I needed a rebirth.

And baby… this was just the beginning.

I just needed to stay consistent.

Stay disciplined.

Stay rooted in my why.

Because I wasn't working for validation anymore.

I was working for longevity.

That year, everything was going so well financially. I was finally operating at my full capacity. My A-game was no longer something I was striving for it was just how I lived.

Thanksgiving that year was stunning quiet, but warm. Just me and my little family: my boys and I. We FaceTimed our extended family, laughed, caught up, and shared how much we missed each other. There weren't a ton of people in the room, but the energy? It was peaceful. It was full.

That same season, I decided I wanted to adopt a few children for Christmas. I didn't just want to do it myself I wanted to include my kids, too. I pulled up the charity list on my laptop and scrolled through dozens of names: kids, teens, even elderly adults in need. I let each of my boys pick two names.

That year, we adopted our first six children for the holidays.

I wanted to buy them whatever was on their list bikes, jackets, toys, warm jeans, new shoes. I wanted them to feel like someone saw them, cared for them, even if we never met face to face.

We didn't get to deliver the gifts directly, but the experience still moved me. I'll never forget the image of my kids sitting at the dining table, eyes locked on the screen, reading bios out loud and taking their decisions seriously. Watching them care like that, love like that, was one of the most beautiful moments of my motherhood journey.

I also told them we'd be making warm meals and passing out plush blankets to the homeless. Texas winters don't freeze, but it still gets cold enough to need shelter, warmth, or at the very least a hot meal and human kindness. I wanted my boys to know: you don't have to be rich to be a blessing. You just have to be willing.

People sometimes say I like to take care of others because I wasn't taken care of in the ways I needed growing up. That it's a trauma response. And maybe that's true. Maybe it is. But you know what? It's also what makes me me. And I wouldn't change that for anything.

While I was still working corporate, I started letting my old boss and my best friend go through my Instagram DMs for fun. I had hundreds probably thousands of unopened messages. They thought I was crazy for not checking them. I couldn't stop laughing.

They were so invested in seeing me go on a date or do something fun for myself for once. All I ever did was work, run my businesses, show up for my kids, go to games, cook, clean, organize, and plan. I was always doing for others always. They knew how laser-focused I was, and they wanted to see me take just a little time to let life flirt back.

But that's the thing.

I hadn't really made time for me in that way.

Not yet.

And deep down, I knew…

Maybe that was about to change, too. There was one guy in particular tall, muscular, gym-fit, attractive, and in business too. He had been following me for years. Always consistent. Always respectful. No pressure. No weird energy. Just… present. He'd send me videos from his day gym clips, work updates, motivational messages. Nothing overbearing. Just little glimpses into his world. It was subtle, but steady. A slow drip of presence that said, I see you, even if you don't see me back yet.

I never replied. I left him on "read" or "seen" for what felt like forever. Not because I wasn't flattered I just didn't have the emotional capacity to entertain anyone. My heart had been through too much. I was in a season of quiet rebuilding. I was protecting myself.

And honestly?

I probably should've left things that way.

But… let me not ruin the story.

Eventually, I gave in.

I told him how he could reach me directly outside of the DMs and started replying. He didn't hesitate. Quick to engage, but never pushy. That balance caught me off guard.

There was one message I'll never forget.

I had posted a picture of myself holding a box of Ferrero Rocher chocolates one of my all-time favorites. He replied, "I knew you weren't basic. That chocolate says it all. You're a woman who knows what she wants."

It was so simple, but thoughtful. Specific. A little flirtation wrapped in genuine attention. It stood out.

My boss, my sister, even my coworkers started teasing me.

"Just let him take you out already!"

So, I did.

For context, we'll call him Virgo.

One morning, Virgo messaged me no back and forth, no guesswork. Just, "Pencil me in. I got VIP tickets to a comedy show. It's your birthday gift December baby, right?"

I paused. I hadn't even told him that. He remembered.

I told him I'd think about it.

And eventually… I said yes.

At first, I offered to meet him there. He said no insisted on picking me up.

That made me nervous.

I hadn't shared my address with anyone. Not since Dallas. Not since everything I'd been through. Especially now, with my social media platforms growing and strangers knowing my name. I had learned how sacred peace and privacy really are.

But Virgo was consistent, and respectful, and persistent in a way that didn't feel intrusive just sure of himself. Eventually… I let him.

I'll never forget that night.

I wore a brand-new white silk maxi dress the kind that flowed and caught the light in all the right places without even trying. Clear high heels, delicate jewelry, a soft glow to my makeup. Minimal, elegant. Clean. I felt beautiful. Not just cute beautiful.

When he pulled up, my house was still the only one built in the neighborhood. Empty lots surrounded us. But that night? There were cars everywhere.

He told me later that as he drove up, his heart dropped.

He thought, "Did she double-book? Am I walking into a competition right now?"

I couldn't stop laughing when he told me.

It was pizza delivery. My boys had their friends over. That was all. Just kids, pizza, and chaos.

Virgo stepped out immediately and opened the car door for me. He was driving a sleek black stick shift BMW classy, clean, powerful. The kind of car that makes a quiet statement. We headed out for the evening, starting with dinner. He wasn't just trying to impress me he wanted to connect. He was intentional.

No surface level stuff.

He wanted real conversation.

And honestly?

He impressed me.

He led the night with quiet confidence opened doors, pulled out chairs, and asked for my preferences before placing the order. He knew I was a gym junkie, so grilled chicken, steak, salads he got it right. I didn't lift a finger. He handled it all. Even the drinks.

He looked at the waitress and said, "Keep them coming for the lady."

The way he moved…

It was effortless.

And for once, I didn't feel like I had to perform.

Didn't feel like I had to control anything.

I could just be.

That felt new.

That felt refreshing.

And even though I wasn't sure where it would lead…

That night reminded me what it felt like to be seen not for what I did, not for what I built, not for what I gave…

But simply for who I was.

As I stepped out of the car that night, Virgo looked at me like he was seeing a dream in real time. His eyes scanned my dress, then locked onto mine with a stunned, almost reverent expression.

"I can't believe you're my date tonight," he said, almost breathless.

"You look absolutely stunning."

At the comedy show, it was the same. People kept stopping us, complimenting the dress, the way it flowed, the way I carried it. I could feel their eyes not in a per formative way, but in a damn, she's glowing kind of way. That night was dreamy. Soft. Surreal.

After that, we kept seeing each other. Virgo would send good morning messages every day without fail. Sometimes he brought me coffee, sometimes lunch. He'd check in just because. We worked out together a few times light banter between sets, shared playlists, and matching soreness the next day.

The holidays were around the corner, and we were both knee-deep in charity work. He had his own supplement store and ran toy drives through his business. I did the same through mine offering nail discounts in exchange for toys, helping local families give their children a Christmas worth remembering. We bonded over that. The giving. The purpose behind the hustle.

I even helped him decorate his store for the holidays. We hung lights, set up display tables, made jokes about Santa protein powder. It was fun. Easy. We laughed, worked, lifted weights, and swapped business strategies.

It was refreshing being around someone who understood my world without me having to explain it.

Then came a surprise that would stay with me forever.

My coworkers, my boss, my best friend they orchestrated the most thoughtful, heart-filling gesture I'd ever experienced. My birthday is December 30. My best friend's is December 28. They tricked me into thinking I was planning her surprise party. My only job? Pick her up and bring her to Topgolf.

But when I walked in?

Two full sections had been reserved. One for her.

One for me.

Balloons. Banners. Decor. My favorite carrot cake sat on the table, already sliced. Dove dark chocolate the exact kind I keep in my nightstand was tucked into a gift bag. Jars of pickles, because they know I'm obsessed. Books I'd mentioned in passing were gift-wrapped and stacked neatly. It was like walking into a room that had listened to me for years.

I've always planned my own birthdays.

Bought my own cake.

Set up my own camera to take my own pictures.

But that night?

They did everything. For me.

And I felt so incredibly loved.

I'll never forget that.

But life… life has a way of keeping you humble.

On New Year's Eve, Virgo told me he was heading to New York with his son. Just a few days, he said. Nothing major. He'd be back before I knew it. I told him okay. I trusted it. I believed it.

Then… silence.

Days passed. No good morning text. No check-ins. No "landed safe" message. Nothing.

At first, I was concerned. Something felt off. I had friends help me search online and what we found?

He had gone to New York… and gotten married.

Apparently, he had been in a whole relationship with someone else the entire time.

I was blindsided.

But it didn't break me.

Maybe it bruised me a little.

Maybe it left a sting.

But I got through it.

Because I've felt worse pain. And I've survived every version of it.

What it did do was remind me of something important:

That I can open the door again without letting the whole world walk through it.

That I can flirt with the idea of love without handing over the keys to my peace.

I wasn't in love with him. Not even close. But I was open cautiously, intentionally.

And that alone was a milestone.

A quiet win.

A trial run.

It didn't lead anywhere permanent.

But it showed me how much I've grown.

How much I've healed.

Because the old me?

She would've spiraled.

She might've chased closure.

She might've begged for an explanation.

But this version of me?

She poured a glass of wine.

Peeled off her lashes.

Laughed it off.

And let the door close without burning the house down.

No bitterness.

No chaos.

Just grace.

Because sometimes healing isn't about who hurt you.

It's about who you didn't let destroy you.

And this time?

I walked away with all my softness intact…

And my standards even higher.

The old me would've lost sleep.

The only thing I lost this time…

Was interest.

Chapter 29

The Woman San Antonio Softened

Well… Happy New Year, everyone.

The calendar flipped, a fresh chapter began and just like that, poof… we never heard from Virgo again. But hey, back to work we go.

Because let's be real:

A smooth sea never made a skilled sailor, right?

Sigh.

Life was actually going really well aside from the little sting Virgo left behind. But we won't give him too much airtime here. It was what it was. It didn't break me. It didn't even bend me. I brushed it off, took the lesson, and kept it moving.

The truth is, everything else around me was beautiful.

I felt steady. I felt strong.

I felt… softened, in the best way.

One of my close girlfriends at the time a woman I met shortly after moving to San Antonio, back when I was still finding my rhythm and showing up at the gym in oversized t-shirts and ponytails had become a real light in my life. We'd grab salads for lunch here and there, swap stories about healing and hustle, and she ended up taking me out for my birthday that year to the cutest little Italian spot. She even brought a birthday sash. I swear, it was the most adorable gesture thoughtful, lighthearted, and exactly what I needed after closing the Virgo chapter.

After all the birthday dinners, Christmas parties, and New Year's toasts, life picked up pace again quickly especially with my oldest son's school schedule and basket ball games.

From the jump, I made a promise to myself:

I wouldn't miss a single game. Not one.

I wasn't going to let content creation, clients, or even my corporate schedule interfere with that.

My role as a mother would always come first.

At the time, I was still working an overnight shift 8 PM to 5 AM which was brutal on my sleep schedule, but it bought me time with my boys during the day. If I ever needed to leave early or log in a little late, I'd send a quick message to my boss, and thankfully, he always had my back. I was tired, sure. But showing up for my kids? That energized me in a whole different way.

I'd film TikToks after every win his big smile, our cheers, the scoreboard in the background. We'd celebrate with wings, pizza, or late-night ice cream runs. And when the team lost, I still made the night count. I turned every disappointment into a memory.

Because that's when the real lessons sink in in the losses.

My son would get frustrated after a tough game, but I'd always tell him: "You have no idea how many times I've lost before I ever got my win. But I kept going. That's how I built what we have now."

He heard me. I could tell.

And deep down, I knew he was watching me just as closely as I was watching him.

Meanwhile, business was booming.

My nail clients were keeping me booked and busy. My social media was growing faster than ever. Women were driving in from all over Texas Houston, Austin, even tiny towns I'd never heard of just to sit in my chair. My work was in demand. My content was going viral. I was putting out set after set, and loving every second of it.

And then February rolled around.

That's when I decided:

It was time to start romanticizing my life.

Not just for content.

Not for the aesthetic.

But for me.

Because this shift felt different.

It felt intentional.

It felt sacred.

I wasn't just decorating for the holidays or pouring love into my boys. I wanted to start doing things for me.

That's when I made the decision to go back for more laser hair removal life-changing, by the way and for the first time ever, I booked an appointment for Botox.

I was scared.

I'd never had any type of cosmetic procedure before, aside from my breast augmentation years ago. But forehead movement runs in my family accordion lines, deep expression creases. I was still young, but I wanted to take care of my skin early. I wanted to protect the face that had already carried so much emotion joy, grief, strength, heartbreak.

And to be honest?

Botox ended up being one of the best investments I've ever made. It wasn't painful.

It wasn't outrageously expensive.

And the confidence it gave me?

Worth every single penny.

That Valentine's season, I went all in.

I left my Christmas tree up and transformed it into a full-blown Valentine's Day installation heart ornaments, pink garlands, velvet ribbons, and sparkly tinsel. I placed everlasting luxury roses all over the living room. You know the ones those million-dollar looking preserved roses in crystal clear acrylic boxes? I was obsessed. They made the space feel high-end, romantic, sacred.

My whole home looked and felt soft. Joyful. Feminine.

I drank water out of wine glasses, made fancy coffee every morning, and played Dirty Dancing in the background while I danced around with my little emoji heart headband on, mopping the floors like it was a scene from a music video.

I was healing and thriving at the same time.

Weddings were rolling in fast. My Valentine's sets were getting reposted left and right. And around this time, my encapsulated 3D rose nails started blowing up on TikTok and Instagram.

Back then, my nail Instagram was sitting somewhere between 6,000 and 10,000 followers. I remember praying for the day it would finally take off. I already had a separate fitness page with tons of followers, but my priorities had shifted. I wasn't competing anymore. That wasn't my lane anymore.

Now I was focused on what I loved… and what was making me money:

Nails. Storytelling. Presence.

I made tons of trending "transaction" videos using Dirty Dancing soundtracks. I was just in flow creating, designing, sharing, laughing. It was fun. It was fulfilling.

It felt like me.

Business was booming so much that I finally bought a mini fridge for my studio. I filmed the unboxing like it was Christmas, then filled it with every drink you could imagine sparkling waters, juices, energy drinks, wine. I even added chilled wine glasses, all complimentary for my girls.

Because I didn't want them to feel like they were just getting their nails done I wanted them to feel like they were stepping into a sanctuary.

A sacred space.

A moment of pause.

A little pocket of luxury.

I made it clear:

No kids.

No pets.

No chaos.

Just you time.

My space was about them every single client. I wanted them to walk in and feel like the world could wait. That they could decompress, gossip if they wanted to, vent, heal, or sit in total silence and just breathe.

Because I knew what it felt like to pour into everyone else and never have anywhere to refill.

So I built that place.

And it started with a mini fridge… but it meant so much more.

Eventually, I invested in a TV for the studio. I had no idea how to mount it, but with the help of my assistant and a few YouTube tutorials we figured it out. I filmed the whole process, of course. That clip went viral.

From then on, my clients could watch Netflix, catch up on their favorite shows, or vibe out to music during their appointments. Some preferred silent services. Others loved to chat. The TV was positioned just right no twisting, no turning. Just comfort. Ease. Flow.

Everything was designed with care. Every detail had intention behind it.

My passion was fully back.

I wasn't thinking about anyone else not men, not dating, not distractions.

Just me. My kids. My clients. And the work I loved.

And the money? It wasn't being split with anyone.

No one was asking for a cut.

No one was clocking my checks.

It was mine.

And I poured it right back into the business high-end products, luxury tools, premium supplies all the things that elevated my craft.

Eventually, I even started duetting videos with other nail techs and beauty creators online. That was new for me. Because if I'm being honest?

I didn't always vibe with other women.

I had a past.

I was once a mean girl.

I had my walls up built high and thick. I was defensive, guarded. I had been bullied, picked apart, judged for how I dressed, how I walked, how I existed. And instead of healing... I projected that pain back onto others.

But San Antonio softened me.

The woman I was becoming here?

She was different.

I started to see that when women truly support one another not with envy, but with love we all rise higher.

There's enough room for all of us to win.

And honestly? That changed me.

Now, more than ever, I proudly consider myself a girls' girl and I love it that way.

I support women loudly, intentionally, and without competition.

That's my energy now and it will always stay that way.

I want to see all of my women succeed. Period.

And the more I looked back, the more I understood something I had missed before:

Every single obstacle that ever blocked my path wasn't sent to break me it was sent to build me.

I've never truly been stuck.

I've been strengthening.

I'm not behind.

I'm not in ruins.

I'm becoming.

Every setback built me a little stronger. Every challenge added muscle.

And those muscles? They're the ones I'll need to carry the bigger blessings coming next.

Now that I've learned that…

I want to teach it.

I want to hand out the same tools I had to build from scratch.

Because nobody handed me a map I had to draw one.

And now that I've found the path?

I want to light it for someone else.

That's when I started filming my Big Sister Advice videos soft but strong little check-ins from me to whoever needed them. I'd sit down, heart open, voice calm, and pour wisdom into every word like I was speaking to the version of me who once needed it most.

I had lived so much by that point heartbreak, parenting, grief, survival mode, rebuilding and I just had so much love to give. So I did.

And it felt so right.

I paired those videos with Big Sister Energy captions, the kind that hugged your soul and gently reminded you: "You're doing better than you think." I wasn't trying to be perfect. I wasn't giving expert advice. I was just being me raw, reflective, and real.

And right around this time, I made a huge decision though if I'm being honest, it didn't come entirely from me.

I was still working my corporate job, juggling everything: nails, content, motherhood, late-night shifts, growing pains, big dreams and it was catching up to me. But I wasn't ready to let go.

Not until my boss looked me dead in the eye one day and said,

"You're too good for this. I'm going to force you to go full-time in your dream."

At first, I laughed. I thought he was joking. But he wasn't. He meant every word. And deep down? I knew he was right.

If he hadn't pushed me if he hadn't challenged me to actually leave I probably would've stayed. Still juggling. Still surviving. Still dimming my light to fit into a role I had already outgrown.

But it was time.

It was time to leap.

The only thing I knew I'd miss was my coworker we had grown close. But even that didn't stop the growth. We still saw each other outside of work, and I even did her nails a few times after I left. It was a bittersweet goodbye… but a powerful one.

Around Valentine's Day, something unexpected happened my anti-Valentine's sets started going viral.

I had started making these bold, moody, unapologetic black Valentine's nails full of edge, sass, and silent strength. Chains, chrome, broken hearts, even custom lettering. And to my surprise? Women loved them. They resonated. They reposted.

I leaned into it.

Because sometimes, we don't want red roses and sweet pinks.

Sometimes we want black hearts, nails that say "I'm healing and you're not him," and just a little bit of bite.

It worked.

Meanwhile, I stayed close with one of my corporate friends. We'd hit local spots for lunch, film random little videos, laugh till our stomachs hurt, and make the most of our new freedom. Most places were finally open again after the shutdowns even if they were short-staffed. We didn't care.

We just needed the girl time.

The normalcy.

And then…

The Texas freeze hit.

Total chaos.

Power outages. Plumbing issues. Wrecks on every freeway.

Apartments flooding. Pipes bursting. Families displaced.

It was like everything shut down all over again.

But somehow by some miracle my place stayed safe.

I had a generator on standby, just in case, but I never lost power. Not once. I was so grateful.

So instead of panicking, I leaned into peace. I stayed in with my boys, made chocolate-covered strawberries, fed my fur babies organic pumpkin with their food, and sipped wine in my cozy pajamas while candles glowed in the background.

And I couldn't help but laugh a little because listen,

I'm from Oregon.

We used to walk to school in the snow, uphill, both ways. (Okay, maybe not both ways but you get it.)

Texas was not built for this.

The moment a single snowflake touched the ground, schools shut down, roads froze, and everyone lost their minds. There was no salt, no prep, no plan. It was like a Hallmark movie gone wrong.

But for me?

Just another winter day.

Still, we needed something to lift our spirits a real getaway. So my

family and I planned a trip to Ruidoso, New Mexico.

We packed snow boots, snow pants, jackets the whole setup and hit the road.

We rented the cutest Airbnb tucked into the forest and celebrated my brother's birthday there, too. It was like a dream. Snow tubing, ziplining, cooking together, laughing until we cried. The Airbnb had a hot tub, a pool table, a cozy fireplace everything. So even when we didn't leave the cabin, we were good.

And the snow?

The snow fed my soul.

I hadn't seen that many trees or that much white powder in so long.

Texas could never.

I almost wanted to cry because God knew how much I'd needed this.

That stillness. That beauty. That breath.

I filmed tons of TikToks while I was out there transitions with my boys, cute clips with my baby nieces, cozy family content in pajamas, in snow gear, in full-blown joy.

And because I had already batched my nail content ahead of time, I didn't fall behind. I prepped captions, saved drafts, and stayed on schedule even on vacation. That's how locked in I was.

I even packed number balloons in the back of the car to celebrate each new follower milestone on the road.

Every time I hit a goal? I filmed a cute video.

It was extra, yes but it made it real.

And when we came back from New Mexico?

The celebrations kept rolling.

Even though I had left my corporate job, I was still attending birthday outings with my old coworkers. But these weren't club scenes or loud bar nights they were laid-back, cozy, grown-woman fun.

Pickleball spots. Rooftop lounges. Wine bars with live bands. Out-door patios with heaters and music and laughter.

My kind of fun.

I started filming more restaurant content too ambience shots, menu highlights, outfit details, and little voiceovers.

Those videos blew up.

Some of the restaurants even reposted them, which brought in local collabs, brand invites, and even more exposure.

And around that same time, people started asking me what I ate in a day what I cooked, how I stayed balanced so I added in some healthy meal prep content too.

Not because I was trying to be a fitness page... but because I'm a mom, a business owner, and I know how to make things work.

And surprisingly?

Those videos did really well.

As more income flowed in, I reinvested back into my studio.

I bought a more comfortable chair for my clients something plush, ergonomic, and sleek. I upgraded my lighting to a chandelier fan with a built-in speaker a full vibe. I filmed every part of the makeover, and my followers loved it.

The chandelier had a remote control, soft lighting, and custom music.

It elevated the whole space.

Suddenly, it wasn't just a nail studio. It was a sanctuary.

My sets were getting more intricate.

People were booking me for detailed artwork, 3D roses, sculpted charms things I used to only dream of doing. I was having so much fun.

I even filmed "Work With Me" videos during appointments soft-spoken, behind-the-scenes reels that showed the process.

My audience ate it up.

And this is also when I got... a little spicy.

I started posting what I used to call my "cringe" treadmill dancing videos just me, at home, in my element. Being goofy. Playful. Sassy. 100% myself.

No makeup. No filter. Just fun.

And to my surprise?

They took off.

Millions of views.

Big repost pages.

Brand emails.

Traffic everywhere.

And that's when I realized something that I still carry with me today: Don't kill your own content just because you think is cringe.

Kill the part of you that cringes and post it anyway.

Because you never know what's going to blow up.

My kids helped film a lot of my content especially my second born.

He was always down to hold the camera, make silly videos, vibe with me, and hype me up like my tiny creative director.

Those moments?

They meant everything.

I even documented every single Botox appointment from the before and afters to price breakdowns and real-time reactions. Not because I was trying to sell it or glamorize it…

But because I remembered how scared I once was.

How I sat there Googling side effects and watching shaky YouTube vlogs, unsure of what to expect.

And I wanted to demystify it for women like me curious, but nervous.

I wanted them to feel informed, empowered, and in control of their own choices.

No shame. No secrecy. Just realness.

Because women deserve that.

And thanks to the momentum from my gym content and socalled "cringe" videos, I was gaining traction beyond just nails and before I knew it, I became an official influencer for a gym in San An-tonio.

I signed a real contract.

Filmed workouts there.

Tagged them every time I posted.

It felt surreal.

But if I'm being honest… I hesitated.

I didn't feel like I looked "fit" enough anymore.

I wasn't as lean, toned, or competitive as I used to be.

And truthfully? I didn't want to be.

I had zero interest in going back to that world the endless pressure, the comparison, the grind of prepping for shows and shrinking myself for approval.

That chapter had closed. And I had no plans of reopening it.

At the time, I still had a contract with Universal Supplements one I intended to finish out respectfully but I had already made peace with that phase ending.

My heart was fully in nails, content creation, motherhood, and building a life that lit me up from the inside.

I didn't want to go back to being "that girl" again not when I was becoming this woman.

Plus, my fitness page?

Full of men in the DMs.

But my nail page?

90% women.

My girls.

My tribe. My audience. My people.

And I loved it that way.

Still, I honored the season I was in showed up for the campaign and stayed grounded in my why.

And then…

Hawaii.

Later that year, I took a dream trip with one of my best friends someone I'd gotten close to during my corporate days.

We booked our flights. Packed light. And left real life behind.

And it was one of the most healing, vibrant, soul-nourishing trips I've ever taken.

We even filmed a fun transition video from rocking my branded merch in San Antonio to twinning in bikinis in the middle of paradise. It was playful. It was silly It was… full circle.

We did oyster pearl jewelry together, laughed until our stomachs hurt, and soaked in every single day we were there.

COVID restrictions were still heavy masks everywhere but we didn't let that ruin it.

We stayed at a humble little hotel right in front of the beach, walking distance from everything.

It wasn't luxury.

It wasn't five stars.

But it felt like freedom.

The sunrises. The sunsets. The swing hanging from a massive oceanside tree.

It was breathtaking.

That moment swinging barefoot over the ocean was one of the most peaceful I've ever felt in my life.

And what made it even more special?

This trip wasn't for content.

It wasn't for my kids.

It wasn't even for work.

It was for me.

A reward for everything I had survived and pushed through.

A pause in the chaos.

A thank you to my own soul.

We hiked waterfalls.

We didn't care about makeup, hair, or outfits.

We were just women in the wild laughing, resting, living. And that version of me?

She was glowing.

From the inside out.

One of my friend's connections on the island hosted a family dinner for us, and it was one of the most beautiful, humbling nights I've ever experienced.

They made white rice, walnut shrimp, and a spread of dishes I couldn't even name but every bite was soul food.

The table was full.

Bowls were passed hand to hand.

And laughter floated through the air like music.

We ate outside with a view of the mountains.

Every morning, the rain would fall just enough to make the world feel soft and sacred.

At night, we'd run through the drizzle and soak up the good vibes.

No filter.

No pressure.

No rush.

Just presence.

Their house was full of mirrors and I couldn't help but compliment it.

If you know me, you know I love mirrors.

In my room, the hallway, the bathroom everywhere.

Something about reflections has always spoken to me. I like to see light bounce back. I like to be reminded I exist that I'm real that I'm here.

One of her cousins or uncles said something like,

"You must be confident if you like to see yourself that much."

It was meant playfully.

But later, I found out that someone in the house had wondered if I was transgender.

It caught me completely off guard.

I've always had a sharp chin.

And in that moment, a wave of old insecurities I thought I'd buried came rushing back like when one of my aunts used to say I had a "horse face."

I think I mentioned that earlier in the book, but this?

This was different.

It brought the old shame to the surface in a new way.

When I got back home, I told one of my best friends about it.

She didn't let me spiral.

She told me not to overthink it that I was beautiful exactly as I was, naturally, just as God made me.

That comment? Nonsense.

And she was right.

Still, it lingered.

Not because I believed it now but because I had believed it once.

And those are the kinds of wounds that take the longest to fully heal.

I've gotten hateful comments online before.

People have said I "look like a man" or "look transgender" because of my chin.

But this is the face I was given.

I have my father's chin.

I have his hands.

His side of the family's feet.

I'm not tall, but I'm not short either I'm 5'3".

People say I look taller on social media, but this is just who I am.

And I've finally, fully, learned to love myself all of myself.

I don't respond to hate anymore.

I don't explain myself.

I don't shrink.

I've made peace with my reflection.

But once I landed back in Texas, it was right back to grind mode.

Orders were pouring in from my Etsy shop and surprisingly, men were shopping too.

One customer stood out.

He kept sending me random Amazon gifts and buying all my merch.

He even sent birthday presents.

I didn't know who he was at first, but I recognized the name.

He had messaged me on Snapchat years ago back when I was competing in 2016 or 2017.

He'd always comment on my milestones, and now here he was again, showing support like a ghost from the internet.

I didn't overthink it.

I was just… grateful.

Around that same time, I made a bold investment:

I bought a nail printer.

I wasn't sure I'd even use it.

I just loved how sleek and white it was it matched my studio perfectly.

But after I posted a video about it, the company saw it and loved it so much, they reached out to collaborate.

That printer turned out to be a hit.

I started using it for baby showers, Disney sets, and couple photos printed directly onto nail tips.

I printed sonograms.

MICKEY MOUSE.

Real love stories in tiny detail on gel nails.

I didn't expect to fall in love with it but I did.

It brought a new level of creativity and personalization to my work, and my clients couldn't get enough.

Summer and fall were packed.

I started filming peaceful, full process videos using calming background tracks like "You're as Pretty as a Picture" by Al Bowlly and people loved them.

They weren't just watching for nails anymore.

They were watching for the energy.

The softness.

The vibe.

Then came Halloween my favorite time of the year.

And if you know, you know I go all in.

Just like some people do 30 days of Christmas or "Vlogmas," I did my version:

30 Days of Halloween.

Every single year.

I did it all creepy gore sets, Freddy Krueger, IT, Scream, Chucky, Michael Myers.

I made custom press-ons, full client sets, and wild freestyle nails.

People lived for it.

I even had clients asking for Halloween-themed nails during Christmas.

That's how iconic it became.

Outside of nails, I was still filming daily mom-life content dropping off my kids, shopping for supplies, prepping for holidays.

Halloween.

Thanksgiving.

Christmas.

Even Easter.

Those last three months of the year?

They became some of my busiest and most profitable and for that, I'll always be grateful.

Then came Christmas.

And this one was special.

It was my first time hosting Christmas for my entire family in our new home in San Antonio.

Everyone was coming into town.

No hotel rooms.

No checking in and out.

No separation.

I wanted everyone under one roof like we used to be.

I made sure we had everything:

Extra towels, paper plates, pillows, blankets so everyone could sleep side by side.

Couches. Floors. Bedrooms.

It didn't matter.

I planned the meals.

Bought board games, jumbo Jenga, yard games for the kids.

And of course...

I picked a theme:

Grinchmas.

And baby, you already know I don't do basic.

I got a talking animated Grinch that my nieces could take photos with.

I built a balloon arch.

Created custom invitations with everyone's names on them even though they already knew the party was happening.

I filled jars with Grinch-themed candy, swapped my bathroom décor with themed shower curtains, rugs, and towels, and even bought

Grinch inflatables for the yard.

I kept my classic white tree up in the dining room but everything else?

Green, red, and chaotic joy.

It was the first time I didn't do an elegant silver or neutral holiday setup.

But this year?

This one was for the kids.

And it was a hit.

Then my birthday rolled around.

And my family went all out.

My sister-in-law celebrated with me, and I felt so loved.

And that mystery man from Amazon?

He went crazy with the gifts.

He sent full outfits, gym gear, accessories I ended up wearing for New Year's, a G-Shock watch, and even a set of sleek white pots and pans I had saved on my wishlist.

It felt like I had a secret Santa who actually paid attention.

To this day, I don't even know his face.

But the love I felt from those small acts of kindness?

It was real.

I'm trying not to cry as I write this because moments like that…

The ones nobody sees, the ones not posted or performed…

Those are the ones that stay with you.

I just wish it could've stayed that way.

But we'll get to that soon.

And my kids?

They were thriving.

Some of their friends weren't as fortunate.

And they asked me if we could buy gifts for them shirts, games, little things just to make their holidays brighter.

Of course I said yes.

That's the kind of heart they have.

And that's what made me proud.

I used to worry about how they'd feel when we left our fancy townhome the one with the garage, the upgrades, the "bougie" finishings and moved into something simpler.

No garage.

No sleek details.

Just a home.

But they didn't complain.

Not once.

They loved it.

They felt safe.

Happy.

Content.

And in that moment, I realized…

I'm doing a damn good job as a mom.

And sometimes?

That's all the validation I need.

Chapter 30

Soft Season, Strong Heart

Nothing really changed after the holidays and for once, that felt like a blessing.

No chaos. No major shifts. Just consistency.

Christmas was calm and beautiful.

My birthday passed with love.

The New Year arrived without pressure or expectation.

Everything just… flowed.

It all felt aligned in a quiet, grounded kind of way.

I slipped into a steady rhythm that winter one I had long craved.

A peace I hadn't felt in years wrapped itself around my mornings like a soft robe.

Each day, I woke up before the kids. I'd let Sasha and Whiskey out into the yard while the world was still hushed. Then I'd start brewing my coffee in the dim morning light, the kitchen slowly warming with the sounds of soft music, a podcast, or sometimes just the birds outside stirring awake.

I'd light incense or a candle something calming. Maybe sandalwood. Maybe cinnamon.

Then I'd start making breakfast.

The smell of eggs, toast, and fresh coffee would mix with the gentle scent in the air, and just like that… it felt like a home built with rhythm and love.

And every single morning, I filmed.

Not just for content but because it was part of how I documented the life I was rebuilding. Even the smallest, most ordinary moments felt worthy of capturing. I'd prop my phone near the coffee pot and let it roll catching glimpses of me dancing in my robe, flipping toast with one hand, or plating breakfast for the boys while they sat at the table, still half-asleep but smiling.

The content never stopped and neither did my drive.

I was posting consistently.

Showing up online in ways that finally felt like me.

And slowly but surely, it started to pay off.

My inbox began to fill with emails from brands.

I started landing paid collaborations, brand partnerships, and PR packages.

I'd open my email and see subject lines like "We'd love to work with you" or "Let's talk paid partnership" and I'd just sit there for a moment, breathing it in like, Wait... is this really happening?

For the first time, I wasn't just creating content I was monetizing my lifestyle.

And it didn't feel forced. It didn't feel per-formative.

It felt earned.

I did contact lens reviews and partnered with brands that actually aligned with what I liked and was genuinely curious about.

Not everything went viral.

Not everything sold out.

But I enjoyed it.

I got to try new things, speak honestly, play around creatively and that in itself felt like a gift.

My hair was thick and healthy again.

My skin was glowing.

I was sleeping better, eating better, and dressing in ways that felt good to me not just following what was trending.

The dogs were calm. The kids were happy.

We had our own little ecosystem of love, routines, and joy that felt sacred in its simplicity.

My Etsy store was still running small but steady.

And every single time I got a new order, it felt like a little whisper from the universe saying, "Keep going, mama. You're doing it."

I'd pack orders with music playing full blast twirling around in the kitchen with shipping labels in one hand and custom nail sets in the other, dancing to songs like "Linger" by The Cranberries.

There was something so healing in the joy of that in romanticizing the hustle, in finding softness inside structure.

It might not have looked flashy from the outside, but this season was one of the most real chapters I'd lived.

I wasn't trying to prove anything to anyone.

I was just living with full intention.

And the momentum didn't stop there.

My gym content was thriving. I was working out, filming consistently, and for the first time I started showing my kids more on social media. That was a boundary I had always kept tight, but they started joining me at the gym more often, and it just happened naturally. They'd pop up in my workout videos, goofing around or hyping me up in the background. It was fun. It felt like us.

Then one day boom. An email came in from Ethika.

Yes… that Ethika.

They wanted to collaborate. But what got me what moved me

was that they didn't just want to work with me…

They wanted to include my boys.

They sent us a massive PR box I'm talking hundreds of items. Socks, boxer briefs, hoodies, joggers, athletic sets, you name it all in our sizes. The boys tore into that box like it was Christmas morning. They went wild with excitement, and we filmed the whole unboxing and shared it online. It was one of the most heartwarming moments we'd had in a long time.

Even better? They gave me my own custom code and shoppable link which I still have to this day.

It felt like a full-circle moment. Not just because Ethika is a dope brand… but because they saw me as a mother, as a creator, and as a whole human. They didn't just see the numbers. They saw my life.

That meant everything to me.

I also had a few local supplement and gymwear companies reach out and they, too, made sure to include my boys in the gifting.

I don't know what it is, but the mother in me just lights up any time my kids are thought of, included, or celebrated in something meant for me.

That kind of love gets me emotional every time.

Watching their eyes light up, seeing their little proud smiles, hearing them say things like, "Wait, this is for us too?" it makes every long night of building this life feel so worth it. That's the real flex.

Not the free gear or the emails but those moments where they felt seen, valued, and included.

I also got sponsored by Path Water, and let me just say I have nothing but love for that brand. I'm a sucker for alkaline water.

And listen… if you drink water for real, then you know not all water tastes the same. Path Water is hands-down one of my top favorites. It's smooth, crisp, and tastes clean. The bottles are sleek and refillable, which makes it even better and eco-friendly.

If you haven't tried them yet, here's your shameless plug.

You can find them on my Amazon storefront and if you're holding this book, chances are you already follow me, or there's a QR code nearby.

Go ahead and scan it. I got you. You won't regret it.

Another full-circle moment? My very first nail product collaboration with none other than Beetles Gel Polish. They reached out and offered to send me their entire collection to create content with, and I would also earn commission from sales made through my personalized link. I remember how surreal it felt when that box arrived.

It was my first official nail brand collab, and I was so proud.

Since then, I've been lucky enough to collaborate with them at least once a year and I genuinely love it. The products are affordable, long-lasting, and perfect for both professional nail techs and everyday girls who just want to do their own sets at home. That collab reminded me that everything I had been working toward late nights, filming, editing, packaging, showing up was slowly building a path forward.

And then… there were the gifts.

Y'all remember that Secret Santa I mentioned earlier in the book?

Yeah… he didn't stop after the holidays.

The surprises just kept coming.

He sent the cutest two-piece outfits perfect for lake days, beach trips, or just casual hot Texas weather (which, let's be real, is every season down here). I wore all of them. And the gesture alone? It was just thoughtful in a way I hadn't experienced in a long time.

But let's talk about the wildest gift he sent…

A touchscreen toaster.

Yes. A touchscreen. Toaster.

I didn't even know toasters could do all that. I was so hyped. This thing had more settings than my last TV. It practically spoke to me. It made my kitchen feel like I had a smart home chef on standby. When I unboxed it, I literally stood there speechless like... who buys someone a toaster this fancy?

It was crazy expensive luxury appliance status. But it was also, oddly, one of the best gifts I'd ever received. Because it was so random. So extra. And so me. I was obsessed.

I actually wore one of the outfits he sent on Mother's Day that year. I took my kids out for a little brunch date just the three of us. We went shopping afterward and they basically just tagged along while I sipped mimosas and lived my best life. I was giggling through aisles with a buzz, walking around in my cute little two piece, and they were right there, letting me have my moment.

The boys have always been supportive of me celebrating myself even if that meant letting mom get a little tipsy on her own day.

They've seen how hard I work. They've seen me pour myself into everyone else.

They know I deserve to enjoy life too.

They just want to see me happy.

They've lived through everything with me every heartbreak, every loss, every win.

Every chapter, they've been by my side.

And as much as I've raised them, I feel like in many ways... they've helped raise me too.

I remember filming TikToks that day while we waited for our food. People at the brunch spot recognized us smiling, waving, saying kind things. The whole energy just felt warm, welcoming, and full of life. I was glowing, laughing, and holding space for the version of me that had fought so hard to feel light again.

It was nothing but good vibes, good food, and loud laughs.

And like I always say:

My favorite dates will always be brunch and shopping with my two broke best friends a.k.a. my kids.

And I stand by that.

That year, I also made them a promise.

I told them I'd take them to Hawaii just the three of us.

I had recently gone on a trip with one of my best friends and had the most amazing experience. It was healing. It was breathtaking. It was something I knew I wanted to share with them. I told myself that if I saved consistently, we wouldn't have to go on a budget. We'd go right and we'd do it all.

I pictured us hiking, exploring the island, eating incredible food, and doing those iconic 5 AM surf lessons. I couldn't stop talking about the McDonald's rice and egg breakfast yes, McDonald's. I know it sounds random, but it was my first time trying it in Hawaii, and I swear… it hit. I craved it for weeks after I got back.

And I decided right then and there that every time I returned to Hawaii, I'd buy myself a new piece of oyster-made jewelry. I had bought a ring on that first trip, and I told myself it would become my personal tradition: one piece per visit. A small reward. A sacred reminder of how far I'd come, and how much beauty life still had to offer.

And let's not get it twisted I still rewarded myself from time to time.

I got my brows permanently tattooed and let me tell you, that's not some cheap little beauty appointment. That's a whole luxury procedure. But I went for it. And I have zero regrets. I've been obsessed ever since.

I'm not someone who wears a full face of makeup every day, but between my brows, my Botox, and yes let's not forget the lashes I barely needed anything else. Those little enhancements gave me confidence. They made me feel polished without needing to try hard. And honestly? Little rewards like that kept me motivated.

They were proof that I could take care of myself in every sense emotionally, mentally, physically, financially.

They reminded me to keep pushing. To keep growing.

Social media, though… whew. That's a whole other beast.

There's this unspoken pressure to create masterpieces every day.

Like if your content isn't a viral production, it doesn't matter.

The algorithm wants to be fed. People want to be entertained. And creators we end up burning out trying to keep up.

But I had to slow down. I had to fall in love with the process again.

I stopped pressuring myself to be perfect. I started showing just bits and pieces of the beauty in the making. I celebrated every small win. I gave myself permission to recycle content just by editing it differently. I stopped overthinking the posts and just started living.

If you're a creator, take note:

You don't have to post every moment to prove you're living it.

I've learned to tread gently. To live life softly.

To stop treating my creativity like a machine that owes the world something.

Honestly, I think all of my experiences especially losing my dad completely reshaped how I see life. I view the world through a different lens now. My perspective isn't like most people's.

Don't get me wrong I love nice things.

I love being successful.

I love a good purse and a clean car just like the next girl.

But if you really know me, you know I live under my means. I'm smart about how I move because I never want to lose myself in the noise. I want time for travel. I want time for my family. I want to be able to enjoy the things that actually matter.

Because when we leave this world?

We don't take anything with us. Not the money. Not the homes. Not the cars. Nothing.

What we do leave behind are our memories.

Our businesses.

The laughs and stories shared with our children.

The seeds we plant those grow into legacy.

And that's what I'm building. Something that will carry on.

Not just for me but for my kids, and their kids, and generations to come.

Of course I still want the beautiful home, the dream car, the soft life.

But it's not my obsession.

Because I've learned that when you do what you love with your whole heart, the money comes.

The blessings flow.

The right people find you.

And you'll still have your soul intact.

That's why I started using the DND feature on my iPhone. I needed boundaries especially from social media. I'd post, maybe scroll for a bit, and then log out. Because I had caught myself working 24/7... and for what?

Balance, baby. Balance.

That balance also made me fall in love with the gym again.

And honestly? This was my prime era in the gym.

I was hitting my legs like never before smashing PRs on squats, building strength, sculpting my back. I've always said the most beautiful physical feature a woman can have aside from her smile is a stunning back.

Just my opinion. Lol.

And while I was locked in…

Of course.

Here we go.

I met someone.

He was shy at first when he talked to me. But during one of our conversations, I cracked a joke and said, "You must be a Cancer."

And he goes, "I actually am."

So boom that's what we're calling him in this book: Cancer.

He was Latino. Tall tall I mean, I'm 5'3 and this man had to be 6'6 or close. Definitely over 200 pounds. Not the overly buff, steroid-type guy but he was big. Solid. Strong. He could lift heavy. And anytime I needed a spotter or felt unsure about pushing more weight, he'd show up encouraging, steady, helpful.

He became a solid gym partner. Sometimes he'd pop up in my videos, too. We had fun little shits and giggles here and there. It was light.

Then we started grabbing food after workouts. Or hanging out on our days off.

He built homes for a living and did a few other things on the side. I really admired his work ethic. I even tagged along a couple of times just to see what he did, and it felt nice to connect with someone who seemed to be on a similar level as me.

I'd give him tips on networking and branding because I was way more social and tapped into that world than he was. We went out to brunch a few times, and honestly, I don't think he had ever done anything like that before. I was pulling him into a softer world.

But something felt off.

He would disappear sometimes said he was out of town for work.

At first, I didn't question it. Until I started feeling it.

Then one night, he invited me to grab drinks and dinner.

I said yes. But when we got there… things got weird.

He started tipping the bartenders and waitresses $100 bills casually, like it was nothing. But he wasn't okay. He got way too drunk. He couldn't drive. He handed me his phone and his money and told me to get him a place to stay. I got him a hotel and went home to my own place.

And then… I saw something.

A message.

A notification.

A whole second life.

Turns out he was in another relationship.

The entire time.

And then her phone number popped up.

She called me.

We talked. She told me she knew who I was.

She had seen my number. My photos. My texts.

She had seen me. At the gym. In real life.

She had just… kept quiet. For reasons I won't go into, because that's not my story to tell.

But it shook me.

He was her son's coach. A stepfather figure. Her son even called him daddy.

This man had built a full-on double life.

And just like that… I was done.

The entire thing lasted maybe two months. But when I found out, I didn't wait around for more lies. I blocked him. Switched gyms. Disappeared from his orbit completely.

And just like that, my first attempt at dating again after almost two years…

Ended like that.

So I shut it down again. I went back to my little bubble.

If I went out to dance? I danced.

If I hit the club? I had fun.

But I was not opening the door for another man.

Or so I thought…

Because just two months later, I met another man this time at a bar.

I was out with one of my close friends (funny enough, another friend I met at the gym). It was Latin night. We were dancing, vibing, having a good time.

He came up to the bar, paid for our drinks, and asked for my number.

I said no.

Fast forward a few weeks later… I ran into him again at my new gym.

He walked straight up to my treadmill while I was doing cardio and asked again.

This time, I said yes.

We went out to dinner. We sat down at the table, ordered drinks.

I got water and some oysters as an appetizer. I was excited, hungry, and ready to enjoy the night.

The waiter brought the oysters, set them on the table and this man looked at them, made a face, and said:

"Ew."

I don't know who raised him, but in my family? That's disrespectful.

You don't react like that to someone's food especially not on a date.

So you know what I did?

I reached into my purse. Pulled out a crisp $50 bill.

Laid it gently on the table to cover my drink and appetizer.

And I walked. Right. Out.

Didn't say a word.

Didn't look back.

Blocked his number the second I got to the car.

Because at this point in my life?

I know my worth.

I know my boundaries.

And if something feels off, I'm not sticking around to explain why.

That $50 was the price of peace and I paid it gladly.

And don't get me wrong. He tried to reach out. Again and again.

He was attractive. He was successful. He drove a Maserati.

But let me be real with you:

I don't care what car you drive.

It's not about a man giving me everything.

It's about what he gives when he doesn't have much.

It's about respect. Character. Intentions.

It's about a man who has $20 and still gives you $10.

Who has no time and still makes time.

Who respects women. Loves his mama. Stands on his word.

And he just wasn't that.

So my decision was final.

When I placed that $50 on the table… I knew I wasn't just walking out on the date.

I was walking into my power.

Back to being locked in.

Back to my peace.

Back to my soft season.

Living. Working. Glowing.

I booked our dream trip to Hawaii with both my boys, Julian and Isaac.

I planned everything to the T.

From the excursions we'd take, to the hotel we'd stay in, to the exact rental car I'd be driving I handled every detail myself. I built a full itinerary: hiking trails, beach days, Jurassic Park tours, sunrises, sunsets, local food spots, and everything in between. I paid for everything in advance so that once we got there, it was all about spending money on what we wanted, not worrying about budgets or limitations. The trip was set for early fall right after summer break, which meant the boys would miss about a week of school.

And let me be honest: I'd rather them miss a few days of school to make unforgettable memories than wait for some "perfect time" that may never come.

I told them they could make up their work during the year, or I'd write a note but what we weren't going to do was let an opportunity like this pass us by.

Because yes, I traveled as a kid, but I didn't get vacations like this. I didn't grow up with beach trips or full itineraries. I didn't get luxury experiences.

So now? I give my kids the life I wished I had.

And I do it guilt-free.

I wanted to create memories that would last forever.

I wanted them to enjoy life with no stress, no fear, no guilt.

And I was making that happen.

We were all counting down the days we were so excited we could barely sit still.

I even hopped on SHEIN and let the boys pick all their beach shorts and outfits pieces they could wear, mess up, or leave behind with-out worrying about cost. I did the same for myself. I ordered bikinis, beach cover-ups, hiking fits, and cute sets that were inexpensive, easy to pack, and perfect for adventure. I didn't want to risk ruining anything name-brand or designer I wanted to be comfortable and cute, not worried about scuffing up my wardrobe on a trail.

When the month finally arrived, I kicked into full-on business mode.

Like I'd done for previous trips, I batch created a ton of content in advance. I edited videos, wrote captions, and scheduled posts across all my platforms. The time difference between Texas and Hawaii was going to be major, and I wanted everything to run smoothly while I was gone.

My Etsy store? Handled. I made sure my assistant had everything she needed to pack and ship orders while I was away. I had seen clients late into the night some past midnight just to make sure everyone was taken care of before I left.

My loyalty to my clients has always been a top priority.

I even asked my ex-husband if he wanted to join us.

Not because we're together we're not.

But because we've always been good friends, and truthfully, he's never really traveled either.

He ended up declining for personal and work reasons and that was fine. But for those who may be raising an eyebrow: yes, our co-parenting relationship is that solid.

We've known each other since I was 16.

We've had our rocky moments, sure but we've always been great friends.

It's the relationship stuff that got messy.

But trips? Vacations? As friends?

They've always been a blast.

While we were in Hawaii, he even sent us some extra money to shop and enjoy ourselves and he upgraded our rental car too. That's just the kind of co-parenting energy we keep. Supportive, respectful, and focused on what's best for the boys.

And Hawaii?

Hawaii was everything I dreamed of and more.

We hiked through lush trails, chased waterfalls, and soaked in every moment except for one hike where we got super lost and thought we might need to be rescued. We couldn't find our way out for a while and legit panicked. But thankfully, we had our phones and were able to GPS our way back to the car.

We laughed about it later but in the moment, we were shook. We

ate so much food.

Did some light shopping.

Caught a few football games and even hung out in some of the local restaurants and bars.

And with two boys? Trust me any moment involving sports is

automatically a good time.

When we got back to Texas, we were glowing.

Refreshed. Recharged.

The boys were in great spirits and jumped right back into school.

They didn't fall behind and even if they had, it would've been worth every second.

That trip was soul food.

It gave us memories I know they'll carry for the rest of their lives.

And just a few days after Hawaii, I took another quick vacation this time to Las Vegas.

It was still hot when I got there, so pool parties were on. I had a great time.

And funny enough, my ex-husband ended up meeting me there.

We ate tacos on the street, walked the Strip, and talked about everything the trip to Hawaii, the boys, life.

We've always had open conversations about what we missed out on as kids, and what we want our children to experience now. Our conversations aren't bitter. They're real. Thoughtful. Honest. He listens. I talk (a lot), and somehow we always meet each other in that middle ground of mutual understanding.

Was it a lot going from Hawaii to Vegas in the same week?

Absolutely.

But I also learned something on that trip Vegas is not a "vacation" destination for me.

It's more like a weekend escape. A vibe.

Somewhere I can shop, walk the Strip, and reset for a second.

And let me just say this:

If you've never been to a Ross in Las Vegas… you're missing out.

I swear, they take all my money every time.

I'll fly out with an empty suitcase and fly back with a brand new wardrobe.

Vegas Ross hits different.

Anytime my ex and I have taken small trips like this or met up for a quick weekend, we always end up talking about life. He asks about what's going on in my world, and I update him from social media chaos to business wins to failed dating attempts (which we always end up laughing about).

It might seem weird to some people but to us? It works.

We've known each other for so long that there's just a mutual respect that's never gone away

Even if we're not in a relationship, we've always known how to be good to one another as co-parents… and friends. Even in disagreements, we've kept it cordial or at least tried.

When I got back from all the traveling, something unexpected made me even more excited For the first time since moving in, there were homes being built all around me. I finally had neighbors. A real sense of community was starting to form and I was ready for it.

The timing couldn't have been more perfect. Fall was creeping in… and that meant one thing:

Halloween season.

I was so excited words honestly can't even describe it.

This year, I decided to go all out and make Halloween Boo Baskets for my new neighbors.

Each basket was filled with mini bags of chocolate chip cookies, cans of Diet Coke, mini liquor bottles (a little Jack Daniels, some rum, or something fun), a variety of candy, and cute little Halloween toys or spooky knickknacks. It was playful, thoughtful, and my love

471

language in every way.

And this wasn't just any Halloween it was the first year I fully invested in outdoor decor.

We're talking haunted house displays, 12-foot skeletons, fog machines, creepy lights, the works.

I was so committed, I set my alarm for 5 AM and waited in virtual lines to grab limited-edition decorations before they sold out. That's how serious I was.

The boys and I got our costumes early and even started dancing around the house in them. I was teaching both of my sons a little Halloween dance because... let's be real:

Who doesn't love a man who can dance and has a sense of humor?

Since more families had moved in, more kids were out trick-or-treating that year so I went all out and handed out full-size candy bars. My house became that house.

And guess what?

I won House of the Month for the neighborhood because of all my Halloween decorations.

And I didn't stop there.

For Christmas, I changed the entire theme of my home. Since I wasn't going to be hosting family that year, I decided to finally do something just for me a dreamy, elegant all-white Christmas.

White reindeer.

White snowball lights.

A glowing snow arch at the front entrance.

Drizzling snow effects outside the house.

It was magical. This was also my second year starting Christmas shopping in September, because let's be honest from September to December, my life gets hectic. Between business, content, corporate work, and personal life, I don't have time to run around last minute in December like everyone else.

Plus, I don't like rushing gifts. I like giving people good gifts not just "whatever was left on the shelf." Shopping early meant I didn't have to stress or stick to a tight budget. I could plan it right.

I got my boys gaming chairs, a new basketball goal, all kinds of cool gadgets including both a PlayStation and an Xbox.

There's nothing that fills my heart more than seeing my kids light up over something they love especially when I'm able to give them the kind of joy I once felt as a kid.

Making their dreams come true filled my heart more than words can explain.

Even my birthday that year was amazing.

I invited some of my closest friends a mix of corporate coworkers and gym friends and we all went out for brunch.

One of my besties came over to my house that morning to help me get dressed and ride with me to the brunch spot. It was beautiful seeing people from different parts of my life all show up and vibe together the gym girls, the work fam everyone.

And of course... my mysterious Secret Santa from earlier chapters?

He was still around.

He sent me the most thoughtful birthday gifts and we actually started messaging back and forth on Snapchat. I didn't know who he was not really but I considered him a social media friend. A sweet little online mystery. And honestly?

It was cute.

We sent each other pics and little birthday updates. It was fun and harmless and it made me smile.

I also hosted a New Year's lunch and dinner at my place to bring in the new year right.

Some of my closest friends came over including a few new ones who had just moved to Texas from New York.

We had fireworks, food, and a playlist that had everything from Mexican music, soca, hip hop, and even country. We danced, laughed, and celebrated the end of another wild, beautiful year.

It was loud.

It was warm.

It was perfect.

We crossed over into the new year surrounded by joy, music, and genuine people.

And most importantly?

I felt present.

I felt proud.

I felt like I was truly healing and living in my prime.

Healing didn't look like silence anymore.

It looked like music, candy baskets, laughter, fireworks, and saying yes to myself in every season.

And just like that I closed out the year soft, strong, and steady. Fully me.

Finally home.

Chapter 31

This Season, I Chose Me

This was the year I fully learned that yes my dad taught me how to be street smart but I taught myself how to be book smart. I think I've mentioned this before, but even if I haven't, it's worth repeating: my dad used to say that women were like roses. We were beautiful, yes but we had thorns. We needed to be handled with care. We weren't meant to be picked up and tossed aside.

Women, he said, were like gardens. And men? Men were like the gardeners meant to tend to them.

But somewhere along the way, I became both.

At this point in my life, I was the rose with thorns and the gardener with calloused hands. I watered myself. I took care of myself. I treated myself as fragile and as sacred as I would something I deeply loved. I wasn't waiting for anyone to rescue me from the dirt. I bloomed on my own.

This was the year I learned to hold the kind of power that didn't have to be loud to be strong. I learned when to stay silent, and when to speak. I realized that "killing them with kindness" was more than just a saying it was a tool, a quiet kind of fire. And everyone has access to that power, but not everyone knows how to use it.

I meditated. I burned incense. I prayed. I connected with the universe in ways I never had before. I used affirmations and manifestations daily not just to attract things, but to stay in alignment with who I was becoming.

I knew deep down that I wasn't just chasing success I was choosing legacy. I didn't care about having shiny things just for show. I was planting seeds for something that would outlive me. I wanted roots. I wanted depth. I wanted something that could grow for generations.

After living in San Antonio for several years, I learned to let go of the pressure to perfect everything. I stopped needing to control how life unfolded. I gave myself permission to evolve, to wake up looking different, to feel different. I was healing, slowly, and learning to love that I didn't have to be 100% ready to show up. I just had to be honest with myself, with my life, with the world.

I stopped waiting for inspiration and started creating it. Anywhere. With anyone. At any time. It became second nature.

January was a slow start to the year, but I didn't let it throw me off. I stayed locked in every single day creating business plans, content calendars, and writing everything down like always. I've always been a visual person; if I don't see it, it doesn't feel real to me. I needed that paper trail. That roadmap.

I had also planned a vacation yes, another one. This time, with one of my girlfriends who had moved from New York to Texas. We decided we were going to celebrate Galentine's in the most fabulous way back in New York City. The plan was to indulge in delicious food, go shopping, stay in a bougie and comfortable hotel, and live our best girly-girl weekend.

We got tickets to the SUMMIT at One Vanderbilt. The views were insane. The Edge has a glass sky deck that makes you feel like you're floating 1,130 feet above the city. It was unreal.

We also took a cruise to see the Statue of Liberty, and in my opinion, the experience was completely worth it. The boat had a bar, music, photographers, and all the vibes. The weather was cold and crisp true winter energy and our outfits were giving New York Fashion Week. Short dresses, black tights, booties, trench coats, and scarves to match. It was a dream.

We had lunch in Chinatown still one of my favorite memories. It's located in Lower Manhattan and is one of the oldest and largest Chinese communities in the Western Hemisphere. The streets were alive with culture, food, and tradition. We ate so good. 10/10 rec-ommend.

Later that night, we had the most romantic Galentine's dinner in Little Italy. Pasta, pizza, a side dish, and a bottle of chilled Chardonnay. The energy was perfect. The vibes were immaculate. And then… it snowed. Like movie scene snow. We had brunch at this incredible spot called Dudley's (you have to go), and on the walk back to our hotel, the flurries started falling. We took so many pictures. The whole trip felt like a reset. A breath of fresh air.

And listen I'm not gonna lie. New York streets did smell a little rough at times. I have a sensitive stomach, so I kept covering my mouth and nose with my scarf to keep from gagging. But that didn't stop me from enjoying every moment. I took tons of pictures, laughed nonstop, and made the best memories. Because my friend had lived in the city before, she had a ton of connections, so we ended up at a drag show club one night and it was amazing. The entire place was filled with women. We danced and laughed until the early morning. I had so much fun.

And call me dramatic, but I've always wanted to ride the train in New York. I didn't care what anyone said I wanted the full experience. My friend told me we didn't need to, but I insisted. So we did. And yep, I saw people knocked out cold, drunk, and curled up in their seats. It was hilarious. I soaked it all in. Wouldn't trade it for anything.

Before and after that trip, I'd been filming tons of Valentine's Day nail sets. I'd even done my own nails this was during my long-nail era when I wore the longest, most extra sets on myself too.

When I got back home, my house was overflowing with roses. I mean it bouquets at the door, in the kitchen, everywhere. Some from friends. Some from family. Some from old clients and even acquaintances. A few people found my business address on my book-ing website and sent flowers there. The effort… it meant something, even if it confused me. I got chocolates, strawberries, Amazon wish-list gifts it was a lot.

I made funny TikToks with my kids and all the flowers. It was a vibe. From the outside, it probably looked like a dream. But inside… I don't know. I still felt a little empty.

A part of me wondered if some people were sending things because they wanted something in return. I didn't feel like much of it was genuine. But I still smiled. I still said thank you. I still carried on with my day.

Truthfully, I had given up on everything except my kids and my business. Love? Dating? Going out? Doing anything for myself? That was all at the very bottom of my list.

My oldest son had been going to the gym with me a lot this year, and I kept posting little clips on social media especially Snapchat. It's funny because I had sworn off Snapchat for a while. It wasn't bringing in money like the other platforms, and at that point, I was only interested in social media that could generate income. But I kept Snapchat anyway.

Why? Because most of my family was on there my sisters-in-law, nieces, nephews. It felt like a private way to stay connected with the people who mattered. And even though it didn't make sense financially, emotionally it did. So I kept it. And I'm so glad I did.

Because you know who was still watching my stories on there?

Secret Santa.

Yeah him.

He would always reply to my workout stories or send little laughing emojis when I posted funny stuff with my kids. He seemed to genuinely enjoy the fact that I was always telling stories, cracking jokes, and being myself even during our gym sessions. He told me once that he loved how excited I always looked when I talked about my kids or life in general. I guess I never realized how much of that joy translated through the screen until he said it.

Then one day… he sent me a photo.

I don't remember if he was wearing a hoodie or a T-shirt from my merch line but he had finally purchased something and wanted to show it off. That was the first time I ever saw his face. And when I did… whewww. He was fine.

I mean fine fine.

He had these piercing marble eyes a mix of icy blue and pale green, like the sky right before a storm. They were striking. He was tall, attractive, confident, and he had supported my business without ever asking for attention in return. I'd later find out he'd been following me for years since maybe 2016 or 2017, back when I was competing on stage. But I never knew who he was until that moment.

Secret Santa finally had a face.

After that, I started entertaining our conversations more. I'm not gonna lie part of it was because he was attractive, but another part of me respected the fact that he'd been silently cheering me on for so long. There's something powerful about consistency. Especially when it's quiet.

A lot of my friends used to ask me why I hadn't given him a chance yet. Why hadn't we flown out to meet? Why wasn't I open to something that clearly had history?

The truth?

He was an Aries. "A fire sign".

And that scared the hell out of me.

It might sound silly, but after that traumatic situation in Dallas with that Aries man… I just couldn't shake the fear. I didn't even bring that chapter up earlier in the book because it was such a dark time. But that experience truly traumatized me, and I wasn't ready to re-live anything even remotely close to it.

So anytime someone asked, my response was the same:

"He's an Aries. I just can't do it."

"He's an Aries. I don't want to go through that again."

"He's an Aries. End of story."

And that was that. That became my excuse for years. Secret Santa stayed just that a secret.

This year also happened to be another peak season for my TikTok. My account was blowing up again. I had crossed over 200,000 followers, and my Instagram went from around 6,000 to over 40,000. That kind of growth on IG doesn't come easy, either it's a slow grind on that platform, so every follower felt like a win.

I still had my fitness page too, and my DMs were full. But I wasn't entertaining anyone except for one strange, generous man who booked an entire week of appointments on my booking site... just so I could take time off. No joke. At first, I was confused. Then I got a message on Instagram from someone saying, "Hey, I just wanted you to rest and do something for yourself. That was me."

Can you imagine?

I never met him. Never called him. Never even had a conversation outside of that one thank-you message. But it stuck with me. People were always watching. And some were actually rooting for me in ways I didn't expect. Even still, I wasn't the best at replying to DMs. I never have been. I've always been a little dry with messages. Not because I'm rude just because I'm not really a "people person" like that. I'm social on social media, but in real life? I'm quiet. I take time to warm up. And when I do... then you see my personality. But until then, I stay in my bubble.

This year, I stayed dedicated to work. Obsessed, actually.

I had started planning my own brand, even though I didn't have all the answers yet. I didn't know when it would launch. I didn't have a team. I wasn't even asking other nail techs for help. I didn't even know where to begin but I was determined.

I made YouTube, TikTok, and Instagram they became my personal university. I sat down and studied. I consumed videos, tutorials, packaging tips, shipping ideas anything I could find. If it existed online, I could learn it. I just had to show up and be willing to do the work.

My schedule was insane, up by 5 AM to hit the gym. By 8 AM, I was back home making breakfast and editing videos. By noon, I was already doing nails and I'd keep going until midnight, sometimes later. I'd schedule my content for 6 PM and post while my clients were washing their hands.

And then? Repeat. Every. Single. Day. It was non-stop. But it was necessary.

I know I had already been off of the corporate world for a while, but for some reason, my sleep schedule was all messed up, so I had my blackout curtains still installed in my room and would need to completely shut those to get some rest.

Sometimes I felt like I was slacking a little with my son's basketball or foot-ball games. And mom guilt? It was real. But I had to explain to the boys if they wanted a good life, if they wanted nice things, if they wanted to keep the stability we had mom had to work. I didn't miss all their games. Just some. I still had control over my schedule, but I was in a zone. Tunnel vision. Locked in. Laser-focused.

Focused in a way that only women with something to prove can be.

That summer brought a little softness to all the hustle. I finally carved out time to hit the beach and escape to the lake with my best friend aka my wife, as most of my followers know her. We'd pack the kids, grab drinks, and head out to the water for the day. Sometimes we'd go tubing, sometimes we'd just lay in the sun and recharge with music, laughter, and good energy. Afterward, we'd stop for finger foods and cocktails with the kids, making those lazy, sun-kissed afternoons feel like a reward.

Back at home, business was booming. I had started filming live nail consultations on TikTok and they went insanely viral. It got to a point where I couldn't even take new clients anymore because I was so booked. I hosted TikTok Lives too, and yep... those started bringing in consistent income. I had already passed 200,000 followers and the numbers just kept rising by the day. My page was hot. I had mountains of PR packages waiting to be unboxed, so I did what I do best turned them into content. I showed the process: the unboxing, the packaging, my honest reactions, and the behind-the-scenes of content creation. My filming schedule was heavy, but I thrived in that energy. I applied pressure in all the right places and it showed.

One thing that always hit? Me doing my own nails on camera. Those videos never missed. People loved seeing the long sets I created on myself and especially loved when I talked to the camera while working. It was personal, real, and fun. That year, I was rocking extremely long nails and people were obsessed. The sets were dramatic, feminine, and totally me.

And somewhere in the middle of all that momentum, I made a decision I was going to buy a new car.

I had two visions in mind: either an SUV that could handle my traveling, content equipment, and nail supplies… or something luxurious, like a BMW. Every time I drove by the BMW dealership, I chickened out. I kept telling my best friend, "I don't feel like I belong there." I would literally avoid walking in. Something about it felt intimidating.

I wished I could just click and order it online like I did with my white Camaro. But this was different.

Eventually, I mustered the courage and walked into BMW. And I'm so glad I did.

I custom-ordered my dream car: a white BMW X3 with wine-colored leather seats. She was classy. She was cute. She was mine.

It would take about three months for delivery, but I didn't care. I chose what felt good for me: a heated steering wheel, touchscreen motion screen, XL sunroof, heated seats nothing over-the-top, just clean, functional luxury. I didn't need the biggest, the flashiest, or the most expensive. I just wanted something that felt comfortable and worked for my life. I had finally entered an era where I wasn't trying to prove anything. I just wanted peace and tools that supported my business and lifestyle.

But just as I was in my groove, I got hit with the worst flu. It felt like I caught COVID three years late, and it knocked me out. I was down bad congested, aching, miserable.

That's when my best friend introduced me to what's called a hot toddy basically tea, honey, lemon, and whiskey. And if you know me, you know whiskey is my thing, so I wasn't mad about it. I said, "Girl, pour me three shots. Let's fix this." We actually filmed a PR unboxing video on TikTok while sipping hot toddies… and it went viral. People loved it. We were sick, unfiltered, cozy, and hilarious and they ate it up.

During those days inside, I treated myself to something I'd always wanted as a little girl: Barbie LEGOs. It might sound silly, but it was healing. The little version of me never got to have those toys, and here I was now, finally giving her everything she ever wanted.

And with the new Barbie movie coming out, I was hyped. I never really considered myself a "Barbie girl" growing up but the healed version of me? Oh, she loved Barbie. She loved soft pink. She loved glam. She loved joy.

Anytime I left the house, people would recognize me. I was being stopped in public at gas stations, grocery stores, malls. People wanted hugs, selfies, quick convos. They'd say things like, "I follow you for the nail content," or "Girl, your videos crack me up!" Some didn't even know I was a nail tech they followed me purely for my humor or my vibe.

Even my kids' friends and coaches knew who I was. At first, it definitely embarrassed the boys. But after a while, they adjusted and started proudly saying, "Yeah, that's my mom. She's that girl." LOL.

When the Barbie movie finally dropped, you already know I had to show out. I was one of the first in the theater. I wore a pink leather dress I had ordered online just for the occasion, paired it with pink lipstick, and styled my hair to match the Barbie aesthetic. I took my oldest son with me as my date and we had the best time.

We went to the fancy theater by my house the bougie one with an open bar, full kitchen, and servers that bring everything straight to your seat. No lines. No waiting. Just vibes.

That night felt magical.

I posted photos and videos on Snapchat and across my socials. I was glowing.

And then… I got a Snapchat message from him.

Secret Santa.

"You're the real Barbie," he wrote.

"Barbie's got nothing on you."

I won't lie I blushed. Just reading that from him, picturing his face, remembering those stunning eyes... whewww. I liked him. I didn't even know him like that, but I liked him.

That summer, my clients were also catching the Barbie fever. Everyone wanted pink nails soft pinks, hot pinks, glitter, rhinestones. I was booked and busy with Barbie sets left and right.

And during that time, I also got really close to one of my regular clients. She came so often that eventually we started hanging out outside the salon. We shared wine, went on little girls' nights, and eventually became best friends. What started as a business relationship turned into a beautiful sisterhood. I guess being a nail tech does come with some perks.

I was surrounded by a powerful circle of women and it felt safe.

Later that year, I decided to revamp my merch line. I upgraded all my logos, got new hoodie and t-shirt designs, and re-listed everything on Etsy. I even added the merch to my booking site so clients could purchase in person during appointments. The new logo was so me my hair, my outfit, the red bottoms, my favorite color white it captured my essence perfectly.

And of course, my clients supported it fully. Almost everyone who sat in my chair bought a shirt or a hoodie.

And Secret Santa?

Yep he bought his too.

It was a small gesture, but it made me smile.

Because even when I didn't fully believe in love, people like him reminded me... that I was still being seen. One of the highlights of that year was planning my first trip ever with my best friend my wife, as my followers know her. I had invited her to my uncle's annual formal birthday party, one of the most iconic family events I go to every year. It was being hosted at one of his own ballrooms. He owns several venues, insurance offices, and businesses, and honestly, I've always looked up to him as a mentor. He even has his own published books. Watching him build his empire over the years has inspired me deeply

I hyped her up and told her, "Girl, we're not pulling up casual. We're giving FORMAL. Grown woman. Red carpet." So we did our shopping, locked in on our health goals, ate clean, worked out, and made sure we were feeling and looking our best. We prepped our outfits months in advance. I reserved the hotel room early and made sure every single detail was set in place. No last-minute chaos. I'm just that way I love being prepared. I'm not controlling in a bad way, I just like things to go smoothly. I like to be ahead of schedule, always.

At this point, I had been talking more consistently with my Secret Santa. The girls started jokingly calling him "my sugar" because he was always sending sweet gifts and even sweeter messages. LOL. He had become a daily part of my life checking in, complimenting me, making me laugh. During the trip, I was messaging him back and forth and had a lot to drink that night. That party? WHEW. It was the first time my best friend had seen me fully let loose. Usually, I'm the mom of the group. I'm the one driving everyone home, checking the time, making sure people get home safe. I'm the one who has it together.

But that night? I was just me.

We took shots straight from the bottle. We danced, laughed, and partied so hard I couldn't even get out of bed the next morning. I sent my Secret Santa some post-party videos, half hungover, and even then, he still called me beautiful. Even on my tired, makeup-smudged mornings the made me feel adored.

My best friend loved seeing me like that. She said it was refreshing to see me unwind, because I rarely do. I'm the type to clock out of work and pour a glass of whiskey or wine to relax but rarely do I get shitfaced. But that night? We went all out. And it felt earned. As soon as the trip was over, it was back to grind mode. Halloween content was coming up fast and everything felt like it was on fast-forward. The months were flying by like days. It was GO time, and I was locked in.

And then... Drake announced his tour stop in Austin.

My kids were dying to go, and honestly, I wanted to see him too so I decided to get us tickets. Around that time, I sent my Secret Santa a snap and told him I was heading to the concert. By then, he felt like my little online boyfriend. We talked every single day, and on Snapchat, he was definitely the one with the little heart next to his name. My favorite person.

I don't know what it was about him, but he brought out such a soft side of me.

Right before the concert, I posted a video of me getting ready and singing along to that song that goes, "they done took me off the market."

He replied, "You're officially off the market."

I laughed at first, but deep down, it made me pause. I didn't even know him in person... and yet, something about the way we connected felt real. Well- at least to me.

I've always believed in love.

And what's meant to be... will always find its way.

For years, we had talked about finally meeting in person, but the timing never lined up. I told myself that this year, I'd find a way to make it happen. But I was juggling so much. My schedule was insane between collabs, paid partnerships, nail appointments, content creation, motherhood, dog mom life, managing a household, teaching classes, and traveling. I was doing it all. And somehow, still being a loyal friend... and yeah, I guess, an online girlfriend too. Or so I thought.

I was juggling a lot in my head like usual, Some people say that I've never heard the word "No" before or that I don't know how to take "no" for an answer. The fact of the matter is that I got told "no" a lot when I was a kid let's not forget I couldn't even have a stereo in my room or a TV or trendy clothes or anything like that at a younger age all the luxuries came a little bit after And I liked it and I got used to it and I demanded it and I wanted it and now I do it for myself therefore, no I will no longer take "no" for an answer. I don't think that it's being spoiled. I think it's called standards. I have those standards for myself because I feel and know that I deserve it. And why would I accept crumbs and an appetizer when I can give myself the whole meal? I wanted everything for myself. The good, the calm, the house. THE TRUE LOVE!

Despite the work and goal chaos, I kept pushing out content because I had a goal:

My veneers.

I had dreamed of getting my teeth done for years, but I knew it would be expensive. So I planned to do the bottom row first, then the top. I booked consultations with multiple dentists, got quotes, and started saving. Once I locked in a provider, I reserved my hotel and prepped for the trip. It wasn't in San Antonio, so I'd need to travel and stay overnight.

Each tooth was about $1,000, and I was getting 14 veneers, plus having all my wisdom teeth pulled, a full dental cleaning, and a quote for the top row. It was a lot of money—but I was ready. I wanted this for myself.

On the drive to the appointment about three hours away I stayed on the phone with Secret Santa. We talked about everything. Goals. Dreams. Life. The future. I found out he was about six years older than me, which I found incredibly attractive. Something about older men who have wisdom and can teach you things you don't know? That's a whole different type of intimacy.

At the same time, I didn't know if I was ready to give my heart a real shot again.

I thought I needed to be fully healed first.

But that's not how healing works.

We don't heal first and love later.

We heal in love.

Through love.

Around love.

In the presence of people who are safe enough, stable enough, and willing enough to walk with us through the hard stuff.

A part of me really thought this might be it.

Our conversations were deep.

Our goals were aligned.

Our careers were similar.

We didn't have kids in common he didn't want any, and I already had two older boys and didn't want more. That felt like fate. Like for once, I might have found someone who could love me fully as I am, without needing to change me or break me down.

Someone who could protect me, pour into me, spoil me, and help build something beautiful with me.

This wasn't about anyone else.

This was about us.

About me finally being loved the way I deserved to be.

And I know some people might roll their eyes and say, "Girl, you didn't even know him in person."

But I swear… the emotional intimacy, the mental connection, the comfort we had through the phone it hit different. There's no other way to explain it.

And because I had focused so much on healing, self-care, and rebuilding my peace…

I knew I had it in me to love again.

To give again.

To believe again.

Everything in my life felt aligned almost perfect. I had just bought my brand-new BMW X3, and my TikTok had officially hit 300,000 followers. I was glowing, building, and finally standing in the woman I had worked so hard to become. Life was flowing with momentum, and I didn't want to risk it not for the wrong man, not for another heartbreak.

I was cautious. I had worked too hard to build what I had. I wasn't about to invite in someone who might carry a secret life a wife, a kid, a second family in another state, or emotional baggage I wasn't willing to unpack. My past had taught me to double check everything... and then check it again. But despite the fear, something about him felt different. A quiet part of me hoped I wasn't wrong this time.

After months of voice messages and daily snaps, I finally worked up the courage to ask if we could FaceTime. I just wanted to see him. To know without a doubt that the man I'd been talking to was real. That he really looked like the photos. That his expressions matched his energy. That I wasn't getting catfished or played. And honestly... I just wanted to see him smile. Hear him laugh. Watch how his eyes moved when he was deep in thought.

I already knew he was attractive he had muscles, a beard, and those sky-colored eyes that were somewhere between blue and green marble. But FaceTime made it feel official. We set it up like a date, like a doctor's appointment we didn't want to miss.

When the call connected, I was so shy. My stomach had butterflies like I was sixteen again. My cheeks hurt from smiling so much. And I don't know what it was... but something about that call hit me in a way I didn't expect.

Tears welled up in my eyes while writing this, because in that moment it meant more to me than I knew how to explain. We hadn't even met in person yet, and still... I felt something. Something deep. It wasn't about the gifts. It wasn't about the flirtation. It was the conversations. The connection. The way he comprehended me.

The way he made space for my dreams, fed my ambition, supported my mindset.

We could talk about anything religion, politics, business, love, culture. And even when we didn't agree, we respected each other's views. There was no power struggle. No tension. Just understanding. Just flow.

That FaceTime call? It was the cherry on top.

We ended up talking for over an hour, and I was still shy by the end of it but I called every single one of my friends afterward, telling them, "I finally met Secret Santa on FaceTime… and he's dreamy. Like, actual dream material."

After that, we kept talking like usual. Every day. Little check-ins, snaps, random thoughts, good mornings and goodnights. It became routine. Natural. Easy.

That summer was everything.

The fall? Even better.

When Halloween rolled around again, I went all out like I always do. I won House of the Year again. Bought even more decorations. Made gift bags for my clients. Filmed endless Halloween nail

content. My creativity was on fire.

And then I signed a contract with a major nail company, and they invited me to do a meet-and-greet at one of the top beauty expos: the Premiere Show in San Antonio. It was surreal. I knew the turnout would be big this was my city, and my socials were buzzing. But that didn't stop the anxiety.

This man called me super early to make sure I was up and ready! He watched me on FaceTime get ready and I broke out in hives. He helped me stay cool and I took breaks throughout the day to call him and stay in touch with him since it was going to be a long day. He was very supportive and understanding of me being busy with my career! I loved that!

My nerves were everywhere. I blasted the A/C, slathered my skin in eczema cream, and did deep breathing to calm myself down. I had planned my outfits weeks in advance, but nothing could calm the butterflies in my chest except him.

I had told him I was nervous. He told me I was going to kill it. That I was built for this. He believed in me in ways that made me believe in myself. He really was my number one hype man.

Honestly throughout the event, I'd step outside the convention center just to send him updates. Or I'd sneak away to the bathroom and text him, just to feel grounded again.

Yeah… I was really falling for a man I had never even met in person. LOL.

As the year began winding down, something in me clicked. He had been following me since 2016 or 2017 we had talked for the entire year consistently. And now, I finally felt ready. I wanted to meet in person. I wanted to see if the magic translated offline. So when one of my clients invited me to her formal wedding, I decided to ask him if he'd be my plus-one.

I was nervous. I had never brought anyone around my family. Not to weddings. Not to big events. It felt like such a big step, and I was scared of rejection. But when I asked… he said yes.

I helped him pick out his outfit it was an all-black wedding, so he needed to match the vibe. I found my own formal dress and made sure every detail was perfect. He made reservations at a beautiful resort, and just like that… it was countdown mode.

He was flying into Austin, so I planned to drive about an hour to go pick him up. I didn't mind. Honestly, I welcomed the drive, it gave me time to calm my nerves, breathe, mentally prepare. But I'd be lying if I said I wasn't nervous.

In my head, I imagined him walking out of the airport and pulling me into a hug maybe even lifting me off the floor. Real Hallmark movie energy. I know, I know. I've always been a softie deep down.

At the core of it all, I just wanted to feel safe enough to be soft again.

To be held. To trust.

I wanted to be loved out loud.

To be adored gently.

To be poured into with intention.

Because I had already built the empire. I had the business, the body, the bank account, the BMW, the brand coming soon.

But my heart?

My heart still wanted connection.

My heart still wanted home.

And maybe just maybe he was it.

The day had finally come. Wedding weekend.

I had told my clients and friends that he'd be flying in, and everyone was so excited for me especially because I had spoken about him for months. In my heart, I really felt like this might be it for me. I was nervous but glowing. Hopeful. Expectant. Giddy like a teenager again.

He landed at the Austin airport early that morning. I had already taken my everything shower, prepped my hair, makeup, and packed my formal dress with care. I loaded everything into my car and hit the road, heading toward Austin to pick him up. I was so early two hours early but I didn't mind. I didn't want to just pull up curbside and rush through the moment. I wanted to meet him. To greet him face to face. Walk with him to the car. Ease his nerves. Let him know I cared enough to show up fully.

I parked at the airport and hopped on a shuttle to the terminal. I checked his Snapchat and saw he had only posted a vague photo of his leg no caption or context.

I laughed to myself.

"He's such a guy."

He rarely posted anyway, and this wasn't out of character.

Then I saw him.

Walking out of the terminal. I ran to him and wrapped my arms around him... but he didn't greet me with the same warmth I expected. It wasn't mean. It just felt... off. A little cold. I brushed it off, telling myself it was nerves. He was from a small town. This was unfamiliar territory. A new city. A new experience. And let's be real I might've looked different in person. He used to joke that I looked 5'8" online, but I had warned him I'm barely 5'3" in real life. We laughed about that on the drive. I tried to keep things light.

After he grabbed his luggage, the first thing he did was search for a smoking area. He was a smoker not a dealbreaker for me. I was used to it. Most of my friends smoked, and I've always been the only one who didn't. Still, the whole energy between us felt... weird. It wasn't bad. Just awkward. Like we had all this online chemistry, but didn't quite know how to translate it into real life. I didn't expect it to be that hard, especially after everything we'd shared for almost a year.

We stopped at Buc-ee's for brisket sandwiches and headed to the resort. It was stunning two balconies, patio chairs, and the perfect view of the wedding set-up below. You could see the team setting out white chairs and floral arches for the ceremony the next morning. It was dreamy.

That night, I just wanted to sleep. I knew the next day would be long and full of eyes watching us. Everyone I knew was stalking my stories. My DMs were blowing up. People knew he had flown in. And I noticed... he did post some photos to his Snapchat story but only of the patio, or a leg again, or scenery. Nothing about me. Not even a hint. And I started spiraling a little.

"Why wouldn't someone want to show off their date?"

"Does he not like me?"

"Am I not what he expected?"

"Does he regret coming?"

The next morning, we got ready for the wedding. I wore my formal dress, and he cleaned up well. The event was absolutely beautiful. The bride my client had planned everything perfectly. The food, the open bar, the flowers, the music. It was the kind of wedding you dream of. The kind you remember.

He stayed serious for most of it. Quiet. And he kept going outside to smoke. I didn't take it personally I knew he was out of his element. Different state, different people, and let's be honest no matter how much we had talked, I was still a stranger in real life.

But what I didn't expect was… me being the one to ruin the night.

Let's just say… I got shitfaced.

I had one too many shots with my girls, and by the end of the night, I was gone. I blacked out. Not the best impression on a first date, huh? LOL.

I vaguely remember us walking back to the resort afterward. He walked ahead of me the whole time never reached for my hand, never guided me to the room. I stumbled behind him like a tipsy toddler in heels. It was strange. Cold. And it kind of hurt. But I was too drunk to process any of it in the moment.

I passed out on the bed like a full-on starfish. Then, in the middle of the night drunk and disoriented I woke him up, trying to have a heart-to-heart. Why? I don't even know. I just needed some kind of connection. Needed to feel him there. I think I annoyed him. He told me gently to go back to sleep. I asked if he was upset with me, and he said no but I could tell he wasn't thrilled either.

The next day, we spent it at Topgolf. Then dinner, I paid for our meal to be sweet and make up for the night before. I wanted him to feel appreciated. That Sunday night, we had dinner together and just relaxed. On Monday, I took him to the airport. We had breakfast before his flight. I didn't know if I'd ever see him again.

But it was beautiful, in its own weird way.

Meeting my Secret Santa in real life.

When he got back home, things felt a little… off. At first. But we fell back into rhythm. He sent me the most beautiful roses for Friendsgiving, and I used them as the centerpiece at my dinner table. I was so proud to show them off. For the first time in a long time, I felt like I had someone to call my man.

He even went out of his way trying to find peach cobbler because he knew it was my favorite and I had mentioned I wanted to serve it for Friendsgiving. The little details mattered to him. And they mattered to me.

By December, I was planning a trip to see him. I bought the ticket and everything I was ready to experience things on his turf. Let him show me his world. But the day before my flight, he got sick and we had to cancel.

I was crushed.

I had looked forward to it so much. And when I found out he was sick, something maternal in me activated. All I wanted was to go take care of him. Bring him soup. Rub his back. Be soft. Be there. But he insisted I stay home. And so I did. But I still called and FaceTimed him every day. He sounded drained. He had lost weight. I knew he wasn't well, and my heart ached for him.

For Christmas, he sent me a pair of Tiffany & Co. hoop earrings. We did a FaceTime call so he could watch me open the gift. I still remember his face on the screen pale, a little thinner, still handsome, but tired. He was sick most of that month.

Then came my birthday and he outdid himself.

He gifted me the giant Clase Azul Tequila bottle.

Yes, that one. The one I had told him about months earlier. The one I'd always wanted but never wanted to splurge on. He remembered. He paid attention.

It was honestly one of the best gifts I've ever received.

Not because it was expensive.

But because it was thoughtful.

Because it meant… he listened.

And what made it even funnier?

That was the same exact tequila I had gotten drunk on during our first date the wedding night.

I had genuinely thought I'd never see him again after that night.

But here we were.

I took a winery trip with my girlfriends that day too, and I filled him in and snapchatted him tons of pictures and videos while I was out. I missed him and I felt that I was catching a cold too.

That whole season of my life was so many things at once. Beautiful. Awkward. Emotional. Real. Imperfect. Hopeful. And even if it didn't turn into some long-term fairytale, I'll always be grateful for it.

Because it reminded me that I could still believe in people.

That I could still feel butterflies.

That I could still love without losing myself.

And most importantly…

That I deserved someone who listens.

Who remembers.

Who shows up.

Even if just for a season.

Chapter 32

Soft Life, Heavy Heart

A new year did true love finally find me?!

All my life, I've been a hopeless romantic. I kind of blame this on my dad and being Latina. Like, how can you compare a "te amo," "mi reina," "mi princesa," or "mi corazón" to just "I love you" in English? I want my man to struggle to breathe when I'm not around because he loves me that much. Lol.

Some people might say I have daddy issues, but I say I have reverse daddy issues. That's a thing, right? I mean, you already know I didn't have the best relationship with my dad but I also didn't have the worst. We had a pretty good last decade together, even though he was behind bars.

Whatever my mom got for gifts, I usually got a mini version too. Don't forget, I'm the only girl with three brothers. So, for example, if my mom got 100 roses on Valentine's Day, I would get 50. If she got a necklace, I got a bracelet. If she got roses, a necklace, a ring, and a huge bear I'd get the roses, the bracelet, and the mini bear. Okay, okay, you get me!

If there's one thing about my dad he was a very detailed person. Very materialistic, too. I feel like his love language was gift-giving, never receiving. The man wasn't perfect I'm not saying that at all but he knew how to give a good gift.

Okay, enough of the mushy stuff. Let's get into the meat and potatoes.

Was I still seeing Secret Santa? I was.

Our relationship actually got closer after the holidays. I told you we went through a rough patch after our first time together in November me getting drunk didn't help then he got sick, and I got sick too. But for some reason, he always called to check on me. Even with raspy throats and a nasty cough, we'd still FaceTime. It was embarrassing I even had a fever blister on my lip. Probably the worst winter for both of us, but somehow, it brought us closer.

I wanted to see him so badly while he was sick. I just wanted to fly out and take care of him, but he didn't let me. I'm glad he didn't, because I ended up getting sick too.

I had to reschedule some appointments in January because the sickness lasted longer than I expected. I even had a trip planned with my kids to Colorado that I had to cancel I was that sick. I was stuck in bed for more than two weeks. No appointments, no shopping, no stepping out, nothing.

Honestly, I don't even know how I got through my birthday, New Year's Eve, and the new year. It was rough. I guess the mom in me has always taught me to suck it up. I could be going through the worst time ever, and you'd never know.

And because I wasn't seeing clients or working, I didn't have much content to film. I wasn't going to the gym, I wasn't stepping out I was just trying to survive. My favorite neighbor would come over and bring me homemade soup and food. Lots of comfort food, just to make sure I was eating. She knows I'm always taking care of everyone else, so she stepped in and took care of me. She was all I had, to be honest. I have no family or anyone to fall back on here in San Antonio.

To push out content, I started looking up recipes on Pinterest and TikTok. I'd recreate soups and simple meals just so I had something to post.

Secret Santa and I both started feeling better after a couple of weeks. He had a snowmobile trip coming up that annual one he always did with his friends. I think he had already done it once or twice before, so it was turning into a tradition. I was genuinely excited for him. I knew he'd been sick and working nonstop before that, and he deserved to get away.

Not gonna lie, though I was still a little upset. I didn't get to see him in November when I originally bought my ticket. I had to cancel the night before my flight. So part of me was sad, but I was still happy he got to spend time with his friends.

Honestly, I've always wanted to be in a relationship with someone who had their own circle. Someone who could go out to eat or spend time with their friends and not always have to be with me. In all my previous relationships, they never really had their own life they wanted to do everything with me. And while that sounds cute, I had already created a circle of friends that I liked to travel with, hang out with, and do my own thing. I wanted a partner who could do the same.

Of course I want my partner to choose me as their forever best friend, but I still think it's healthy for both people to have their own friendships outside the relationship. And honestly, everything was going so good between us.

Just to throw this in I'm so glad I took Christmas photos with my kids before all of this. If I had waited, I wouldn't have been able to take our annual pajama Christmas pictures. And this year's photos? They came out amazing.

As the day got closer to his trip, he told me he wanted to spend as much time as possible talking to me on the phone to give me the time and attention I deserved because while he was on vacation, he wouldn't be able to.

He mentioned he'd be staying in a winter cabin with no service and would be out snowmobiling all day in remote areas that also had no signal. I understood that.

Not only did this man own his own company, but he also had another job which I loved, because I had finally met someone who thought like me. I owned my own business and worked in corporate too. A lot of people don't understand that hustle or why we do it, but I understood him completely. We had so much in common.

Monday through Thursday, while he was at work, he'd call me every single day around the same time. It became a routine. At first, he would ask if it was okay to call me and I eventually told him he didn't need to ask. We were in a relationship. He could call me whenever he needed or wanted to. I wanted him to feel safe in that.

But after he left work, I wouldn't hear from him much. He might check in here and there or send one message in the evening asking how my day was and that would be it. Sometimes, we'd even go to bed without saying goodnight, which felt strange to me. Still, I didn't bring it up. He was older than me, and I didn't know if I was just being immature about it, so I let it go.

Every day leading up to his trip, I was genuinely excited for him. I'd ask him, "Are you excited? Are you ready to see your friends? Ready to unwind?" But he always sounded irritated, like he didn't want to go. I tried to be understanding. He had just gotten over a bad cold or flu, had lost a lot of weight, and wasn't fully recovered. He wasn't feeling his best, and I could hear that in his tone. But I stayed positive and reminded him I wasn't upset about the trip I wasn't the type of woman to guilt him for taking time with his friends. I genuinely wanted him to enjoy himself.

The night before he flew out, we talked on the phone pretty late. I told him I'd miss him. I had gotten used to hearing from him every day. But after that call, I didn't hear from him at all. Not a single phone call for six full days.

No airport updates.

No morning calls.

No goodnight texts.

Nothing.

He would only send me Snapchats or short messages. I'd send him videos of me working with clients or pictures from my day. A part of me started to feel uneasy like maybe he was doing something he wasn't supposed to but I asked him for a picture, and he sent one of him laying down in his Airbnb room. That helped me calm down a little.

While I worked, my clients would often ask how my relationship was going. I always said it was going great. I'd tell them about the snowmobile trip, about how he was in a remote place with no service. I made excuses for him because I believed him. He had never given me a reason not to trust him.

But on day six of that trip, I snapped.

I decided to break up with him.

I sent him a message on Snapchat. Calm. Collected. I told him I didn't think I could do this anymore not because I didn't care, but because six days of silence felt really wrong. It wasn't anger. It was just me being honest.

This man was a business owner. He had a company to run. I knew he had to be checking in on his business. So in my mind, if he could make a phone call for his company he could have made one for me too.

When he saw my message, he replied saying we needed to talk and that he didn't want to text about it.

But even then... he still didn't call.

He finally called the next day once he was home.

I took his call, and we worked things out. We stayed on the phone, and I told him I never wanted to go through something like that again in our relationship. He agreed. We promised each other that we'd never go days without speaking again. I told him I don't ask for much, but that was one of my non-negotiables. I can't be in a relationship where we just disappear on each other.

To be honest, I was already super busy with my own projects. Like I mentioned before, I was working on building my future brand, and that kept me occupied day and night. I didn't ask for help, and I didn't have any. I was doing everything on my own, and I knew staying busy was the best way to stay grounded.

A few days later, Valentine's Day was right around the corner I want to say about nine days out. Don't quote me on that, but one day, I received the most beautiful bouquet I had ever seen. It was full of vibrant red roses, with a heartfelt card, balloons, and a plush animal. I was genuinely surprised and so freaking happy.

That morning, we FaceTimed for hours. I couldn't stop smiling. We talked about the most random things, just to stay on the phone together. Before the bouquet arrived, he said he had been getting nervous because it hadn't been delivered yet while we were on the call. I wasn't expecting anything from him at all, but when it arrived? I was over the moon. The roses, the card, the effort it made me feel so seen.

He always added handwritten notes to the gifts or flowers he sent, and those notes made everything feel even more special. We hadn't said "I love you" to each other yet, but I would send him little messages with "143" in them and when he sent me those Valentine's Day roses, he wrote "143" on the card too.

My inner Yesi was screaming.

I gifted him a custom-made blue bouquet from The Million Roses elegant and timeless. I added a personalized video slideshow with pictures and videos of us from the past year. I can't even remember what song I picked the website gave a few options and I chose the one that felt sweet and light. I also wrote him a small note that said, "To our first Valentine's… and many more to come."

I loved those roses because they were everlasting just like how I wanted our relationship to be. That same week, I hosted a Galentine's Day for my best friends. It was such a vibe pasta, wine, and DIY canvas paintings I had ordered. I decorated the entire house with heart-shaped balloons, red everything, Valentine's napkins, and themed plates in the kitchen. I even used the bouquet he sent me as the centerpiece for the table. I was so proud to show them off. He had sent so many balloons, I felt like the luckiest girl alive.

My girlfriends came over, we smiled, laughed, took pictures we pulled an all-nighter. They couldn't believe I had never seen The Notebook before, so they made me watch it. It was hilarious and chaotic in the best way. And since I was still awake around two or three in the morning, I kept messaging him on Snapchat, and he replied everytime.

He had trouble sleeping, so our random late-night conversations flowed easily.

I also made Valentine's bags for every one of my clients. Each bag had a mini sugar scrub for their hands, a brush, cuticle oil, candy little touches that made people feel loved and appreciated. Every detail mattered. Love was in the air, baby.

I didn't forget about my boys either. I took them out on little Valentine's dates and made them their own baskets filled with their favorite candies and goodies. We even went to see the new Bob Marley movie. I had been so excited to watch it. It wasn't my favorite, but I've always been a fan of his music. Something about it reminds me of the beach peaceful, timeless.

Everything just felt so aligned. My business was thriving. I was building my brand quietly in the background. My friends were doing well. And for the first time in a long time, I had a real relationship one that felt healthy and mutual.

My life finally felt... full.

This whole time, I had been working on my brand and honestly, it was starting to stress me out. I was constantly rejecting samples, and not to mention, I had to pay for every single one. It was draining a lot of my money. I had to file for a trademark to secure my brand name, and because I wanted my brand to be available nationwide, I knew I needed help from someone who actually knew what they were doing.

So I hired a lawyer someone experienced in handling the application preparation, registration, Amazon brand registry, and all the government office filings. I didn't want to risk messing it up by trying to do it alone. Having someone manage it professionally brought me a lot of peace of mind.

I also hired an e-commerce specialist to help with all the backend work. I wanted my products to be available on Amazon so customers could receive their items quickly Prime shipping, two-day delivery, or even overnight. Some areas in San Antonio even had same-day shipping. That was the goal.

The e-commerce specialist handled everything on Seller Central: uploading listings, fixing pricing issues, doing keyword research, creating optimized titles, and solving listing problems like suppressed items or parent-child variation errors. He also input all the related attributes for a perfect listing, loaded high-volume keywords into the search term fields, and created FBA shipments for fulfillment.

To be honest, I was putting in double shifts doing nails just to pay these people. I knew I wasn't educated enough to handle all of this on my own, and I didn't want to add more stress on top of everything I was already managing. Hiring help was the smartest choice. I stuck to what I knew and paid professionals for the rest. It was the only way to keep moving forward without burning out.

There was so much happening behind the scenes way more than just being a nail tech or a mom.

On the brighter side, I had just surprised one of my brothers and his wife with a Christmas, birthday, and anniversary gift all in one. I got them a winery trip. It was hilarious because I printed out the vouchers, folded them up, and put them in a box with both their names on it. In another box, I included a separate "voucher" that said Free Babysitting meaning I'd take care of all their kids for the weekend. I knew they didn't get much time to themselves as a couple, so I wanted to give them something thoughtful.

And it worked out perfectly, because the trip was scheduled for February right around my brother's birthday and their anniversary . They came into town, and I watched all their kids while they went on the trip and let me tell you, I give all the credit to my sister-in-law. I don't know how she does it every day. I even forgot I needed to use the bathroom at one point because I was so busy. But I man-aged. They had a great time, and it was a total success.

And of course, I made TikTok videos with my nieces and nephew while they were here. I couldn't let the content opportunity pass me by.

Social media was booming. Life felt so good this year my social platforms, my family, my business, my finances, my children.

Everything was in sync. Everything was working.

I even took a girls trip with my best friends to Austin, Texas. We went to Sixth Street to party and celebrate one of their birthdays. We had booked an Airbnb, which ended up being a complete mess but it's hilarious now when we talk about it. One day, we'll probably tell the whole story on a podcast or something, because what happened that night was wild.

But that night? I was in full girlfriend mode. I blew up my boyfriend's Snapchat, text messages, and phone calls all night long. Isn't that what normal girlfriends do when they're in love? I wanted him to see everything I was doing, like "Look babe, we're out!" It was funny and cute. Oh and that Airbnb? If I could give it one star or even half a star, I would. It was that bad.

Life just felt soft.

My kids and I also took a weekend trip to TX2K24 an annual racing event with tons of cars, loud engines, and fast energy. It's the kind of thing you say yes to without hesitation when you're a boy mom. We had a blast but it was definitely expensive. Still worth every moment.

Any chance I got to go out with my friends or spend time with my kids, I took it. Because work was heavy behind the scenes. I was taking in way more clients than usual because I had so much to pay for with my brand. It was starting to consume me. It was taking my time, my money, and my energy. For months, it felt like the brand was only taking and giving nothing in return.

I was reaching a point where I didn't know if I wanted to keep pushing forward…

Or just quit altogether.

I asked the boys if they wanted to start a new tradition going to the movies every Wednesday. Not only did I need the quality time with them, but I needed time away from work too. And to top it off, it was five-dollar Wednesdays. We'd go see whatever was playing, grab some chicken wraps or wings, and enjoy our drinks. And when I say drinks I mean they were getting Dr. Pepper, and I was

Getting a Bahama Mama. Mama needed a break.

On Sundays, we'd go out for brunch together. My oldest was already old enough to drive, so I'd sit in the passenger seat, sometimes even ride in the back while they sat up front. I'd sip my mimosa and we'd go shopping afterward. It became a routine I truly looked forward to.

I was also working with a brand I had signed with the year prior creating content, promoting their products, and earning commission through my discount code. It was going really well.

If you haven't noticed by now, this was finally the season where I was living a softer life. I was able to take more time off and lean more into social media. My streams had increased. I wasn't just making money doing nails anymore I was earning from TikTok, Instagram, my Amazon storefront, my Etsy shop, and the nail brand I was partnered with. I was still receiving commission from Ethika and picking up occasional collabs with other companies too.

The boys and I made it a point to do something fun at least once a month. One of our favorite things we did was take a trip to see the Astros play in Houston. It was so much fun. We had done it before, and I wanted it to become an annual thing a fun little tradition just for us. Unlimited popcorn, gummies, drinks, and jerseys. It was pure joy. Humbly, I was no longer just the Michael Kors mom driving a Chrysler, building a salon with her kids asleep in the waiting room. I wasn't just the Tory Burch woman juggling nail clients and corporate hours while speeding off in a Camaro like an untamed lion.

Now, I was the Louis Vuitton woman.

The one with multiple income streams.

The one building her own brand.

The one driving her dream BMW SUV.

The one learning to take time for herself.

The one living a somewhat balanced life…

and finally happy in a mature, long-distance relationship.

This mom? She felt like she was winning.

I started doing more educational nail classes with the brand I was working with. I'd go teach at cosmetology schools, local workshops, and universities. It became another income stream and a great networking opportunity. The grind never slowed down.

Part of me loved staying busy it was growth, momentum, expansion but another part of me needed it. Because I was in a long-distance relationship, and it was hard. So hard. I loved him deeply, and sometimes FaceTime just wasn't enough.

You have to remember we had only seen each other in person once, at that formal wedding. We FaceTimed often, almost daily. But that's not the same.

I craved a hug.

Warmth.

Closeness.

I was a boss in the streets but I wanted to be a baby in my man's arms.

I was a little upset I didn't get to spend his birthday with him. I really wanted to do something special, but we couldn't make it happen. So I sent him a Louis Vuitton cologne with his initials engraved. Of course, I still called him I wasn't going to miss that. He spent his birthday getting another tattoo.

He was fully tatted up to his neck.

And I'm not gonna lie… I loved that. ALOT!

But long-distance?

It was hard.

Mother's Day came around, and I had originally planned to launch my brand that month. But everything seemed to be going wrong or not exactly wrong, just delayed. So my launch date got pushed back.

What stressed me out the most was that I was already paying everyone I'd hired. On top of that, I had all these recurring business expenses: subscriptions, my Amazon seller membership, GS1 barcodes, packaging, shipping materials, branding fees, logo design all of it was costing me. And once again, I was receiving nothing in return.

Finally, I did my first run. I launched one morning and within 72 hours, I was completely sold out.

I made my first $42,000 in just three days.

But don't get too excited.

Yes, things were going well... until they weren't.

I got in trouble because my trademark hadn't been finalized yet. And there was already another company with the name YNS. I ended up having to make last-minute adjustments to my brand name adding a period at the end just so I wouldn't get sued. Then my entire Amazon account got flagged. Multiple times. For multiple reasons.

Orders stopped. The account was frozen. Nothing could be processed until every correction was submitted, reviewed, and approved. So just when I thought I was finally recovering the money I had poured into this brand, there I was again spending more to fix everything. This is the part people don't talk about when they say they want to be a boss.

Everyone wants to own a business. Everyone wants to launch something. But no one talks about the actual struggle behind it.

I was pulling all-nighters just to keep everything afloat.

I even picked up a nasty habit of vaping out of pure stress.

I'd FaceTime my boyfriend and vent about everything I was dealing with and he was so supportive. For the first time, I was in a relationship where I felt heard. Seen. Understood. Because he was a business owner too, he got it. He understood the hustle. He understood the wins and the losses. He knew what it felt like to invest everything into something, only to see it fall apart and then keep going anyway.

Business is like a gamble:

You lose some. You win some.

And sometimes the losses come big…

just like the wins.

He and I could talk for hours about my plans, my goals, his dreams, his growth. We talked about family, our pets, business moves, personal struggles. All of it. It was such a comfort to have someone who didn't just sit on the other end of the phone nodding but someone who understood every word.

It brought me peace.

It gave me the strength to keep pushing.

He'd tell me, "Focus on the goal."

He'd say, "The struggle is always hardest at the beginning, because the reward God has for you at the end is that much bigger."

He was a God-fearing man and I trusted him when he said those things. His words brought me calm. I felt genuinely honored to have someone like him in my life. A man of faith. A man with a business mindset. Someone who matched my ambition.

We shared so much in common not just religion and politics, but our passion for fitness, too. And I'd already told you he supported my business early on. He'd bought merch and cheered me on, not because I needed it, but because he genuinely believed in me. I loved that.

As the months went by, I stayed extremely busy. I was traveling a lot with the kids, taking trips, living life. We went back to Hawaii, came home, and the hustle continued. I started mentioning him here and there to my family mostly my brothers. Nothing major. After all, yes, we were deeply connected through FaceTime and calls, but we still hadn't spent much time together in person.

And I'd catch a little attitude with him sometimes because I wanted more of him.

We'd talk consistently Monday through Thursday during his work week, usually in the mornings. On the weekends, communication was more sporadic. But I craved more than that. I wanted evenings together even if it was just a virtual dinner through FaceTime. Watching a movie at the same time from different homes. Corny, cheesy things like that. Things that keep the romance alive in long-distance.

But he thought those ideas were childish. He said he was too exhausted after work. I mean I was too, so fair.

So... we never did any of that.

And I didn't push it.

He kept sending me cute gifts. Every six weeks or so, I'd get a surprise bouquet of flowers and sometimes he'd go a little longer, and then suddenly send them back-to-back just because. Each one came with a sweet, handwritten note that I saved and used as book-marks in my Bible.

I loved this man so deeply.

Every time the florist showed up at my door, I'd get so excited. He knew me by name at that point. I'd hear him on the Ring camera say, "Your boyfriend sent you flowers," and I'd run to the door. He was a funny Mexican man and his deliveries always made my day.

By the time June came around, I couldn't hold it in anymore. I told my boyfriend I didn't think I could do this long-distance relationship much longer. I felt like I was constantly breaking up with him but it wasn't because I didn't want to be with him. It was just hard. Really hard. All I wanted was to see him.

It had been six full months since I'd last seen him in person. And it was driving me nuts.

I had an upcoming beauty show in Florida one of the biggest of the year. I was scheduled to be on stage, meeting people, doing videos, pictures, the whole thing. I had already shopped for all my outfits, formal gowns I was genuinely excited for it. But I took a chance and asked if I could fly to see him for a day or two before heading to Florida.

The plan was to fly to him first, spend a day together, and then continue on to Florida. I had already paid for the main flight, I just needed to add a stop and he said yes. He paid the difference for my flight so I could come see him.

I've always been about my money and my business, but I was desperate to be near the man I loved. So the fact that he said yes? It filled me with joy.

When I landed and saw him waiting at the airport, I was nervous but mostly excited. I wanted to see what it would feel like to be with him in his space, his world. When he came to visit me months before, it had felt slightly awkward. He wasn't in his city, not around his friends, not in his element. But this? This felt different.

As we were driving to his house, my mind wouldn't stop racing. I was excited, but scared. I hadn't been with a man like this in so many years. I couldn't help but think what if something happens to me? What if history repeats itself? What if Dallas repeats itself? What if I get hurt?

But I was also so hopeful.

When we took the final turn, and I saw the GPS screen with his address pulling up I could feel the adrenaline in my body. My palms were sweating. My chest got hot. I felt like I might throw up. But I didn't say anything. I just took deep breaths and played it off. I was embarrassed to admit how nervous I really was.

But when we got to his house, it all faded. I was shy at first, but everything felt calm. He said I was acting different and I probably was. Now I was the one in a new city, a new state, completely out of my element.

But it was beautiful.

The views mountains, trees, wide open skies it felt like Oregon all over again. A huge part of me lit up. There was something about it that touched my roots. It was a confusing feeling. Because yes, I've always felt like a city girl... but if we're being honest, I was born and raised in a trailer home in one of the smallest towns in Oregon. There's a country girl in me too.

In that moment, I felt safe.

I felt secure.

Like no one could touch me or talk to me because I knew he would protect me.

I felt pretty.

He had made dinner reservations. I wore my silver, pointy red bottoms and a casual summer dress. The restaurant was elegant country on the outside, but so classy on the inside. The view from our table was stunning. The appetizers were perfect. Crab cakes. A bottle of wine. It was everything I could've hoped for.

But I was still in my head.

Still nervous.

Still trying to enjoy every moment while holding back a thousand thoughts.

I found myself wondering again Where am I from?

Where do I belong?

Could I move here?

I felt like I was Ni de aquí, ni de allá.

Not from here. Not from there.

Floating between two worlds.

It scared me because I had worked so hard to build what I had in San Antonio. And I wasn't dating just to pass time. I was dating for marriage. For longevity. I knew if things got serious, I'd be the one to move. He had a business rooted there. I was fortunate that my job could travel with me, but let's be honest the volume of nail clients and business I had built in San Antonio? It wouldn't be the same anywhere else.

Still… money isn't everything.

I've always thought deeper than that.

I grew up watching my dad play soccer on the weekends. We didn't have a lot, but we had time. And love. And simplicity.

Of course, I love a good life. Who doesn't?

But I've learned that it goes way beyond finances.

The second I got to his house, I texted my friend. I told her everything how excited I was, how nervous, how surreal it all felt. And of course, I shared my location. Safety first.

That didn't last long because I immediately had to catch a flight to Florida for my show. And honestly? It was a blast. Everything about it was amazing the energy, the people, the talent. Some of the most incredible content creators were there: hairstylists, nail techs, tattoo artists, DJs, photo booths, food trucks. The whole thing had a vibe like no other. It was everything you could possibly imagine.

But after that trip, my relationship started to feel… awkward.

Why? Because I would message him, and he would take forever to reply. I wouldn't hear from him as often. He would say he was super busy or that he didn't have his phone with him. He told me he left his phone at home while he worked on the farm and didn't get home until late. He'd say there was no reception at the farm. His messages became dry. Something about it just didn't feel right.

I shook it off. A part of me thought, maybe because of my past experiences, I was overthinking. Maybe I was being too much. I never let him know what I was feeling, but in my head, I couldn't stop questioning it. Meanwhile, I was enjoying the palm trees, the warm air, the drinks, the Florida restaurants, the amazing food. During our time off from the show, I relaxed by the pool, went to the beach, and explored with some of my colleagues. And when I flew back home, I arrived to the most beautiful gift.

I was so excited.

This man had heard me mention, more than once, how much I loved vacuuming my floors every day because my two puppies shed so much hair. My old vacuum barely worked, and I'd told him the one I really wanted was a Dyson. But it was expensive. I always spent my money on gifts for others, on my kids, on my home. When it came to spending money on myself, I was tight. Not because I was greedy with myself, but because for the longest time I didn't feel like I deserved it. My job was to be a mother. To make them the priority. I always came last.

So when I walked in and saw the Dyson, I was stunned.

I filmed an unboxing video, put it together, and FaceTimed him. I still remember it like it was yesterday me, grinning from ear to ear, showing him my new vacuum. And all he said was, "Was that the one you wanted?"

I died.

I couldn't even find the words to thank him. This wasn't about the gift it was about him paying attention. About him noticing something I needed, something I wanted, and quietly making it happen. But things were still the same. Monday through Thursday mornings, he'd call, and I'd sometimes hear from him sporadically on the weekends. But we never went a full day without at least a text. And every single day, without fail, I had my good morning message. Always at five in the morning, sometimes even 3:30am or 4:00am because he was an hour ahead of me.

We'd been talking for almost a year, and that good morning message never failed. I remember one specific morning when I woke up and it wasn't there. I sent him a dramatic message saying, "Did you forget about me? Where's my man?" He started laughing and said, "Dang, I forgot to message my girl." It was funny, but it also reminded me of how consistent he had been with that one little thing.

Back home, my hustle didn't stop. YNS had launched. Everything was fixed now. New designs were coming out. Amazing content was being pushed. I was still taking trips with my kids. We had our weekly date nights. I started going to concerts with my friends. I'd never been much of a concert girl, but I was trying to stay busy, trying to have a life outside of work. Many of my friends had boyfriends, some were even married. I felt left out. I wanted more of my man. I wanted to see him, touch him, cuddle with him. I wanted all those things but I couldn't have them. So going out with the girls, going to a concert or dinner, doing brunch with my kids, shopping with them, hitting the gym that became my escape, my small joys. I'm a workaholic. What can I say?

I also started sending out PR boxes for my brand, mailing them to influencers. I hosted giveaways on my social platforms. I was going live which was another stream of income I hadn't even mentioned before. The streams were stacking up.

My mom life was beautifully balanced.

My love life finally existed even though it was long-distance.

My business was thriving.

Everything was… perfect.

Until it wasn't.

Chapter 33

"It Was a Tiffany Kind of Love. I Gave Everything Soft in Me In Case This Was Forever. But It Was Matching Pajamas & Mismatched Energy."

Yes, you heard that right my TikTok account, my biggest social media platform, got hacked.

And it happened right before my payout.

That month's payout was nearly $8,000.

TikTok had become a major income stream for me. I was making thousands a month sometimes even that much from a single video and all of it was being reinvested directly into my brand. Everything felt perfectly balanced in my mind.

Doing nails? That covered my bills.

Instagram, Amazon storefront, collaborations all of that was my extra play money, the kind I could use for trips, fun experiences, or treating my kids.

But TikTok?

TikTok was funding my future.

It was the stream I was using to build up savings toward real estate. I was putting away a percentage of every payout to use as a down payment. I was also paying off debts so that when the time came to get a mortgage, my debt-to-income ratio would be in perfect shape.

Not that I had much debt to begin with I've always run my businesses cash-based. No major loans. Just my vehicles and the usual cost-of-living bills.

The only thing I'd ever borrowed was a Stripe Capital loan through my booking system, which I highly recommend for anyone starting a business. It automatically pulls a small percentage from each transaction, and no credit check is required. The amount they offer is based on your business's existing income and activity. It's an amazing safety net when you need it.

But when I got hacked, it impacted everything.

It didn't just hurt my TikTok it trickled down into every area of my life.

It affected my YNS brand, my Amazon storefront sales, and even my Instagram momentum, where I had just hit 60,000 followers and was getting over 6 million views a month.

That may not sound like a lot to some people but to me, it meant everything.

TikTok was my main platform and my marketing engine. I had linked all my YNS nail tip videos with my shop URLs, and I relied on that traffic for conversions.

So when the account went down, my sales started dropping.

I tried throwing money into advertising to compensate, but it didn't match the organic reach I'd built.

On top of that, I had to pay my e-commerce specialist to help troubleshoot campaigns and adjust ads because I'm not super tech savvy with the backend of things. So here I was investing again, pouring more money out and getting less and less in return.

I remember one day, sitting with my best friend and going through the paper trail in my agenda.

I've always been super visual I need things on paper. My journals, planners, and notebooks are how I process.

And as I looked over my bank statements, I saw it clear as day.

I had nearly $82,000 saved.

I had worked so hard for that. And I was finally at a point where I could consider stepping back, taking a break from nonstop work, and seriously deciding if I was ready to invest in a property. I wanted to slow down, just for a second, and look at where I wanted to root myself.

But I didn't pull the trigger. I held off on house shopping and real estate deals because of the long-distance relationship I was in. I wanted to be sure.

I knew deep in my heart that I wanted to be with this man. And I didn't know what the future held but I also didn't want to be locked down in Texas if he turned around and told me I was the one.

If that happened, I wanted to be ready.

I wanted the option to pack up and go to start a life with the man I loved.

That mattered to me more than money or business ever could.

Because for me, it's never just been about the money.

It's about the freedom money gives you.

The ability to choose your joy, your peace, your home.

To spend your time and holidays with the people you love.

And I've always believed I could be successful anywhere.

Even before the relationship, I told my kids:

"I'm building something so I can be free."

I wanted to create a business I could take anywhere. And when they eventually moved out off to college or their own paths I told them I'd probably move somewhere different. Maybe somewhere by the beach.

Maybe I'd launch a course or run an online store from afar.

Maybe I'd keep doing nails wherever I went.

Hell, I even joked about moving to Dubai one day.

Because the dream has never been to stay stuck.

The dream has always been freedom.

I knew exactly what it was like to start from nothing.

I wasn't afraid of moving to a different city or even a different state and starting over. I had done it before. The idea didn't scare me.

I also knew that he came from a very small town, so if I ever did move with him, my life wouldn't look anything like what I had built in San Antonio. But still, a huge part of me felt like maybe this was finally my time.

Maybe I was finally entering the season where I could be soft.

Where a man could love me and take care of me.

Where I could sit outside with my morning coffee, rocking gently on a porch chair while the sun rose and the deer walked across the back pasture.

I pictured myself cooking and baking in a cozy kitchen for the love of my life.

A simple life. A soft one. A humble one.

Don't get me wrong I still wanted success. I still had ambition.

But I also wanted the kind of love that made your skin glow.

The kind where all you need is a little tinted moisturizer and some lashes because you're that happy. That radiant. That full.

Still, while I was dreaming of that future, I was fighting for my present. I tried everything to recover my hacked TikTok account. I had my followers tagging TikTok hundreds of times a day, praying it would help me get noticed. I even opened a second TikTok page. But none of it felt right I just wanted my page back. My community. My audience. My brand.

This was one of those times in life when I was especially grateful that I'd always lived below my means. I didn't have a $3,000 mortgage or some luxury lifestyle to maintain. That decision saved me.

Because when you're self-employed, these moments are your version of a layoff.

Your version of losing everything in a blink.

Eventually, I did get my TikTok account back.

But when I logged in, it didn't feel the same.

It felt like when someone breaks into your home. Even after everything's "fixed," something in you doesn't feel safe anymore. It's like your space has been violated. Like the energy shifted.

The algorithm was completely thrown off. My views were tanked.

It felt like starting from scratch all over again.

But I reminded myself I'd built it once. I'd built it twice.

And if I had to, I'd do it again. I wasn't going to stop.

I remember the exact moment I hit my breaking point.

I was lying in the hot tub in my backyard, crying just done emotionally.

I had worked so hard for everything I had. The hours, the sacrifices, the content, the pressure. It was all unraveling so fast.

I was on the phone with my boyfriend, trying to explain what this meant for me, how deeply it was affecting me financially, mentally, emotionally.

And all he said was:

"Yeah, I bet that sucks. It's like someone stripped your livelihood from you."

I don't know what I expected.

But it wasn't that. lol

It felt like a punch in the gut.

I remember thinking: Is this the kind of response a future husband gives? I was so lost for a minute.

Wouldn't the man I was planning a life with want to do something?

Wouldn't he offer some kind of encouragement some support, anything?

Would he help me pay a bill? Would he step in, just a little?

Would he see me?

I started questioning everything.

Was this really the man I was holding space for?

Was this truly the love of my life?

Or was I building a soft life with someone who wasn't building it with me?

I had access to some things, like his HBO Max account and things like that and don't get me wrong, I appreciated those gestures But I was in my head. BAD...

And to top it all off right after getting hacked my brand YNS started going through one of the hardest seasons ever.

A lot of my packages were being returned. I was losing money left and right. Some of the boxes for my nail tips were breaking during shipment, and when customers received them damaged, they would immediately return them. That meant I wasn't just losing the sale I was being charged again.

I was still paying for the Amazon FBA membership, the taxes, the transaction fees, and now on top of that, I was getting billed for returns. And if a delivery arrived a day late and the customer complained, they were issued a partial refund which came out of my pocket.

It wasn't just one or two packages here and there either. It was bulk orders. It was bad.

Eventually, I had to request a product removal from Amazon FBA, which meant all my inventory got shipped back to me. My house ended up looking like a warehouse.

I had boxes everywhere.

I went through every single one by hand checking which were damaged, which were still good, reboxing the good ones, printing fresh labels, and shipping them back out to Amazon warehouses. At that point, my products were already stocked in over 48 fulfillment centers across the U.S. And in some states, there were three to five warehouses per region. I also had products listed and shipping internationally in Mexico, Canada, and Brazil.

It was a massive mess.

A complete failure.

And it was costing me thousands.

I was stressed in every way imaginable physically, emotionally, financially but I was still trying to push out content. Still smiling online. Still promoting brand deals, working on my online stores, being a mom, a fur mom, and maintaining a long-distance relationship.

I was doing the most.

I felt like a lemon being squeezed for every last drop of juice.

But I'll tell you what I never lost my passion. I never lost my drive.

No matter how exhausted I was, I knew I had it in me to keep growing.

The only nasty habit I picked up during that time was vaping. I was so stressed, I started to lose my voice. I wasn't sleeping well. I had nightmares. I would wake up in the middle of the night for no reason, or stay up all night working on my business. I was trying to post content, make sales, answer DMs, manage emails, stay relevant. I was trying to keep my body in shape so I'd still feel beautiful and attractive for myself and my boyfriend.

There were mornings I would wake up at 4 AM just to talk to the universe. I'd pray for my business. I'd pray over his business too. I prayed for my children.

I was trying so hard to hold it all together.

But I could feel myself burning out.

Some of my clients started to get upset because I wasn't as available, or because I was taking weekends off to rest, sleep in, go out for a meal, hit the gym to nourish myself.

Even when I wasn't doing okay, I still made sure to take care of them.

Nobody on social media knew what I was going through.

No friends knew either.

Nobody saw that side of me.

I've always been good at hiding what's really going on behind the scenes.

The only person who ever saw the reality the crying, the yelling, the exhaustion, the 12-hour sleeps, the 2 AM wake-ups was my boyfriend.

My secret Santa.

He saw the prettiest version of me, and he also saw the ugliest.

And that's something I will always be grateful for.

"You do not build a profitable brand by trying to cater to everybody.

You build it by showing up for the clients who value you and your work."

However in my personal life, I genuinely just needed a break. I needed time with my man to reset and feel loved.

If I'm being honest, I needed a moment away from everything work, kids, clients, social media.

And I still hadn't seen him since the Florida show.

We had also started arguing a bit more.

Nothing major just little things. But most of it stemmed from me missing him.

I would tell him how hard it was to be apart. How all of my friends had their husbands or boyfriends around and I just wanted time with mine.

And he'd always say:

"We're building something real. Let's not rush anything. We're building for longevity, not just for fun."

And truthfully? He was right.

I tried my best to be patient. I really did.

Patience isn't my strongest trait, but I'm a pretty boring person. I'm super disciplined.

Waiting wasn't going to kill me.

I'm a Capricorn, okay? All I do is make money, shop online, and stay home.

And I love it that way.

Finally, August came and I got to see my man again.

I made sure my kids had meals prepped, the house was spotless, the pets were either at home and cared for or dropped off at doggy daycare.

I scheduled all my clients before leaving, even though I wasn't going to be gone long.

But even two days away from home two days away from work made a huge difference.

I told him that it was better for me to travel to him, because I could stay at his house. If he came to San Antonio, he'd have to book a hotel, eat out for every meal it would've been way more expensive, and I didn't want to add to his stress.

At least if I was there, I could cook at home and we didn't have to go out.

Not to mention I've told y'all this before I'm a huge homebody.

I love being at home.

I'm the type to wear a formal dress and red bottoms just to read a book on the couch.

I will glam up and still refuse to leave the house.

Fashionably homebound. Lol.

Time with my boyfriend felt like I could completely shut off. I didn't care about social media, my phone, or anything outside of that house when I was with him. Everything was peaceful. Everything was calm. He'd wake up in the mornings and bring me breakfast in bed not that he cooked it, but he'd go out and pick it up for us. He hooked me up with some Livermush. Try it if you haven't!

I'd catch little moments of him vacuuming the house while I was still laying in bed, and it was the cutest thing ever. Since the weather was warm but not too hot, he even took me out on his Harley. Well once. He took me for one ride. Not gonna lie, it wasn't really my thing. I even lost a pair of Ray-Bans during the ride.

What can I say? I've never been an outside girl.

I can't help but laugh about it now.

But we had such a good time. Just being around his house, seeing all his trophies on the wall, it made me feel like we had even more in common than I realized. I had competed in bodybuilding in the past and had been involved in nail competitions too. So seeing that he had a competitive streak in him that he had earned those trophies that tickled something in me.

I was only there for two days before heading back home, but I left hoping we'd start seeing each other more often.

Once I got back home, I jumped right back into business. YNS was finally settling again. My nail clients were steady, and the business was still doing amazing. San Antonio had brought me close to so many incredible women. I felt loved and supported. They would bring me the most creative nail sets and designs, and they'd let me film their sessions without hesitation.

Everyone around me was genuinely happy that I had finally found a relationship someone to love and be loved by.

I had spoken to my mother and my brothers, of course. I share my location with them, so they knew I was traveling not just for work anymore but for my relationship too. And I was excited. For the first time, everything felt like it was falling into place.

I was a little nervous about what the future might hold, but I would reassure my clients that I wasn't moving anytime soon and if I ever did, I'd give them plenty of notice. I was still choosing myself, but I wasn't rushing anything.

This time, we only went about two months without seeing each other before I flew back out in August.

And that's when it happened.

I met the parents.

I'm screaming inside even writing that because he told me I was going to meet his parents literally the night before I flew out. I was so excited. That was the moment I knew things were getting serious.

We had been arguing a little more over the phone like a real married couple. I had even told him I was having trouble sleeping sometimes, like something was bothering me and I couldn't quite place it. So going out there more often and now getting to meet his parents really helped ease my mind.

When I arrived, he took us out to a fancy restaurant. We took pictures together, and he looked so fine. I mean fine fine. He wore these gray slacks with a white shirt and his crisp, clean white Vans. It was simple but sexy.

And yes he smoked cigarettes.

I don't know if I've told you this, but he didn't hold a cigarette like most people. He gripped it like a madman tucked it inside his hand between his thumb and pointer finger. That grown man grip.

I had never dated anyone who smoked before, but with him? I didn't care.

I used to tell him all the time that when I was back home, if I stepped outside and caught a whiff of cigarette smoke, I'd immediately turn around thinking it was him. Isn't that wild? One scent. One place. And it's like your whole body remembers.

You're going to think this is gross, but when we were riding in his truck or laying in bed, I loved sniffing his hands. I know so weird, especially since I've always hated the smell of smoke. But with him? It was different. I just wanted to smell him. All day. All night.

He wasn't an affectionate man, and there were already a few things that had me feeling some type of way. Even that night, at dinner with his parents, I noticed it.

When we got out of the truck, his mom walked beside me and he just took off walking ahead.

That bothered me. I felt gorgeous that night. I wore a beautiful fall dress with matching boots. My hair was curled. My makeup looked flawless. I wanted to feel like he was proud of me. Proud that I was his. I wanted to walk beside him, hand in hand but he was already ten steps ahead, barely looking back.

That stung.

It didn't take long for me to realize that's just who he was. He wasn't overly affectionate, and maybe he never would be.

So I made peace with the fact that I'd probably always be the clingy one and honestly, I didn't mind.

That was our balance.

He was night. I was day.

He was quiet. I was loud.

He was a little boring, and I was a whole lot of fun. LOL

You get it.

After that trip, seeing him became more consistent. We fell into a rhythm every four to six weeks I'd fly out to see him. It became our thing. That season, we even did haunted houses with his family, and I spent more time with his sister and met some of his mom's friends too.

There was this one moment that stuck with me. We were out together, and someone he knew introduced me to a group. One of the ladies there looked me up and down and said, "Oh my goodness, she's gorgeous. Where have you been keeping her hidden?" She kept complimenting me, holding my hands, gassing me up like a proud auntie.

And all he said in response was, "Well, what am I? Chopped liver?"

I didn't understand what that meant at first. I kind of laughed it off. But deep down, I took it a little personal. That wasn't the response I was hoping for. I thought he'd say something like, "I know, right? I'm lucky," or "She's mine now," or even "She's been hiding from me!"something to show he was proud. But that's not what he said.

And I didn't bring it up. I just smiled and nodded, telling myself maybe it was just southern humor or something I didn't fully understand.

That month ended up being one of the hardest we had in our relationship.

We both still had Snapchat, and sometimes we'd go hours without talking. He'd tell me he was busy working on the farm, didn't have his phone on him. But I'd notice his Snapchat score going up.

I wasn't trying to be toxic I swear I wasn't. BUT I WAS.

But when I brought it up to my friends, they'd say, "Maybe you should check his Snap score. Just see if anything's weird." So I did. Eventually, it turned into an argument.

I finally asked him, straight up: "I feel like you're talking to someone else. Is it just me?"

He told me I was the only one. That I was who he talked to.

But a part of me didn't believe it.

Yes, I had met his mom, his sister, even some of her friends… but this was still long distance. And something inside me felt off.

Maybe I was just making it up.

Maybe I was projecting.

Maybe we'll never really know.

I told myself maybe my past relationships were dragging these insecurities into something new something that didn't deserve that. I wanted to be better. I wanted to do better. And the truth was, my past wasn't his fault.

Around this time, though, his tone changed. He got more comfortable, but in a way that started to feel a little disrespectful.

When I'd try to talk to him about how I felt calmly, just expressing myself he'd get irritated. Dismissive. Defensive.

If I asked to FaceTime, or told him something didn't feel right, it would become a whole issue.

There were nights where we'd say goodnight, and he'd say he was going to bed… and then 30 minutes later, I'd see his Snap score go up again. So I knew he was still on his phone.

And it wasn't even about the app. It was about honesty. I didn't expect to be glued to him 24/7, but I hated the feeling of being lied to even in small ways.

When I brought it up, he'd flip it on me. He'd tell me I was crazy. That I needed to "use my head." And I'm saying that nicely

because the words he used were a lot harsher.

Eventually, I snapped too and got ugly.

I cursed right back.

I told him to watch his mouth and stop talking to me like that.

All I wanted was to communicate. I wanted to feel safe enough to say, "Hey, this bothers me," without it turning into a war.

From the start, he always told me I was a flight risk. He'd say I was going to leave him one day. That if I got upset, I'd run. That I was always the one to want to break up.

He also used to tell me that when we needed to have serious conversations, I would shut down. So I worked on that.

I tried.

I didn't want to be guarded anymore. I wanted to share more. Communicate better. So I opened up.

I told him my whole life story everything I'd written in this book. Even the deepest, hardest parts. The kind of stuff I'd never told

anyone before. I truly loved him and confided in him.

He would always say, "You should write a book. Use it as a testimony."

He wasn't the only one who told me that. My friends had said it too.

Little did he or anyone know I had journaled my whole life and already started a book but had told no one. It was my secret.

I'm not going to lie, I was excited to tell him, I knew he'd be proud. He always was. It just wasn't the time yet.

But I was scared. Terrified.

I'd been judged my whole life.

And the idea of opening up to the world? That level of exposure?

It felt unbearable.

But eventually I realized:

To grow in life, you have to get comfortable doing uncomfortable things.

And not everybody is going to like you. And that's okay.

I was so soft with this man. I would cry over little things. Big things. Everything. I was sensitive with him in a way I hadn't been with anyone else. I was different.

I was transparent.

I think because I had held so much in for so long...

Because I had played tough for so many years...

Being next to him made me want to put the armor down.

He was the alpha.

And around him, I just wanted to be soft.

To be held.

To be protected.

On another trip back to his house, the Snapchat conversation came up all over again. I finally told him, "Okay, then let me see your Snapchat," and he didn't let me.

That moment felt like a punch in the gut.

I had already noticed how he posted random things from time to time, not often but never once did he post me. Never a picture of us. Never a soft glimpse into our relationship. Nothing.

Now, I'm not saying every man needs to post his partner some people are private and I respect that but it felt weird to be kept in the shadows. Especially when everything else in my life was out in the open.

Of course, bringing it up turned into an argument. And once again, I let it go.

But then... I found a hair clip on the nightstand beside his bed.

I picked it up and looked at him.

He told me it was mine.

That I had left it there.

That no one else had been at his house.

Did I believe him?

No.

But I still shook it off.

Because the truth is, this man had been married before. He wasn't new to this. He had a life before me. He had dated other people. I wasn't the only woman who had ever stayed in that house. So technically, I had no reason to trip.

Still, I told him to toss the clip.

And I let it go.

Again.

He never really spoke about his past relationships. He always said I could ask him anything that he was an open book. But I rarely did. I think deep down, I didn't want the answers.

Meanwhile, I told him everything. I rambled, overshared, and opened up because I wanted him to know who I was. The real me.

All I knew was that he had never dated a woman with kids before. He had never dated someone who'd been married. And he had never dated someone my age.

He always dated younger.

And I don't mean a few years younger. I mean younger younger.

He was six or seven years older than me, and the girls before me were still younger than me which meant they were in their early 20s.

No kids.

No past.

Maybe no career, no job, no responsibilities who knows. I say that because when I was in my early 20s, my life was a mess. I wasn't put together yet.

And I won't lie knowing that made me feel a little insecure.

I had stretch marks.

I had two grown kids.

I had baggage.

I had been through hell and back.

I felt like he was used to a completely different version of "woman" the kind that still wore innocence and freedom like perfume.

And here I was grown, layered, complex.

But I also knew what I wanted.

I wasn't some project.

I wanted to be loved.

Taken care of.

Seen.

Chosen.

And I can't judge him too harshly, because honestly? My past relationships didn't even feel like real relationships either. I never lived with anyone. Never let a man borrow my car. Never invited anyone fully into my home or my world.

So in some ways... I guess I could relate.

But as the trips continued, and I got closer to his family, more truths started to surface. Some things I didn't like. Some things I didn't want to know.

But I brushed them off.

I kept showing him love.

When I was in town, I'd cook for him. Love on his dog and feed her too. She's adorable! I would do his laundry. Help around the house just to feel useful.

He had a home gym, and I'd use it to stay active while I was away from home. And honestly? From the outside, everything seemed great.

He'd still send me gifts.

Still surprise me with packages at my door.

And the roses... oh my God, the roses.

But the truth is, being in love makes me stupid.

It makes me forget my power.

Forget where I come from.

Forget who I really am.

My friends have always said I thrive the most when I'm single.

And they're not lying.

Anytime I've been on my own, I've bossed up the hardest. Built the most. Achieved more.

Not because I wanted to

Because I had to.

I didn't have the luxury of slowing down. I had to work hard. I had to build. I had to keep pushing... for my kids, and for myself.

For some reason I still felt the need to prove that I could do everything that my dad did, but legally

That's something I told him early on.

And he always said he knew I was in survival mode.

He'd send me videos, soft songs, quotes things to remind me that I could rest. That he wanted to be the one to help me relax.

He'd tell me he might not be able to give me every luxury, but he wanted to be the man I could lean on.

Which is what made it confusing later…

Because as our relationship deepened, his tone changed.

He started saying things like:

"What do women really bring to the table?"

Or

"I want a woman who has her own. I don't want someone to rely on me."

And I'm not mad at the idea of a woman having her own.

Because I do.

I always have.

But there was a shift in energy.

What started off soft and protective started to feel more like… testing me. Seeing if I could carry it all by myself.

Some of our conversations got deep.

And honestly, I think he started to shift too.

Maybe he realized I wasn't just anyone.

Maybe he saw I had value beyond the surface.

And that's probably why I stayed.

I won't lie and say I didn't notice the signs in the beginning.

Because I did.

When we first met, he'd send me videos of his house, his land, his backyard… and say things like:

"This is all going to be yours, baby girl."

I'd laugh and roll my eyes, brushing it off as a pickup line.

And that's exactly what it was.

Back then, we barely knew each other.

But looking back now…

Maybe I should've paid closer attention.

Fast forward,

We had our first official one-year anniversary coming up, and I wanted to take advantage of the trip just in case it took me longer to come back.

I had custom-ordered one of those silver Zippo lighters with his initial engraved on it.

He loved everything silver.

Along with the lighter, I included a beautiful, heartfelt note.

In it, I reassured him that I loved him…

That he was the love of my life…

That I really wanted to build a future with him…

And that I genuinely believed he might be my forever.

Because that's how I truly felt.

I felt honored to be his even with all the arguments, even with all the misunderstandings.

Because sometimes, when it was good…

It was something I can't even explain.

Our conversations had depth.

Our connection felt real.

When I gave him the gift, he didn't want to take it at first.

He said he hadn't gotten me anything for our anniversary.

I don't even think he realized it had already been a year.

But I could tell something in him softened.

His eyes got a little red while he read my note.

I was sitting on the kitchen counter by the sink, watching him, and in that moment I felt so genuinely happy.

Gift giving has always been one of my love languages.

Later that day, when we went to his parents' house, I kept telling his sister how excited I was that we had hit one year.

I even asked him to show off the Zippo lighter.

I was just… happy.

For that moment, everything felt aligned.

Not long after, I ended up feeling stupid.

But… we can talk about that later.

Chapter 34

A Biltmore Birthday and Tamales on the Plane - I Gave My Holidays and My Heart

At home?

At home, everything was actually going great.

My business was picking up again.

And listen I might not be the best at relationships, but when it comes to business or money? That's my arena. That's what I know. That's where I shine.

You know that scene in The Wolf of Wall Street, where he says "Sell me this pen"?

That line has always stayed with me.

Because that's exactly how I feel I could sell anything.

I could talk myself into a job. Sell something through a phone screen, a text, online, in person… it didn't matter. My selling skills were pretty damn elite.

And yet, for someone who knows how to make money and build things from the ground up, money has never really phased me.

Anyone can give you money when they have money.

Anyone can order you a gift online and have it delivered straight to your door with no real effort just a few clicks, a few buttons, a confirmation email.

But time?

Time is different.

Time is precious.

Time is a currency you can't refund or get back.

When you've lived a life where you've had everything except freedom your view changes.

Yes, money is great. Gifts are sweet.

But nothing compares to peace.

Nothing compares to freedom.

Nothing compares to the ability to travel and live and move how you want when you want.

I will never forget where I came from.

I know exactly what it feels like to have and to have not.

I know I've said that a hundred times in this book, but that's because it's the truth. And it matters.

Of course, I still appreciate the smell of my new car.

Of course, I still enjoy an original breakfast at a local café or a cute little brunch spot with fresh coffee and a flaky croissant.

But I don't take any of that for granted.

I don't think I'm better than anybody else.

I know I'm fortunate. I know I'm blessed.

And that's why I'll always support small local businesses.

That's why I'll always be a good tipper, speak with manners, and give great customer service even when I'm on the receiving end.

Because money doesn't make you a good person. Character does.

I love owning a business.

But more than that, I love sharing what I've learned.

I use my social media platforms to speak publicly now about everything:

Business. Nails. Motherhood. Heartbreak. Healing. Hustling. Grieving. Building.

I want people to see it all.

I want them to know what's real.

If I can help someone else by sharing my own experiences then why wouldn't I?

This year, I was invited onto a podcast to talk about my journey my brand, my salons, relocating my business.

We talked about everything: religion, culture, tradition, motherhood, healing.

The only thing I kept private was my relationship.

Because I didn't know where it was going.

When it was good, it was really good.

But when it was bad, it hurt deep.

Still, overall, the podcast was amazing.

And Priscilla if you're reading this book I love you, and I hope you'll have me back again someday.

I also took another trip with my best friend you know her as my wife.

We went down to South Texas for my uncle's annual birthday party.

It was our second time attending, and we had the best road trip.

I drove there, she drove back. We were cracking up the whole way watching videos, reading horoscopes, playing music.

I even remember being on the phone with my boyfriend during that trip.

Since both he and my best friend are white, they understood each other's little slang phrases and country sayings it was hilarious to hear!

That whole trip was just right.

After the party, he and I stayed on the phone for hours.

I remember laying in the hotel bed having deep conversations about relationships, marriage, finances… all the "big picture" stuff.

The next morning, my best friend and I got brunch, visited my dad's gravesite at the cemetery, and then drove back to San Antonio.

That trip became a tradition.

A getaway for the soul.

But when the holidays rolled around, I'll be honest,

I was drained.

Physically.

Mentally.

Emotionally.

Business, social media, the brand, travel… I was doing so much.

So this year, I chose not to host a Friendsgiving.

I was tired of being the one who always did.

The one who always gave.

I was the one coordinating gifts, hosting dinners, planning parties.

I wanted things to be perfect and most of the time, no one matched that energy.

People would show up late.

Show up empty-handed.

Show up with no offer to help.

And I'm not saying I gave to get something in return.

That's not my heart.

But even the strongest givers get tired of giving into emptiness.

So this year, I just didn't.

My holiday décor was simpler too.

I still decorated, but nowhere near the usual level.

Normally, I go BIG.

This time, I kept it small.

I stayed in with my kids.

We watched football games.

I FaceTimed my boyfriend.

I saw him more often.

And yes we argued.

Words were exchanged that shouldn't have been.

But we moved forward.

Because that's what relationships do.

All I ever really wanted was to:

– Be the best mom possible

– Triple my income

– And love someone in a way no one else ever could

I wished I could spend the holidays with him in person.

I stayed close to his family his sister, his mom they checked in on me often.

They loved on my kids, too.

And no, he didn't show much affection toward my kids.

But that was okay.

Because they didn't need another dad.

They just needed to see me happy.

I still took photos of them.

Of our food.

Of the moments.

And I spammed his inbox with them.

I hated feeling like I had to dim myself.

Like I had to show less love.

Or care less.

I hate that feeling.

Because my purest form is soft.

My love is loud.

My caring is deep.

My nurturing is constant.

And none of those things are flaws.

I didn't want to quit.

I didn't want to shrink.

I wanted to fight for us.

Even when it was hard.

Even when the conversations got uncomfortable.

Because love real love is worth the discomfort.

And I wanted to believe that so badly!

There's a quote I came across online that I absolutely loved and I want to share it with you here:

A good relationship is just two people saying:

"Hey, life is hard, but I want to do it with you."

That's it.

It's not a highlight reel.

It's not always romantic dinners or grand gestures.

Sometimes it's folding laundry together,

sending each other memes

when words feel like too much.

Love isn't always loud.

Sometimes it's just choosing each other again.

Isn't that beautiful?

Simple, soft, but so real.

One of the funniest memories I have from that season was when we all went to a haunted house together.

His whole family came along his mom, his dad, all of us packed into a truck and headed out to this huge open field with a corn maze on one side and creepy trailers lined up on the other.

Before the haunted walk through even began, we were dropped off on a wagon, and his mom insisted I use the porta potty.

Let me just say this: I had never used a porta potty in my life and I had literally said so in an earlier chapter.

But she wasn't having it.

"You better go now before we get dropped off," she told me.

And she was right.

Because otherwise? I would've peed my pants.

That haunted house was like nothing I had ever seen before.
We had to crawl through certain parts, duck under broken-down trailers, walk through beat-up cars and dark, narrow hallways.

It was so freaking scary and so much fun.

I kept thinking, my parents would NEVER do something like this.

And the fact that his mom and dad were right there with us laughing, screaming, pushing through like teenagers made it one of the best nights of my life.

It felt wild and silly and unforgettable.

I was literally holding onto him for dear life in some parts, and we were both cracking up the entire time.

It was pure chaos and pure joy.

The kind of memory that stays with you forever.

I felt so close to all of them.

I finally felt loved and accepted.

And his mom always showed love toward my kids.

Christmas was also just around the corner, and while I was in town with him, I made it a point to make his house feel like home. I put up the

Christmas trees. I baked cookies. I mopped the floors, cleaned, did all the wifey stuff.

I loved being in town with him.

I loved cooking for him.

Feeding him.

Pouring into him.

Those were the things that made my heart happy the domestic, quiet,

intentional love.

He let me use his truck to get around town.

I'd go run errands, grab groceries, pick up little things I needed. I even bought a bottle of Prosecco just for myself to make mimosas while I cleaned.

I'd take over the kitchen while he watched TV in the bedroom.

And I remember this one time I was feeling playful, wearing socks,

sliding across the floor as my music played on my phone. I slid right into his room, smiling, dancing like a goofball.

He looked over at me, still lying in bed, and said,

"Are you drunk?"

Ugh. That moment crushed me.

I wasn't drunk I was just happy.

I was just trying to be to enjoy a rare quiet moment together. No kids. No pets. No distractions.

Just him and I.

I wanted to sip a drink, cook dinner, and have a good time.

But that moment was like a pin in a balloon. The air just escaped.

And to make things harder, I was already dealing with tons of flight delays and cancellations around that time too. I was trying so hard to stay patient and positive.

I had to reschedule so many of my clients back home, and that wasn't easy.

My professional life was already chaotic but I was trying to keep my cool.

I knew I was losing a few clients in the shuffle, but my real ones understood. They knew I couldn't control the airlines. They knew as soon as I landed, it would be back to work no days off.

Every year, October through December is go-time for me.

I work past midnight most nights.

I'm booked and busy nonstop.

But now, I had a personal life to balance too

a relationship I wanted to pour into.

I told my boyfriend that I didn't want anything for Christmas or my birthday.

I just wanted to spend time with him.

"If you buy my ticket to come see you, that's all I want."

And I meant it.

Of course, he still got me a gift. Lol.

In December, when I flew out to see him again,

he took me to the Biltmore Estate

somewhere I had never been,

and one of the most breathtaking experiences of my life.

We toured the mansion together huge, elegant, filled with history. I

had a Baileys coffee in my hand. He was beside me.

It felt like something out of a movie.

We walked through the mansion, sipping that Baileys coffee,

exploring every corner together.

We even went into the glass conservatory next door he had booked

us the full experience with the tour package. Afterward, we drove

around the massive Biltmore property hundreds of acres of dreamy

countryside and talked deeply about our dreams and goals,

what we wanted for the future. I still remember walking into the

gift shop at the end of our tour, and he surprised me with a special

Biltmore wine collection

to take back home with me to Texas.

I packed it in my luggage with so much care

like it was a memory I never wanted to lose.

Earlier that day, when he picked me up from the airport,

he had a Diet Coke and some candy waiting for me in the truck.

He told me he was "being a husband" that day. Lol.

I had teased him so much in the past

"You never ask if I need shampoo or toothpaste…

you don't even pull up with a drink!"

So to see him show up like that, it made me smile.

It was sweet.

That whole weekend, he really did try.

We opened some of our Christmas gifts early

and planned to open the rest over FaceTime on Christmas Day.

I had gone all out for his family

bought gifts for everyone I could.

I truly wanted to make his Christmas special.

Throughout the year, I'd paid close attention

to the little things he mentioned the things he liked.

He had wanted a Blackstone grill,

so I secretly ordered one and had it shipped to his mom's house to surprise him.

I even paid extra to have it assembled

because I knew he didn't have the patience for that kind of thing.

He always used the word "aggravated,"

and I didn't want this gift to turn into something frustrating.

But when the grill arrived?

It looked used. It was a mess.

I filed a complaint, and they agreed to send another one

this time in a box and refund the assembly fee.

So I bought a second grill and asked them to pick up the first one…

but they never did.

I told his mom to just keep the first one for his dad.

They never gave me the refund either,

but honestly? Whatever.

It wasn't about the money.

I didn't even care.

Because when I love, I love all the way.

I even got him a Movado watch.

I'm not saying it to brag

I just saw it and thought,

He would look SO good in this.

Even though I knew he didn't wear watches much,

I had noticed he collected them.

And I thought… maybe one day when we live together,

he'll have a walk-in closet

with an island in the center.

His watches neatly displayed.

And this one?

This one would be the first

the watch from the first Christmas we actually spent together.

This was actually our second Christmas together,

but the first one we got to spend in person.

And that meant everything to me.

I was so excited, I brought matching pajamas for us.

I even packed my tripod and Bluetooth remote

so we could take real photos

not selfies, but actual memories.

They turned out so pretty.

Just us. Cozy. Smiling.

Happy in our little holiday bubble.

I gave him other thoughtful things too

like knee wraps for his workouts,

and a custom stocking I made just for him,

filled with his favorite chocolates and silly knickknacks.

I wanted to make him feel cared for

loved in all the small ways.

And in return, he spoiled me.

He got me Tiffany & Co. jewelry.

Not just one piece but several.

He really had good taste.

The thing is… I've never been great at receiving gifts.

Not because I'm ungrateful,

but because I've rarely received good ones.

I'm not trying to compare,

but my ex-husband used to get me the most random,

unthoughtful things weird makeup kits or clearance boxes.

I was always the one giving the bigger, more meaningful gifts.

So when I opened those little blue Tiffany boxes,

I was genuinely in shock.

I didn't know how to react.

I froze a little.

I smiled.

But inside?

My heart was glowing.

He had gotten me Tiffany the year before too,

so it started to feel like our thing.

Like our signature.

Our tradition.

And as silly as it might sound,

I started to imagine…

What if one day I got a promise ring from him?

Or even an engagement ring…

from Tiffany & Co.

That little turquoise box had become sentimental to me because it represented us.

I know some people think promise rings are childish or outdated,

but to me?

It would've meant the world.

I'd never had that before.

No one had ever made that kind of promise to me.

And I had told him how much I wished for it.

He brushed it off said it was silly.

But he didn't understand...

It wasn't about the ring.

It was about what it symbolized

to a woman like me a woman who had been through so much

and still believed in love anyway.

That Christmas, I also traveled with tamales in my luggage.

I felt like a whole narc smuggling contraband through TSA

tamales wrapped in aluminum foil, tucked into my suitcase like bricks. LMAO.

But I knew how much he wanted them,

and I wanted to bring some for his family too.

When I got there,

I made homemade arroz con leche

and packed some up for his mom.

I had a favorite pair of pajamas that were technically his

but they had a huge tear right down the butt crack.

And I still wore them.

When I heard his mom pull up outside,

I ran out with one hand holding the Tupperware

and the other hand covering my butt

just to deliver what I had cooked.

I looked like a hot mess

but I didn't care.

I was happy, his mom had even offered to sew the pajamas since I mentioned to her how much I loved them. lol "She was a doll".

I even had my mom hand-make a custom crochet poncho for him,

just to make it all feel a little more personal.

A little more us.

That December, I decided not to host a big birthday party.

No Christmas party.

No gift exchanges with friends.

This month was about me,

my kids,

and my relationship.

I pulled back from social things.

I didn't feel like doing it all this time.

I wanted peace.

I spoiled my kids with amazing gifts things I knew they'd love. We had the best time together.

And on my birthday, I kept it simple:

Brunch, a really beautiful dress, and my babies by my side.

My boyfriend sent me so many flower bouquets and balloons,

and the cutest white plush bear that I absolutely adored.

And then he surprised me with "Bob."

LOL.

If you know, you know.

It's that freestanding punching dummy.

I had wanted one forever.

I kept saying I wanted to slap it around

whenever I was stressed or film funny videos with it.

And he actually got it for me!

I laughed so hard when it arrived.

That gift felt personal. Thoughtful. Me. The man spoiled me, I'll give him that!

Later that day, I went to the store to buy my own birthday cake.

And while I was waiting in line,

there was an elderly woman in front of me

trying to pay for her groceries.

She looked so fragile.

She was alone.

And her card kept declining.

After a few moments, I couldn't just stand there.

I reached forward and paid for her groceries.

She thanked me softly.

When I got home, I broke down crying.

Not because of the money.

But because I had done something kind for someone

who reminded me of the loneliness I fear.

I kept wondering,

Why was she alone?

Who took her to the store?

Did she drive herself?

Could she even walk safely?

That small act of kindness

left a deep ache in my chest.

It made me grateful for my life.

And afraid of growing old alone.

I talked to my boyfriend about it over the phone that night.

And yes, I had been sipping mimosas earlier,

so I was emotional.

But it came from a real place.

The next day was New Year's Eve.

I prepped everything so my kids,

their friends, and maybe some of mine could come over. I

made individual cups with 12 grapes in each

our little tradition.

We lit fireworks.

Played music.

I cooked food and set the tone for a sweet night in.

When midnight struck,

I grabbed my phone and messaged him right away.

I told him how much I loved him.

How I felt, deep in my heart,

that he was the love of my life.

That I wanted to spend the rest of my life with him.

I truly believed that at the time.

I had never felt a love like this.

I ate my 12 grapes.

Made 12 wishes.

Kissed my boys goodnight.

And went to bed with a full heart.

Just like that,

another year came to a close.

Chapter 35

City Girl Meets Farmer: The Promise Ring, the Gut Punch, the Moonshine, and the Heartbreak

Happy New Year. You won't even believe what I did. I went back to corporate again. Yup.

I did.

I was traveling so much with my boyfriend, and things were starting to feel more serious. I wanted more time with him. I wanted the kind of job that would let me work remotely without losing myself financially. I wanted the PTO for summer trips, holiday visits, spontaneous weekends. I wanted to be able to move with him, if that time ever came, and not be terrified of starting from scratch. I needed the security of a consistent paycheck.

I also wanted him to grow closer to my kids or for my kids to grow closer to him. I had already told him that spending a few weeks together over the summer would be a good start. They had said hello through FaceTime and little moments like that, but I was hoping for something more formal. Something real. In person.

Business was still doing well, but I wanted more options. I needed flexibility the ability to come and go as I pleased without it impacting my income.

Because, like I've said before, social media and business are like buying a lottery ticket.

You work.

You post.

You show up, even when no one's watching.

Just like you buy the ticket... and then another... and then another. Sometimes you lose. Sometimes you win $1.05. But once in a while? You hit the jackpot.

That's the gamble of entrepreneurship especially online. You post every single day, even when your views are low. Even when your views are high and then crash again. Even when your views are all over the place. Because it only takes one video to go viral. One moment to change everything.

The key is discipline.

Consistency.

Tenacity.

And tenacity holds more power than people think. It's a level of grit most people don't have. People give up too easily because they don't see instant results. But building a brand or a business isn't like clocking in and out at a 9-to-5. There's no guaranteed check every week. No financial comfort zone. And that's what scares people the most the risk.

Because that's what business is: a gamble.

Some days you lose.

Some days you win.

Even though I was never afraid to gamble, I still knew I needed something stable. Something consistent. And deep down, I just wanted to spend more time with him. I honestly believed that the time would come when he'd ask me to move in or take things to the next level to really come together as a couple.

Somewhere in Between Softness and Survival

There are a million little moments I didn't plan on writing abouthings I thought were too small or too silly to matter. But now, look-ing back, I realize those were the moments that said the most.

Like the mornings I flew into town just to stay at his place, waking up at five a.m. to help him do chickens.

That's right me. A city girl with off-white, almond-shaped nails, dressed in a blue protective jumpsuit that made me look like a minion, walking into a hot, humid chicken house before the sun even rose. Hair tied up. Gloves on. Bucket in hand and yes I picked up the dead chickens too. lol

It was nasty. The smell was awful pure ammonia. But honestly? It didn't bother me as much as it should have. I'm an NAIL TECH, baby. I've been breathing in monomer and acetone for years. My lungs are built different.

When his mom found out I had been doing chickens with him, I feel like she might have howled. lol I did it out of love. I did it because I wanted to make myself useful because I wanted to show up for the man I loved in any way I could. I wasn't afraid to get my hands dirty if it meant building something with someone.

And I really tried to. Cooking meals. Folding laundry. Adjusting my schedule around his. Helping prep chicken houses like it was second nature. My clients even started joking that I should launch a "Chicken Salad" vlog series once I moved in with the chicken man. I'd just laugh and say, "Don't tempt me."

But let me tell you… that smell stayed with me. I remember taking a shower after one of those mornings, and the second the water hit my hair it activated something foul. I had to wash it twice just to feel clean again. And that, honestly, was one of the reasons I eventually stopped helping him with the farm work. Once I went back to corporate and had to show up polished on Zoom meetings, I couldn't risk clocking in with chicken funk in my strands. Washing was the easy part. Prepping for a blow-dry? That was the real labor.

Still I don't regret a second of it.

When we first started dating, he only had one farm. Toward the end, he had two. I watched his world grow. I watched us grow... and then quietly start to grow apart. Our lives split into two different rhythms. I was clocking in from his house, building my brand, doing nails, filming content, and balancing motherhood and corporate. And he was deep in his own world of farm work, errands, and exhaustion. We loved each other but we started moving like two people who were always one beat off.

The love I gave didn't disappear overnight. But the version of me who molded herself to fit someone else's life slowly began to fade.

And maybe that's the point of this whole book:

To show you what love, grit, and healing look like when no one's watching.

To remind you that the most meaningful chapters aren't always the prettiest.

Sometimes, they smell like ammonia and perseverance.

And sometimes, the girl who used to do chickens becomes the woman who writes her own damn book.

He also had a truck that needed repairs, and I offered to help pay for half of it. That way, when I was in town, I'd have something to drive without always relying on his second vehicle. But it was deeper than that I wanted to show I was invested. That I cared about his world, his responsibilities, his goals. There were things he wanted to upgrade around the farm, and I wanted to be part of that too. I didn't want to feel like a burden. I didn't want him to ever feel like he was pulling dead weight.

Let me explain.

One time, we had a conversation where he said he never wanted to feel like the truck in the relationship, constantly pulling a trailer.

I know... it sounds harsh. But I got it.

He wanted someone who could carry their own. Someone who wasn't always weighing him down. And in my mind, I'd always thought isn't that what a man is supposed to do?

Lead. Protect. Provide.

Set the pace.

And the woman? She follows.

But in that moment, I didn't argue. I just listened.

Because even though I knew I wasn't a trailer, I understood what it felt like to be the truck to be the one pulling everything forward in a relationship while someone else dragged behind. I knew what it felt like to want to fly, to build something, to dream big and to be partnered with someone who anchored me. Who slowed me down. Who made me feel stuck.

I never wanted him to feel that way with me.

I wanted him to know that together, we could go further.

That when we pulled in the same direction, we were stronger.

We still had small arguments, though.

And he'd often say, "I'm not gonna change. This is who I am. You're always trying to change me." But I wasn't trying to change him. I just wanted to be understood. To be seen. To feel heard when something hurt me. When something bothered me. We also made time to head up the mountains to a breakfast spot I loved. And I finally got to meet one of his best friends, too. That meant a lot to me it felt like I was being welcomed a little more into his world, his circle. We even went on a drive with him and his wife. It was peaceful. I had packed snacks for the ride because I knew how much of a snacker he was he was always hungry,

562

always munching on something. I genuinely just wanted to take care of him. Not mother him. Just love him like a true partner. The kind of woman who shows up and stays.

He used to say that in all his past relationships, the women always left. That no one ever stayed. And all he wanted now was a relationship where someone wouldn't walk away. I did. I stayed.

I tried my hardest to balance it all spending time with him, keeping my business running, and being the best mom I could to my boys. I made time for everyone. I gave my all, every time I was around. And when I was home, I still made sure to prioritize my kids. We did our date nights like we always had. I loved taking them to the mall or just walking the dogs around the outlets and outdoor shopping centers.

While I was with my Secret Santa, I made time for his family too. It was a great time! We'd go shopping, spend time together, and I even bought things for his house. Things I paid for with my own money. I never asked him for anything. But he always told me he wanted me to feel comfortable like his home was mine too. And everything he had, he wanted to share it with me. I felt the same way. We'd even had the prenup conversation early on, just to make sure everything would be fair if our future did grow more serious. He had been through a really bad divorce, and I knew that changed how he saw certain things. And I respected that.

On my end, when I got divorced, I didn't ask for anything. No alimony, no child support. I didn't care. I didn't want anything from him. I get that not every woman operates that way and that's okay but that's just me. My freedom doesn't have a price. No amount of money could ever anchor me down or make me bitter.

I wasn't created and I'm not here for an easy or cozy life.

I'm here for a powerful one.

Around that same time, he was getting ready for his annual trip with his guy friends the snowmobile trip. And this time, he invited me. I felt honored. But deep down... I didn't feel safe.

He mentioned I'd have to drive my own snowmobile. I had never done that before. It sounded exciting but risky. He told me it wasn't going to be a couples' trip he wouldn't be by my side the whole time and he didn't want me to feel uncomfortable if I didn't enjoy the outdoors. I asked if I could ride with him, but he said that wouldn't be possible.

I brought it up to my mom, and she didn't feel comfortable either. I had driven in snow before, sure in regular cars. And I had experience riding motorcycles and dirt bikes with my brothers growing up. But a snowmobile? In unfamiliar terrain? That was different. And I wouldn't be under supervision like I used to be. I knew it wouldn't be safe not for me.

So I told him the truth. That I would still love to travel with him, and I'd be perfectly happy staying in a hotel while he rode with his friends. I could Uber to brunch or find a bookstore and lose myself in a novel until he came back. We could still spend the evenings together, go out to dinner, sleep next to each other. I didn't mind that. But I felt bad that he'd be spending so much money, and I wouldn't be out there with him.

He reassured me and promised that we'd take a trip together in the summer something I'd actually enjoy. A beach. An all-inclusive resort. Something relaxing and fun. That sounded perfect. So I declined the invitation and told him to have the best time with his friends.

And I really was okay with that.

Especially because... I already had a flight booked to see him again that same week.

I was going to fly in that Thursday and head back home Sunday. He would be leaving for his trip on Wednesday. The timing lined up beautifully. It felt like everything was aligned.

Not long after the holidays, I also posted a New Year video on my social media. I created a recap of all my favorite moments from the year monthly highlights, little victories, core memories. And for the first time, I made my relationship public. I posted it on both Instagram and TikTok.

And you won't believe what happened next…

I got the "Hey girl" message.

Yup. I did.

And it happened just two days before my flight to go see him.

I found out that on his first snowmobile trip the one from the year before he had taken another woman with him. Yes, it was a group trip with friends, but still… he took her.

As it turned out, he had been spending time with her during the same months we were already together. She sent me photos of herself inside his home. Little moments that didn't lie. I could see her in the places that felt sacred to me. The places I thought were ours.

She even mentioned how they used to hang out over the summer, going shooting together, doing things we never did. And suddenly it all made sense well assuming in my head this was why he was acting so strange and distant when I left for my Florida show. Things really felt off in my heart, I just didn't know why.

What broke me most was realizing that his family had known about her too, yes she was just a friend but still. In all fairness, they hadn't met me until the fall, so if he had been seeing someone that summer, they probably didn't even know I existed yet. Still, it crushed me. I felt erased. Replaced. My mind kept flashing back to that one night at his mom's house how proud I had been, telling everyone we'd just celebrated a year together. How I had given him that custom Zippo lighter with his initials engraved in silver. How his nephews and family looked a little puzzled when I said "a year." I didn't think much of it then. But now, it all made sense.

And it stung even worse remembering the dinner table moments with his friends the same friends from the snowmobile trips. They'd talk and laugh about that past trip, and I'd smile along, saying how I already knew about it, that he and I had been talking during that time. I didn't realize that while I was on the other end of the phone thinking I was his girlfriend… he was on that trip with her.

He kept saying she was just a friend, but that still didn't make it right.

Have you ever been sitting in a room full of people, and suddenly you realize you're the only one who doesn't know the truth? That's exactly how I felt. Like everyone else had been in on something that I wasn't. Like I was the only one living in a different version of the story.

I felt small.

I felt stupid.

And more than anything, I felt embarrassed.

It was like the floor had disappeared under me. Everything I believed in started collapsing right in front of me and there was nothing I could do to stop it.

That same week, I already had my flight booked to go see him. It was paid for, planned a trip I had been looking forward to for weeks. But now? I didn't even know if I could stomach the thought of looking at him.

When I confronted him, he denied it at first.

I begged him to be honest with me. I needed the truth, even if it broke me.

And finally he admitted it.

He said yes, it was true. But he swore it was just a friend, that nothing happened.

I wanted to believe him so badly.

But the damage was done.

I cried harder than I had in a long time. I felt hollow. My chest physically hurt. I didn't even recognize the sound of my own crying anymore. I wanted to cancel my flight. I wanted to block him, delete everything, walk away.

But then... I couldn't. Because I still loved him.

He didn't want me to cancel. He asked me to move the flight up instead to leave right away. He said he'd even fly out to come see me because he didn't want to lose me. But I couldn't make sense of it. I told him I just needed time.

As the days passed and the trip grew closer, he checked on me every single day. I was so emotional. Torn between my heart and my pride. I told him I didn't want to go because I didn't feel like myself. I didn't want things to be awkward or forced.

His mom was also planning a family dinner, and I couldn't imagine sitting at that table pretending everything was fine. Pretending I hadn't seen what I saw. Pretending I wasn't breaking inside.

But when the day came, I decided to go anyway.

Because that's who I am. I don't quit easily. I don't give up on people I love. God knows I did love him.

I told myself that maybe just maybe we could work through it. We all make mistakes, right?

When I landed, I wasn't feeling great. I was catching a cold, running a fever, coughing nonstop. I told him I didn't feel well enough to go to his mom's dinner, but he said we had to go that it was already planned.

So I went. I smiled through it. I tried to make the best of it.

But the truth is… I felt like a ghost of myself that night.

Later that evening, I broke down in his arms and cried. Cried like I hadn't cried in years or ever if I can be real.

And let me repeat that I cried in the arms of the man who had just broken my heart.

He held me close and told me everything would be okay. He made me tea, gave me a couple of pills for my fever, and even poured me some moonshine to help me relax. I remember slipping into a hot bath afterward, sitting there for nearly an hour, sobbing quietly while he watched TV in the next room.

When I finally came out, I crawled into bed beside him and I just stared at the ceiling.

It's a strange kind of pain when you realize the person you love most is also the one you can't trust.

I wanted to believe in us so badly. But something in me already knew nothing would ever feel the same again.

The following day, I was doing my hair and makeup in one of his bathrooms when I opened the cabinet and my stomach dropped. There it was. A whole bunch of girl stuff. Products. Tools. Leftovers from someone else. A reminder that I wasn't the only woman who had stood in that exact spot, doing what I was doing now.

It felt like another punch to the gut. One after the other.

I quietly mentioned it to him, trying not to fall apart. He looked at me for a second, almost frozen then immediately jumped up and grabbed a trash bag. He got down on his knees, opened every cabinet, and started cleaning them out one by one.

I told him I could do it, but he insisted.

Watching him on the floor like that, tossing it all out, bagging it up and walking it out to the trash broke my heart in a different way.

Because I could see that he knew. He knew how badly I hurt.

"I knew he loved me and he spoiled me when he could". This situation sucked.

He came back inside, wrapped his arms around me, and kissed me gently. I didn't say much. I just nodded and tried to shake it off. I kept telling myself we had to get past this.

We all have a past. And we could both do better.

A few months before, he'd deleted Snapchat completely. So did I. It wasn't a big deal for me since it didn't impact my business or socials, but it felt like a fresh start. Something symbolic. A gesture of cutting ties and cleaning house.

Still, my trust was broken. And when trust is broken, even little things feel loud.

I loved him so much. I truly believed that at his age, in his early 40s, and with me in my mid-30s, we were both mature enough to make the right decisions for love, for growth. I really did believe that if we both wanted to, we could rebuild something strong. We could fix what was cracked.

Mine. My trust. That's what needed fixing.

Because the truth is, no relationship is perfect. We both just needed to keep fighting for this.

But the aftermath was hard. I would wake up in the middle of the night crying. Tears rolling down before I even opened my eyes. Sometimes I would cry myself to sleep and then wake up crying all over again.

And that didn't just last a few days. It went on for weeks if not months.

But eventually, we did get through it. The relationship, for a little while, felt perfect.

That storm almost brought us closer. He became extra patient. He was more attentive. When he took his next trip with his friends, he made sure to FaceTime me, to call me constantly, to check in. I could feel he was trying to reassure me.

And I appreciated it deeply.

The pain was still fresh though. My heart still bruised. I would still lose it sometimes. I'm not gonna lie I think I yelled at him two, maybe three times during that trip.

And I felt bad.

But I also couldn't control how hurt I was. Even when he was being present with me now, all I could think about was, Why didn't he do this last year? Why didn't he check on me then?

Still, I tried. I told him I was trying. I promised I was working on it.

And then February came around.

I was so excited to finally spend Valentine's Day with him. This wasn't our first Valentine's together, but it was the first one we would get to spend in person.

He was really busy with work, so I already knew we wouldn't do anything over the top. No fancy restaurants or big plans. But just like the holidays I didn't care. All I wanted was time with him.

We could've cooked steaks at home, made some waffle fries, watched movies, cuddled on the couch. That would've been more than enough for me.

I just wanted to melt into his arms.

I wanted to make the day feel special for him too. I spent so much time thinking about the perfect Valentine's gift. I was crazy over this man. I don't even know how to explain it. Maybe it was the way we talked the deep conversations that somehow made the world feel quiet.

Yeah, we had arguments. Plenty. But our conversations? They were powerful. The chemistry? Insane.

I was nuts about him.

So, I searched for creative gift ideas and finally came up with the five senses gift.

Something he could touch

Something he could smell

Something he could taste

Something he could hear

Something he could see

Cheesy, huh? Lol. But I thought it was cute.

I even thought about getting him a new phone. His had been broken for the longest time. I knew he had AT&T, just like me, and one of my clients actually worked there.

We got to talking about Valentine's gifts one day and I mentioned the phone. She offered to help me surprise him with it. She even joked, saying, "Hell, I could pull up his records for you." It was one of those toxic girl jokes, but we both laughed.

I didn't end up getting the phone, but the idea alone showed how much I cared. I just wanted to make him feel loved. Cared for. Considered.

Because despite everything despite the hurt, the broken trust, the sleepless nights I still wanted us to work.

I was still all in.

I had also bought him one of those Alexa devices with a screen and camera. I thought it would be cute to set it up in his kitchen something he could use to play music while cooking or working. I imagined him connecting it to Wi-Fi, jamming to his favorite songs, and maybe even hearing my voice pop in when I missed him. I could connect from my phone and say hi whenever I wanted to.

At the time, I thought it was one of the most adorable things I could gift him.

But I ended up loving the idea way too much... so I kept it. Lol.

Overall, Valentine's was perfect. He picked me up at the airport, and while he was working during the day, we planned a cozy dinner at home. I went to the store, bought steaks, and made my signature truffle fries.

But before any of that happened right when we got to his house he told me he wanted to give me my Valentine's gift. I told him to wait. I wasn't ready yet. I still needed to unpack, set up his gift, and I had even considered running to the store to buy balloons to decorate the house a bit. I wanted everything to be perfect.

But he insisted.

And then he handed me a small, beautiful blue box.

Can you guess what it was?

Yep. You're right. Tiffany & Co. Ahhh!!!

Inside was a promise ring. On Valentine's Day!

I jumped with so much excitement, I could've cried. It even came with a little handwritten note that said, "I love you, babe."

I officially had a ring on my finger.

I knew he wasn't the type to care much about promise rings, but he knew how much it would mean to me. It was the attention to detail that mattered. The fact that he remembered, that he made the effort.

I immediately FaceTimed my best friend. Then my sister-in-law. And of course, I told my mom. I wanted to show it off to everyone. I felt like I was living in my very own fairytale my own Hallmark movie.

All my clients would say it was "city girl meets farmer." Lol.

I was genuinely in love.

And honestly? After everything we had been through the ups, the fights, the hard conversations I felt even closer to him. Because we were getting through it together. We were both mature enough to admit when we were wrong. And we kept choosing each other.

I don't want to sound like a downer, but I'd be lying if I didn't admit I had one ugly thought lingering in the back of my mind: "What if he got this for me as a hush ring?" You know… to soften the blow of everything that had just happened.

But I shook it off just like I had with everything else. I let myself enjoy the trip. Enjoy the ring. Enjoy my man.

At this point in my life, I was juggling it all.

I was working a corporate job, doing nails, running my YNS brand, still doing collabs, promoting my Amazon storefront, running my Etsy shop, creating merch, working out, being a mom, a dog mom, traveling to see him, loving on his dog, connecting with his family, and even taking care of his home like it was mine.

Anytime I had the chance, I'd pick up something small for the house a rug, new towels, a cute seasonal wreath. I just wanted it to feel like a home for us.

When his dog got sick, I did everything in my power to help calling vets, texting his sister or mom, checking on updates, trying to lighten the load for him in any way I could. I don't even know why I loved him so much... I just did.

His mom and sister would call me at 5 a.m. even with the time difference, since he was an hour ahead of me. And I loved that they felt that comfortable with me. I always appreciated the way they checked up on me, especially when I was flying in or out.

Sometimes, I wouldn't land back in Texas until past midnight, and his mom would still be up waiting for my text.

When I forgot to send it, she'd message me the next morning:

"Hello, little lady. Did you make it home safe? I stayed up late waiting for your text, but I didn't receive anything."

How sweet is that? Seriously. I'll forever hold love for them in my heart.

We were getting so comfortable, too. At one point, he even gave me his debit card.

I never used it unless it was for a Starbucks coffee, and even then, I always asked for his approval before I swiped. I never wanted him to feel like I was taking advantage of him. Even if it was just for something cute, like a pair of shoes on Amazon, I would still tell him, "I feel so spoiled."

Because to me, it wasn't about the money.

It was about the thought behind it all.

His birthday was coming up, and I wanted everything to be perfect. Almost two months in advance, I started secretly prepping what I was going to do. I messaged his best friend's wife and let his mom in on the plan I wanted to host a small dinner for him. Something intimate. Something thoughtful. Something just for him.

For his gift, I decided on a Louis Vuitton wallet. The one he had was already worn down and falling apart. I even went out of my way to measure the wallet while I was at his house quietly comparing sizes so I wouldn't get one that was too bulky or too small. I wanted it to be just right the kind of gift he'd actually use. That mattered to me.

I flew into town the day of his birthday.

We got dressed together that evening and ended up in matching outfits. It was the cutest thing ever. I took pictures of us in that big, gorgeous mirror he had in his bathroom. He didn't usually like pictures, but he did it for me and we even took some silly ones that made us laugh.

Before we left, I had already given him his gift.

He loved it.

I told him we had dinner reservations, and when we arrived at the restaurant, his best friend was already there waiting.

That's when he low-key threw a tantrum.

He didn't want to get out of the truck and said he was going to drive back home. He told me he hated surprises.

I couldn't help but laugh. I shrugged and teased him, told him to stop being such a girl and to just enjoy the evening. I reassured him nobody else was coming. It was just a private little dinner, personal and relaxed. I told him I knew he needed time with his boys, and that's what I wanted for him.

He was always working. Always doing so much. I just wanted to give him a moment to breathe and be celebrated.I figured he could catch up with his best friend while I sat with the girls or chatted with his best friend's wife. The vibe was casual no pressure, no heavy relationship talk. I didn't want the whole night to feel like it was just about us or like I needed anything from him. I just wanted him to enjoy his birthday. I wanted him to feel free and appreciated.

I knew how much he loved biking, hanging out, just having real conversation and I thought this night could give him all that.

His mom and dad came too, which made it even more special. I was so glad I had the opportunity to treat everyone to dinner that night. He almost didn't let me pay, but I looked at him and told him gently not to block my blessing.

This was something I had planned for a long time. I wanted it to be amazing. I wanted it to be unforgettable.

And it was.

After dinner, we all stood outside the restaurant talking for nearly an hour. The air was cool, and the night felt peaceful. I stood off to the side for a moment, just staring at him while he stood there cigarette in hand, talking and laughing with his people.

God... I was so in love with him.

Mesmerized. Dickmatized. Spellbound whatever you wanna call it.

I don't know what it was about that man, but I just wanted him to feel happiness. Real happiness. I wanted to be the person who gave him peace. Who gave him a home within my love.

I really thought I could be that person.

But that didn't last long.

Chapter 36

"I Fought for Us. He Fought for His Peace.

And He Let Me Lose."

There were little things here and there.

I had left my Alexa camera behind at his house. The one I originally bought as part of his Valentine's Day gift the one I was so excited about. I thought it was sweet at first, just a way to feel close. But little by little, it became something else. There were things he would say things he claimed he was doing and they wouldn't always add up. Small lies. Harmless, maybe. But still lies.

And I had a camera there.

That's how I found out the truth, over and over again. They weren't huge betrayals. But they were still dishonesty. And I so badly wanted to call him out on it. I hinted. I danced around it. I poked a little but I never outright said it. I never told him. Part of me was scared of what would happen if I did. Would he explode? Would he hate me? Would he press charges? God knows, he always joked about being strict about privacy. I don't know. I just stayed quiet.

It wasn't right not on my part either and I knew that. Deep down, I was hurting myself more than anything. So I flew back out almost immediately. I packed up the Alexa and brought it back home with me. I told myself if I really wanted this relationship to survive, I had to try to trust him again. That was the only way forward. "He found out about it eventually". We even got into another argument when he dropped me off at the airport. I don't even remember how it started. But I do remember asking him if he had his exes or any girls he used to talk to blocked on his phone. And his response?

"I don't do that."

It crushed me. I wasn't trying to control him I was trying to feel safe. Maybe I was asking for too much. Maybe I was being too much. But I needed something to help rebuild the trust that was already cracked. His response just made the wound feel fresh again. He dropped me off without saying much, stormed off, and I walked into the airport holding back tears. " I was in my head and I just thought I couldn't possibly be in a relationship with somebody who was still friends with their ex, a person they were intimate with before, I just couldn't".

But like always, he called me when he got home. He was usually the first to say sorry. That night was no different. We talked before I boarded the plane and, just like every time, I got over it. I didn't want to quit. I wanted to believe in us. I wanted to believe love could fix it.

But the arguments got deeper. The silence got louder.

He said he was busy. Always busy. And I started spiraling. I became that girl the one constantly questioning everything. Every move, every text, every plan. I hated that version of myself, but I couldn't stop. He had taken a trip with his friends not long before, and I couldn't let it go. I was still bleeding from it. Still haunted.

The truth? In my eyes, he was sleeping peacefully in bed while I stayed up crying, hurting over everything I couldn't say out loud.

Still, I took another trip to see him. I asked first, of course. He said he'd be busy, but it was fine if I came. So I did.

But nothing about that trip felt easy. The delays were insane constant rescheduling, hours of waiting. I tried to stay calm, but it was wearing me down. Every time there was a change in the flight plan, he got frustrated. Not necessarily at me, but at the inconvenience. At how it interfered with his farm work. At how much time it would take to pick me up.

And I get it he had a business to run. But I couldn't help but think... What about me?

Because every time I came to see him, I cleared my entire schedule. Not just an hour or two my entire weekend. Sometimes longer. I shifted nail clients. I paused brand deals. I reshuffled mom duties. I gave everything. And when delays happened? I didn't complain. I didn't take it out on him. I'd sit at the bar, order a drink, and try to stay calm. Cool. Collected. The last thing I wanted to do was make his life harder or stress him out more. So I swallowed my own stress and smiled through it.

But quietly, a question echoed in my head.

Would he ever do the same for me?

Would he fly out, deal with delays, clear his whole weekend? Would he sit on a plane for hours just to spend time with me? Would he ever rearrange his world to show up the way I was constantly doing for him?

And I think deep down... I already knew the answer.

For this trip, he had told me that if the flight got delayed, I should just rent a car but if it didn't, to call or text him in the morning and he'd pick me up. That was our agreement.

He didn't pick me up at the airport.

To be fair, the trip was my idea, not his. I knew he had a lot going on, but I genuinely believed the only way this relationship would work was if I spent more time with him. I wanted to show up. I wanted to keep choosing us.

Thirty minutes before landing, he texted me saying he was still busy at the farm. Thank God I had paid for Wi-Fi, because the moment I read that message, my chest tightened. I got a mini anxiety attack right there on the plane my legs shaking, my heart pounding, trying to stay calm while people around me were excited to land.

I was upset. Confused. Disappointed.

I figured it out, though. I got the rental car.

But I was terrified. I had never driven by myself in his state before. My hands were trembling on the steering wheel when I got into that car. Sure, I had GPS, but everything still felt foreign. Cold. Lonely. Especially after realizing that our "agreement" apparently didn't mean much to him.

He had told me he'd make dinner reservations in the city and that we could take the rental car because his truck was too big for parking but I didn't remember agreeing to that. I thought the plan was simple: if the flight wasn't delayed, he'd pick me up. I had even canceled my original rental car reservation that morning after confirming the flight was on time. So having to scramble last minute to get one again? It just made me feel small.

When I finally arrived at his house, he still wasn't there.

That's when I knew

something had shifted.

He started procrastinating. "That's how I felt".

He filled his hours with work and errands instead of me.

No matter how often I came every two weeks, every month he never seemed to make room for us.

I got so ugly with him.

There was a moment I'll never forget I cornered him and told him I'd access his phone bill. It wasn't true.

But I remembered a client once telling me she worked for AT&T and had access to his account back when I tried to surprise him with a phone for Valentine's Day. I held onto that information. Not to use it, but to keep it as a kind of weapon.

Because I felt so insecure.

Because I was spiraling.

Because I felt like he was constantly lying to me.

And to be honest I got out of hand.

I was going nuts trying to hold on to something that no longer held me.

I just wanted him to make me feel safe.

I wanted him to reassure me that I was still his, that he loved me, and that he wouldn't hurt me again.

But instead, he blew up.

He threatened to take me to court.

He said the woman who worked for AT&T wasn't welcome at his home.

He accused me of things I hadn't even done.

It crushed me to hear those words come out of his mouth.

I wasn't scared of court. I wasn't scared of him.

Because I knew who I was. I would never actually do something like that.

I said it because I wanted him to react to show me the truth. But it only made things worse.

That weekend, we got into another ugly fight.

And once again, I flew back home.

The following week, I threw myself into everything I could.

Corporate. Nails. My brand. My boys.

My world was stacked full and heavy, and I didn't have much left to give.

My son's graduation was coming up, too, and my mind was spinning in a hundred directions.

He would still text or call sometimes, usually when he had time.

But this time, I didn't drop everything like I used to.

I didn't rush to reply.

I was learning how to hold some of myself back.

I was learning how to balance again.

Then came the message.

He told me he was going to the rodeo that weekend.

He said he'd be leaving around 6 p.m., and I casually asked how long he'd be there.

He snapped back with an attitude:

"Until it's over. Does it matter?"

It did matter.

Not because I didn't trust him.

Not because I cared where he went.

But because every time I was in town, he never had time for me.

Not like that.

I never got full days together.

At best, I'd get a few hours on a Saturday maybe.

And Sundays?

Always reserved for him. His couch. His races.

Don't get me wrong the chemistry was still there.

The laughter, the spark, the way we clicked.

When it was good, it was so good.

But toward the end, I could feel the shift.

The way his energy changed.

The way he filled his days with busy work chores, errands, distractions anything to avoid being present.

Even when I brought my laptop to his house to work remotely, he found reasons to leave.

Farm tasks. Projects. Last-minute things that somehow couldn't wait.

It broke my heart.

Because I still wanted to believe in us.

And then the next day, he went to the rodeo again.

Same time. Same story.

And again, it wasn't the rodeo that bothered me.

It was the fact that he could make time for everything else but never for me.

Late at night, when my body was tired and my mind finally slowed down, all I wanted was to feel close.

To talk. To share. To laugh. To tell him about work or my kids.

To sit in silence on FaceTime, even if we didn't say a word.

But he didn't even give me that.

So after another fight, another tearful call, another sleepless night…

I ended it.

I ended us.

Just like that.

I was confused.

Empty.

My body was going through changes I couldn't fully understand cramping, aching, hurting in ways I couldn't even put into words. My emotions were scattered and sharp. One minute I was calm, the next I was breaking down in tears over nothing. I felt fragile and out of control at the same time, like something in me was unraveling and I couldn't hold it together anymore.

And he knew.

He knew what was happening.

He knew my body was in pain. He knew something was wrong. He could hear it in my voice, feel it in my silences. And still… he pulled away.

Instead of showing up, he shut down.

Instead of asking if I was okay, he buried himself in work.

I tried to tell myself that maybe that was how he coped by staying busy, by avoiding but it didn't make it hurt any less.

Because while I was quietly breaking, he was nowhere to be found.

While my heart begged for comfort, the person I loved most made me feel like an inconvenience.

He didn't call.

He didn't check in.

He didn't ask if I needed anything.

He didn't try to fix what was breaking.

He just… let me fall apart quietly.

And I'll never forget that kind of silence the kind that makes you realize someone can know you're hurting and still choose not to care.

Still choose to look away.

Still choose not to show up.

He didn't even try to save the relationship.

Only a few days later, my firstborn had his graduation. And I was so tempted to send him pictures. I held my phone in my hand for way too long, thinking about it. I didn't.

But I thought about it because a part of me still clung to the memory of how, weeks before, he had sent my son $500 to buy his prom suit. That was the first time he had ever really shown my kids some love and I was so grateful for it. So were they.

Then Mother's Day came. And passed.

A small part of me thought maybe he'd send flowers... maybe he'd want to reach out. He didn't have to, but I thought maybe just maybe he would.

But I was wrong.

I heard crickets.

Nothing.

It was like the relationship never happened. Like we never happened.

Like we were strangers again.

No messages. No check-ins.

No "I hope you're okay."

Nothing.

And what hurt the most wasn't just the breakup. I was grieving so much more than that.

I wasn't just grieving the man I loved.

I was grieving the friendship.

I was grieving the silly moments, the little traditions, the "secret Santa" gifts.

I was grieving the person I thought would always show up for me.

And the person I thought I was becoming with him.

I had known this man on social media since 2016 or 2017 not closely, but I always knew he was there. And somehow, all of that history now felt like it meant nothing.

Like I meant nothing.

It was as if I had been erased.

Deleted.

Like I never mattered at all.

And as much as I hate admitting this part I still reached out.

Multiple times.

I couldn't help it.

I even caught a flight.

I paid over $600 for a last-minute ticket, another $400 for a rental car, and showed up at his house unannounced. Not because I was trying to be dramatic. I just genuinely thought maybe if he saw me in person, we could talk. Maybe we could fix it.

Please don't judge me. Or do. I don't care.

But when I arrived…

he looked right through me.

There was no reaction. No warmth. No smile.

Just confusion.

"How did you get here?"

"What are you doing here?"

"How long are you staying?"

I felt so stupid.

He gave me a side hug the coldest, driest, most distant hug I've ever received in my life. It was like hugging someone who didn't want to be touched. Someone who couldn't even pretend to care.

I later found out he made a comment about me showing up and said, "he didn't like surprise visits".

Anyway, I stepped out to get something to eat, I still hadn't had breakfast that day. On the way, I stopped to say hi to his sister. I gave her the biggest hug. It was just so good to see her. Something familiar. Something kind.

When I got back to his house, he was already getting ready for bed.

It felt like I didn't know him anymore.

Like I had stepped into a stranger's house.

Even when he took a bath, he closed the door. When he came out, he was fully dressed like I hadn't ever seen him without clothes before. It was cold. Awkward. Unwelcoming.

I knew I wasn't wanted there.

I started looking up hotel rooms, ready to leave. But he told me I could stay, that I didn't have to go. So I sat quietly on the couch in his bedroom while the TV played. Eventually, I dozed off.

But I couldn't sleep with the TV on. He knew that.

He left it on all night anyway.

So I got up, grabbed my blanket, and went to sleep in the living room instead.

That's when I broke.

I got on my knees and cried.

Not just a few tears. I cried. For what must've been an hour or two, maybe longer. I prayed. I sobbed. I begged God for peace, for clarity, for strength.

I cried for everything I had lost.

For the lies I felt but couldn't prove.

For the love I still had but couldn't hold.

For the words he never said.

For the things I knew he was hiding.

And for the version of me that still hoped he'd come around.

The following morning, he got up to go to work.

We ended up arguing again.

He kept repeating that we weren't in a relationship as if I didn't already know that. His tone was cold. Detached. Empty.

It was like every word he said was meant to remind me that I no longer belonged there.

I couldn't get a flight for that same day, so I booked one for the following afternoon. I'd be flying out Sunday at 5 p.m.

To be honest, I only bought a one-way ticket. I didn't know how things would go.

Maybe we'd talk. Maybe we'd work it out. Maybe breakfast would soften the tension.

Or maybe I'd just leave and never come back.

He was gone most of that day.

He avoided me.

Didn't talk much.

So I tried to distract myself. I took my rental car, went to the gym, tried to shake off the heaviness in my chest. When I got back, the house was still empty. Eventually, we went to dinner, but barely spoke. He just sat there watching TV like I wasn't even in the room.

All I could think about was how bad I wanted to go home.

Two arguments in one day. Two people who used to love each other now sitting in silence, pretending they didn't feel the distance.

That night, he told me I could sleep in the bed that I didn't have to stay on the couch. The second time he offered, I finally agreed. I slipped onto my usual side of the bed, quietly, like muscle memory. It was awkward. Cold. I should've left and booked a hotel. But I didn't. I stayed.

Sunday morning came.

I asked if he wanted to get breakfast with me before I left, and he said he had too many things to do on the farm.

That hurt.

Because I'd seen him leave his chores before to grab breakfast with others. But for me? He couldn't spare the time.

So I went alone.

I sat at the bar of a small café, FaceTimed my mom, and cried. I told her everything. She listened, calm and gentle like always, and told me, "Still be kind. Be loving. Be you."

So I wiped my tears, ordered food to go, and took him breakfast.

When I got back, guess what? He was still home. He hadn't even left for work. Could he have gone with me? Of course he could have. But he didn't.

I told him I brought him breakfast. He thanked me, heated it up in the microwave, and walked to the room to eat alone. No conversation. No eye contact. Just distance.

In that moment, I saw the ugliest version of him the one who didn't care if he broke me.

But I wasn't the same either. I was tired. My hair was falling out from stress. My skin was breaking out. My voice was gone. I was drained physically, mentally, emotionally. I barely recognized myself anymore.

And that's when I realized—

I was being stupid. "Damn it took that long huh".

With a heavy heart and tears in my eyes, I packed my things, loaded the car, and walked up to him. He was lying on the couch. I told him I was leaving. It wasn't even noon yet, and my flight wasn't until 5:30 p.m. But I didn't care. I would rather spend five hours at an airport than five more minutes feeling unwanted in that house.

I cried as I said goodbye.

I wrapped my arms around him so tightly, my face pressed against his chest, tears running down my cheeks and he just sat there. Still. Unmoved.

He hardly hugged me back.

Didn't kiss me.

Didn't stop me.

He simply said, "Everything's gonna be okay."

I kissed him anyway. A small, desperate kiss. Just one. And then I walked out.

He closed the door behind me.

When I got in the car, I stayed parked for a while, waiting for the air to cool down, trying to calm my breathing. I was crying too hard to drive.

A part of me still hoped stupidly that he'd come outside. That he'd tell me to stay. That he'd love me enough to stop me from leaving.

But he didn't.

He never came.

I returned the rental car. I boarded my flight.

And I cried the whole way home.

He never called.

He never texted.

He never looked for me.

I think I drunk-called him once, crying like a child. I don't even remember what I said. Probably begged. Probably embarrassed myself. I was broken. Lost. Still in love. Or maybe just addicted to the idea of love.

At one point, I asked him if flying out there wasn't proof enough of how much I loved him.

And he said,

"Getting a ticket is easy. Flying is easy. Renting a car and taking a trip is easy."

Easy?

Says the man who never took a single flight for me.

The man who never rented a car.

The man who said he couldn't "just up and go."

But now it was easy?

He told me being needy was a turn-off.

That I loved him too much.

He said, "It's like holding a bird in your hand it's suffocating."

The last conversation we had together at his house, he told me I was beautiful, smart, that I "checked all the boxes"… but that he was tired. That my emotions, my arguments, my needs they were just too much.

He clapped his hands together, brushing them clean like he was done with it all, and said, "I'm not doing that. I don't need a mother. I don't want to check in all the time. I don't want to have to keep my phone on me."

Then he looked me in the eyes and said, "You've been through a lot. Like… a lot. You've got things to work on."

He wasn't wrong I had.

But so had he.

And I really thought love meant working through it together.

We had this conversation while sitting on the back porch of his house. His phone kept lighting up with notifications, the alert sound chiming. I ignored it. I didn't want to think about whether he was already talking to someone else or if maybe he'd been talking to someone else this whole time. I didn't want to spiral. I didn't want to leave.

I just wanted to fix things.

But then he said he needed to find peace again.

That he needed to get right with God.

That he needed time alone.

So I tried to respect that.

But for months after that, I went through withdrawals like losing a drug.

I couldn't eat. Couldn't sleep. Couldn't focus.

I had the worst depression of my life. I lost an incredible amount of weight.

It was bad.

It affected my whole life.

My kids heard me cry.

It hit my gym performance, my work ethic, my energy to show up for anything. I didn't want to be seen. I didn't want to do nails. I didn't want to film content.

But I still did.

I showed up anyway filming what I could, forcing a smile when I needed to. Most of my followers and clients could tell something was off. I think they knew I was going through a hard time, but I tried to keep it private.

I missed his dog. I missed him. I missed his family.

But I had to keep it together.

I had to travel for work. And even arriving at the airport was too much for me sometimes. I'd walk into those terminals, pass the pickup areas, and I'd break down in the bathroom silently, painfully every single time I flew to the city where he used to meet me.

And that's something he'll never understand.

Because he never did that part.

He never packed outfits and luggage each month.

He never rearranged his schedule.

He never met my family or built a bond with my dogs or kids. His

routines never changed. His life stayed still.

I was the one in constant motion.

I was the one changing everything my calendar, my appointments, my client schedules, my time away from my kids, my dogs, my home. I was the one navigating the ache of homesickness while staying in a house that wasn't mine, hoping for connection that never came.

And every now and then, I'd catch myself reaching for the spot on my hand where I used to fiddle with my ring…

Only to remember it wasn't there anymore.

I had given that back, too.

I started reading.

Book after book.

In one month, I even read five.

Some were:

Let Them.

The Subtle Art of Not Giving a Fck.*

Fervent.

The Handmaid's Tale.

The Intelligent Investor.

Atomic Habits.

And the one that cracked something wide open in me Psychopath Free.

And finally, The Mountain Is You.

I started therapy.

I got prescribed antidepressants "Fluoxetine", to be exact.

I began caring for myself again, piece by piece.

My grind never stopped. Even when my soul was exhausted.

I slowed down,

but I didn't stop.

I still cried for him, often.

And I'll admit it I'd mess up and call him again.

Every five or six weeks, like clockwork.

Each month that passed felt like peeling off another layer of pain.

And I couldn't understand how the man who used to end every phone call with "I love you more" didn't care enough to check on me once.

Especially knowing how deeply I struggled with anxiety.

Knowing I'd cry until I couldn't breathe.

Not for attention. Not to manipulate. Just from the ache. From the loss. From being unseen.

I was hurting beyond hurting.

One night, I think I was under the influence, and I called him crying. I told him how much I missed him. I brought up the fact that I found out he had spoken to one of his exes the one he lived with before me. She knew about me. Knew about my social media pages. She knew who I was.

Even if the conversation meant nothing, it still bothered me.

Why hadn't he just told me?

Why did I always have to find things out from someone else?

He brushed it off, his tone sharp and detached.

"I'm a grown man," he said. "I don't need a mother. I handled it."

Then he said something I'll never forget

words that landed like a slap to my soul:

"You just added another nail to your coffin."

I didn't even know what he meant.

But I knew it wasn't good.

And I felt crushed.

Every time I reached out, it only hurt worse.

Some calls ended with nothing but silence and tears.

Other times, I'd break down, and he'd snap,

"How old are you? Stop crying and act like it. Control yourself."

But over time thankfully

the love began to fade.

The heart-shaped glasses came off.

And for the first time,

I finally saw him clearly.

He once said he'd never change.

And he didn't.

He meant it.

He wore it like a badge of honor

as if change was weakness.

As if growth was betrayal.

But I was never asking him to become someone else.

I just wanted to feel considered.

To feel safe.

To feel chosen.

When you love someone,

you don't have to give up who you are

but you do learn how to love them better.

You adjust. You communicate.

You meet them in the middle.

You evolve together.

He didn't.

And I finally stopped trying to convince him.

Because the truth is,

I had grown into a woman who no longer needed to be loved.

He didn't change.

I just outgrew the version of me who needed him.

I had given myself permission to lead and love,

to run a business and still try to be soft.

To pour into my children.

To try again, even when I was scared.

I had finally given my heart permission to open.

And that's not something to be ashamed of.

And my chapter doesn't end here.

I'm still a businesswoman.

I'm still successful.

And I'm a damn good mother.

I'll say this though. I do not regret any of it. He holds a huge part in my heart and always will.

Chapter 37

For the Girls Who Keep Surviving.

THE END!

I didn't write this book to make anyone look bad.

I wrote it so I could finally look at myself and say, "You made it out."

There were so many times I could've closed the chapter early.

Times I could've made the pain prettier, or the healing sound faster.

I could've skipped the parts that made me look weak.

But that wouldn't have been the truth.

And if there's one thing this book taught me it's that my truth deserves the light.

I have lived so many lives in one.

The daughter. The wife. The mother.

The lost girl. The girl who gave everything.

The girl who kept starting over. The one who stayed quiet to protect everyone else.

The one who finally said, enough.

I've been poor. I've been in love. I've been betrayed. I've been praised.

I've made money from scratch. I've moved across states with kids and no real plan.

I've trusted the wrong people and walked away from the right ones out of fear.

I've been the woman who gave too much and the woman who finally gave it to herself.

And now?

I'm the woman who wrote the damn book.

What I've Learned

I learned that peace isn't something someone else can hand you. You have to fight for it sometimes harder than you fought for them.

I learned that family doesn't always mean safe.

That sometimes the people closest to you are the ones who break you the most.

But I also learned that healing doesn't mean you have to hate them.

I learned that grief comes in waves

and just when you think you've caught your breath,

a memory can knock the wind out of you again.

But I also learned how to swim through it.

How to breathe anyway.

How to build a life with the grief, not around it.

I learned that love is not proof of worth and begging for love doesn't make it stay.

I learned that my softness is sacred.

That my anger was holy.

And that boundaries are the bridge between who I was and who I now am.

Who I've Become

I became a mother who can lead with grace and grit.

I became a businesswoman who can write invoices and wipe tears on the same day.

I became a writer who doesn't need a fancy degree or a fancy desk just her story, her heart, and her voice.

I became a woman I'm finally proud to be.

I still have days I question myself. I still cry.

I still grieve the versions of me that nobody clapped for the one who didn't know better, the one who stayed too long, the one who had to survive before she could heal.

But I also thank her.

Because she built this.

What I Want You to Take With You

If you're holding this book, I hope you feel less alone.

I hope you see that broken doesn't mean unworthy.

That soft doesn't mean weak.

That choosing yourself isn't selfish it's survival.

I hope you realize healing won't always look like peace signs and yoga mats.

Sometimes it'll look like crying in your car,

restarting your life for the fifth time,

or learning how to stop calling them back.

It's messy. It's nonlinear. It's real.

But damn, it's worth it.

To the girl who started this story:

I'm sorry no one protected you.

I'm sorry they made you feel like you had to earn your softness back.

But I'm so proud of you.

You made it here.

You made it out.

And now you're free.

The Soul Fighter's Truth

I used this time to truly heal.

To go to therapy.

To stay committed to my medication.

To bring my body to the gym.

To speak gently to my mind.

To rest my soul.

I closed on my first half-million-dollar property.

I kept showing up to corporate, doing nails, building my brand, packing up orders, being a content creator, filming brand deals, running beauty booths, giving speeches all while raising my boys and being the dog mom to our chaotic little family.

I built this whole thing with my own two hands.

No one handed it to me.

I didn't have a financial safety net.

No rich ex. No silent investor. No family saving me behind the scenes.

I did my own homework. I pulled the all-nighters.

I worked overtime. I worked multiple jobs and still do.

That's how this book got published.

From my own sweat. My own prayers. My own hustle.

I learned that sometimes, you have to get sick of your own shit. You have to be hungry I mean starving to get tired of where you are and finally rise above it.

Discipline is the bridge.

Faith is the engine.

And your story is the light.

You weren't born to convince anyone of your worth.

You are somebody's missing rib

and they better rise to the occasion if they want to meet you where you stand.

Don't ever step off your high shelf just because someone can't reach it.

And never accept breadcrumbs when you could feed yourself a whole damn meal.

I read The Four Agreements by Don Miguel Ruiz.

The first time? It didn't hit.

The second time? I sobbed.

You receive it differently depending on where you are in life.

One chapter said:

"Life is a dream"

And it stuck with me.

When we're born, we don't choose our names.

Our religion. Our language. Our beliefs.

They're programmed into us by our parents, society, school, culture.

But adulthood? That's where your power begins.

Because now I dream my own dream. I choose my language. My

behaviors. My boundaries. My business. My beliefs.

My life.

And baby, don't be shy with your prayers.

Ask for more.

God is not on a budget.

I know now I have a whole set of needs that must be met and I have

so much love to give.

So protect your peace.

Protect your softness.

Protect your growth.

And surround yourself with women who get it.

My best friends? The girls who've held me up?

You know who you are.

You've been part of my healing.

And I will forever be a girls' girl.

At any age.

At any stage.

Writing Through the Storm

A few days ago, I was curled up at the quiet beach house

the kind that sits peacefully on stilts, facing the sea.

It was storming outside.

The sky was dark and dramatic.

Thunder rumbled through the walls while the rain painted streaks on the windows.

But inside?

Inside it was warm. Safe. Sacred.

I sat there barefoot, hoodie on, coffee in hand just typing my heart away while the storm passed around me.

The dogs snored. My phone was off.

And for once, the only thing I was trying to "fix" was the ending of this book.

I'll remember that moment forever.

Because it reminded me that storms can still bring peace.

That writing can be a shelter.

That sometimes the most powerful healing doesn't happen in loud moments but in the quiet ones.

So to the girls who keep surviving:

I see you.

I believe in you.

And I'll be cheering for you.

No matter what age.

No matter what storm.

With love, Yesenia ♡

ACKNOWLEDGEMENTS

First and foremost, thank you to my babies Julian and Issac.

MY WORLD. MIS AMORES.

You are the reason I keep showing up, keep writing, and keep healing. Every page of this book carries pieces of your mama's love for you.

To the father of my children, thank you for always showing up through everything, you've never let me drown. Divorce didn't break the friendship, and I'll forever respect the way you've stood beside meand the boys as a co-parent, a dad, and a friend.

To my mother

My three amazing brothers who I love with my entire heart, and my beautiful sisters-in-law who I love like true sisters thank you.

To my family. My friends, the real ones who stood beside me through every season: thank you for believing in me, even when I didn't believe in myself.

To my dad in heaven (RIP — Que en paz descanse) love you, Papi.

To my dream team, My web babe-Mercy, My awesome formatter Dorian, my designer Rony, my second designer Olivia and Faith and last but not least my third designer Sarah AND of course... To my assistant and right hand Nova! You guys made this happen!

♡

Thank you for helping me bring this vision to life. For pushing me on the days I wanted to quit, for handling every detail with love and professionalism, and for making this process feel possible. I'm so honored and blessed to have created this alongside such a beautiful team.

To everyone who's ever felt like the black sheep in the family... out of place, out of bounds, or like you were "too much" to belong this book was written for you.

To the ones who hurt me, thank you too. You gave me the fire. The edge. The story.

And this is me turning pain into power.

To my followers and readers you mean the entire world to me. Thank you for holding these pages with care. May you see yourself in my words, and may they remind you that you are never alone.

And to the little girl inside me

You made it, baby. Look at what we did.

You're free now.

With love,

Yesenia Garcia ♡

www.ingramcontent.com/pod-product-compliance
Lightning Source LLC
Chambersburg PA
CBHW060400130626
46555CB00005B/1957